Written Space in the Latin West, 200 BC to AD 300

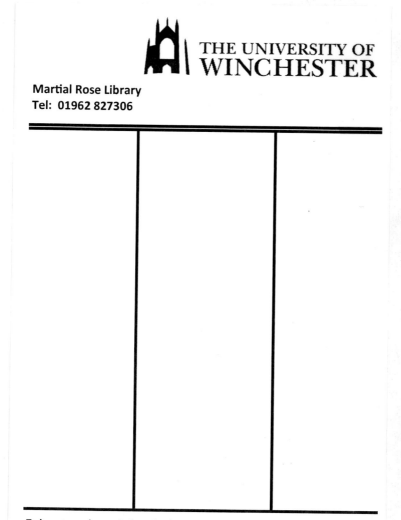

THE UNIVERSITY OF
WINCHESTER

Martial Rose Library
Tel: 01962 827306

To be returned on or before the day marked above, subject to recall.

Written Space in the Latin West, 200 BC to AD 300

Gareth Sears, Peter Keegan and Ray Laurence

B L O O M S B U R Y
LONDON • NEW DELHI • NEW YORK • SYDNEY

Bloomsbury Academic
An imprint of Bloomsbury Publishing Plc

50 Bedford Square	1385 Broadway
London	New York
WC1B 3DP	NY 10018
UK	USA

www.bloomsbury.com

First published 2013
Paperback edition first published 2015

Introduction and editorial arrangement © 2013 by
Gareth Sears, Peter Keegan & Ray Laurence

British Library Cataloguing-in-Publication Data
A catalogue record for this book is available from the British Library.

ISBN: HB: 978-1-44112-304-6
PB: 978-1-4742-1708-8
ISBN: ePUB: 978-1-44116-162-8
ISBN: ePDF: 978-1-44118-876-2

Library of Congress Cataloging-in-Publication Data
Written space in the Latin West, 200 BC to AD 300/[edited by] Peter Keegan, Ray
Laurence & Gareth Sears.
pages cm
Includes bibliographical references.
ISBN 978-1-4411-2304-6 (hardback)–ISBN 978-1-4411-8876-2 (epdf)–ISBN 978-1-4411-
6162-8 (epub) 1. Inscriptions, Latin–Rome. 2. Public spaces–Rome–History. 3. Rome–Social
life and customs. 4. Inscriptions, Latin–Europe, Western. 5. Inscriptions, Latin–Africa,
Northwest. I. Keegan, Peter. II. Laurence, Ray, 1963- III. Sears, Gareth, 1977-
CN525.W75 2013
411'.7093763–dc23
2013002703

Typeset by Fakenham Prepress Solutions, Fakenham, Norfolk NR21 8NN

Contents

Part 3   Written Space and Building Type

Part 4   Regional Written Spaces?

List of Contributors

Eamonn Baldwin is a Research Associate in Remote Sensing at the IBM VISTA Centre in the Institute of Archaeology and Antiquity, Birmingham. He specializes in archaeological survey methods including: geophysical, topographical and terrestrial laser scanning surveys and standing building recording. His research interests lie in the investigation, interpretation and presentation of archaeological landscapes through remote sensing technologies.

Alison E. Cooley is a Reader in the Department of Classics and Ancient History at the University of Warwick. She has published extensively upon topics relating to Latin epigraphy and Roman Italy, most recently *The Cambridge Manual of Latin Epigraphy*.

Mireille Corbier is presently a Directeur de recherche emerita at the Centre National de Recherche Scientifique and Director of *L'Année épigraphique* since 1992. She is a graduate of the École Normale Supérieure (1966) and a former member of the École Française de Rome (1972–5). She has taught ancient history at the University of Paris X Nanterre and at the École Normale Supérieure, as well as anthropology in the Department of Anthropology at the University of Paris VIII. She received her doctorate in 1972 and published her thesis in 1974: *L' 'Aerarium Saturni' et L' 'Aerarium Militaire'. Administration et Prosopographie Sénatoriale* (coll. EFR, n° 24). She has published extensively on various aspects of Roman history, and a complete bibliography of her work can be found on the web at http://www.anneeepigraphique. msh-paris.fr

Simon Esmonde Cleary is Professor of Roman Archaeology at the University of Birmingham. His research interests include the late Roman period in Britain and Western Europe and in particular the relationship between archaeology and textual sources, Roman urbanism, Roman numismatics and Roman funerary archaeology. He has excavated in south-western France at Éauze and St-Bertrand-de-Comminges.

Renata Senna Garraffoni is a Lecturer at Paraná Federal University (Curitiba, Brazil). She works on Roman history and archaeology and in particular on gladiators and Pompeiian graffiti. She held a visiting British Academy Fellowship from December 2008 to March 2009 at the University of Birmingham, UK, to study Roman graffiti from Pompeii.

Robert Hannah is Professor of Classics at the University of Otago, New Zealand, and a Fellow of the Society of Antiquaries of London. He has written extensively on the uses of astronomy in Greek and Roman culture, particularly in relation to calendars and the perception of time. His most recent publications include the books *Greek and Roman Calendars: Constructions of Time in the Classical World* (2005), and *Time in Antiquity* (2009).

Emily A. Hemelrijk is Professor of Ancient History at the University of Amsterdam. She has published numerous works on Roman women including: *Matrona Docta.*

Educated Women in the Roman Elite from Cornelia to Julia Domna (1999; paperback 2004). She is currently preparing a book on women's public roles in the cities of the Latin West: *Hidden lives – Public Personae. Women and Civic Life in Italy and the Latin West during the Roman Principate.*

Tom Hillard teaches Roman history in the Department of Ancient History at Macquarie University. He has also excavated on archaeological sites in Greece, Israel and Syria.

Dr Peter Keegan is a Senior Lecturer in Roman History in the Department of Ancient History at Macquarie University. His fields of research and teaching include Latin epigraphic culture, the history of gender, sexuality and the body in the Mediterranean world, late Republican and early Imperial Roman historiography and historical theory. He is currently working on a survey of non-official epigraphic practices in the ancient Mediterranean (*Graffiti in Antiquity*, forthcoming 2013).

Ray Laurence is Professor of Roman History and Archaeology at the University of Kent. His publications include: *Roman Pompeii: Space and Society* (2nd edition 2007); *Roman Passions* (2009); *The City in the Roman West* (with Gareth Sears and Simon Esmonde Cleary 2011); *Rome, Ostia, Pompeii: Movement and Space* (with David Newsome 2011); and *Roman Archaeology for Historians* (2012).

Helen Moulden is a Research Associate in Artefact Scanning, Modelling and Reconstruction for IBM VISTA at the University of Birmingham. She specializes in the application of 3D scanning technologies (both object and terrestrial), with particular focus on the convergence of 3D object representations and digital archiving as a means to enhance accessibility and research practices.

David J. Newsome completed his PhD at the University of Birmingham in 2010 on the relationship between movement, the representation of space, and fora in Rome and Roman Italy. With Professor Ray Laurence, he edited the volume *Rome, Ostia, Pompeii: Movement and Space* (2011). His primary research interest is the examination of movement as a key variable in the development of both the Roman city and Roman social relations.

Louise Revell is lecturer in Roman Archaeology at the University of Southampton. She works mainly on Roman architecture and inscriptions, focusing on questions of imperialism and identity. She is author of *Roman Imperialism and Local Identities*.

Gareth Sears is lecturer in Roman History at the University of Birmingham. He works on Roman urbanism, particularly in North Africa, and the Christianization of the city. He is the author of the *Cities of Roman Africa* and *The City in the Roman West* with Ray Laurence and Simon Esmonde Cleary.

Francesco Trifilò is a Research Associate at the University of Kent. He specializes in Roman Archaeology and History, particularly urbanism, architecture, epigraphy, and everyday life, the subject of his latest publication: 'Movement, Gaming and the Use of Space in the Forum' in: Newsome, D. and Laurence, R. (eds), *Rome, Ostia, Pompeii. Movement and Space* (2011).

List of Figures

Abbreviations

Journal abbreviations are as in L'Année Philologique. Other abbreviations are as the Oxford Classical Dictionary; the exception is ILS. In addition the following abbreviations are used:

BAR	*British Archaeological Reports*
BEFAR	*Bibliothèque des Ecoles Franchises d'Athènes et de Rome*
CILA	*Corpus de Inscripciones Latinas de Andalucia, Sevilla 1991–*
EAOR	*Epigrafia anfiteatrale dell'Occidente Romano*
IAM	*Inscriptions antiques du Maroc*
ILA	*Inscriptions Latines d'Aquitaine*
ILAfr.	*Inscriptions Latines d'Afrique*
ILM	*Inscriptions Latines du Maroc*
ILMMalaga	Serrano Ramos, E. and Atencia Páez, R. (1981), *Inscripciones latinas del museo de Málaga*. Madrid.
ILS	*Inscriptiones Latinae Selectae*
ILSard	Sotgiu, G. (1961), *Iscrizioni latine della Sardegna*. Padua.
ILSicilia	Manganaro, G. (1989), Iscrizioni latine nuove e vecchie della Sicilia, *Epigraphica*, 51, 161–209.
ILTun.	*Inscriptions Latines de la Tunisie*
IMCCatania	Korhonen, K. (2004), *Le iscrizioni del museo civico di Catania*, Tammisaari.
IRBaelo	Bonneville, J., Dardaine, S. and LeRoux, P. (1988), Belo 5: l'Épigraphie. *Les inscriptions romaines de Baelo Claudia*. Madrid.
IRPCadiz	Gonzalez, J. (1982), *Inscripciones Romanas de la Provincia de Cadiz*. Cadiz.
LTUR	*Lexicon Topographicum Urbis Romae*

Written Space

Ray Laurence and Gareth Sears

Today, we inhabit urban environments that are full of writing. Sitting down on the London Underground, for instance, one can read sets of 100 to 200 words in what might be described as 'textboxes'; advertisements, instructions, maps, poetry and the less official graffiti that, despite official attempts to eradicate them, are untameable by authority. The volume's concept began, as a simple idea, voiced in discussion between Gareth Sears, Simon Esmonde Cleary and Ray Laurence towards the end of the writing of *The City in the Roman West* (2011). Public space tended to be associated with writing carved on stone and that writing created a different sort of space worthy of study. This viewpoint was also informed by David Newsome's (at the time a PhD student in Birmingham) development of a better understanding of movement and space.[1] Yet, it would seem that Written Space has not been a subject of discussion in either the Humanities nor in the Social Sciences. The closest that we found was Robert Harrist's *The Landscape of Words: Stone Inscriptions from Early and Medieval China*.[2] However, Harrist tends to discuss stone inscriptions in relation to the landscape of peak sanctuary sites, rather than the city that is the focus of our volume. Interestingly, far fewer stone inscriptions survive from Classical China than the Roman Empire – instead the focus was on construction in wood and, perhaps, writing on wood, which prevented the preservation of texts.[3]

Most societies develop forms of written space in cities, notably inscriptions on public buildings, but this does not necessarily equate with an indication of literacy. Yet, it has been demonstrated in the study of Arabic as a written language that nomads learnt to read inscriptions and in turn to write graffiti on rocks in the desert.[4] The relationship between literacy and the written inscription is neatly defined by Macdonald: in societies with oral memories, there need to be fixed points in terms of genealogy that defines not just a record of the past, but also a means to define the rights, identity, and personal circumstances of an individual or group; oral cultures can use writing for graffiti and writing can be learnt from the observation of public inscriptions or from legal documents.[5] The use of writing created fixed points within a society which was more usually dependent on oral traditions of re-telling the past and re-shaping the past to the context of the present.

Writing is a particular form of language delivery quite distinct from its oral expression.[6] We might further suggest that the use of writing in a certain context should also be considered as an aspect of linguistic study. Thus, an inscription on a building provides the expectation that the text will refer to the structure, who built it or oversaw the building, and where the money came from. The language of public writing in Latin is somewhat formulaic, but can be individualized through the use of names, gods, and so on. It may be cross referenced to statuary that provided a visualization of the individual.[7] However, whatever other clues there are, language is needed and writing is a necessity for public space in the Roman Empire. The problem is, to what extent does this act in the manner of a museum label, providing a name to the person represented or an explanation of the building's purpose that may or may not be needed by the viewer? In Roman society it is clear that a statue needed an inscription and, if a restoration was undertaken, care was needed to maintain the right inscription with the right statue when it was moved to be re-erected in a different written space.[8] In other words, writing went together with statues or buildings which were located in spaces associated with them. However, the question over the level of literacy needed to understand these written spaces and how many people could read these spaces needs further investigation by relating these forms of public writing to both the oral culture of Rome, studied by Nicholas Horsfall,[9] and the use of graffiti. Here we would agree with Thomas Habinek that the ability to write confers agency upon the writer to differentiate him from those who cannot write.[10] *Written Space*, as a book, opens with four chapters that as a group seek to understand the everyday actions of writing against the concepts of physical movement in the city and the role of time (chapters by Corbier, Keegan, Newsome and Hannah). The focus shifts then to a series of chapters (by Hillard, Garraffoni and Laurence, Hemelrijk, and Baldwin, Moulden and Laurence) that relate writing to socio-political/cultural groups that produced that writing in quite distinct places. Two space-specific studies comprise a short section that brings into focus building types that have been somewhat neglected when compared to the forum or the cemeteries of Roman cities: the baths (Cooley) and the *platea* (Trifilò). The final section examines the manifestation of written space in the provinces of the Roman Empire: the North African provinces (Sears); a sample of *municipia* in Spain (Revell) and within the province of Aquitania (Esmonde Cleary). There is, of course, another dialogue underpinning the chapters in the book – the development of *Written Space* as an area of study in its own right. In this introduction, we wish to draw out the key findings of the chapters that shift the focus of study from inscriptions and their context towards a better understanding of *Written Space* as an urban phenomenon.

Mireille Corbier set out the importance of studying communication via text in a key article from the 1980s.[11] Her chapter, translated in this volume as Chapter 2,[12] distinguished those texts that were viewed as one moved through the city, often monumental writing, and those that were smaller and would require a person to stop to read them. Corbier also points to the politics of writing in imperial spaces and reactions to it. There is also another important consideration in this chapter. Some texts were set up as permanent long-term forms of communication that over time were read and re-read; whereas more ephemeral texts, such as graffiti, scratched into plaster may be more poignant but short lived. The convergences of larger or more prominent letters with permanent texts and the smaller letters with temporary or short-lived existences, also maps onto the modes of reading – glancing in motion or being stationary and reading. This emphasis on the relationship between movement and text provides David Newsome with the means to discuss the role of graffiti as a spatial tactic, and a role for writing in the alteration of the use of space – for example writing can cause people to stop or provide a means of locating a place in space, such as the bookseller in Rome's Argiletum.[13] The convergence between the selling of texts and writing on the walls of the bookseller's shop should not be seen as coincidental, as Newsome points out. There is a correlation between spatial practice and its representation in a text: the advertising of a book for sale, its actual sale and the location of the writing/advertisement on the walls in Martial's book of epigrams that was also for sale in the shop in the Argiletum. The reporting of the use of graffiti as a spatial tactic in republican politics is a theme pursued by Tom Hillard. Graffiti had a role in motivating politicians in the narratives of Plutarch and Appian written some two or more centuries after the events happened. The fact that these actions made sense to Appian or Plutarch might suggest that graffiti were a means by which political communication was still conducted in the second century AD. Whatever we may wonder about the authenticity of the content or the location given to these graffiti in these texts, we should notice their importance in creating an explanation of why a politician might follow a course of action or, more broadly, how writing in key locales could influence the course of action directed by the elite. The authorship, identified by Hillard was that of artisans, weavers and shopkeepers/hawkers and, thus, residents in the city rather than supporters from the countryside (the importance of the city as the location, par excellence, for carved stone is re-stated in several of the chapters).

A recent shift from the study of graffiti as texts, to an analysis of the action of writing has led to a focus on the producers of text in recent work.[14] This new focus has been informed by an approach derived from what may be termed 'spatial archaeology', which had its origins in new approaches to archaeology initiated by David Clarke in the 1970s.[15] These initial approaches have led to the evolution of a whole series of methodologies within spatial archaeology that can be applied to the study of graffiti, all of which Eamonn Baldwin, Helen Moulden and Ray Laurence explore to evaluate the location of graffiti in the Villa of San Marco at Stabiae – a suburban/maritime villa on the Bay of Naples. Importantly, this analysis does not simply map locations, but relates these to potential patterns of habitation by groups within the household – particularly to the less archaeologically visible: slaves and children. Approaching the same sorts of problems in a different way, Renata Garraffoni and Ray Laurence explore the spatial archaeology of the graffiti associated with gladiators and those associated with children learning to write – alphabets – at Pompeii. Analysing where in the city of Pompeii we find x or y type of graffiti allows us to begin to understand writing (and drawing) as an urban phenomenon. Perhaps surprisingly they find that it is not flat surfaces, but the convex spaces of columns, that are the preferred location for graffiti as graffiti increase with an increase in the incidence of columns. Spaces with columns – temples, *palaestrae*, *plateae*, basilicas, fora, peristyle courtyards in rich houses – may have been seen as symbols of power architecturally and in consequence attracted the graffiti writer to them. Columns as non-verbal signifiers of power could have that message enhanced, altered or indeed subverted through the act of writing upon their surface. We may conjecture that columns made of hard stones (for instance the granite of the Pantheon's columns) may have been graffiti resistant, when compared to brick columns covered in plaster. The use of writing as a weapon in the contesting of space – a phenomenon widely reported in the study of the modern city[16] – can be seen in several cases. The development of architecture in the Roman city, for example the basilica/stoa of the second century BC, may have provided new opportunities for pertinent political messages. Tom Hillard highlights, amongst other examples, how Gracchan supporters daubed their message to Tiberius Gracchus on the Portico of the Metelli over-writing a monument of their opposition built a mere 13 years previously. The intention of the builder was to create an architectural space to promote the Metelli, yet such spaces could still be appropriated and subverted, at least temporarily, by writers of signs and graffiti.

In contrast to these social and political studies, Francesco Trifilò moves the discussion of the evolving nature of space in a different direction. His chapter looks at the recognition of a space as a *platea* – a term that defines an urban setting as much more than a street: a broad street or an informal piazza or perhaps a form between these two. Intriguingly, the presence of a *platea* is recognized through the use of writing and establishes the *platea* as a *locus* of euergetism to sit alongside spaces already recognized, for example fora with their associated statues and monuments. What we find with the *platea* was the recognition of the development of formal space from activities associated with that locale; monumental writing essentially helped to codify the space.

The intersection between the development of an epigraphy of place and the transformation of the Roman landscape lies at the heart of Peter Keegan's chapter. The development of epitaphs set up on tombs in extramural cemeteries, around Rome from the first century BC and at Isola Sacra between Ostia and Portus from the late first century AD, should be seen not in isolation, but in relation to the major agricultural landscape transformation that is known today as centuriation. Both developments create a marking of space with an identity and, in the case of the epitaph, include an inscribed stone from which we may understand choices made in the commemoration of both men and women. This phenomenon is not unique to Rome or to Latin epigraphy, but can be found in Italic inscriptions.[17] The corpus of more than 100 Oscan inscriptions from Pompeii point up the role of magistrates and the use of fines for urban development (public buildings and roads) alongside graffiti in the form of Oscan alphabets.[18] It is a clear indication that it was not just in Rome, that we can identify the development of urbanism and writing being linked together. Habinek's analysis of forms of inscriptions in the Republic confirm a pattern in which the third and second centuries BC were the time at which writing found associated with the state shifted to the cemetery and the commemoration of the dead at tombs.[19] Keegan argues that the roads running through these cemeteries need more attention, in order to understand how the identity of the viewer was constituted through movement along these roads. In moving around Rome the viewer/reader of epitaphs on tombs was able to relate their own social position to that of the dead enhancing their understanding of society. For Keegan, this causes the cemetery with its epitaphs to have a role not dissimilar to that of, say, the Forum of Augustus in the development of individual identity and power relations at Rome. Thus, his chapter draws out the role of the cemetery as a written space to be considered alongside the monumental centre of Rome itself as a place of identity formation and long-term memorialization of the present that inevitably in the future becomes the past.

Robert Hannah in his chapter on the writing of time in space reminds us that the first public calendar appeared in 187 BC somewhat before the landscape changes examined by Keegan. The location of the calendar as part of the decoration of the Temple of Hercules Musarum can be seen as an addition to a programme of urban development that had its origins with the building of the Circus Flaminius (220 BC). Only fragments of the calendar are known, but there is some convergence with that set up in the forum at Praeneste in the first decade of the first century AD; it sets out festival days, but also provides explanation of their origin. As Hannah notes, these were to be read and should be associated with a literate body of people in the forum, who could use them. Yet, calendars are also found as 'graffiti' scratched into the walls of Pompeii – pointing to the need for access to a calendar that indicated when market days and festivals occurred. Other calendars, e.g. *Fasti Capitolini* listed the consuls and would seem to be the community's means of recalling their past; just as individuals were written into the landscape of the suburbs of Rome. The two phenomena taken together are indicators of societal development and the desire to recall in writing, and to even copy for private use, those public documents (e.g. *Fasti Antiates*) that list and organize social activities in space. There is also some convergence here with Hillard's observations on the writing of graffiti on monuments from the time of Tiberius Gracchus to contest the authority of the builder of the monument. Some two centuries on from the first known Roman calendar, Augustus systematically recalibrated written space to ensure there was a sense of time that was centred on his own identity.

The development of writing in architectural space in the provinces is the focus of Louise Revell's chapter. She looks at the forum in three Spanish *municipia*: Munigua, Singilia Barba and Baelo Claudia to set out the formation of written space and the role of writing in the production of space. Her choice of location is deliberate. None of these places was a colony (such as Mérida), nor could these be seen as provincial capitals (such as Tarragona); instead these are archaeologically well-attested sites at which writing played a role in the definition of the forum as a 'Roman' space. That space was not just constituted through building inscriptions and statue bases, but also by the erection of bronze tablets recording decisions made with regard to the cities. In most cases, these would be signified in the archaeological record by the presence of nail holes in the fabric of a wall and, thus, are seldom identified or, if identified, even noted. Revell pulls together these varied forms of writing to identify how these texts maintained the evolving ideology of Roman-ness and an on-going sense of civic harmony with a past as well as a present and a future.

Inscriptions on stone in Aquitania are the subject of Simon Esmonde Cleary's chapter. At cities such as Bordeaux, Périgueux and Saintes tombstones were by far the most common form of inscription memorializing the identity of the deceased and providing a place to commemorate them. However, in these cities the adoption of other forms of writing was far from uniform; Périgueux and Saintes have many more dedications than Bordeaux, and no altars have been found in Saintes. The development of space over time leads to a synchronic space that, according to Esmonde Cleary, acted as a *lieu de mémoire*. We might suggest further that the oral stories associated with statues or gravestones were fixed through writing, whereas images without text could refer to quite unspecified persons whose identity could become a subject of debate. What we might be seeing in Aquitania is a phenomenon identified by Greg Woolf in the epigraphy of Britain – the state has an inscribed place but there is a different pattern to the use of writing from that found in, for example, Italy. This reshapes the nature of written space and may be, in part, determined by the nature of connectivity with and distance from the centre of empire.[20]

The temporal framing of the construction of space and the commemoration of that action provides Gareth Sears with a focus in his chapter. He tests the assumption that the accession of Septimius Severus, the so-called 'African Emperor', marked a dramatic change in euergetism in the cities of the provinces of North Africa. His study points to an increase in public building in North Africa across the second century that provides the context for this continuing pattern through the Severan period and on into the third century. His case studies of Cuicul, Lepcis Magna, and Thamugadi demonstrate a variation in the creation of new written spaces in these cities. The chapter as a whole points to the on-going and continuous expansion of public space in African cities in the second and third centuries – something of a contrast to the patterns of development of written space found elsewhere in the Roman Empire. Sears is adamant that we should not see the development of written space as having a relationship to the fact that a person from a city, or indeed region, had become emperor. Instead, we see development of written space over a *longue durée* through more than a century, yet in the Severan period the earlier developments are added to, occasionally given new meanings, and expand written space.

Gender and epigraphy of the city has not been a subject that has attracted much attention. All will know that there are more epitaphs surviving from the Roman Empire set up to men than to women (although the gender gap may not be as great as is often assumed; a ratio of men to women at c. 60: 40 for epitaphs). Emily Hemelrijk's chapter provides a corrective to this, drawing on her long-term project to understand the role of women in urban (Roman) societies from public inscriptions. Statues of women including a written record of their identity were to be found in the cities of the Roman Empire and, more importantly, women were involved in the funding of public building projects that are recorded in Italy and the Western Provinces. One of the features that has perhaps excluded women from the discussion of the Roman city in the past, is a modern preoccupation with elections and a view that magistrates had primarily a political role. If we adjust our focus to view an elite (male and female) concerned with ritual and religion that included the celebration of games and payment for public building projects, we would write a history that saw both men and women altering the landscape of the Roman city.

The language of public inscriptions tends to refer to the virtues of men and women, especially if the inscription was set up in the forum. However, there is one space in the Roman city where a shift in the language of inscriptions can be seen – the baths. As Alison Cooley points out in her chapter, it is in the baths that we find the greatest usage of words such as *splendor* and *ornamenta*. There is a difference in language and a difference in space – the baths were seen to be places in which pleasure could be experienced.[21] In many Roman cities, there was direct competition for custom between bath complexes. It was through the development of novelties, including window glass, that the baths became differentiated from one another and might attract custom to them. Writing in space was extended into this realm of luxury and was to be experienced by the discerning customer who sought an experience that could be described in an inscription as urban (*urbico more*). Inscriptions were embellishments, deepening and reinforcing the positive aspects of bathing in general, and individual bath houses in particular, for the literate bather; text in the baths and well-known literary texts acted in concert.[22]

Our book has privileged the use of Latin as the medium for creating written space in the Roman West. This is for a practical reason – inscriptions in Latin are far more common than those in other languages and Latin did eclipse other languages. The presence of Neo-Punic and Latino-Punic inscriptions in North Africa raises interesting questions about the use of language in an epigraphic context. Robert Kerr suggests that there was a fundamental difference in the epigraphic cultures of pre-Roman and Roman Tripolitania. The Punic focus was on epitaphs and religious matters and a much broader epigraphic culture came from Italy, in which writing was associated with other areas of life.[23] Like the Italian Oscan texts, Kerr identifies in the Neo-Punic inscriptions the influence of epigraphic formulae in Latin on the development of these epitaphs: *vixit annis* being translated into the formula *avo sanvth*, and the utilization of Roman numerals to indicate age.[24] There is a sense in which the language used is of less importance than the usage of text and its role in defining a written space when seen from the perspective of a multilingual empire in which Latin was the official or dominant language. It is beyond the scope of this book to deal with this issue, but we raise it here and wonder whether use of a specific language alters the phenomenon of written space.[25]

This introduction has focused on key aspects of each chapter that we see as both poignant for the development of the study of 'Written Space', and provides a distinctive element in the delineation of different forms of 'Written Space'. The process of shifting from a conference session at the Roman Archaeology Conference held in Ann Arbor in 2009 to the completion of the manuscript of 15 chapters has involved us in setting the authors of the volume the new and distinctive task of thinking about neither simply inscriptions nor their archaeological context, but a hybrid form – *Written Space*. It has been with some pleasure that we have watched authors shift from wary acceptance when faced with the concept towards total engagement as they pulled together thoughts about bodies of evidence for this fundamental aspect of the Roman city. There is a sense that this book is a product of interdisciplinary collaboration across two hemispheres from the Department of Ancient History at Macquarie University, and the Institute of Archaeology and Antiquity at the University of Birmingham. Two groups with their local contacts created a dialogue that took place initially at the Roman Archaeology Conference in 2009 at the University of Michigan.[26] Underpinning the work is a conception of the study of epigraphy in antiquity that draws on both archaeology and ancient history. In 2009, at the start of the project, two out of the 17 authors were in the Department of Ancient History at Macquarie University and nine were based in the Institute of Archaeology and Antiquity; the concentration points to the vitality of the research culture at the interface between ancient history and archaeology. The three month visit of Renata Garraffoni to the IAA (thanks to the British Academy Visiting Fellowship scheme) brought an additional dimension; whilst Eamonn Baldwin and Helen Moulden drew on their experience of working on the Restoring Ancient Stabiae project (part funded by the British Academy) to experiment with spatial techniques to engage with the elusive slaves and children of that villa. With glaring gaps evident in our coverage, Robert Hannah, Alison Cooley and Emily Hemelrijk all contributed further chapters and the addition of the translation of Mireille Corbier's chapter has helped to structure the book, as well as providing a firm basis for the development of the regional, socio-cultural and specific building-type studies. In addition to the British Academy which funded various projects associated with this book, the editors wish to thank the authors for their patience and understanding in dealing with our demands, schedule and comments with remarkable good humour, to Celine Murphy who produced the initial translation of Mireille Corbier's chapter as well as the index, the illustrators Harry Buglass in Birmingham and Lloyd Bosworth in Kent, for their efforts, our commissioning editor Michael Greenwood for his encouragement and Dhara Patel for seeing the project to its conclusion. We also wish to thank colleagues based at the University of Birmingham, the University of Kent and at Macquarie University for supporting this endeavour.

Notes

1 That was to produce Laurence and Newsome (eds), *Rome, Ostia, Pompeii: Movement and Space* (2011).
2 Harrist, 2008.
3 Nylan, 2012 can only report 400 inscriptions on stone surviving from the Classical period.
4 Macdonald, 2010.
5 Macdonald, 2010, p. 22.
6 Sampson, 1985 for distinction of the linguistics of the written compared to the spoken.
7 See papers in Newby and Leader-Newby, 2007 and Corbier, 2006, pp. 90–146.
8 Suet. *Cal.* 34; for discussion see Stewart, 2003, pp. 131–2.
9 Horsfall, 2003.
10 Habinek, 2009; Woolf, 2009.
11 Corbier, 1987a, 2006.
12 The development of the English version owes much to the work of Celine Murphy who produced the first draft for the editors.
13 Mart. *Ep.* 1.2.7–8; 1.117.9–12.
14 See, for instance Milnor, 2009; and essays in Baird and Taylor, 2011
15 For instance: Raper, 1977; Clarke, 1978.
16 Harvey, 1989, pp. 200–29.
17 Crawford, 2011 with others provides a full catalogue in three volumes.
18 Crawford, 2011 vol. 2.
19 Habinek, 2009, Table 6.2.
20 Woolf, 2009, pp. 53–6.

21 For instance: Tac. *Agr.* 19–21.
22 A very different type of writing in baths – graffiti – can be seen in Garrafoni and Laurence and Laurence, Baldwin and Moulden.
23 Kerr, 2010, pp. 13–24.
24 Kerr, 2010, pp. 145–6.
25 On bilingualism see: Adams, 2003; on regional variation of Latin see: Adams, 2007.
26 At which Esmonde Cleary, Garraffoni and Laurence, Keegan, Revell, Sears, and Trifilò delivered papers – Sears and Esmonde Cleary were funded by the British Academy Overseas Conference grant scheme.

Writing, Reading,
Movement and Time

2

Writing in Roman Public Space

Mireille Corbier[1]

As Armando Petrucci highlighted in one of his essays,[2] the contrast existing between the omnipresence of writing in the Roman city during the Imperial Age and its almost total absence during the medieval period, is the necessary starting point for a new examination of writing in Roman public space. This contrast underlines the specificity of the urban space, identified and imitated as such during the Renaissance.[3] The study of writing has been regenerated, from the very heart of the discipline,[4] in three areas: first, the written output in its broadest sense, including its purposes, forms and authors;[5] second, its reception, in terms of the recipients' levels of literacy[6] and in terms of individual or collective reading;[7] and third, the quality of writing and not just its quantity, with particular attention dedicated to the fine line existing between writing and drawing. This last approach, involving the identification of learning techniques especially, is owed mainly to palaeographers.[8]

It is tempting to engage in comparative studies for this topic,[9] but it soon becomes evident that such an approach is limited. Indeed, the anthropological paradigms adopted by historians – notably Jack Goody's model of distinction between illiterate societies, societies with restricted literacy and widely literate societies[10] – are too broad for studies of imperial Rome intending to go beyond mere classification. As a matter of fact, Rome is almost entirely absent from Goody's studies,[11] as if the city had nothing innovative to contribute on this issue. Rome is indeed chronologically distant from the origins of writing, occurring in the third millennium BC in Mesopotamia; from the revolution which was represented by the Phoenicians' completion, and the Greeks' diffusion, of the alphabet;[12] and indeed from the political achievement defined by the transition to written and published law adopted by Greek cities of the sixth century BC (even if royal and republican Rome experienced a similar decisive transition).[13] These turning points were strongly consolidated by the beginning of our era. Conversely, the other revolutionary moment marked by the invention of printing[14] was too far in the future and took place in a radically different context of societies – which subsequently developed different uses and demands for reading and writing – born from the dissolution of the Empire. For the Romans, printing was still a distant speck on the horizon.

From this perspective, imperial Rome did not mark any transitions or turning points, except maybe in introducing the usage of writing for administrative purposes for an immense empire, not uniquely for a city or an average sized state. This does not mean, however, that the uses Rome made of writing and reading are not worth studying. These uses, on the contrary, present a remarkable coherence and indisputable originality, best seen when we avoid attempts at comparison with earlier or later situations, from which partial or anachronistic conclusions are often drawn. Rather, such qualities are most clear when unbiased inventories are composed. An inventory will therefore be my starting point, since it allows for the observation of parallels more than of evolutions. For indeed Rome, and other cities in its image, '[were] full of things to read'.[15] I shall then try to draw certain observations from this inventory, some of which will be pertinent for Rome alone, others for the other cities of the Roman world, and some even for the whole Empire insofar as Rome was simultaneously an urban and administrative model. It is also tempting to attribute to Rome what can be found in Pompeii.[16]

But let us avoid any ambiguities. Rome witnessed many public and private uses for writing: administrative archives, contracts, correspondence, literature and so forth, written and destined for a group of individuals who could read and write – either as a result of general education or for professional needs. In the period which we are studying these particular uses witnessed technical transformations with the progressive appearance of the *codex*.[17] My approach, however, will be different: I shall keep to epigraphic texts regardless of their sources, be they official or private, engraved or displayed on a wide variety of supports, so that they would or could be read, by all, in various locations of the urban space and its natural extensions such as roads. These texts allow us to delimit the field of public communication, or at least communication destined to undifferentiated audiences, as opposed to other categories of texts concerned with the crystallizing and transmission of facts and knowledge.

Inventory

These epigraphic urban 'texts' represent (outside Egypt) a large part of the written documents we possess:[18] deliberately public writings have, overall, been better preserved than private ones.[19] In this regard, we must not forget that the totality of public writings is not preserved and that writing, in fact, held an even stronger place in society than the texts we possess today suggest. Some of the lost texts might have been the texts which, in Roman public space, attracted most gazes or provided the readers with most information. Be it of private or public nature, monumental inscriptions must be brought closer to other, more or less 'spontaneous', practices of writing, even if the needs of scholarship often tend to keep these separate.[20]

These imbalances in preservation (if we put chance in parentheses) indicate in turn the existence of other distortions. That of the supports for the written texts is the most obvious, and corresponds, at least partly, to the inequality of importance assigned to these different categories of texts by contemporaneous individuals themselves. Those carved *in aere* (in bronze), where the status of the text might appear as a guarantee of durability – and here we could cite a whole series of ancient authors on this topic[21]

– were victims of later reuse of the material; they have, paradoxically, survived less well than graffiti.

Other imbalances in the surviving material are also important, including: those of subjects, authors, public or private, individuals or collectives, the place of display or posting, the modes of writing, and still more, notably among them the indirect knowledge of lost writings or writing practices that left no trace. All of these elements outline a hierarchy which will be examined in detail at a later stage. Large numbers of the following have survived to our times:

- Texts embodied in the monument: public building dedications, altar dedications, honorific inscriptions on bases which have mostly lost their statues, epitaphs especially[22] – a partial response to the wish of their authors, identical or not to that of the memorialized persons (we are well acquainted with the fear of *oblivium* expressed in prose or verse).[23] The trap of history is that in the case of statues and tombs, the object itself, the monument, has often disappeared.

- There are also texts carved on stones, most frequently on boundary markers[24] which map out public space inside and outside the city: altars at junctions, the limits of the *pomoerium* (extended by Claudius) or the city walls, boundary stones linked to the city tolls, the markers of the banks of the Tiber, the markers of the aqueducts which crossed the city, 'milestones' from which distances were calculated from the 'golden milestone' (*miliarium aureum*) raised on the Roman forum in front of the Temple of Saturn and so forth. Road names, carved on tombstones for the convenience and glance of passers-by, must also be added to this list. Moreover, we must not forget the representation of the *Urbs* (Rome, the city par excellence) in a plan, carved in marble in the *Forum Pacis*, from the time of Septimius Severus,[25] the representations of the *oikoumene* placed under the *Porticus Vipsania* on the Campus Martius by Agrippa,[26] and the 'list of stations' carved in marble or displayed.[27]

- Authorization documents – either requested or granted (by public administrations or simple *collegia*) – which individuals commissioned to protect themselves and their descendants from vexatious proceedings.[28] An example is the permission to build a small house on public soil, or a tomb in a private garden, obtained respectively by the guardian of Marcus Aurelius' column[29] and the *colonus* of the gardens of the *collegium magnum arkarum divarum Faustinarum*.[30]

Public documents, written on wooden and bronze plaques designed to be durably displayed on durable monuments such as temples or Augustus' Mausoleum, or even the words of the Prince, transmitted by ancient authors or through the Theodosian and Justinianic Codes, are often lost. Some of these are, however, known from copies discovered elsewhere[31] or authors' citations.[32] Only one account, that of Vespasian's edict on doctors' privileges, seems to indicate, through the mention of the term '*en leukômati*', that is '*in albo*', that emperors, like republican magistrates, published their edicts on wooden boards painted white.[33]

Turning to written documents for temporary display, be they regular (invitations for tenders, sales by auction, pantomime shows, gladiatorial combats, and so forth), and therefore given specific advertisement space,[34] or clandestine (for the 'placards', political pamphlets), survival in the city was not likely, although luckily some did nevertheless survive thanks to literary annotations.

The same can be said for signs. Despite its uncertain provenance, we must dedicate special treatment to the marble plaque decorated with images and relief letters, a technique rarely used on marble, which possibly belonged to a farmer of weights and measures, whose activities Margherita Guarducci[35] situated in the Temple of Concord (Figure 2.1). Be that as it may, signs of this type may have been affixed on the Temples of Castor and Ops where such verifications could be carried out using the standard measures.[36]

Paul Veyne drew attention to an even more ephemeral practice of writing, but one which is also more efficient for attracting passers-by: the placard – the *titulus* – borne at the end of a pole in various circumstances (by the religious person going to the temple for an offering or sacrifice, the executioner or lictor accompanying the sentenced individual and the like).[37] Most particularly, these banners were carried during ceremonies of triumph or imperial funerals that bore triumphal connotations. The placards held by lictors, which we still see on the Arch of Titus (Figure 2.2),[38] preceding the most remarkable item in the triumph over the Jews, the seven branched candelabrum brought back from the temple of Jerusalem, are clear of text. Were they painted? Only one extant marble plaque, from Cherchel,[39] presents the combination of *ferculum* (a litter) and *titulus*: the *ferculum* supports a model bridge[40] while the *titulus* indicates its name, the '*Pons Milvius*' (Figure 2.3).

Information designed to be seen (and maybe to be heard too if the 'public cry' was associated with movement) was quite diverse. During Claudius' triumph over

Figure 2.1 Relief with a representation of the Temple of Concord (the sign of a farmer of weights and measures?) Rome, Musei Vaticani (photo Musei Vaticani, Archivio fotografico)

Figure 2.2 Arch of Titus: Triumph against the Jews. Rome (after Bianchi Bandinelli, 1969, p. 215, Figure 238)

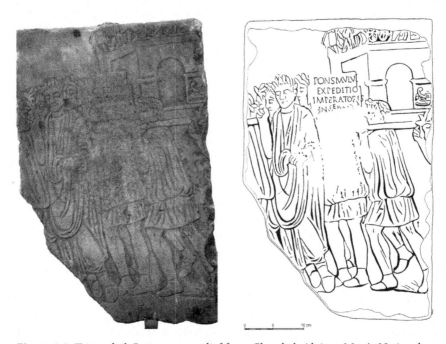

Figure 2.3 Triumphal Cortege on a relief from Cherchel, Algiers, Musée National des Antiquités (photo A. Teatini)

Britain, the *fercula* bearing the golden wreaths offered by the Gauls and the Spanish were preceded on this occasion, according to Pliny the Elder, by *tituli* presenting the name of the donor provinces and the exceptional weight of both wreaths.[41] Aurelian's triumph would have also included a procession of golden wreaths, accompanied by the enumeration of the various cities of the Empire which participated in this homage.[42] These signs, however, also provided opportunities for imagination: captives exhibited during Aurelian's triumph were promoted to being 'amazons'.[43] In the same vein, Pliny the Younger was fascinated by the exotic names of captive princes who walked behind placards bearing their names.[44]

Placards were also borne during the funeral of Augustus, where the ceremonial was inspired by the triumph. Some recalled the name of the laws initiated by the *princeps*, and others the names of nations defeated by him (or defeated in his name).[45] Upon his return from Greece, Nero staged a very peculiar triumph which did not lead him to the temple of Capitoline Jupiter but rather to the temple of Palatine Apollo. The motive of the triumph was to commemorate his victories during the artistic contests (or chariot races), which were indicated by notices.[46]

Were dignitaries also, in normal circumstances, preceded by banners indicating their rank? Such a practice would have probably left traces in literature. It is attested for legates while they exercised their authority, notably by stucco reliefs on a mausoleum at Carthage which present a soldier bearing a *vexillum* with word *legatus* before a mounted officer.[47] In this case the inscription also serves as a 'key' for the scene depicted on the funerary monument.

Graffiti were also created to be read, and literature has recorded some of those that contained political messages.[48] The walls of certain public or semi-public places[49] – a basilica, the *vigiles'* post in Trastevere, waiting rooms and ante-chamber of the pages in the imperial palace, taverns (let us note that these places are all virtually exclusively masculine) – prove that at least some people could write.

If Rome presented us with reading material, it also, as we know, presented us with material to look at. News and propaganda also came across through images as well as through writing. Such images would have been either ephemeral, such as battle scenes displayed during triumphs,[50] or durable, such as 'historical reliefs',[51] with the first category serving sometimes as models for the second (for instance the four panels showing the seizure of cities which decorate the Arch of Septimius Severus, Figures 2.4 and 2.13).[52]

The multiple references to the practice of writing on reliefs are also of interest. For instance: the depiction of the burning of the archives to demonstrate the finality of the fiscal amnesty (Figure 2.5);[53] the registering of citizens during the *census* (Figure 2.6);[54] the aforementioned *tituli* of the triumphal processions; the banal symbolism widespread on all monuments and supports of Victory writing on a *clipeus virtutis* (Figure 2.7).[55]

The list gives one the impression of overlapping uses of images and writing, made to be seen and read individually, but also associated. This overlap is probably best represented by coins[56] which are the only signs capable of being reproduced identically in thousands or tens of thousands of copies and invested with a strong symbolic power.

Figure 2.4a–b Arch of Septimius Severus. Rome, Forum (photo Deutsches Archäologisches Institut Rom)

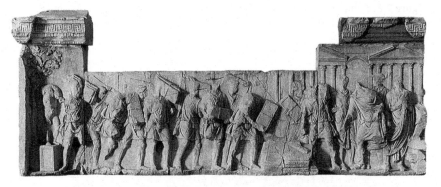

Figure 2.5 'Plutei Triani': The burning of the archives, Rome, Curia (photo Deutsches Archäologisches Institut Rom; Felbermeyer, Neg. 1968.2783, D-Dai-Rom 68.2785)

Observations

This inventory allows for a few observations concerning the use of writing in Rome, and on its place and function in public space, which I will now summarize.

Durable display and publication

In Rome, publication means posting up the written word. It gives the contents of the latter an autonomous existence, independent from mankind and speech, and which

Figure 2.6 Scene of a census from the relief called 'of Domitius Ahenobarbus' (photo M. and P. Chuzeville)

Figure 2.7 Base of the 'decennals', AD 303: 'Caesarum decennalia feliciter', Rome, forum (photo Deutsches Archäologisches Institut Rom; Faraglia, D-Dai-Rom 35.734)

also prevents it from being forgotten or worn away over time. In other words, publication gives the contents spatio-temporal continuity which guarantees the artefact's identity. Publication is regarded as necessary for a certain number of texts of interest to the city and its institutions. Here it plays a central role – which can no longer be seen in later periods. From this perspective, in which writing and power are joined together, and which Armando Petrucci[57] made an important long-term constant, Rome represents a real peak.

Religious affairs only occupy a limited place in these publications. Roman religion is not a religion of the book and, significantly, texts of a religious nature[58] usually imitate the contents of official acts: *leges templorum*, dedications to gods, minutes of sessions (acts of the *Fratres Arvales* ...), ceremony arrangements (secular games ...), etc.

The principal use of these publications is, on the contrary, tied to politics in the broadest sense. This primacy of politics thus explains:

• The topics covered in the texts which were brought to the knowledge, effective or potential, of all citizens by the authorities (law and legislation; urbanism and maintenance of monuments; armies and war; administration and finance; taxation).
• The varied choices of supports and writings, in order to promote their greater majesty and longevity.
• And finally, the choice of the spaces reserved for this 'publication'.

Thus, public space presents, on the one hand, monumental letters which imposed upon the gaze of the passer-by regardless of whether they intended to read them and regardless of their movements, and on the other hand, texts in small characters which require one to stop and to deliberately spend time reading them.[59] Among the first category, we must reserve a special place for monumental arches placed directly in line with traffic circulation, and particularly for the anamorphosis, (the technique of engraving the lines in letters of increasing height as they get more distant from the viewer, in order to give the impression that the letters are all of the same height when the reader is at the foot of the monument) of the lines of the Arch of Titus[60] which are still clearly visible today for those descending from the Palatine side on to the monument (Figure 2.8).

No other society after the Romans will recognize the same importance in durable displays. In our society, permanent public writing is limited to commemorative uses, and the law – which no-one can ignore – is simply printed in the official government register, which has few real readers but which all may consult.

The status of the original

Writing thus invades public space, (a problem which the Ancients also experienced with statues[61]), but it also hierarchizes and organizes it.

Of course, not all legal and administrative texts had always been displayed like this. But Rome, since the Law of the Twelve Tables, lived under the regime of published law. The Republic did display propositions for laws although it did not

Figure 2.8 Inscription of the Arch of Titus. Rome (photo Deutsches Archäologisches Institut Rom; Schwanke, D-Dai-Rom 79.2014)

feel the need to proceed in the same systematic manner for these laws once they had been voted, insomuch as they had been voted by the people. Only the most important ones were on display (Figure 2.9).[62] It was always this way under the Empire (Figure 2.10). The decision to display the *senatus consulta*, the laws, the most important edicts, but also simple administrative responses, was, in Rome, made by the originating authorities themselves; while in Italy or in the provinces, it was made by individuals or *collegia* and local authorities who published arrangements made in their favour or which pertained to them in one way or another. It is probable, if not certain, that systematic displays would have been arranged for all regulations directly relating to the people of Rome (urbanism, taxes …).[63] The conflict between Caligula and the people of Rome testifies *a contrario* to regular publication of tax regulations. The emperor had promulgated a series of new taxes 'announced, but not displayed' (*vectigalibus indictis neque propositis*) in order to multiply the number of offenders. Pressed by public opinion, he resolved to display the law (*proposuit quidem legem*) 'but in minute letters, in a very tight place, so that no one may take a copy of it'. This parodic passage takes up the inverse of the formula devoted to the publication of official texts: *unde de plano recte legi possit*, discussed below. Nero, on his part, sought popularity by demanding that levels of charges imposed by tax farmers (*publicani*) be displayed.[64]

Figure 2.9 *Lex Antonia de Termessibus* (fragment), 68 BC? Naples, National Archaeological Museum (after ILLRP. Imagines, n. 388; by kind permission of the Ministry for Cultural Assets and Activities – Soprintendenza Speciale per i Beni Archeologici di Napoli e Pompei)

Publication marks – in principle – a point of no return. That Domitian went back on his decision regarding an edict on the destruction of the vines, which had already been displayed, was noted. What was the motive for this withdrawal? A pamphlet: *ut edicti de excidendis vineis propositi gratiam faceret …*[65]

Overall, the frontier between documents which are simply archived[66] and those documents displayed on a support of bronze, which had pretensions to durability, remains unclear. Durability was marked by the performance of a gesture – the fixing of a nail (*figere*) in a wall, usually that of a temple[67] – which was also a magical act.[68] This is what raises the question of the status of the original text – a unique piece – from which a copy (*exemplar*) is delivered or taken. In order to restore the 3,000 bronze tables destroyed in the fire of the Capitol in AD 69, Vespasian ordered a search for existing copies of: 'senatus consulta and plebiscites, relating to the alliances, to the treaties, to the privileges granted', a collection of texts defined as *instrumentum imperii*.[69] What, then, is an original? The text recorded in the archives? Or the text carved in bronze to potentially be placed under the gaze of all? The very conditions of the texts' reproduction and the absence of any kind of signature place us in a world where authentication follows other rules than our own, and where a copy can easily replace the original, the destruction of which casts it into oblivion.

It is as if the validity of a text, even when produced by the state's highest authorities, is identified with the continuity of its support. Public space is thus invested with a fundamental function: it is its role to preserve, unchanged, under the uninterrupted gaze of all, and sheltered from all manipulation, the texts essential to the life of the city and the status of individuals. The duration of the *monumentum* (the bronze plaque

Figure 2.10 *Lex de imperio Vespasiani* (missing the start) AD 69–70, Rome, Musei Capitolini (photo Deutsches Archäologisches Institut Rom; Singer, D-Dai-Rom 71.1939; CIL 6.930 = 31207 = ILS 244). See also Gregori and Mattei, 1999, p. 595

itself) appears as the only solution to the fragility of wooden or wax tablets... A law of Constantine, directed to the African decurions, preserved in the Theodosian Code, specifies: 'For this to be perpetually observed, we ordain that this law, carved in bronze tablets, be publicly exposed'.[70]

The use of plaques affixed to the wall – mobile by definition – contrasts, however, with the practice of incising the actual walls of temples and public monuments in Classical Greece (of which the sanctuary of Apollo at Delphi offers fine examples). The notion of duration does not exclude the sentiment of provisionality, or predictable discontinuities, that the Empire may have, in a certain way, accentuated.

The Empire in any case seems to have spread the practice of honorific displays in bronze, be they durable or not: notably with the institution of imperial constitutions in favour of the veterans.[71] Independently from involuntary destructions related to the fires of the Capitol in AD 69 and 80, it is reasonable to envisage reworking of the plaques a few decades after their exposure, once the beneficiaries were deceased: some military diplomas were made from these plaques. History gives way to current events, and the past gives way to the present, which is itself the subject of these displays.

Traces of *senatus consulta* in Pallas' honour, the freed slave and the person responsible for Claudius' finances, remained, of course, in the Senate's session reports (*acta senatus*), where Pliny the Younger consulted the text 50 years later, but also on Pallas' funerary monument raised on the Via Tiburtina, a private space protected by the rights of tombs.[72] However, the commemorative bronze plaque affixed, during Pallas' life, *ad statuam loricatam divi Iulii* – presumably in Caesar's Forum – had apparently been 'removed'.[73] This symbolic practice is similar to the knocking down of statues.

The finest documents related to similar commemorative displays '*in aere*' are incontestably the *senatus consulta* concerning the death of Germanicus: the (second) *senatus consultum* of December AD 19 on the posthumous honours to be held for Germanicus, and the *senatus consultum* on Piso's condemnation a year later on 10 December AD 20. Both texts have been transmitted to us through copies found outside Rome.[74]

Legibility and the choice of the most frequented place within the city were two required conditions for the display of the text. From these conditions issued the famous epigraphic formula: *celeberrimo loco proponendum curent, unde de plano recte legi possit* ('may they take care that it be displayed in a highly frequented place, in a location where one may read it easily').[75] We find the same *celeberrimus locus* in Pliny the Younger's indignant letter regarding the display of the *senatus consultum* in Pallas' honour.[76] *A contrario*, Caligula, as we have seen, had new taxes printed 'in minute letters in a very tight place' (*minutissimis litteris et angustissimo loco*).[77] This situation raises the question of place. Carefully chosen, these places are never neutral but contributed to the creation of spatial references, which, for contemporaries, already held, or were in the process of taking on, a particular meaning.

Places of display

The space dedicated to publicity, which was initially limited, progressively expanded. At the same time there was an equally progressive specialization of places for display. (On the value of the *meson* – the centre – in the Greek city's political vocabulary, we have works such as those of Jean-Pierre Vernant and Marcel Detienne).[78]

In republican Rome,[79] the Rostra and the Temple of Saturn appear as favoured supports for legal texts. The Capitol, which also hosted these texts, is tied to the sphere of international relations (for instance treaties or concessions of privileges).[80]

In imperial Rome, an exemplary case concerning the delimitation of a zone for display is brought to us by constitutions in favour of veterans.[81] In Claudius' reign there was an initial symbolic choice: the wall of the temple of *Fides*, the deity guaranteeing engagements, an exhibit *in aede*. The whole essence of this display invites us to identify this wall with the temple's external wall rather than its *cella*.[82] Next, diffusion of texts on the *aera Capitolina* was not, according to Slobodan Dušanić, due to the simple chance of available surfaces, but instead could have had a more concrete significance; hence the constitutions relating to veterans of the German wars under Domitian on the monument dedicated to Germanicus. A first attempt at defining a space for official display might be to suggest the *ara gentis Iuliae*[83] in AD 69–71; a construction where the external wall would have intentionally been left clear of all decoration, as opposed, for example, to that of the *ara Pacis*. Finally, the delimitation of a definite display zone or, more precisely, a wall, between the forum and the Palatine behind the Temple of the Divine Augustus: *in muro post templum divi Augusti ad Minervam* (according to F. Coarelli, this cult of 'Minerva' could have given its name to the Athenaeum).[84]

This evolution, in the sense of specialization, must be linked to the new administrative role, clarified by F. Castagnoli,[85] granted to a certain number of locales in the urban space, notably those bearing the name *atrium*. The preference accorded to the city's central spaces, for the display of these texts, such as the forum, the Capitol, the imperial forums, and the monuments within these spaces (temples, altars, bases), whose principal function was not this type of use, is important. Whether it was of an administrative, legal or political nature, the displayed document needed a sanctification which erased its ties with the authority which had produced it, so that it may be placed under superior protection and given another type of existence. The Curia was just one meeting place for a Senate which could as easily hold its meetings elsewhere. The *senatus consulta* of December AD 19 carved in bronze and concerned with Germanicus' posthumous honours were displayed: 'on the Palatine, in the portico of Apollo's temple, in the *templum* in which the Senate had met'.[86] The people no longer voted for or against laws, whereas previously they had met in the open to vote. Moreover, the Emperor's offices preserved the official status of a domesticity which depended uniquely on him. The *senatus consulta* in Pallas' honour were probably displayed in proximity to the administrative services he had run, imperial finances, for which it would have then been necessary to search the locales in the Forum of Caesar.[87]

It would be worth following how the institutions, clearly defined and having set up their own buildings, such as that of the Prefecture of the City,[88] managed to develop their own functional and 'secularized' display areas. 'Secularized' insomuch as this term makes sense for Rome where certain administrative services were placed under divine protection, hence, Ceres and Flora for the *annona*[89] and Juturna for the administration of the waters ... [90] According to F. Coarelli,[91] the Severan marble map of the Temple of Peace, the *Forma Urbis Romae*, was tied to the Prefecture of the City at that time. As for the display of the prefects' edicts, this had been done since the 330s under the Prefecture's very porticoes. It is precisely the discovery of some of the fragments of these edicts, but also the location of the bases of the prefects' honorific statues near the Basilica of Maxentius which confirms the Prefecture's location in the immediate vicinity.[92]

These various display practices – and notably the indication, on copies, of the 'original's' location, or to be more precise, the displayed copy of the original, invite us to recognize them as being for *reference*, rather than for information. Writing legitimizes. Nothing about it is banal. Writing has all the juridical value of the documentary proof of which our erudition has maintained the practice: one must give the exact text but also, simultaneously, the exact location at which it can be consulted and verified. Many ancient authors cited inscriptions to support their narratives.[93] Among the grounds for pride of Lucius Iulius Agrippa of Apamea, a contemporary of Trajan but a descendent of the tetrarchs, appear ancestors 'inscribed on the Capitol on bronze plaques as allies of the Romans...',[94] a privilege accorded by Augustus a century earlier and of which a copy had been preserved in the archives at Apamea.

Power and the practice of writing

The Roman practice of power (with its succession of magistracies, recourse to euergetism, rights of the victorious general over booty) was revived by emperors for their own benefit. It allowed the individual holding the authority of the Roman people, and who acts in their name or in their favour, to sign acts and carry them out. By inscribing one's name on an edifice, and primarily on a temple (which does not always carry the name of the divinity), one is appropriating it. Moreover, the prestige of one restoring an earlier monument is no less important: in effect the restorer participates in its foundation.[95]

On the *Haterii*'s funerary monument (Figure 2.11), the course of action taken by that family of contractors to label the arches,[96] using inscriptions, is interesting since these inscriptions are both incorrect. The commissioner and/or the artist used the space which would have normally been reserved for the building's dedication to name these arches '*arcus ad Isis*' and '*arcus in sacra via summa*'. The family had laid a claim to the arches by inserting them on their tomb, and recreating their exact dedications would have meant restoring them to their dedicator.

In Rome, dedication of a public monument was no small affair. Already during the Republic, anecdotes regarding disappointment over the lack of inscription of one's name, or 'cheating' occurring in a way that someone's name was inscribed alone,[97] already abounded.[98] The builder had the right to leave his name on the monument,[99] and it was an obligation for descendants to maintain those erected by their ancestors.[100] However, from the beginning of the Principate, individuals lost their right to build public edifices in the capital city, although they still held it in the provinces.[101]

Even though the contemporary official discourse – the *Res Gestae* and the funerary eulogy pronounced by Tiberius[102] – credits Augustus with 'discretion' for having reconstructed the temple of Capitoline Jupiter and the theatre of Pompey without carving his name on them, it was nevertheless a systematic policy of Augustus' to inscribe the name *Iulius* on all the edifices surrounding the Forum Romanum, as modern authors have noted.[103] After the construction of the *porticus Iulia* in honour of Gaius and Lucius Caesar in AD 12, the last act of this regime, all the passers-by in the centre of the forum could, in looking around, read the name of the *Iulii* on the four sides of the plaza.

Figure 2.11 Funerary monument of the *Haterii*. Detail. Rome, Musei Vaticani (photo Musei Vaticani. Archivio fotografico)

The emperors demonstrated the whole range of possible attitudes. Some were discrete: Augustus according to official propaganda, as we have already seen, Tiberius, Claudius, and also Hadrian, who was respectful of Agrippa's name.[104] Others went to the other extreme: they either put their name everywhere, with (for instance Septimius Severus) or without (Nero) the pretext of a reconstruction,[105] or they built too much, like Domitian.[106] The latter's constructions consisted especially of arches which did not have any utilitarian purpose, but instead served to make the emperor's name appear everywhere, in the very axis of the street – from where it could be seen from far afield and from both sides. There were also emperors who exaggerated over legalism or humility. This phenomenon is however also a programme of government: for instance Nerva had *publicae aedes* (a public building) inscribed on the imperial palace.[107] In normal circumstances, the name of the emperor himself sufficed.

If the *Res Gestae* includes the monuments built or restored by Augustus through his patrimony,[108] the distinction between the emperor's private finances and public finances becomes difficult to gauge. At Rome, Claudius was the first to present himself as responsible for the expenditure by applying the typical epigraphic formula for personal benefaction to the inscription carved on his aqueduct cutting the Via Labicana and the Via Praenestina with two arches: '*sua impensa in Urbem (aquas) perducendas curauit*'.[109] This inscription attracted two others: that of Vespasian then that of his son Titus, who both restored the aqueduct (Figure 2.12).[110] This type of precision becomes rarer later.[111]

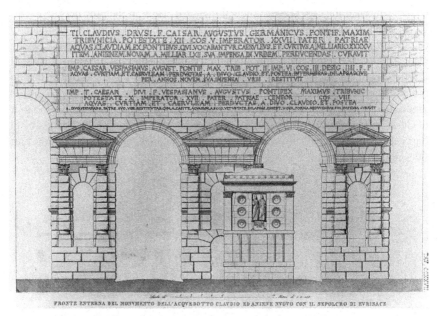

Figure 2.12 Dedication of the aqueduct of Claudius; restorations of Vespasian and Titus. At front, the tomb of Eurysaces. Rome, Porta Maggiore (drawing; photo Deutsches Archäologisches Institut Rom)

The famous inscription '*ex manubiis*' ('from booty') was deployed on Trajan's Forum in order to tie the expenditure of the prince with his victory, thus legitimizing it, and accorded with the decorative programme commemorating the conquest of Dacia.[112] The money had been taken from booty, and was not the product of regular taxes. Unlike Greek temples, or at least some of them, the walls of Roman temples did not display the financial accounts of their construction.[113]

A parallel situation to the anxiety over carving one's name, is its removal in a case of *abolitio nominis*[114] through erasure and potentially the eventual engraving of an anodyne text in the empty space.[115] At Rome, was the gaze of passers-by towards these alterations and regrets (of which the Arch of Septimius Severus offers the best example[116]; Figure 2.13), sharp like that of Piranesi, whose imaginary inscriptions were riddled with erased lines?[117] Or was it the indifference of the architects of the Villa Medicis on their famous 'envoys'?[118]

The very act of erasure is a source of information – as is the contrary act of not erasing. Thus, the preservation of the Plautilla's name on the Arch of the *argentarii*, long after her repudiation, has been attributed by modern authors to Caracalla's fear of causing popular upheaval.[119] Previously, the people of Rome had supported Claudius' daughter Octavia's cause against her husband Nero who wished to renounce her.

Once, the simple fact that Livia had her son's, the emperor Tiberius, name inscribed after hers on the base of a statue of *divus Augustus* caused gossip.[120] The prince took umbrage at this.

Figure 2.13 The mutilated and reinscribed inscription of the Arch of Septimius Severus. Rome, Forum (photo Soprintendenza archeologica di Roma). See Figure 2.4 above

This public use of a name simultaneously marks the behaviour of individuals who inscribe their names on their tomb[121] and the behaviour of communities: religious and artisanal colleges or corps of troops stationed in the city. Each person's survival (dependent on political status and social condition) was limited to a name inscribed in letters of variable size. The name of the emperor formed a cartouche which develops throughout a reign, but which, above all, increased in size and solemnity over centuries.[122] Conversely, Propertius wrote: 'when I am nothing but a tiny name on a tiny marble plaque'.[123] It is the 'name', we know, that authors of graffiti prioritize in their writings. This is a revealing choice, in a society in which the use of a signature, as attested in Egypt on papyri, is less frequent than the use of the seal.[124]

A practice on which historians of antiquity have not placed sufficient value deserves special attention here. Rome is a place in which lists could be read everywhere: lists of names in particular (Figure 2.14), but also those of units of soldiers or simply place names on itineraries. The list is, nevertheless, a form of written text which stands apart from spoken word and communication, and whose presence in the initial phases of literate cultures was the object of a remarkable study by Jack Goody.[125] Even better,

Figure 2.14 Homage to the family of Septimius Severus from a group of *vigiles* (firemen), Rome, Musei Capitolini (after Gordon, 1983, p. 47)

the list is often accompanied by a formula. The list can be retrospective, thus, the *fasti* of the republican period that Augustus reconstituted on his arch in the forum[126]; or it can be set in the present, the 'real' *fasti*, such as those found in Ostia[127] (Figure 2.15); or the list can be a witness, photographing at a precise moment the composition of a specific group: units of troops (Figure 2.14), professional colleges, etc.[128] Neither are lists absent from the cities of Italy or the provinces; Canosa, in Puglia, yielded to us the *album*, the orderly list, of the city's decurions of AD 223, preceded by the names of the patrons of the city (Figure 2.16), and Timgad, in Algeria, gave us a municipal album from the fourth century.[129]

The list implies a form of spatial structure: a vertical arrangement in columns which can demonstrate chronological order. The information contained in the list, however, can also be reclassified under several separate columns. Examples of such arrangements would be the constitutions in favour of veterans, which, carved in bronze, appeared during Claudius' reign and which associated a formula related to privileges granted, a list of the relevant corps of troops and the nominative list of liberated soldiers.[130] The slight modifications to the formulary over time and to the concessions accorded to the benefit of the soldiers do not concern us here. No original

Figure 2.15 Fragment of the Fasti Ostienses (AD 94–96), Ostia (photo Soprintendenza archeologica di Ostia, by kind permission of the Soprintendenza Speciale per i Beni Archeologici di Roma e Ostia).

Figure 2.16 The album of Canusium (*CIL* 10.338 = ERCanosa 35) AD 223 (photo Marcella Chelotti)

has been preserved, but we can consider as a prototype the edict by which Gnaeus Pompeius Strabo gave Roman citizenship to Spanish horsemen in 89 BC; an edict carved in bronze with a list of the beneficiaries in columns (Figure 2.17). It was found near the Capitol on which it had presumably been displayed.

In their strict hierarchical presentation, the dedications of the cohorts of the *vigiles* to the emperors also form an interesting series to observe; in actual fact for the arrangement of the lists the bases are even more interesting than the bronze plaque reproduced here (Figure 2.14). The latter presents in effect the facsimile of a written page layout, offering, with letters decreasing in height, imperial titles followed by authorities and officers, and names of the *vigiles* dedicators in a column. The peculiarity of this piece is that it is adorned with bronze appliqués, the only original being young Caracalla's head on the right.[131] The three-dimensional bases (not reproduced here) display the contrast of: one smoothed face, clearly delimited by a border, where, under the name of the Emperor, those of the officers on the full page albeit with letters of decreasing height, as is proper; and roughly levelled-off sides presenting the names of simple soldiers (*vigiles*) in very small letters in columnar format.[132]

The list can become an instrument of government propaganda. In Rome there was knowledge (possibly through the dissemination of copies) of the 'edict' which Trajan used, during his stay in Germania, to publish lists (possibly on two columns) of the requisitions (*statio* by *statio*) levied by himself and his predecessor Domitian, just to

Figure 2.17 Edict of Cn. Pompeius Strabo, 89 BC, Musei Capitolini, Rome (after *ILLRP*. Imagines n. 397, see also Gregori and Mattei, 1999, p. 597). The plaque itself could be a copy of AD 70

show that his own levies were lighter.[133] Was this appeal to provincial opinion also diffused in Rome? Mommsen associated a fragment of an 'itinerary' found at Rome to publications of this type.[134] Such a use of the list invites us to consider the relation existing between displayed writing and public opinion.

Finally, the list is also an instrument of power when the names of those whose possessions were confiscated[135] were displayed – as were the names of the proscribed in the last century of the Republic.[136]

Writing and communication

Rome presents a society in which the imperial power seeks to *communicate*, and where, potentially, it seeks it all the more because it had dispossessed the Senate and the people of all decision-making political power. Augustus' autobiography, the *Res Gestae*, or, close to three centuries later, the Preamble of the Maximum Price Edict, present nice epigraphic testimonies of this.[137] The former presents a directed vision of Augustus' seizure of power and the imperial regime, which, it is worth mentioning, did not deceive all the ancients, as shown by the start of the *Annales* of Tacitus,[138] but which strongly influenced historiography up to our own time. The latter presents the motives of the edict of 301 issued by Diocletian to limit prices.

Among the noticeable forms of this communication, notably figure the pair *oratio* of the emperor to the Senate and *edictum apud populum*, diffused, without a doubt, simultaneously through public announcement and through the display of the text. The contents of these imperial edicts were, it seems, most varied:[139]

- Didactic texts: in this way Augustus justified his decision to place around his forum statues of illustrious men with corresponding *elogia*.[140]
- Sermonizing texts: Tiberius blamed the people for their excesses in mourning following the death of Germanicus, by affirming that princes were mortal, but that the Republic was eternal.[141]
- Self-justifications: an official version of the details of Piso's conspiracy was thus circulated by Nero.[142]
- Various promises and unilateral undertakings were announced in the same medium.[143]

By pronouncing an *oratio* to the Senate himself or by having it take the form of a message read in his absence, the Emperor could put in the order of the day the creation of a *senatus consultum*.[144] In the end, consultation was transformed into a vote, pure and simple, without discussion, on these messages to the Senate.

When examining the form of the speeches to the Senate and the people (*in senatu aut in contione populi*), one will remember Fronto's advice to Marcus Aurelius Caesar[145] regarding the avoidance of rare words, obscure or unusual metaphors (which would have no echoes in the memory of the audience). This advice is emphasized by a comparison of the *eloquentia Caesaris* with the sound of the bugle rather than with the clarinet, which was less sonorous and more difficult to listen to. Mass communication aiming at a large public needs simple speech without ambiguities or nuances. To my knowledge, however, there exist no accounts of messages written to the praetorians, to whom the Princeps addresses himself through an *adlocutio*.[146] Without a doubt the 'sound of the bugle' was appropriated for them. It is worth remembering here Claudius' amusing harangue, after the secret divorce and remarriage of his wife, Messalina, in which he promised the praetorians that 'he would never marry again, since marriage was not a success for him'.[147]

This type of communication, it is true, is by definition a one-way communication, which makes it somewhat trivial. There is no other way of verifying its impact other than through negative reactions, through the satirical writings, 'graffiti', jokes and songs, which it provokes and which the governing power is condemned to either ignore and neglect or, as Augustus did, laboriously refute.[148] He answered point by point (in written form?) (*magna cura redarguit*) the *famosi libelli* against him, which circulated *in curia*, and he struck back with an edict (*contradixit edicto*) against the jokes (*ioci*) of the streets of which he had become the victim.

The expression of public opinion

A public opinion was expressed through writing and it places us on the borderline of oral and written communication. This counter-communication usually took the shape of graffiti which reused the same supports offered by the official monuments, but this time for contestation. Suetonius,[149] for instance, described the indirect calls for the assassination of the dictator written on the bases of the statues of Lucius Brutus, the first consul of the Republic, who according to legend had rid Rome of the last Etruscan king, and those of Caesar himself as being 'subscribed' (written below). Conversely, the base of one of Agrippina's statues received, after her assassination, this reproach addressed to Nero: 'I, I am ashamed of you; but you, do you not blush?'[150] The most famous of these graffiti,[151] made in response to the multiplication of arches erected by Domitian, is the word *arci* appended in Greek letters on one of them. The play on words assimilates the plural of the word *arcus* to the Greek verb *arkei*, 'it's enough', which were both pronounced 'arki'; a true 'boomerang' effect.

Yet the displayed pamphlet (*libellus*, always *propositus*), from the popular usage of the song (*carmina vulgata*) with which it was associated, pushes our analysis of the written on, towards the oral. We will in fact not confuse these simple 'placards' with what we call 'the literature of invective',[152] those brochures and pamphletic letters which were circulating inside the political class during the civil wars. A passage by Ulpian included in the Digest is dedicated to such edited, malicious, *libri*, reproduced in a certain number of copies (*quis librum ... scripserit, composuerit, ediderit ...* 'whoever wrote, composed, edited a book...').[153]

So, too, the *libellus*, which was displayed (*propositus*) against the peregrines admitted to the Senate by Caesar[154] and which was, in fact, very brief: '*Bonum Factum* (a reprise of the formula placed at the heading of the edicts). No-one should indicate the Road of the Curia to a new senator'. It echoed the couplet chanted in the streets (*illa vulgo canebantur*):

'After having triumphed over the Gauls, Caesar led them into the Curia.
The Gauls have removed their breeches to put on the laticlave'.

Essential to our study is a textual analysis of a passage of Tacitus' *Annales* which mentions Augustus' extension of the law of treason to simple *dicta*.[155] Until Augustus, 'acts (*facta*) were addressed, words (*dicta*) remained unpunished'. *Primus Augustus*, Augustus first covered himself with this treason law in order to handle a trial *de famosis libellis*, defined in the following line as *procacibus scriptis* – 'insolent writings' – which did not even strike at him, but at 'high ranking men and women'. *Scripta*, even of an insolent nature, which had been considered until then as *dicta* in turn became *facta*, and therefore likely to be pursued. If we believe Tacitus, the pamphlet now only needed to be written to become blameworthy. To further mutate the words into a 'placard' was to compete with official texts, to proceed to a 'publication' in the strongest sense of the term. A similar attitude can be seen on the part of Tiberius, still in the same passage of Tacitus, who was exasperated by the *carmina incertibus auctoribus vulgata* (their means of diffusion are not detailed), which were directed against him at this time. Suetonius, it is true, offers us a more gentle account of these episodes, during which Augustus answers these satirical writings disseminated *in curia*, as we saw above, and settles for simply chasing up those written under a false name.[156] Cassius Dio confirms both types of intervention. Augustus punished the authors and destroyed the pamphlets (in Greek, *biblia*) containing attacks on 'certain people', and led an investigation to clarify whether Publius Plautius Rufus was really responsible for the display of pamphlets by night following the fire of Rome, or whether others were using his name.[157] Even though the contents of these writings appear quite weak, usually being limited to personal accusations, they were perceived at the time as a form of political opposition.

I believe that there is no comparison in form or content between these *famosi libelli*, or at least for those that are still extant, and mazarinades, also named 'libelles' ('pasquinades', satirical writings) which Christian Jouhaud analysed for seventeenth-century France.[158] We have retrieved, it is true, songs which accompanied these texts, which could be more easily learnt and repeated. These songs would not exist, however, if they had not benefited from the support and diffusion of printing (about 50 copies at a time, so we are told). Also these French texts, much longer and more complex than the Roman examples, appear as the result of a clever game (or at least wished to appear so), set up to manipulate a fairly large number of readers, but, even more so, the principal political actors, during the troubled period of the Fronde.[159]

We could indeed apply Roger Chartier's formulation regarding printing to these satirical texts of imperial Rome, and for that matter to a large part of writing in Rome: 'Being communally manipulated, taught by some and deciphered by others, deeply integrated into communal life, it (writing in this case, not printing) is the hallmark of urban culture for most people'.[160]

This practice of the capital city spread around Italy under Tiberius. How can we not think of imitation when an ex-soldier of the praetorian cohorts issues a call to freedom to the slaves of the region of *Brundisium* in the form of these same 'placards' (*positis propalam libellis*), which he had seen on the walls of Rome when he was in the garrison?[161] Such a call for sedition through the means of writing demonstrates the belief that at least a sufficient number of slaves could read the text to others.

These *libelli*, regardless of whether they are in prose or verse, are always brief and are written in both Greek and Latin.[162] This is of course a sign of bilingualism but also, potentially, a sign of a coded language for 'initiates'. Let us not forget that *utraque lingua* can be obscene.[163] These *festivos libellos quos statuae sciunt* ('these mocking pamphlets which are well known to statues'), in Tertullian's formula,[164] did not have a special place for display in imperial Rome, unlike, according to Jean Delumeau, the 'pasquinades' of Sixtus V's Rome.[165] In Rome, 'graffiti' and placards used the same supports.

From the use of puns[166] and versified texts with songs – *carmina et epigrammata proscripta aut vulgata*,[167] we can tell how much the 'oral', and the possibilities of memorization, influence the structure of these satirical writings (which may have known several levels of composition) and other uses of non-displayed writings. Famously, these puns include Tiberius' nickname Caprineus, which means 'the man from Capri',[168] but also 'old goat'.[169]

Games of writing and reading

This taste for formulae and plays on words – which is evident in the slogan '*Tiberius ad Tiberim*' chanted by the people of Rome after Tiberius' death[170] – is in effect a verbal response to the pictorial games of which Paavo Castrén published a whole wall from Rome (which was found under Santa Maria Maggiore and, according to the author, probably belonging to a 'tavern').[171] On it we can see the reproduction of the alphabet (let us face it, the simplest of lists), groups of letters, palindromes and squares, whether 'magical' or not, in Greek and Latin, without, of course, forgetting (Roman) number sequences (Figure 2.18). The term 'magic square' (which can be read both horizontally and vertically) is attributed to the letter groups SATOR-AREPO-TENET-OPERA-ROTAS, to which certain modern scholars had wrongly attributed a crypto-Christian meaning.[172] On the other hand, the most widespread palindrome (to be read from left to right and right to left) in Rome and the Roman West is certainly the simple ROMA-AMOR.

Giancarlo Susini's correct observation regarding the role ready-made expressions, proverbs, may have played in the process of acculturation[173] is not only significant for Italy and its provinces, but is most relevant for a cosmopolitan city like Rome. This leads us to a first conclusion.

Rome, and Roman civilization in the strong sense of the term, presents us with two complementary aspects of the uses of reading and writing. The first aspect, which we can restrict without an excessive risk of being mistaken to a limited and cultivated elite, consists of literature, which harnesses eloquence. Even when pronounced in public, harangues and pleas were, as we know, written and rewritten before circulating among the 'happy few'. These have been taken up by our classical education, which made them the basis of the humanities, inscribing our culture into a past of two millennia ago. We have learnt them at school, before being able to read them, today, with a historian's approach. The second aspect must not consequently be regarded *a priori*, and

Figure 2.18 Graffiti on a wall of an Augustan edifice discovered under the Basilica Santa Maria Maggiore. Rome (photo Musei Vaticani Archivio fotografico)

without any analysis, as the popular form. It associates, through a permanent dialogue with many exchanges, elites and the masses, the masters of power and the multitude of citizens and soldiers; these are mostly men, as the issue is predominantly, if not always, political, and thus excludes women and children from a struggle which takes place, in the last resort, openly in public.

Who are these readers, or rather these reader-writers, about whom historians of other eras,[174] or Claude Nicolet in his *Metier de Citoyen*,[175] and Guglielmo Cavallo for Rome,[176] raise questions? Indeed, it is not possible to escape a question on this subject – is it possible to have texts, and in the case of Rome, widespread and ever present texts, without a large number of readers? Would Roman society have consisted of – at a political level – the first male, literate, society in history? In fact, notions of writing and reading remain too vague to be usefully employed while they have not been given concrete form. Large, contemporary, Indian cities present a similar contrasting profusion of writing (with or without the support of an image) – such as signs or notices – offered to the gaze of a population with low rates of literacy.

Public writing, and on this point I agree with Guglielmo Cavallo,[177] is compatible with a low level of capacity among its readers. The widely cited Hermeros' *'lapidarias litteras scio'*[178] from the *Satyricon* – which should not be separated from the rest of the sentence 'and I can divide to the hundredth-part metal, weight, and coinage' – depicts a character who can read each letter, in large capitals, one by one, but also undoubtedly a certain number of words. The mnemonic systems practised by cultivated men themselves (for instance learning by heart a text which had deliberately been written for memorization purposes, as Quintilian advised[179]) were available to semi-literate individuals. It is these same mnemonic capacities, which relate to forms of writing (palindromes and magic squares) used in hopscotch, and often cut into the paving and pavements of roads and public squares, in which words have a value relating to the number of their letters, and of their order (left to right, right to left, top to bottom) independently of any phrase. Not everyone was able to recite Virgil backwards, nor was this practice very useful. It was nevertheless an appreciated piece of knowledge, a curiosity at the least.[180] As Jack Goody has shown us, writing stimulates memory, on the first reading at least, as it freezes the text and allows controls. Writing maintains the 'oral' and imposes certain demands on it.

The ability to recognize capital letters, the only requirement of readers of epigraphic texts, is of interest to us when considering cognitive processes:[181] recognition of monumental letters requires less effort than cursive texts, which at this period in Rome used also an alphabet of small capitals.

Public writing in Rome – as opposed to literary writing – belongs, in my opinion, to a category which is not the same as limited literacy, nor mass literacy, but a form which I would be tempted to call 'weak literacy', widespread in Roman society. 'Weak literacy' is conceived of here as the recognition and assimilation of the contents of a simple text, the fumbling mastery of writing with letters more frequently recognized than known and used, the important role attributed to memory which allows the crystallization of a limited number of relatively simple words and associations (where terms could be modified or replaced and through which plays on words or puns would be created) and by the constant link it maintains between the 'oral' and the written.

The application of methods of frequency analysis, employed on literary texts in the laboratory in Liège,[182] to graffiti (and why not to inscriptions themselves, or at least to all those which seek to attract the passer-by's gaze such as dedications, epitaphs, signs and so on and which do not reproduce, unlike law, reference texts?), might well reveal the existence of a form of 'basic Latin' adapted by a 'basic writing' for the needs of a 'basic reading'. Such 'basic Latin' may have allowed a large number of people to read, recognize, or to have read to them, a relatively limited number of words or strongly coded, current abbreviations, which were integrated into a deliberately simplified syntax: without relative or subordinate clauses; around a verb in the present or perfect tense (the verb would sometimes have been omitted), with a series of datives, nominatives in apposition and absolute ablatives. This basic knowledge and use is the very basis of communication. It associates the written to the spoken, discovery to recognition, and relies upon the easy comprehension and memorization of already internalized schema; this does not exclude the effects of surprise.

Notes

1 I would like to thank Jacques Baudoin, the director of CNRS éditions, for permission to reproduce in English the first chapter of my book, *Donner à voir, donner à lire: mémoire et communication dans la Rome ancienne*, Paris, 2006. An earlier version of this text was presented at the conference entitled 'L'Urbs: espace urbain et histoire', organized by l'École française de France in May 1985 (Corbier, 1987a).

2 Petrucci, 1980, pp. 5–123. This essay was further developed in 1986.

3 See Sparrow, 1969, whose study deserves to be described as pioneering.

4 See Susini, 1982, in which bibliographical resources on Latin epigraphy at that date are both listed and classified. See also Susini, 1988 and 1989; Lassère, 2005.

5 See Susini, 1966 and 1985a; as well as previous *Epigrafia e Antichità* volumes (published in Faenza), managed by the same author. See also Sanders, 1984 and 1991, and Veyne, 1985, pp. 168–71.

6 Youtie, 1975–81; Cavallo, 1978; MacMullen, 1982; Harris, 1983 and 1989.

7 Knox, 1968. Important texts were read out loud, but silent reading was also practised. See also Petrucci, 1984, p. 604, and Valette-Cagnac, 1997.

8 See, notably, Mallon, 1982–96; Marichal, 1973, pp. 1265–317; the works of Petrucci and of Cavallo; on the intrinsic beauty of Greek and Latin epigraphy Fitchtenau, 1946, pp. 75–88.

9 See, notably, the different issues of the journal *Scrittura e civiltà* created in 1977; the collection *Alfabetismo e cultura scritta…*, 1978; Cardona, 1977, 1981, 1982; Basso, 1974.

10 Goody, 1968, pp. 1–26, 27–68. The expression 'restricted literacy' is applied by the author to the uses of writing which remain inscribed in the system of oral culture.

11 Goody, 1977–9, 1986, 1987–94.

12 For a brief synthesis see the exhibition catalogue *Naissance de l'écriture: cunéiformes et hiéroglyphes (Paris, Galeries nationales du Grand Palais 7 mai–9 août 1982)*, Paris, 1982. Read Havelock, 1973, 1982; Havelock and Hershbell, 1976–81.

13 Detienne, 1964 and 1988.

14 Eisenstein, 1979. The important stage of the twelfth to thirteenth centuries, which

saw the double diffusion of writing in the administration, and the reading of
manuscript books, does not directly concern our argument (see Clanchy, 1979,
Petrucci, 1984, pp. 603–16).

15 Harris, 1983, p. 91.

16 See, notably, Gigante, 1979; Franklin, 1980 and 1991; Sabbatini Tumolesi, 1980;
    Chiavia, 2002.

17 Roberts and Skeat, 1983; Blanchard, 1989.

18 One finds a number of examples brought together in the books of Gordon, 1958–65
    and 1983.

19 On this see the publications of Bowman and Thomas, 1983, 1994, 2003; and
    Lalou, 1992. Thanks to Alan Bowman I had the pleasure to see, and touch, at the
    Ashmolean Library, in 1985, the tablets discovered during the course of that summer.

20 Read 'Epigrafia e palaeografia. Inchiesta sui rapporti fra due discipline,' in *Scrittura e
    civiltà*, 5, 1981, pp. 265–312.

21 Plin. *HN* 34.99: *Usus aeris ad perpetuitatem monimentorum iam pridem tralatus
    est tabulis aereis, in quibus publicae constitutiones inciduntur* ('The employment of
    bronze was a long time ago applied to securing the perpetuity of monuments, by
    means of bronze tablets on which records of official enactments are made' trans.
    Rackham, Loeb Classical Library 394, p. 201); but see, for example, Cic. *Cat.* 3.19:
    legum aera, and *Phil.* 1.16 *acta Caesaris firma erunt, quae ille in aes incidit…* ('that
    the acts of Caesar will be unshakeable; whereas measures that Caesar inscribed
    on bronze …' trans. Shackleton Bailey, revised by Ramsey and Manuwald, Loeb
    Classical Library 189, p. 23) and Plin. *Pan.* 75: *quae uos, patres conscripti, ne qua
    interciperet obliuio, et in publica acta mittenda et incidenda in aere censuitis* ('all that
    you, Conscript Fathers, decided to save from oblivion by publishing in the official
    records and inscribing on bronze.' trans. Shackleton Bailey, revised by Ramsey
    and Manuwald, Loeb Classical Library 59, p. 499). In 1987 Williamson published
    interesting research devoted to the symbolic value of this display, which could not
    take into account the *senatus consulta* of 19/20 transmitted by the bronze tables of
    Andalucía; see also Williamson, 2005.

22 MacMullen, 1982, has observed that the eruption of epitaphs which started in the
    first century, diminished, bit by bit, during the third century. A hundred thousand
    epitaphs have been found; according to Veyne, 1985, p. 170 'elles ne dérivent pas
    d'une idée élémentaire de la mort mais d'un règne de la parole publique et du
    contrôle public'. On the other hand, as has been pointed out to me by Paul Veyne
    'une particularité de la province de Syrie (hellénisée en surface) est que, malgré de
    très grandes villes, il n'y a que très peu d'épitaphes'.

23 Sanders, 1984, p. 98.

24 See Gordon, 1983, pp. 78–80, no. 4 (*cippus* of the *forum Romanum*); pp. 87–8, no.
    12 (mile stone); p. 118, no. 43 (limit of the *pomerium*). On the markers attesting the
    obligation of paying city tolls, Le Gall, 1979, pp. 121–6.

25 Carettoni et al. 1960; Rodríguez-Almeida, 1981. The *Templum Pacis* (or, alternatively,
    Forum of Peace) had been in effect, most likely, the seat of the prefecture of the city
    in its first development; Coarelli, 2005, pp. 152–3.

26 Plin. *HN* 3.17; see Roddaz, 1984, p. 293.

27 On these 'schedules of journeys' incorrectly called 'itineraries' in the past, read
    Arnaud, 1992, whose work has underlined notably that they did not include any
    indication of the distance, but on the contrary indicated dates. Levi, 1967, pp.
    25–32 gives a list, pp. 27–8, n. 29. The Roman inscription on marble (*CIL* 6.5076)

is a fragment of a list of stages which concerns the Emperor Hadrian (Syme, 1988, p. 160). It has been commented on briefly by Miller, 1916, p. 664. Following the *Historia Augusta* (*Alex. Sev.*, 45), Severus Alexander, the ideal emperor, had affixed the schedule of his journeys (at Rome and in the relevant provinces?) before embarking upon an expedition. An inscription from Syria has conserved a memory of a journey of Caracalla: *IGLS*, IV, 1346.

28 The formula is that of Veyne, 1976, p. 756, n. 236.

29 *CIL* 6.1585a and b and pp. 4715–6 (= *ILS* 5920); see Gordon, 1983, pp. 152–4, no. 69.

30 *CIL* 6.33840 = *FIRA²*, III, no. 147; see Gordon, 1983, pp. 161–2, no. 76.

31 For instance the text of the *Res Gestae* of Augustus found at Ancyra (Ankara); see Gordon, 1983, pp. 108–10; Gagé, 1977.

32 See the classic study of Stein, 1931 and that of Chevallier, 1972, pp. 11–13. On Suetonius' interest regarding inscriptions, but also public notices and graffiti, read Gascou, 1984, pp. 515–35 and 565 (in particular Suetonius had used the text of the *Res Gestae*, readable in his day on the bronze plaques attached to the two quadrangular pillars erected in front of the Mausoleum of Augustus). And, on the utilization of inscriptions by Tacitus, see Bérard, 1991, pp. 3015–25.

33 An edict known from an inscription of Pergamum: *FIRA²*, I, no. 73 = Oliver, 1989, no. 38. On the practice of painting the heading in red, see Fol, 1877, pp. 1325–31, *s.v. color*.

34 For instance at Rome the column of Maenius close to the basilica of Porcia was, at the end of the Republic, the location of display devoted to public auctions, Veyne, 1983–91, pp. 21–2 (see Schol. Bob. ad Cic., *Pro Sestio*, 8.18: '*columna etiam Maenia, apud quam debitores a creditoribus proscribebantur*'). See the plan of the area proposed by Coarelli, 1983, p. 139, and *LTUR*, I, *s.v. Columna Maenia*).

35 Guarducci, 1962, pp. 93–110; see Becatti, 1973–4, pp. 30–3.

36 See Platner and Ashby, 1929, *s.v. Castor* and *Ops*; and *LTUR*, I, *s.v. Castor*, and III *s.v. Ops Opifera*.

37 Veyne, 1983.

38 Pfanner, 1983, pl. 54.

39 Torelli, 1982, pp. 124–5, and pl. V.6; and 1998, p. 139. Read also Mastino and Teatini, 2001.

40 On these monuments as reduced models Gros, 1976, pp. 60–1.

41 Plin. *HN*, 33.54: '*Claudius ..., cum de Brittania triumpharet, inter coronas aureas VII pondo habere, quam contulisset Hispania citerior, VIIII quam Gallia comata, titulis indicauit*' ('Claudius when celebrating a triumph after the conquest of Britain, advertised by placards that among the coronets there was one having a weight of 7000 pounds contributed by Hither Spain and one of 9000 from Gallia Comata' trans. Rackham, Loeb Classical Library 394, p. 45).

42 S.H.A. *Aurel.* 34.3: *praeferebantur coronae omnium ciuitatum aureae titulis eminentibus proditae.*

43 S.H.A. *Aurel.* 34.1: *ductae sunt et decem mulieres ... quas de Amazonum genere titulus indicabat – praelati sunt tituli gentium nomina continentes.*

44 Plin. *Pan.* 17. See on the same issue n. 43, the Triumph of Aurelian.

45 Tac. *Ann.* 1.8.3.

46 Suet. *Ner.* 25.

47 Veyne, 1961, pp. 34–5; Romanelli, 1970, p. 321 with pl. 259b (a detail of the scene which unfortunately excludes the bearer of the *vexillum*...) – references which I owe to René Rebuffat, as is true for the suggestion of Dio Cassius, 40.18.3: among the

unfavourable omens of the war of Crassus against the Parthians, figured the takeoff and fall into the Euphrates of a *vexillum* 'which indicated in scarlet letters the name of the legion and that of its general'. For other references read MacMullen, 1984, p. 446. See also Corbier, 2006, pp. 97–9 (inscribed *vexilla*).

48 Gascou, 1984, pp. 517–8 and pp. 565–6; Susini, 1982, pp. 122–3.

49 See notably: Della Corte, 1933, pp. 111–30; Solin and Itkonen-Kaila, 1966; Castrén and Lilius, 1970; CIL 6.2998–3091 and 32751 (for the guard-house of the seventh cohort of the vigils in Trastevere); Castrén, 1972 (for the tavern (?) found under the Basilica of Santa Maria Maggiore).

50 Following Herodian 3.9.12, Septimius Severus had displayed at Rome several large tableaus representing the episodes of his conquest of the East. Napoleon was accompanied by painters on his campaigns.

51 On historical reliefs see Torelli, 1982 and 1998; on the reliefs of Trajan's column Veyne 1991.

52 Bianchi Bandinelli et al., 1964, p. 39.

53 Represented on the reliefs conserved today in front of the Curia and considered, following the authors, as the *anaglypha Traiani* or *Hadriani*, and in the same way that on the Chatsworth relief: see Rüdiger, 1973, pp. 161–73, in particular pp. 168–9, with pl. 4, 9 and 10; Torelli, 1982, pp. 105–9, with pl. IV.2, IV.9–11, IV.16.

54 On the relief called 'of Domitius Ahenobarbus', see Torelli, 1982, pp. 9–10, with pl. I, 4a; and 1998, p. 142.

55 For instance: on monuments such as the Column of Trajan and the Column of Marcus Aurelius (Wegner, 1931, Figure 1 p. 62 and Figure 1 p. 63); on the base of the *decennalia* erected on the *forum Romanum* in 303 (Castagnoli, 1957, p. 45 '*Caesarum decennalia feliciter*'); on sarcophagi (Février, 1961, p. 11–17); on coins (Wegner, 1931, p. 67, Figure 3: coins of Galba, Vitellius, Vespasian, Trajan, Marcus Aurelius, Septimius Severus; Maurice, 1908–12, III, pl. VIII.5, and pl. XXI.5: coins of Licinius and Constantine), etc.; it is the logo which has been chosen for *L'Année épigraphique*.

56 See Belloni, 1974 and 1976; Crawford, 1983, pp. 47–67.

57 Petrucci, 1985.

58 For the acts of the Arval brothers, see the edition of Scheid, 1998; for the *ludi saeculares*, those of Pighi, 1965 and of Schnegg-Köhler, 2002. On the *leges templorum*, read Magdelain, 1978, pp. 18–19 and 29–31. Finally, on the relationship between religion and writing, Beard, 1991.

59 A distinction illustrated by Giancarlo Susini in his article 'Compitare per via': Susini, 1988.

60 Pfanner, 1983, p. 16, with pl. 12–13.

61 For this reason Augustus cleared the *area Capitolina* of the statues which cluttered it up; transported to the *Campus Martius* they were later destroyed on the orders of Caligula: Suet., *Calig.*, 34.1; see Lahusen, 1983; Eck 1984–96.

62 But any bill, although previously displayed, must be read aloud before the vote: see, particularly, Magdelain, 1978, pp. 17–19. On the display of the laws, Rotondi, 1912 (1966), pp. 167–73 and *Dizionario epigrafico*, IV.23, 1956, pp. 707–10, *s.v. lex*; on the *senatus consulta* Volterra, 1969, pp. 1055–8; and on the whole of the problem Von Schwind, 1940. On the promulgation of the imperial constitutions from the fourth century, Seeck, 1919, pp. 8–10. To these classic studies one adds Crawford, 1996, I (introduction) and Coriat, 1997 (on the promulgation of the edicts in the Severan period).

63 Suet. *Calig.* 41.1. See also Corbier, 2006, pp. 43–4.

64 Tac. *Ann.* 13.51. Among the consequences of this policy figures the translation into Greek, the engraving in marble and the exhibition at Ephesus, 'capital' of the province of Asia, in AD 62 of the rules of the Customs of Asia (*lex portorii Asiae*) in a location that is unfortunately unknown because the inscription had been reused: *AE* 2008, 102 and 1353.

65 Suet. *Dom.* 14.5.

66 On the Roman archives, Cencetti, 1953, pp. 131–66; Posner, 1972; Nicolet 1985, 1994, 1998; and the collective work on '*Mémoire perdue*'.

67 For an 'exposé des motifs' read Tac. *Ann.* 3.63.4.

68 See Piccaluga, in *Cultura e scuola*, 85, January–March 1983, p. 123, n. 23.

69 Suet. *Vesp.* 8.9.

70 *Cod. Theod.* 12.5.2; see Lepelley, 1981, p. 343.

71 Corbier, 1984a and Corbier, 2006, pp. 131–46; and Dušanić, 1984.

72 Plin. *Ep.* 7.29, 8.6.13 (commented on by Pavis D'Esurac, 1985).

73 Plin. *Ep.* 8.6.13. I have discussed this location elsewhere: first Corbier, 1987b and now Corbier, 2006, 147–62.

74 Corbier, 2006, 183–95.

75 For instance *CIL* 10.4643 (with regard to a municipal document); see Sanders, 1984, p. 100 and Roman Statutes, I, pp. 19–20.

76 See Corbier, 2006, 147–62.

77 On Suetonius' parodic passage see above in the text and Corbier, 2006, pp. 43–4.

78 Vernant, 1962, pp. 44–6; Detienne, 1964, pp. 83–98.

79 Rotondi, 1912; Guittard, 1983, pp. 37–8.

80 The first commentators on the inscribed bronze tablets found close to the church of Sant'Omobono (see Corbier, 2006, p. 25 and above Figure 2.9) believed that they came from the neighbouring Temple of Saturn; they had in fact fallen from the Capitol which was crumbling away in sections. On the importance of display at the Capitol, note the formula of Vespasian assimilating the bronze tablets destroyed in the fire of 69 to the '*instrumenta imperii*'.

81 Corbier, 2006, pp. 131–46.

82 The preposition *in* permits, in effect, both interpretations. The initial display on the walls of the *cella* of the Temple of *Fides* had been suggested by Gros, 1976, pp. 99–100, but without the support of the whole of the dossier.

83 On its possible location see *LTUR* I, *s.v. Ara gentis Iuliae.*

84 Coarelli, 1981a, p. 74, 1987, 2005, p. 94. *LTUR* I, *s.v. Athenaeum* and III *s.v. Minerva.*

85 Castagnoli, 1964, p. 195: '...Il nome atrium divenne un termine ufficale per designare la sede di uffici publici'; *LTUR* I, *s.v. Atrium Libertatis.*

86 Corbier, 2006, pp. 163–95.

87 Corbier, 1987b and Corbier, 2006, pp. 147–62.

88 Chastagnol, 1960, pp. 243–51.

89 On the other hand the traditional localization of the *statio annonae* – at the location of Santa Maria in Cosmedin: Pavis d'Escurac, 1976, pp. 153–6 – is no longer supported; Coarelli, 1981a, p. 323, 1987; *LTUR* I, *s.v. Ceres, Liber, Liberaque, aedes; aedes Cereris.*

90 Coarelli, 1981b, pp. 37–49; 2005, pp. 338–9.

91 Coarelli, 2005, pp. 152–3 which details the stages of its extension.

92 Gatti, 1891; Chastagnol, 1960, pp. 243–51.

93 Practice was variable according to ancient authors; Susini, 1982, pp. 162–4 (in a general fashion); Gascou, 1984, pp. 532–4 (with regard to Suetonius); Bérard, 1991, pp. 3015–25 (with regard to Tacitus).

94 *AE* 1976, 677–8; see also *IGLS* 4.1314.

95 On the desire of leaving one's names (see Dio Chrys., *Or.*, 31.20), see among others, Veyne, 1976, p. 267, 288, etc.; Gros, 1976, p. 53; Eck, 1984–96, etc. For a concrete example, read the history of the *Basilica Aemilia* in Torelli, 1982, p. 92–4, and on the importance accorded in general to building, Bodei Giglione, 1973, pp. 185–94; and Brunt, 1980, pp. 96–8. Read also Malissard, 1983 and La Rocca, 1987. On the prestige of those who restore see Balland, 1984, p. 63.

96 Well reproduced in Brilliant, 1967, Figures 7 and 8.

97 Such would be, after Plin. *HN*. 36.42 (*…ac sua impensa construxisse, inscriptionem sperantes*), the case of two Spartiate architects who constructed at their own expense the two temples of the portico of Metellus. On that 'anecdote d'historicité douteuse', Gros, 1976, p. 53.

98 Frontin. *Aq*. 5.3 delights in recounting the subterfuge by which Appius Claudius Caecus succeeded in only inscribing his name on the Aqua Appia and ousted that of his colleague.

99 A freedman could honour his patron in this way; after Dio Cass. 39.38.6, the theatre bearing the name of Pompey would have been paid for by Demetrius his freedman (see Fabre, 1981, p. 234).

100 Dio Cass. 53.2.4 (see Eck, 1984–96, p. 160, n. 95); but also read Tac. *Ann*. 3.72.1–2 (with regard to the basilica of Paulus Aemilius 'monument of the *Aemilii*' and of the Theatre of Pompey).

101 Tac. *Ann*. 3.72.1–2; Veyne, 1976, p. 639. The texts are reunited by Janvier, 1969 in particular Macer, *Digest*, 50.10.3 'it is not permitted … to inscribe on a public work another name than that of the Prince or the person with whose money the work had been executed' reflects the instructions given to the provincial governors.

102 *Res Gestae* 20.1 (ed. Gagé, 1977, p. 112): *Capitolium et Pompeium theatrum utrumque opus impensa grandi refeci sine ulla inscriptione nominis mei*; on the funerary eulogy for Augustus, pronounced by Tiberius, read Dio Cass. 57.10.1–2.

103 Torelli, 1982, p. 94, 1987.

104 See *supra* n. 102 for Augustus; Dio Cass. 57.10.1–2 and 60.6.8–9 for Tiberius and Claudius; and for Hadrian S.H.A. *Hadr*., 19.9; and *CIL* 6.896, see 31196 (= *ILS* 129), the dedication of the Pantheon: *M. Agrippa L. f. cos. tertium fecit* 'Marcus Agrippa, son of Lucius, consul for the third time, made this'.

105 Dio Cass. 76.16; Suet. *Ner*. 55.

106 Suet. *Dom*. 13.7.

107 Plin. *Pan*. 47.4.

108 *Res Gestae*, 19–21.

109 *CIL* 6.1256 (= *ILS* 218a). Gordon, 1983, pp. 118–19, no. 44; one notes the suggested link between the activity of the emperor and his *cura* on the city of Rome. On the subject of the use of the formula *faciendum curauit* by municipal magistrates on the dedications of Italian aqueducts, read Corbier, 1984b and in particular pp. 247–54.

110 *CIL* 6.1257 and 1258, see p. 3129 (= *ILS* 218b–c).

111 For the period from Claudius to Diocletian, Panciera, 1998, has brought together about ten examples including the three discussed here.

112 Gell. *NA*. 13.25.1; see Zanker, 1970.

113 Burford, 1971, pp. 71–6.

114 Susini, 1982, pp. 122–3.

115 After the assassination of his brother Geta, Caracalla had substituted for the erased name a series of honorific epithets which elongated accordingly his proper

titulature. Here l. 4, *optimis fortissimisque principibus* relates to his father and himself.

116 *CIL* 6.1033 = *ILS* 425; see Gordon, 1983, pp. 158–9, no. 73.

117 The frontispiece of *Le Antichità romane*, Rome, 1757, reproduced in the article of Petrucci, 1980, n. 73, after p. 48, illustrates perfectly the taste for contrasts between erased spaces and letters in relief. Note, as a matter of interest, that the contemporary English painter Richard Shirley Smith was also inspired by Latin inscriptions.

118 On the drawings of architects devoted to the Arch of Septimius Severus, those of A. N. Normand and of C. Moyaux, the erased rectangle containing the name of Geta has not been distinguished. That exposition was presented precisely to the Curia and the Villa Medicis in 1985 at the moment of the colloquium on the *Urbs* where this paper was presented in its first version. See the catalogue *Roma Antiqua*, Rome, 1985, p. 31.

119 Haynes and Hirst, 1939, pp. 3–6.

120 Tac. *Ann.* 3.64.2.

121 Veyne, 1985, pp. 168–70.

122 On this well known evolution of imperial titulature, an important decorative element of honorific arches, see Susini 1982, pp. 120–1 and Gordon, 1983, pp. 27–30.

123 Prop. 2.1.71–2: *quod quandocumque* (…) *breue in exiguo marmore nomen ero*; see Susini, 1982, p. 147.

124 Macqueron, 1982, p. 5; Youtie 1973 and 1981.

125 Goody, 1979, pp. 140–96 (on the 'list') and pp. 197–221 (on the 'formula').

126 *Fasti Capitolini I. Ital.*, 13.1.1; see Eck 1984–96, p. 138.

127 Vidman, 1957–82; see Bargagli and Grosso, 1997.

128 On the professional *collegia* see, for example, *CIL* 6.996, 31220a and p. 4314; *CIL* 6.1060 = 33858 and p. 3071 and 4321; *CIL* 6.10300 = 33857a (= *ILS* 7224–6). On the lists (non-extant) of those eligible for the distribution see Virlouvet, 1987 and 1995.

129 *CIL* 9. 338 = *ILS* 6121 = *ERCanosa* 35; Chastagnol 1978.

130 *CIL* 1².709 and p. 714, 716 = 6.37045 = *ILS* 8888 = *ILLRP* 515. See Degrassi, 1965, no. 397 and Criniti, 1970.

131 See *CIL* 6.220 = *ILS* 2163; see Gordon, 1983, pp. 156–8, n. 72 and Gregori and Mattei, 1999, p. 593. I have studied the changes in the decoration of the bronze plaque and the different interpretations of scholars from its discovery in the first half of the seventeenth century to our days in Corbier, 2008.

132 *CIL* 6.1057–8 (= *ILS* 2157), 31234 and p. 3777 and 4320. See also Gregori and Mattei, 1999, pp. 98–101, nos. 151–2.

133 Plin. *Pan.* 20. On the cohorts of *vigiles*, read Sablayrolles, 1996, who did not make any observations about these lists.

134 *CIL* 6.5076. If the comparison is valid for the arrangement in columns, it is less about the meaning of the display of this 'list of steps' detailed *supra* in note 27.

135 Tac. *Ann.* 6.23.1; a sale of confiscated properties took place in AD 33.

136 Jal, 1967; Hinard, 1985, pp. 17–37.

137 On the *Res Gestae*, see *supra* note 31 and on the Edict of Maximum Prices Giacchero, 1974, pp. 134–7.

138 Tac. *Ann.* 1.

139 Veyne, 1976, pp. 549–51.

140 Suet. *Aug.* 31.8.

141   Tac. *Ann.* 3.6.5; Corbier, 2006, 183–95.

142   Tac. *Ann.* 15.73; the conspiracy of AD 65.

143   Veyne, 1976, p. 733, n. 27 gives several examples: Augustus had promised to repair at his own expense the aqueducts of Rome; Nero, after the fire at Rome, promised to contribute to the reconstruction of private homes; etc.

144   See Corbier, 2006, 147–62, 183–95; Coriat, 1997, pp. 101–4.

145   Fronto, 3.1 (edition of Van den Hout, p. 36).

146   A practice which was celebrated by coins with the legend *adlocut(io) coh(ortium)*. See for example Durry, 1938, pl. III.A. after p. 50.

147   Suet. *Claud.* 26.5 after Veyne, 1983–91, p. 9.

148   Suet. *Aug.* 55–6. On the pamphlets and songs see Veyne, 1983–91, pp. 13–5.

149   Suet. *Iul.* 80.6.

150   Dio Cass. 61.16.2a.

151   Suet. *Dom.* 13.7; see Carradice, 1982. Rodríguez-Almeida has put forward the hypothesis that the *arci* of Domitian were the gates of the *pomerium*.

152   Jal, 1963, pp. 201–30, who also cites, p. 202, n. 3, the important works of A. Kurfess on this theme.

153   Ulp. *Digest*, 47.10.5.9–10.

154   Suet. *Iul.* 80.3.

155   Tac. *Ann.* 1.72.

156   Suet. *Aug.* 55–6. On the chronology and the future of this Augustan legislation read Bauman, 1974, pp. 25–51.

157   Dio Cass. 55.27.1 and 56.27.1.

158   Jouhaud, 1985.

159   Rebellions against the royal power in France between 1648 and 1653 during the minority of Louis XIV and the government of Anne of Austria and Mazarin.

160   Chartier, cited by Jouhaud, 1985, p. 26.

161   Tac. *Ann.* 4.27; Corbier, 2006, pp. 217–32.

162   Suet. *Ner.* 39.3.

163   'The one and the other languages', the usual expression to designate Latin and Greek, the two official languages of the Empire. One finds it, notably in the provinces, on the epitaphs of young boys who had not yet entered into public life but who could, at least, be congratulated on their bilingual culture (*utraque lingua eruditus*).

164   Tert. *Ad Nat.* 1.17.5.

165   Delumeau, 1957, p. 30.

166   Cèbe, 1966, pp. 163–9.

167   Suet. *Ner.* 39.3; see Gascou, 1984, pp. 563–5.

168   The island where Tiberius lived.

169   Suet. *Tib.* 43.

170   Suet. *Tib.* 75: 'Tiberius to the Tiber', the body of a condemned person was often, as is well known, deprived of a tomb and was thrown out in this way; this was not the case for Tiberius.

171   Castrén, 1972.

172   Earlier interpretations: Jerphanion, 1938; Guarducci, 1978; Cartigny, 1984. See now: Veyne, 1968, pp. 427–36; Étienne, 1976, pp. 168–70; Alarcão and Étienne, 1979, pp. 268–70.

173   Susini, 1966; Chevallier, 1972, pp. 43.

174 See notably, for France Furet and Ozouf, 1977; Chartier 1985 and Roche 1985 coming across at several points, for the eighteenth century, my theme.
175 Nicolet, 1976, pp. 517–9.
176 Cavallo, 1978 and 1989.
177 Cavallo, 1978, p. 470.
178 Petron. *Sat.* 58.7.
179 Quint. *Inst.* 11.2.32–3. Read Yates 1975.
180 August. *De anima et eius origine*, 4.7.9 with regard to his friend Simplicius.
181 After Mecacci, 1984, pp. 150–3, recognizing capital letters necessitates only the activity of the left side of the brain; the complementary intervention of the right side, which specializes in the analysis of complex forms, is necessary in order to read cursive script. In fact actual research on the brain does not lead to such a simple analysis. Among the diverse work which I have been able to read thanks to the bibliographic suggestions of my specialist colleagues, none, obviously, addressed the question of the monumental capital and of the cursive writing, 'the common writing', of the Romans. The observation seems to be more orientated towards the study of the relative difficulty of reading printed texts and manuscripts, or of reading printed texts in upper or lower case.
182 See, for example (particularly adapted to our argument, because it concerns the Juvenal's *Satires*), Dubrocard, 1976.

3

Reading Epigraphic Culture, Writing Funerary Space in the Roman City

Peter Keegan

Words and images in the epigraphic landscape

CVIQ
VE SU. [= *suom*
CIPO   *cipom*]

Rome, third/second century BC

Scratched on tufa near the site of the sarcophagus of L. Cornelius Scipio Barbatus ('The Bearded One'), this inscription (*CIL* 1².2660) speaks directly to the subject of this chapter. The Latin is gender neutral, yet the broader context (i.e. the proximity of the elite family monument, the *sepulcrum Scipionum*) imposes a linguistic bias. E. H. Warmington's mid-twentieth-century translation is instructive: 'To every *man his* own gravestone'.[1] How true to the sociocultural historicity of the unknown composer is such a reading? Given the apparent dominance of patriarchal discourse in the late republican *milieu*, how possible is any other interpretation? And in what ways do spatial location and configuration within the written fabric of the Roman cosmopolis dictate the production and consumption of epigraphic and sociocultural meaning?

The presence of this inscription tests the boundaries of our understanding of what it meant to be a part of an oral-literate society and a participating member of a pervasive epigraphic culture. To appreciate the significance underpinning this juxta-position of social and cultural issues, we should consider the implications of a single question: Who made this? Determining 'who' calls for the inquirer to examine how possible it was for any member of the ancient population to formulate – articulate, produce, and transmit – a written message within the extra-mural spaces of Rome's funerary environment. The extent to which the inscription seems to address inter-pretative issues of concern to the composer, the ancient society, and the modern researcher – for instance, the manner and subject of public commemoration – is a necessary addendum to the questions of literacy, epigraphic technique, and the socio-linguistic system in Classical antiquity.[2] This finding must also address how accessible the location chosen was for any individual, and the degree of significance which that person attached to the context of memorialization. These points of inquiry lead the investigator to a discussion of modes of social mobility, kinds and numbers of intended audiences, and the thought processes, values, and beliefs shared by members of different communities under Roman rule.

To address the form and function of epigraphic culture in relation as it pertains to the notion of written space, this chapter explores the contexts in which men and women set up burial monuments and inscriptions: family and collective tombs lining the roads of republican and imperial Rome. As spatio-temporal contexts offering practical engagement with the relationships of art and language, of the real and imagined, Rome's sepulchral roads and ritual spaces provide primary sites for investigation. Defining the context of epigraphic culture in the funerary landscape of Classical Rome is a logical first step. In exploring the nature of written space as it manifests itself within and across Rome's peri-urban environment, it will also be important to assess the range of discursive possibilities – for men and women who lived in, worked in or around, or visited the city as they experienced, interacted with, or participated in the epigraphic exchange of information and self-representation – that characterizes funerary spaces (underestimated, for the most part, in modern scholarship on ancient oral-rhetorical cultures). Moving beyond this potential for participation to conceivable situations for involvement, this chapter will examine a single specific instance of male and female participation in civic activity within written funerary space. This should provide a sense of the degree to which the epigraphic environment permeated the lifeways of the metropolitan Roman population. How different will our standpoint on ancient Roman society be if we take into account this conceptual transformation of epigraphic culture? What 'other' world might be recovered if we accommodate the possibilities of the extant record?

Epigraphic culture[3] in the suburbs: country estates, market gardens, and tombs

The funerary epigraphic environment of the city of Rome – the variegated streetscape of inscribed burial monuments that evolved over centuries within the peri-urban region of the Roman metropolis – may be seen to consist of two important inter-locking aspects: (a) what Greg Woolf regards as the notion of an 'epigraphic culture',[4] which 'depends on taking both the monumental and the written aspects of inscriptions seriously'; and (b) what Nicholas Purcell aptly describes as the development of a Roman landscape of property, 'epiphenomenal to the centuriated landscape which had already been divided and allotted'.[5]

Why did ancient men and women inscribe anything on stone? Ramsey MacMullen regarded the question as 'mere conjecture', opting instead for a distributive investigation of the 'epigraphic habit' in chronological, spatial, and social terms.[6] What the forces which generated the widespread 'impulse' to communicate in inscriptions were, MacMullen had no idea that he felt could be substantiated, other than to suggest that the exercise of the habit was in some way controlled by a 'sense of audience'.[7] Elizabeth Meyer contends that a general belief in the value of Roman citizen status, and a concomitant desire to express that acquired status, interacted with existing testamentary practice, dependent on the obligations of heirship, to generate incremental patterns of self-commemoration in provincial funerary inscriptions until Caracalla's grant of universal citizenship in AD 212 (the *constitutio Antoniniana*).[8]

Beyond these views, once the historian of Classical Roman society takes seriously the monumental and written aspects of private Latin inscriptions constituting written funerary space in Rome's *suburbium*, the potential for recovering distinctive and vital personal expressions of kinship, inheritance, amity, dependence and belief is considerable. Motivation is variable: legal responsibility, familial duty, affective bonds and religious need. Similarly, patterns of funerary commemoration reflect a range of practitioners not limited to the senatorial, equestrian or curial classes. Deriving its purpose from motives integral to a society and displaying a tendency to cross cultural boundaries, the discursive phenomenon of the text engraved on a tombstone enabled the marginalized and subaltern of Rome to encode aspects of their represented identities, their personal affiliations, social statuses, and ethnic origins that would normally have been omitted from the historical record. Speaking directly to issues of literacy and memory, the corpus of burial epigraphy illustrates how diversely men and women of all classes participated within the funerary spaces of Rome's urban fabric.

Naturally, while the statistical studies of funerary text distributions epitomized by MacMullen and Meyer do not help to identify the causes of epigraphic production, and their methods of classification, dating, and periodization may be challenged,[9] they do provide objective correlations with the circulation of symbolic capital, dubbed by some as the 'rhetoric of power', in the provincial Mediterranean world after the first century AD.[10] However, the development of this commemorative phenomenon in late republican and early imperial Rome is generally conflated with or ignored in favour of that period and those regions which provide high epigraphic density. Moreover, even the most rigorous quantitative compilations of dated, situated inscriptions fail to address the significance of sexed participation in epigraphic culture.[11] According to treatments of this type, valuation of the deceased in terms of age or sex preference is effectively represented and perceived as a neuter-male category of 'sentiment'; the habits of commemoration within written funerary spaces are regarded as the expressions of regional, ethnic and cultural practices among a variety of social groups, yet who commemorates is almost invariably a subset of unsexed entities like 'slaves', 'freedmen' (*sic*), 'spouses', and 'children'.[12]

Accordingly, inscriptions may be regarded as a special kind of text *and* a special kind of monument.[13] The monumental epigraphic contexts of private commemoration provide a category of evidence for testing Greg Woolf's claim that 'the desire to fix an individual's place within history, society, and the cosmos provides a plausible background to "the epigraphic impulse"'.[14] Situating the need to define the qualities of written space in the Roman city within the context of a cultural practice of inscribed commemoration highlights the nexus of social relationships among curators of the commemorated and the subjects of memorialization. In sum, epigraphy allowed individual men and women and sexed collectives to 'write their public identities into history'.[15]

Of course, by its very nature written space requires that this historical self-representation is displayed within the urban – or, in the case of funerary commemoration, *sub*urban – fabric of Rome. Here, Purcell's notion of the epiphenomenon of the surveyed Roman landscape takes on interpretative significance. Centuriation[16] was a system of marking out land in squares or rectangles, by means of boundaries (*limites*). Varro attempted to rationalize this distributive system, giving it a patina of homogeneity and Roman order.[17] But in fact, the strategies by which the ever-expanding *ager privatus* (incorporating the concentric circles of pleasure gardens, country estates and smallholdings close to Rome) and *ager publicus* (comprising lands acquired by Rome through conquest from enemies or confiscation from rebellious allies) were set apart could involve anything from a ditch which also served for drainage to a row of markers to a drystone wall.[18] Over time, official boundaries established a network of roadways or baulks and occupied land across the developing strata of Roman urban-rural society. Under Augustus, regulation of the urban centre in what must be understood as a rural environment encompassed the private land of a multitude of statuses.[19] By quantifying what Cicero and the jurists systematized under the rubric of a Roman's changed condition as a citizen (*capitis deminutio*),[20] public surveying and settlement of land registered not just the cultural appropriation of the landscape but also the ambiguity of hierarchical social divisions, with respect to a person's household (*familia*) and the broader civic community of Rome.

These observations are not intended to reject the significance of birth and wealth, honour, place of residence, or markers of distinction as determinants of social, political, and economic divisions under Roman law and in customary practice. What should be clear is the degree to which the orders (*ordines*) of Roman society – whether officially stratified (*patres conscripti, equites, decuriones*) or less formally so (the rest of the free population, including the *ordo libertinorum*) – contradict idealizing legal definitions.[21] This is particularly the case in relation to the potential for localized social associations in urban-rural precincts along the axes of the city's roads.[22]

Consider, for example, Varro's reference to the estates of a certain Scrofa, much visited and admired for their spectacular productivity.[23] How might ancient wayfarers have encountered this display of aristocratic prosperity? It is almost certain that such an encounter took place in close proximity to the small-scale, intensively worked land of myriad allotments and tomb plots. Varro tells us that 'the top end of the Sacred Way, where apples fetch their own weight in gold, is the very likeness of [Scrofa's] orchard'.[24] Epigraphic evidence confirms the literary view. For example, an inscription for a property belonging to a minor corporation which met beneath the arches of the Theatre of Pompey explains that:

TABERNA CVM AEDIFICIO ET CISTERNA
MONIMENTO CVSTODIA CEDIT
LEGE PVBLICA VTI LICEAT ITVM ADITVM AMBIT
HAVSTVM AQVAE LIGNA SVMERE

Rome, first century AD

The shop with the building and the cistern is attached to the tomb for its maintenance in accordance with the law, allowing right of passage in and around, of
drawing water and of collecting firewood.[25]

In the same way that Petronius' freedman-caricature Trimalchio thinks of his tomb
as a measure of space, [26] this diffusion of scale is symptomatic of a heterogeneous,
centuriated landscape – a phenomenon reflected throughout Roman Italy by the
epigraphic habit of setting out the boundaries of a tomb in feet. The landscape, in
turn, reflects practical solutions to the needs of urban growth, resource dependence,
and multiple civil statuses. The Roman *atrium* house in many instances failed to
distinguish between place of occupation and residence.[27] In the same way, citizen,
freed servant, and slave shared space – occupational, productive, recreational, and
(indelibly) written – in life and often enough in death.[28] Likewise, the frontage of
Roman roads displayed a constellation of urban society. Varro's estate owner, Scrofa,
may have regarded himself as a member of Rome's social elite, and his status might
well have differentiated him before the law from the 'more base' (*humiliores*),[29] yet
his peers and their subordinates often shared social contexts. So, too, the corridors of
movement, transport, and communication marking such alignments generated areas
of interaction among otherwise disparate social entities.

In this regard, Michael Koortbojian suggests that the public display of words and
images within the architectural and topographical contexts of burial and commemoration in the late Republic and early Empire 'effected a cultural transaction', namely
'the exercise of *memoria*'.[30] Building on this, I would suggest that the architectural,
sculptural, and textual elements of the ancient Roman streets of the dead may be
interpreted not only in terms of 'the [regularized and repetitive] evocation of common
history' but also as markers of specific socio-cultural densities and diversities. The
factors that determined commission and display of the range of appurtenances
pertaining to funerary commemoration (additional, that is, to the inscribed tomb
marker) – namely, capacity to order or purchase, purpose for selection, audience
intended to view – reflect the ways in which written space expresses the spectrum of
social demographics (who is commemorating, and for whom) and cultural systems of
practice and ideation (how the space is marked for display, and what beliefs or customs
or views the media of display represent) that constituted the city of Rome. One only
need consider the diverse typology of epigraphic remains and surfaces: monuments on
stone supports; standing elements (altars, bases, *cippi*, *stelae*); applied elements (plates,
podial tables); containers (cinerary vessels, sarcophagi, *kline* monuments); structural
elements (blocks, columns, epistyles, *tympani*); furnishings (statue plinths, busts,
reliefs, candelabra, pilasters); and non-stone supports (plaster paintings, bronzes). To
borrow a comparison from Koortbojian, the repertory of the monumental epigraphic
environment is very much 'like that of an "apartment house" teeming with life'.[31]

With regard to modes of travel and perception, interaction with the built
environment of the typical Western urban periphery means something qualitatively
different from the modern city inhabitant or visitor. As Giancarlo Susini rightly
stresses, the human reality of the modern world is replete with 'contrivances and
sensations … which must have been wholly unknown in Classical antiquity'.[32]

Engagement with the contemporary urban fabric is more often than not registered through protective glass, and only in passing as background to established rituals of occupation and leisure. In addition, unregulated pedestrian travel in today's cities – the kind of movement best suited to participation in any multi-faceted, organized urban space – would seem for many either a privileged or socially mitigated activity. For some, walking is therapeutic, good for the circulatory system, environmentally friendly, and a salve for the pressures of modern living. Even so, the activity is usually attuned to the tyranny of urban rhythms. For others, walking is an unavoidable phenomenon, concomitant on economic strictures or social regulation, the territorial prerogative of disenfranchized, marginalized, and deviant urban minorities.[33] In a manner of speaking, only the tourist, the homeless, and the otherwise dislocated make frequent, lasting contact with the assemblages of our built environments. This corresponds with the modern 'sociology of mobilities' advocated by John Urry: that in order to understand the relationships between humans and things, we need to understand, *inter alia*, the socio-spatial practices of corporeal mobility.[34] In this light, the conditions of ancient movement require a different conception of the centuriated Roman landscape. It is necessary to imagine a display of different spatial and relational patterns different from our own along the grid of Roman roads penetrating the peri-urban territory of the city of Rome. This situates the street as a constitutive rather than purely structural unit of public space in the zones of transition between Roman city and country.

What this means for reconstructing the epigraphic environment in the city of Rome is simple. Just as the proportion of interactions as the result of incidental or purposive engagement with written space outside Rome's walls can never be ascertained, so too the number of travellers responding to the imperatives of private Latin inscriptions – 'Stop, traveller, and read'[35] – will always be uncertain. Regardless, the ratio of wayfarers who were citizen, freed, or slave, must be regarded as a significant quantity in any consideration of meaning production and reception in the ancient suburban landscape. This collocation of different viewpoints can be seen, for example, in the relationship between the tomb façades and the surrounding environment of the Isola Sacra streetscape (Figure 3.1). In the first century AD, a road linked the two centres of Ostia and Portus, crossing an island and becoming the main road axis of both settlements. A single, large necropolis grew up alongside the road. The necropolis has buildings, some of which have two storeys, elaborately decorated with paintings, stucco work and mosaics. Marble inscriptions on the façades of the tombs mention the names of the owners, the conditions for use of the tombs and often also their size.

Next to the inscriptions there are often terracotta relief figures, representing the work carried out in life by the tomb inhabitants, mostly of the entrepreneurial class of merchants and freedmen and women. The various types of tombs and their inscriptions, statues, altars, and associated decorations are an integral part of the road between Portus to the north and Ostia to the south. Taken together, this epigraphic landscape represents the tastes, culture and fashions of Roman society in the middle and late period of the Empire (second–fourth centuries AD).

While the allotment patterns of the propertied within the settled periphery of Rome cannot be determined accurately, it stands to reason that any given half-mile frontage

Figure 3.1 The extra-mural epigraphic environment – Isola Sacra (author's photograph)

would have presented to pedestrian traffic a mixture of country estates, pleasure gardens, smallholdings and tomb plots.[36] The pattern of memorialization exemplified in Figure 3.2 reflects the fact that many of these inscriptions were originally located outside or within spaces used or viewed by people other than those responsible for setting them up – individual, family or group tombs in town cemeteries, burial plots that were part of larger family estates beside major roads, communal tombs set aside for household *familia* and members of burial collectives; not to mention sanctuaries, military camps, and neighbourhood shrines. This means that the persons making these inscriptions intended that others would read their sepulchral and dedicatory messages set up as part of a broader social context. At the very least, they would have been aware of the likelihood of some kind of readership for their texts, and so commissioned and/or composed their inscriptions accordingly.

Therefore, in addition to the itinerant and regional visitor to the imperial capital, the travelling population comprised the privileged, freed, and enslaved inhabitants of the periphery with business in the city or with neighbouring estates; and, conversely, city dwellers with investments of some kind in the suburban precincts, whether cultic, residential, agricultural, display, or otherwise. Included in this category is the substantial but far less localized displacement of people generated by the movements of colonists interested in agricultural produce, exchange opportunities, and exploitable labour like the general work provided by the slave. In addition, one can interpolate the standard experiences of leaving home to be a soldier, seeking out an oracle or shrine, attending festivals, or 'taking the waters' for recreational or medical purposes. Economic

Figure 3.2 The extra-mural epigraphic environment – Via Appia Antica (author's photograph)

interdependence involved more people in the pursuit of trade, levels of slave, freed, and free travel arising from this development, and the existence of widespread background mobility and its infrastructure. Such contacts and communications are witnessed by onomastics, epitaphs, papyrus letters, literary anecdote, and more generally by structural categories like cultural uniformity, economic cohesion, and so on.[37]

If we then articulate a gendered component to this traffic, late republican and early imperial men and women (elite, working class, and slave) must be assigned a significant percentage in any calculation of regular, pedestrian movement along the thoroughfares leading to and from Rome. However, in the main, in modern treatments, the sex of the ancient traveller is almost exclusively male. For instance, in Casson's 'first full-scale treatment, in any language, of travel in the ancient world', female participation in 'getting from A to B' is confined historically to the 'service industries';[38] for all intents and purposes, those occupations associated with eating- and drinking-houses (*popinae; cauponae*). One must also deal with a reductive, classist perspective which seems to draw almost consciously on ancient philosophical exposition. For instance, Casson tells us that 'the transient … most often put up at an inn, and even respectable inns … while the kind they called a *caupona* was distinctly low class … and the *caupo* … was of the same social and moral level as his establishment'.[39] Compare this rhetorical antithesis with Seneca's formulation of the cultural character (*ethos*) adhering to different buildings and areas in the city:

> Virtue is something profound, elevated, worthy of a king, invincible and inexhaustible; pleasure is lowly, servile, weak and perishable, whose standing- and dwelling-place are brothels and taverns.[40]

The relatively narrow socio-cultural view adopted in Casson's *Travel in the Ancient World* stipulates a cautionary approach to encyclopaedic treatments of road construction, land division and social mobility.

Reading memory, writing in space and time: the epitaph of C. Hostius C. l. Pamphilus and Nelpia M. l. Hymnis

Here is an example of written space in the Roman epigraphic landscape; that is, an illustration of how private Latin funerary inscriptions represented these complex social and cultural patterns within the context of the ancient epigraphic environment. As a necessary corollary to this exercise, it is useful to read the inscription of C. Hostius C. l. Pamphilus and Nelpia M. l. Hymnis as part of a hypothetical memorial. An external reconstruction of the burial context as it may have been seen from street level is a vital consideration.[41]

C. HOSTIVS C. L. PAMPHILVS
MEDICVS HOC MONVMENTVM
EMIT SIBI ET NELPIAE M. L. HYMNINI
ET LIBERTEIS ET LIBERTABVS OMNIBVS
5 POSTEREISQVE EORVM
HAEC EST DOMVS AETERNA HIC EST
FVNDVS HEIS SVNT HORTI HOC
EST MONVMENTVM NOSTRVM
IN FRONTE P. XIII IN AGRVM P. XXIIII[42]

Rome, first century BC

8. MEVM for NOSTRVM *CIL* 1² with Garr. (erroneous).

Gaius Hostius Pamphilus, freedman of Gaius, a doctor of medicine, bought this monument for himself and for Nelpia Hymnis, freedwoman of Marcus; and for all their freedmen and freedwomen and their posterity. This is our home for ever, this is our farm, these are our gardens, this is our memorial. Width, 13 feet; depth, 24 feet.

If this inscription belonged to a free-standing tomb, the exterior might have been decorated in stone or terracotta relief, with images alluding to the deceased's profession, in this case, surgical instruments like knives, scalpels, or probes. Portraits in the round or in relief of Nelpia and Hostius may have been set into the tomb's façade or the surrounding wall, conceivably identifying the relationship of the figures portrayed. Such portraits may have been bust-length, with hands clasped in the *dextrarum iunctura*; or perhaps the monument displayed a full-figure ensemble.[43] Additionally, the inscription denotes the location of the burial monument as a farm (*fundus*) with gardens (*horti*).[44] While the nature of any horticultural produce remains unspecified (a logical omission, given its visibility to the casual wayfarer), the presence of any, or a combination, of the common produce of suburban/rural allotments – vines, fruit trees, flowers, and/or plants of various kinds, including vegetables, reeds, and trees producing wood for purposes of building or fuel – seems appropriate. Small buildings for the eating of funerary meals, for keeping provisions, or for other forms of social activity, paths and provision for the supply of water might also be imagined as part of the overall sum of what could be seen from the road.[45]

Keeping this proposed context in mind, let us turn to the inscription. Whether released formally or informally from his owner's control,[46] C. Hostius Pamphilus was more than likely the former slave of a certain Gaius Hostius. If Gaius Hostius retained the slave name component in his *tria nomina*, then it is possible that either he himself or his family line originated in the southern coastal plain enclosed by the mountains of eastern Lycia, Pisidia, and Cilicia Tracheia, the rugged western portion of southern Asia Minor. Given that Pamphylia was part of the Roman provincial complex since 133 BC,[47] his or his family's procurement as slave labour through war, piracy and brigandage, trade, or, eventually, natural reproduction from that region is certainly conceivable. His commemorated skills as a medical practitioner (dietetic, pharmacological, surgical, or 'mixed')[48] assured that he would have been assimilated at the very least into a reasonably comfortable domestic context.[49] What can be said is that an ex-slave claims for himself the semi-official status of *medicus*. His declaration of technical skill[50] is situated prominently in the arrangement of the commemorative surface (*medicus* continues and completes the all-important process of identification), and strategically in apposition to the memorializing intention (*hoc monumentum*).

Using the same system of Roman nomenclature, we can similarly consider Nelpia Hymnis as a member of the manumitted social order, though belonging originally or at the last to a slaveowner called Marcus. By applying statistical likelihood to the formation of her names, we may also assign Nelpia a possibly peregrine and almost certainly foreign origin, either for her own or a previous generation. Moreover, Nelpia and Hostius do not appear to have shared an owner, though slaves were known to occupy more than one household during the course of their service. We might assume, then, that they came into contact and formed a union in an intra- rather than inter-familial manner. This is not to say, of course, that an association may have initially developed in the same household (a quasi-marital *contubernium* or simple friendship), only to be temporarily curtailed through procurement of one or the other by a different slave owner; and which was eventually restored by the manumission of one or both – though not the purchase of Nelpia by Hostius[51] – and the confirmation of the *de facto contubernium* or intention of a *iustum matrimonium*.[52] As such, we may allow for the contingency of a union fostered either within or outside the hierarchical spaces of domestic slavery. What remains significant in this relationship is the unstated but considerable degree of personal mobility which may be apportioned to Nelpia and Hostius, and which was eventually ratified formally or otherwise by representatives of the slave-owning class.

In this regard, we should note the social reproduction of the practice of slave ownership in the (childless?) household of two former slaves.[53] Hostius' inscription commemorates not only his equivocal relationship with Nelpia but also their joint ownership of men and women as personal property, not to mention the subsequent manumission of these individuals. While we cannot know if these 'assets' were an element of the commercial and financial activity conducted by Nelpia and Hostius with the *peculium* of either or both, it is hard to avoid the conclusion that historical differentials of power transcended social limits. Just as the slaveowners Gaius and Marcus conferred freedom on a previously enslaved non-citizen woman and man, so

Nelpia and Hostius are complicit in the propagation of a pervasive social reality (*et liberteis et libertabus omnibus/postereisque eorum*).[54]

This conceptualization of the Roman sociology of slavery may seem to be a jejune interpretative ploy; but I would suggest otherwise. Hostius' inscription represents a variety of relational, occupational, and behavioural practices, articulated within the bounds of, and memorialized upon the surface of, a durable cultural artefact within the written space of the commemorative periurban environment. Sexing, reclassifying and deracinating the structural role of slavery in Graeco-Roman society, even on such a microhistorical level, allows historians to observe the ways in which ancient marginal categories ('woman', 'slave', and 'peregrine') intersected, and how individuals belonging to inferior social orders endured by adopting strategies of accommodation and resistance in their daily lives.

Bearing these connections in mind, what if we now incorporate the categories of *fundus* and *horti*? How is a burial plot measuring 312 (Roman) feet^2 – comprising 'monument', 'farm', and 'gardens' – to be understood? Normally, discussions of funerary architecture – the built structure, which incorporates spaces for cremation and storage of the designated deceased, in addition to any affixed inscription – focus on aesthetic, functional, or ritual questions.[55] Conversely, most scholars of classical agriculture concentrate on matters relating to technique, yield, transport, and storage, and are predisposed to the interrelationships of environmental (climate and rainfall, geophysical diversity) and social or political developments (citizen smallholdings, tied tenant labour, estate agriculture).[56] Within which category of interpretation should we locate Nelpia, Hostius, their extended ex-slave household, and the explicit mensuration of an area of land with many functions? It seems to me that making a choice here is the least productive strategy. Instead, it is best to see this *monumentum* as a public registration of multiple social realities.

Imperial Rome was hemmed around by her dead. By the end of the first century BC, the traditional Roman practices of extramural burial and familial commemoration of the dead at gravesites had ringed the urban periphery with a network of cemeteries and tombs. Amidst the web of funerary monuments that fanned out from the city between the spokes of the radial roads, luxury villa estates of the wealthy (euphemistically styled 'gardens', *horti*) vied for space with actual market gardens (*horti* also) and tomb orchards (*cepotaphia*) in the increasingly crowded suburban landscape. In this written space, Nelpia and Hostius found it unnecessary to deny the marginal aspects of their represented identities, their personal affiliations, social statuses, and ethnic origins. Indeed, their participation in the epigraphic culture strongly reflects a felt need to emphasize the achievements, skills, accoutrements, and limitations of their relative positions in Roman society without differentiation. The fact that two ex-slaves and their freed household[57] also assert a continuity of settlement and production on land which modern scholarship designates as a burial plot[58] should be viewed as an opportunity to further illuminate the variegations of ancient landscape and social practice. Nelpia and Hostius probably lived in proximity to the city of Rome; except in terms of plausible speculation, the location is beyond our grasp. But, contemporaneous to this uncertain existence, we have proof of a definite physical, financial, and ideological investment in the suburban landscape of epigraphic culture. Many questions remain unanswered: Who purchased the land? From whom? Who worked the land? For what purposes? and so on. Similarly, the memorialization of these phenomena needs to be viewed in terms of *communes loci*. This refers not so much to the topological formulations of rhetorical declamation with which epigraphic artefacts are usually associated.[59] Rather, we can focus on the 'common places' of the inscribed, built environment wherein monumental commemoration served as a medium (one of a number) for expressing, defining, and reformulating cultural practices of a diverse social community. *That* the modern observer envisions this place – which simultaneously commemorated the dead, advertised individual and familial status, traced the regenerations of a manumitted slaveowning household, and recorded the small-scale practice of pastoralism and cultivation – is as important a conceptual framework as worrying about the 'hows' and the 'whys'.

Notes

1 Warmington, 1953, pp. 8–9, no. 11). For bibliographical references to the *Scipionum elogia*, see *CIL* $1^2/4$: 859.

2 These issues cannot be addressed in this chapter. What can be said is this: the survival of legislative, contractual, testamentary, epitaphic, administrative, military, religious, economic, and social texts from the mid-sixth century BC onwards indicates that the relationship between social environment and cultural media is less than incidental and perhaps cumulative. It is a short step to consider the possibility that men and women of divergent ethnic, social, and political statuses should be situated in the midst of this developing mode of self-expression.
   If we define literacy as the ability to figure out and transmit a short message at a 'functional' or 'craft' rather than 'scribal' level, questions of practice, availability, and transfer across households become less significant in the production of reliable quantitative interpretations. In fact, the impressively large numbers of male and female slave and ex-slave epitaphs – as well as the significant Roman phenomena of political pamphleteering, electoral *programmata*, advertising posters and graffiti (see Corbier, Hemelrijk, Hillard, Newsome in this volume) – tend to support the contention that levels of male and female literacy are not as much of an issue *sui generis* (as purely quantitative ratios). Of comparable importance in any analysis of the ancient epigraphic environment is the existence of cultural strategies designed to underpin, counterpoint, and supplement the range of privileged and subjugated positions comprising late Republican/early Imperial society.

3 For the usefulness of this terminology in preference to MacMullen's 'epigraphic habit' (see n. 7 for citation), I agree with Gordon et al. 1993, p. 153 n. 402.

4 Woolf, 1996, p. 24.

5 Purcell, 1995, p. 168.

6 MacMullen, 1982, adumbrating the work of Stanislaw Mrozek, 1973.

7 MacMullen, 1982, pp. 233, 246.

8 Meyer, 1990, p. 95.

9 Cherry, 1995, pp. 143–50.

10 See Beard, 1991; cf. Purcell, 1987. 'Symbolic capital' is a theoretical concept formulated by Bourdieu, 1977, pp. 171–83, which explains how society conceals

through a variety of cultural discourses the arbitrary character underpinning the reproduction and distribution of economic capital.

11   For instance, the articles by Mrozek, 1988, and (to a lesser extent) Saller and Shaw, 1984. For some doubts about the approach employed by Saller and Shaw, see Martin, 1996; for a critique of Martin's evaluation of Saller and Shaw which nonetheless endorses a reconsideration of regional and cultural variation, see Rawson, 1997.

12   For discussion of gendered epigraphic display in civic written space, see Hemelrijk (Chapter 8); and, in relation to funerary written space (a series of altars associated with the *taurobolium* to the Magna Mater in Lectoure), see Esmonde-Cleary (Chapter 13).

13   Woolf, 1996, p. 28.

14   Woolf, 1996, p. 29. This 'desire' is demonstrated in a negative way by Cato's characteristically sober contentment *not* to have monumental commemoration (Plut., *Cato Mai.* 19: 'I had far rather that people should ask why there is no statue of me than why there is one').

15   Woolf, 1996, p. 39.

16   For research moving beyond pure description of land division to explore the concepts and ideas behind the making of a centuriated landscape, see Palet and Orengo, 2011. Two instances of aerial photography reproducing the centuriated Romanized landscape may be found in the useful encyclopaedic work Cornell and Matthews, 1991, pp. 49, 114: traces of centuriated land in Emilia; the Fosse Way, highway from Exeter to Lincoln, contrasting with the varied patchwork of the field system.

17   Varro, *Rust.* 1. 10.

18   For ancient technical treatises giving detailed descriptions of the nature and practice of land settlement (although badly corrupted in transmission and sometimes obscurely expressed), see Blume et al. 1848–52, repr. 1962; Thulin, 1913, repr. 1971; Bouma, 1993; Campbell, 2000. See also *OLD*³, s.v. centuriation, *gromatici*.

19   I specify this period in the development of the city of Rome and its environs for the following reason. Establishing boundaries on private estates, assessing land for the census and land-tax, and measuring and dividing public land (the *ager publicus*) for the settlement of colonies, were particularly prevalent activities at the end of the republic and in the early Principate when vast amounts of land were distributed to soldiers.
     In these respects, Augustus's benefactions between 30 and 2 BC simultaneously avoided the land confiscations and disruption frequently accompanying land settlements (namely, for veterans without the recognized right to discharge bounties), and radically expanded the integration of statuses by centuriated land-plots already widespread in Italy from the fourth century BC. In this regard, it is edifying to remind oneself that the history of late republican Roman Italy is inscribed across a landscape of demand, acquisition, allocation, shortage, redistribution, proscription and exploitation. From the *lex Licinia* of 159 BC to Augustus's land purchases after Actium, the collective *mentalité* of urban and colonial communities experienced the radical, subversive and often violent contestations of conflicting statuses. It seems only natural that this history of contestation might be reflected by other discursive strategies in the same landscape.

20   Cic. *Top.* 18, 29; Gai. *Inst.* 1. 158–63; *Dig.* 4, 5.

21   In this light, consider Gardner's observation (1997, p. 53): 'Not only was it quite possible … for persons to pass for something that they were not [in lower-class

families], but the law took a relaxed and tolerant attitude about this'. If one allows for the fluidity of statuses which this statement explicitly claims, then it should be clear that our interpretative framework concerning Roman social organization must begin to de-emphasize the still prevalent and influential structural-functional focus on classificatory labels and roles. Weaver, 1990, for example, discusses at length the *Latini Iuniani* (Gaius, *Inst.* 1.22; 3.56). His delineation of a status group in Roman imperial society intermediate between slaves and citizens effectively complicates social and demographic questions of status and adds to the changing sets of alternative statuses extant in Roman society, and which must be integrated into modern research models.

22 For a study of the complex relationship between spatial organization and group life in the urban context of Augustan *vici*, see Lott, 2004.

23 Varro, *Rust.* 1. 2. 9–10.

24 Varro, *Rust.* 1. 2. 10: *huiusce inquam pomarii summa sacra via ubi poma veneunt contra aurum imago.*

25 *CIL* 6.9404: ll. 12–15. For editorial apparatus and commentary, see *CIL* 6.2, p. 1235.

26 Petr. *Sat.* 71.

27 For a detailed overview of the textual and architectural evidence used to assess the use of space in Roman houses, and the need to allow for variegated activities in and dynamic interrelations among these spaces, see Allison, 1992, 2004; cf. *eadem* 1997, esp. p. 352: '… perhaps we should be more critical of our seemingly culturally and gender-biased assumptions concerning the meanings, or even existence, of public and private domestic spaces in Roman houses'.

28 For a view of the Roman household emphasizing the need to take into account the heterogeneous population which used it, see George, 1997a.

29 This is a broad distinction, at first social, but which acquired in the Principate and thereafter an increasing number of legal consequences. The discretionary nature of this classist allocation sits well with the customary weight of much private and criminal Roman law, and aptly illustrates the oftentimes purely rhetorical stress on sociospatial *limites*.

30 Koortbojian, 1996, p. 233.

31 Koortbojian, 1996, p. 221. For a similar symbolic portrait of how the edifice of language regiments the landscape of entities in the form of 'an immense "Roman columbarium"', see Eco, 2000, pp. 45–6.

32 Susini, 1973, p. 55. Susini's discussion of 'the inscription as a cultural monument' (1973, Chapter 6) identifies the standpoint from which the reader must view the 'text' as the fundamental principle for understanding (now as then) meaning production within the ancient epigraphic environment.

33 For a stimulating discussion of the literary, artistic and architectural evidence revealing the crucial role walking played in the performance of social status, the discourse of the body and the representation of space, see O'Sullivan, 2011.

34 Urry 2000, pp. 49–76.

35 E.g., *asta ac pellege* or *siste viator et lege.*

36 For a detailed picture of the horticultural landscape in the environs of ancient cities like Rome, see Carandini, 1985; for a conspectus of opinion on the subject, see Cima and La Rocca, 1998; and for a recent historical perspective on gardens in ancient residential and non-residential contexts, see Farrar, 2000.

37 For a brief excursus on these and related phenomena of ancient Mediterranean levels of mobility, see Casson, 1974, pp. 176–96; and Chevallier, 1976, pp. 178–81.

38 Casson, 1974, p. 9.

39 Casson, 1974, p. 204.
40 Seneca, *De vita beata* 7.3: *altum quidam est Virtus, excelsum et regale, invictum infatigabile: Voluptas humile servile, imbecillum caducum, cuius statio et domicilium fornices et popinae sunt.* As noted above, Seneca's Latin (and Casson's English) genders *virtus* masculine and *voluptas* feminine.
41 Koortbojian, 1996, p. 211 notes that 'discussions of [funerary monuments] often fail to provide a comprehensive account of all their elements in interaction'. His overview of the series of types of monument (wall relief, stele, altar, urn, and sarcophagus) and his reconstruction of the visual and cultural experiences underpinning ancient encounters with the funerary environment attempt, but stop short of, wholesale engagement with the contextual complexities of Roman commemorative practice. Davies, 2000, pp. 119–21 focuses briefly on similar strategies of memory perpetuation. The following discussion hopes to extend Koortbojian's and Davies' analyses considerably. Cf. Cooley, 2000a, p. 1: 'Inscriptions are primarily texts, of course, but they are also archaeological and artistic objects. Consequently, the viewer can respond to an inscribed monument as a whole, or to only part of it – its written message, letter forms, ornamentation, or spatial context'.
42 *CIL* 1^2.1319 = *CIL* 6.9583. For editorial apparatus and commentary, *CIL* 6.2, p.1256. See also Buecheler 274; Diehl^5 694; Dessau 8341; Warmington, 1953, pp. 42–3, no.93; Degrassi 2, 798; *CIL* 1.2/4, p. 976.
43 For a lucid exposition of libertine and freeborn funerary representation from c. 75 BC to the second century AD (identification of materials, figures, types, style, hairstyles, costumes, chronology, and so on), see Kleiner, 1977.
44 While not dismissing out of hand the possibility that these terms signify metaphorical conceptions of space and occupation, I draw attention to the epigraphic assignation of land measurement. At first sight, the enumeration of area seems unimpressive, yet a volumetric reading yields unexpectedly generous results. For the calculations, see the following note. Cf. *CIL* 6.33840 (request for permission to build a funerary monument on a plot 20 feet square).
45 Cumont, 1922, pp. 57, 200 and Toynbee, 1971, pp. 94–100 provide a useful and annotated overview of funerary gardens (*cepotaphia, horti, hortuli*). Jashemski, 1970–1, pp. 97–115; 1979, pp. 141–53 discusses the evidence for funerary gardens in the context of the archaeological remains at Pompeii. See also Carroll, 2004, pp. 98–9 with n. 40; Hope, 2001, pp. 153–4; MacDougall, 1995, p. 188 with n. 4. In this regard, the dimensions of the plot under consideration – 13 × 24 (Roman) feet – may appear too slight an area to contain such an assemblage of built and environmental features. Yet 0.02 per cent (approx.) of a modern acre is still sufficient to accommodate a modest horticultural lease in conjunction with the customary paraphernalia of the burial plot.
46 Formal manumission: by manumission *vindicta, censu,* or *testamento*; informal manumission: under the provisions of the *leges Iunia* (?Norbana), *Fufia Caninia,* or *Aelia Sentia*.
47 A milestone found near Side – belonging to the road built by M'. Aquillius (cos. 129 BC, succeeding M. Perperna in Asia and completing the war against the allies of Aristonicus) between 129 and 126 BC from Pergamum – locates Pamphylia as part of the recently constituted *prouincia Asia*. See French, 1981–8, 11.2.428; Mitchell, 1999, pp. 17–21, esp. Table 1.
48 For a first century AD (perhaps Tiberian) iteration of the traditional division of medical therapy, see the eight books of A. Cornelius Celsus's *de medicina,* in Marx, 1915, reprinted in the Loeb edition of W. G. Spencer 1936–8.

49　The practice of medicine in the ancient world was a profitable profession for many;
　　e.g. Plin. *HN* 29.2.4; Mart. 11.84 (Alcon). On the other hand, Cicero (*Off.* 1.42)
　　and Varro (*Rust.* 1.16.4) – not to mention Martial and his jibes against oculists –
　　represent a variant perspective. In this regard, it is impossible to ascertain if Hostius
　　belonged to a family which in part comprised one or more medical practitioners, or
　　whether he learnt his skills as an apprentice to another doctor, by attending lectures
　　or even public anatomical demonstrations. So, too, we cannot know if his training
　　occurred in a traditional Italian or foreign context, though the available evidence
　　indicates that many doctors were Greek.

50　The concern with establishing the status of medicine as an art (as opposed to the
　　enterprises of philosophers and alternative healers) in many of the theoretical works in
　　the medical corpus may be viewed here as a practical imperative underlying epigraphic
　　registration of libertine identity. For metanarratives treating aspects of the descriptive
　　epistemology in ancient medical treatises, see Scarborough, 1969 and Jackson, 1988.

51　Otherwise, we would read Nelpia C. l. Given the emphasis of the inscription on
　　Hostius's personal pecuniary agency (*emit*), the reverse seems even less probable.

52　All of the foregoing must remain conjectural, however, in the face of the absence of
　　any reference in the inscription to the specific social context or of words like *uxor*
　　and *maritus*.

53　*Dig.* 1.5.4.1.

54　Plin. *HN* 33.134 leavens any surprise the modern social historian may aver in the
　　face of slaves and ex-slaves participating and perpetuating slave-owning attitudes and
　　ideology: C. Caecilius Isidorus, formerly belonging to the *familia Caesaris*, was said
　　to have owned 4,116 slaves at his death.

55　A work which exemplifies the encyclopaedic simplification of these approaches to
　　funerary space in the ancient Roman world is Toynbee, 1971. For a recent collection
　　of works specifically attuned to environmental complexities (i.e. the ways in which
　　the social fabric impinged on the cultural contexts of Roman burial practice), see von
　　Hesberg and Zanker, 1987; cf. Koortbojian, 1996, p. 318, n. 8.

56　Whether general, archaeological, or topically specific, the treatment of Roman
　　agriculture seems characteristically attuned to developmental patterns, regional
　　studies, and Braudelian periodizations. Microhistorical, comparative analysis of
　　interlocking sociocultural and socioeconomic practices in pre-industrial Roman Italy
　　– utilizing textual, archaeological, and epigraphic evidence – is still remarkably 'thin
　　on the ground'.

57　Unless otherwise indicated, ownership of slave labour by libertine commemorators
　　should be regarded as a necessary if problematic given. The accommodation
　　of freedmen and women within the context of a freed household through ties
　　of sentiment, companionship, or occupation is a difficult statistical quantity to
　　determine. Applying the logic of possibility, the manumission of homeborn or
　　purchased slave labour by ex-slave *patronae/i* does not exclude the former category,
　　but is just as, if not more, likely than the transfer of previously known *libertae/i* by
　　virtue of affective or work attachments.

58　A burial plot is, by post-industrial definition, exclusively funerary in nature or
　　marginalized in favour of the aforementioned artistic, structural, or religious
　　scholarly predispositions. In either view, environmental or social contextualization is
　　an unnecessary complication.

59　I refer here to modern scholars' talk of legal, moral, philosophical, and other *topoi* in
　　relation to the heavy use of conventional formulas in *all* inscriptions. Cf. Lattimore, 1942.

4

Movement, Rhythms, and the (Re)production of Written Space[1]

David J. Newsome

Introduction

Piazza di Pasquino

On 9 March 2010, the 'Pasquino' statue group abutting the Palazzo Braschi in Rome was cleared of the messages that had been painted, glued, or affixed to it and had accumulated as a palimpsest of protest for half a millennium.[2] The statue – Menelaus holding the body of Patroclus – was excavated from the newly dug streets of the *Rione di Parione* in 1501 and re-erected by Cardinal Oliviero Carafa, resident of the adjacent palazzo and keen patron of the arts. From 25 April 1509, he would host an annual competition in Latin literacy and composition, at which poems were affixed to the statue base.[3] Before long, the act of posting *pasquinades* extended beyond the competition and the subject matter changed to satirical, at times scathing, commentary on the Papal state. For the next five centuries, Pasquino has served as 'an anonymous organ of public opinion, and part of the social system of Rome' (Figure 4.1).[4]

The *pasquinade*, in its broadest sense, is an attractive form of social commentary for two main reasons. First, it provides exposure for one's message by being located in a busy public space. The Pasquino group stands at the intersection of numerous roads that criss-crossed the *Parione* following a period of urban renewal under Sixtus IV (1471–84), including Via Papale – the principal street through this part of Rome prior to the construction of the new Corso Vittorio Emmanuele II in the 1880s. Movement – of pedestrians and vehicles, of chance passers-by and those who specifically went to look – guaranteed the statue's status as a preferred location for written space.[5]

Alongside space we must also consider the time of writing – at night. The second reason the *pasquinade* is attractive is that it allows the writer anonymity (necessary when the content is critical of authority). This anonymity is not simply a result of choosing not to leave one's name: it is because the act of posting the *pasquinade* has particular temporal as well as spatial considerations. It is a nocturnal activity that seeks to interject in rhythms of urban movement; it appears at night to be read and circulated by day. It is the opportunistic (re-)production of a particular place that

Figure 4.1 Piazza di Pasquino, Rome (author's photo)

began as an 'official' written space – encouraged and endorsed by the city's authorities at certain times for certain purposes – but which was appropriated and remade by the city's inhabitants.

Aims and structure of the present chapter

In this chapter, I examine the production of non-official written space within the Roman city, focusing on the ways in which activities within space were based on the exploitation of rhythms (e.g. of movement, of light). This chapter builds upon my previous work on movement as an important variable in the Roman city.[6] Specifically, it responds to the need to understand the temporal rhythms of the location-specific activities.[7] I consider how the Roman city was structured not only by the configuration of space but by the temporality of spatial behaviours (writing/displaying; discovering/ reading; copying/dispersing). In particular, I examine the production of non-official writing as an act of appropriating 'official' spaces. Several of my examples relate to writing within spaces defined as a *locus celeberrimus* ('the busiest place'), thereby relating movement, visibility, and exposure but also underlining the ways in which non-official written space acted within (responded to and changed expectations of) existing representations of the city.[8]

My interest is the production of non-official writing as a 'spatial tactic' that uses time to transcend the propriety of 'official' urban spaces. This distinguishes my chapter from the work of those who have looked at similar evidence, such as Corbier, in this volume (on the myriad ways in which writing was used for public communication to undifferentiated audiences), Zadorojnyi (on the ancient literary elite view of non-official writing and the embedding of political dissent within the

Graeco-Roman discourse) and Hillard, in this volume (on the efficacy of non-official writing, examining the ways in which this medium might provoke action and become embedded in the historical narrative).[9] While our chapters elide in our interest in location, my interest is in dynamic space – the appearance of non-official texts within rhythms of urban movement – and the appropriation of both space and time.

I begin with a discussion of what I mean by 'spatial tactics', following the theories of Michel de Certeau, and then establish how the production of non-official written space can be considered illegal (and an act of 'the other'), based on Roman legal texts. I then briefly consider the relationship between official texts and their display in spaces of movement, to establish the wider context of non-official writing. Following this, I examine the evidence relating to non-official texts in public space – highlighting those examples that contribute to our understanding of the relationship between movement, time, and the appropriation of official locations. I conclude with some thoughts on what these relationships tell us about the production and reproduction of space in the Roman city.

Before proceeding, it is important to clarify what is meant by non-official texts. My interest is in those texts that were inscribed, painted on to, or written and posted/affixed upon, existing spaces or monuments – whether new or the addition to or alteration of existing texts – without the consent of those who established the site or who were responsible for its maintenance. This is a broader range of material than we might associate with the modern term 'graffiti', for which we do not have a direct ancient equivalent (either noun or verb). It also encompasses a range of different interest groups, all of whom can be considered – at least at the time of their activity – as 'others', acting in opposition to official space.

Non-official writing as 'the other': tactics and legality

Spatial tactics

Throughout this chapter I follow Michel de Certeau's theory of 'spatial tactics' – the use of movement and time to momentarily usurp or appropriate the place of another.[10] Tactics are associated with non-official space, in contrast to 'spatial strategies', which are the product of the official organization and representation of space. We may think here of imperial statues or monuments as spatial strategies, as are legal codifications of what constitutes 'sacred' or 'public' space. Within and around such spaces, de Certeau's interest is in the ways in which people compose a 'network of antidiscipline' – how the everyday 'tactics' of individuals form a subversive response to spatial strategy.[11] 'Tactics' are based on time and opportunism, poaching in space that is conceived and managed by official persons and institutions, and they are both mobile and temporary. Studying spatial tactics allows us to understand the ways in which urban space is creatively reproduced by non-official actions making use 'of the cracks that particular conjunctions open in the surveillance of the proprietary powers'.[12] This includes those between night and day, as well as busyness and emptiness, linked in turn to concepts of public and private. Rhythms – the kinetic and temporal attributes of urban space

– are both time and place specific. One cannot be dissociated from the other. The examination of the spatial practice of non-official writing should consider not just particular spaces but particular rhythms – the relationship between time and space, or as Lefebvre terms it: 'a localized time' or a 'temporalized place'.[13] Lefebvre argues that the more purposeful a given space the less susceptible it is to appropriation by 'everyday' spatial practices, leaving only the opportunities brought by time, and the related variations in intensities of urban movement.

Such themes are evident in an example from Lucian's dialogues, written in the mid-to-late-second century AD. The courtesans Chelidonion and Drosis discuss how to respond to a letter written by the father of one who has been forced to stop frequenting them and turn to philosophy instead. The dialogue is full of references to movement in public spaces of Athens – the streets, the stoa Poikile, the agora – and an awareness of movements informs their actions:

> CHELIDONION: I also think I will write on the wall in Kerameikos where
>   Architeles usually takes his daily walk […]
> DROSIS: How will you write unnoticed?
> CHELIDONION: At night, Drosis, with a piece of charcoal we will pick up on the
>   way.[14]

Key here is awareness and exploitation of movement and rhythm – where Architeles *usually* takes his *daily* walk – and the use of night and opportunism to interject in this 'everyday' space.[15] In Lucian's passage, de Certeau would recognize these actions as spatial tactics: opportunistically poaching in space used by others; requiring and exploiting mobility; demonstrating knowledge of the regular, rhythmic use of space and of existing expectations.[16]

Another example of a spatial tactic is the inscription carved into the temple of Concord in 121 BC: 'at night, beneath the inscription on the temple, somebody carved this verse – "a work of mad discord produces a temple of concord"'.[17] The temple stood in the northwest corner of the Forum Romanum, at the foot of the Capitoline, and its relationship to the forum and the crowds that moved there is evident in numerous sources.[18] This is a space characterized by movement (both to it and past it) in the day, and at which an anonymous perpetrator made their mark during the night. This would have been a highly visible defacement of the new temple and appearing beneath the official inscription it would have been a direct challenge to the representational 'strategies' of the formal dedicatory text.

These are the kinds of themes that we can examine in other non-official writing in the Roman city. In order to discuss the production of non-official written space as a spatial tactic, it is first necessary to establish the extent to which it could be considered an act of 'the other' in the legally-codified spaces of the Roman city.

Legal attitudes to non-official writing in public space

Roman legal texts include numerous prohibitions against the defacement or alteration of public monuments and the production and dissemination of defamatory writing, and a brief survey of evidence establishes the nature of the examples we will encounter throughout this chapter. We can start broadly, regarding prohibitions on interference with public monuments and imperial statues. Such interferences are collated by Ulpian as 'deformations', in contrast to 'adornments'. There is an acknowledgement that motive ('acts committed for the purpose of') should be considered in the prohibition, although elsewhere consequence ('from which injury or inconvenience may result') is given precedence over motive when establishing what is not permitted in 'sacred places'.[19] Injury (*iniuria*) should here be read in its broadest sense, encapsulating not only damage and physical harm but a wider sense of offence and wrongdoing. Such injury is worse when the act is committed in a public space, no doubt because it would be exposed to, visible to, and thereby cause offence to (or stimulate similar sentiments among) a greater audience than comparable actions in private.[20] Imperial statues are treated separately; defacement of them was not only prohibited but could be an act of *laesa maiestas* – an offence against the dignity of the Roman state and the emperor.[21] The legal sources collated in the *Digesta* focus not on what is prohibited but what was exempt from prosecution; by inference those things not exempted were prohibited.[22] This would include non-official writings either carved into or attached to the statue bases – one of the most common types of non-official writing encountered in our sources.

Marcianus, with reference to earlier sources, links location and content when he informs us that: 'it is provided by imperial constitutions that anything placed upon public monuments for the purpose of defaming another shall be removed/destroyed'.[23] As well as removing things already posted, action was taken to try and prevent the production of such material in the first place. We are told that one could be prosecuted for writing, composing, publishing, or procuring to be published, things for the purpose of defaming another (*ad infamiam*) – whether this is done under a false name (*alterius nomine*) or anonymously (*sine nomine*).[24] The same penalties apply, *ex senatus consulto*, to those who write such *epigrammata* and those who cause them to be purchased or sold.[25] This implies a network of dissent and defamation that includes those who conceived of the material and those involved in its distribution.

The evidence presented in the last two paragraphs indicates that steps were taken to dissuade – by the threat of prosecution – the production of certain written materials and their display in public space. However, the examples imply that such non-official writing continued to be produced, disseminated, and displayed in the spaces in which it was prohibited. This brings us to another important consideration in Roman law when establishing how such writings were spatial tactics – the routine coupling of the concepts of violent and clandestine behaviour.[26] Violence has a broader semantic range than we might now give it, meaning – according to a definition of Quintus Mucius which is accepted in the *Digesta* – 'where a person does [something] after he has been forbidden'.[27] This would include the production and publication/display of the kinds of written material described above, which were subject to Senatorial decree and the prohibitions of the *praetor urbanus*. They should be considered – in legal terms – as 'violent' acts. Cassius, via Ulpian, defines clandestine actions as those of one 'who conceals what he is doing from his adversary, and fails to notify him, because he feared, or thought that he had good reason to fear, opposition'.[28] The close relationship between violent acts and clandestine behaviour reveals the manner in which the former were enabled by the latter; people were able to perpetrate violent acts by acting in secret. In the case of the examples presented in this chapter, this meant acting at night.[29]

The prohibition of certain writings, the restriction on what could be done to public monuments and imperial statues in particular, and the conceptual and legal relationship between acting in secret and acting in violence, all help us to understand the ways in which the production of non-official written space in the Roman city should be considered a spatial tactic: they are intrusions in a space that has an 'official' and legally defined status (constituted as sacred/public/imperial); they are composed of the kinds of messaging that is prohibited (designed to cause defamation or disrepute); they are produced clandestinely (at night). One of the clearest indications that these are 'spatial tactics' is their impermanence. As mentioned by Marcianus, above, things placed upon public monuments are to be removed and destroyed; or, as de Certeau would put it, 'whatever it wins, it does not keep'.[30]

Movement, display, and 'written space'

Corbier's contribution to this volume provides substantial detail on the relationship between writing in public space and communication. Here, I need only state a few pertinent examples of the relationships between movement, visibility, and the official production of written space, in order to provide the context in which non-official writings can be understood. I refer the reader to Corbier's chapter for a wider-ranging survey of official and non-official texts in public space.

An idea of the physicality of written space can be gleaned from the frescoes from the atrium of the *Praedia Iuliae Felicis* at Pompeii – scenes that are full of movement and interaction in urban space. They include an image of several pedestrians stood before a banner that has been stretched across at least three equestrian statue bases in front of a portico (Figure 4.2).[31] Still clear are the traces of a darker pigment that represented text on the banner, although it would not have been readable; it is illustrative of where text would have been.[32] The portico and forum depicted in the fresco is a space of mobility and congregation – a focal point for haphazard convergence.[33] This is a written notice in a space of pedestrian traffic, and the positioning of the figures and their feet make clear that they have stopped to read.

The posting of texts in spaces of movement is linked to visibility and the exposure of a message to an audience. The *senatus consultum de Bacchanalibus* of 186 bc includes the recommendation, pertaining to the display of the prohibitions, that: 'you shall […] order it be posted where it can be most easily read'.[34] Location is determined by an assessment of where it might be most easily read, or most easily 'known' (from *nosco*, which has a broader semantic range than *lego*). This suggests that this otherwise unspecified space is one of considerable movement, and potential audience. What the *senatus consultum* and non-official writing have in common is an insistence on the movement of viewers past them.[35] Something similar has been suggested for a dedication in honour of Pallas, the freedman in charge of Claudius' private accounts. In reward for his revenue-enhancing Senatorial decree, among other honours, copies

Figure 4.2 Pedestrians read from a banner stretched across statue bases. From the *Praedia Iuliae Felicis*, Pompeii (II.4.3), *Le pitture antiche d'ercolano e contorni* III (1762), tav. XLIII, p. 227

of the text were to be displayed in public; Pliny the Younger later tells us that a *locus celeberrimus* was chosen.[36] Considering rhythm as well as movement, we should also note the *acta diurna* – a gazette of sorts 'published' from the late-first century BC.[37] Their name evidences their regularity (*diurna* – daily) and rhythmicity. It is likely that they were posted in a busy public space, such as the forum, where they would have an audience, could be examined, and from where copies could be taken. They were routinely displayed in spaces of movement.

We can begin to consider non-official writing and the ways in which they appropriated public space with an example that again relates to movement, visibility, and exposure, but which introduces illegality into our evidence. In around 304 BC, Gnaeus Flavius – a scribe to the consul Appius Claudius – published details of the procedures that took place during litigation, and the *dies fasti*, which stipulated the days on which legal actions were permitted. These had hitherto been known only to the pontiffs and Flavius' actions ended their monopoly on legal knowledge. The event is described in several later sources, relating to movement, display, the acquisition of knowledge, and everyday rhythms. Livy (9.46.5) describes how Flavius 'made public the legal forms and processes which had been hidden away in the archives of the pontiffs, and published the calendar on white tablets around the forum'.[38] Cicero (*Pro Mur.* 11.25) does not give details of the display or its location, but the verb he used to describe Flavius' actions accords with Livy – *propono*, to expose/display. Pliny's use of *publico* captures the essence not only of display but of turning this information over to the people, in both a visual and possessive sense.[39] Cicero relates this to daily rhythms ('records to be learnt by heart every day') while Pliny implies that the display of this information *changed* rhythms in that the people no longer had to ascertain it each day (*cotidie*) from the few who knew.[40] Cicero and the second century AD jurist Sextus Pomponius leave no doubt that Flavius' actions were not sanctioned, and as such the exposure of these texts can be considered an act of appropriating both their contents and the spaces in which they were displayed – the forum.[41] The theft, the display, and the production of a *new* and non-official written space are similar to the 'spatial tactics' of non-official writing we can consider next.[42]

The production of non-official written space

If the act of 'graffiti' is one of *writing* the city, then the spatial tactic of non-official writing first requires a *reading* of the city – an understanding of the choice of site (its associations and expectations, which the graffito will reconfigure) and the rhythms associated with that site. Questions of foreknowledge and preparedness are considered in detail in the early-first century BC *Rhetorica ad Herennium*, which when assessing the nature of crimes asks one to consider, among other things: 'was [the location] frequented or deserted; always a lonely place, or deserted then at the moment of the crime? […] could the victim have been seen or heard? […] whether in day or at night […] and why such a time? […] was it long enough to carry out this act, and did the defendant know there would be enough time to accomplish it?'[43] Imagining that 'the crime' is an act of non-official writing, either attaching to or defacing a public monument, these are all considerations that make that act a spatial tactic in de Certeau's terms. In order for it to be acted upon, opportunity needs to be recognized. This recognition is both spatial and temporal – knowing both *where* and *when* opportunities arise. Of the considerations listed in the *Rhetorica ad Herennium*, the relationship between secrecy, the night, and opportunity is clear.

Spatial practices at night in the Roman city have received little attention compared to those of the day. Lanciani vividly described Rome when the sun went down – 'the solitary streets, plunged into darkness, wore a sinister look' – and Plautus has a character describe the act of walking alone at night as a proxy for bravery.[44] But if night was fearsome to some, and dissuaded them from movement, it was an opportunity for others. The characterization of the night as an opportunity for clandestine activity (discussed above) appears in numerous sources. Cassius Dio provides several references to things being done secretly (11.11) and unobserved (36.48) at night, and considered it 'the greatest of aid for clandestine activity' (48.8). Appian notes how the night afforded concealment and the ability to move unrecognized (2.57; 5.4.70), while Ammianus Marcellinus refers several times (14.11.1; 15.4.8; 25.6.14) to the ways in which the night provides concealment and enables activities that required protection from visibility. The very nature of 'public' and 'private' changed from day to night. Cassius Dio (61.16.1–2) describes how critics of Nero revered him in public but criticized him in private, including defacing one of his statues at night. In essence, the night has turned this public space into a private one.[45]

However, the degree of concealment afforded by the night was subject to natural rhythms as well, and these could have the opposite effect to those described above. Commodus is said to have driven a chariot from Rome on 'a moonless' night to avoid being seen – the night alone does not provide adequate concealment; this depends on a particular kind of night, one in which moonlight did not reveal his activities.[46] This reminds us that, much as we have rhythms of night and day, we have other lunar rhythms that should be associated with the opportunity, and even the ability, to produce non-official texts. We have numerous references to the increasing and decreasing of moonlight, and the Roman calendar itself was based upon the lunar cycle.[47] At its brightest, indeed, Cicero remarks that the moon 'makes a kind of day of the night'.[48] Here, then, we must consider that while night provides concealment, certain degrees of moonlight provide enough light to enable one to produce non-official texts. There is, then, a lunar effect to consider, albeit one of opportunity rather than superstition. Certain conditions are more favourable for the production of texts at night, in otherwise unlit public space, and we should consider how some location-specific behaviours are made more possible (and, perhaps, more likely – particularly when tied to the Roman election calendar) at some times than at others. An example from Pompeii is thought-provoking. Sometime after AD 50, Aemilius Celer wrote, on a wall close to his house, an advert for upcoming gladiatorial games, ending: 'Aemilius Celer wrote this on his own by the light of the moon'.[49] These details are related: the light of the moon enables Aemilius Celer to write on his own, without needing someone to hold a lamp, and this is deemed worthy of comment. Under ordinary circumstances, perhaps when the moon was not so bright, a second person may have been required to facilitate the production of such texts at night. This may imply that the production of texts at night, and the non-official texts described here, may ordinarily have been actions of complicity, involving more than one individual.

Complicity is implied in Plutarch's discussion of the non-official texts left upon the statues of the elder Brutus and tribunal seat of Marcus Iunius Brutus (*Brut.* 9.5). Having learnt that some citizens (plural) have been leaving messages in these places at night, we are told that these actions were provoked by the flatterers (plural) of Caesar who had themselves put crowns upon his statues – at night. Here we have two different campaigns of nocturnal subversion. That the pro-Caesar side do not affix verbal messages, but added imagery, is of less relevance than the fact that we have two opposing groups both using and moving through the city in similar ways and at similar times.[50] Neither has a right to the spaces they are rewriting and repurposing. Both are spatial tactics, as defined above.

Not surprisingly, given their clandestine nature, most of the texts that produce non-official written spaces are anonymous: those responsible are identified mostly by impersonal collective pronouns.[51] According to Suetonius (*Aug.* 55–6), Augustus did not try to discover the authors of critical *libelli* that were distributed in the *Curia*, but did propose that thereafter authors of defamatory notes or verses who wrote under a false name (*sub alieno nomine*), should be called to account.[52] This is not the only time we read of messages circulating in, or from, the Senate under assumed names. Tacitus (*Ann.* 5.4) tells us that fictitious attacks were circulated under consular names (*sub nominibus consularium*), and explicitly links the quantity and the nature of such letters to their anonymity.[53] Suetonius tells us that gibes were written about Nero and either posted on walls or circulated around the city, in both Greek and Latin, but the identity of those responsible remains anonymous, collective, and unspecific: 'those who said', or, simply, 'authors'.[54] This is similar to the identification of the graffitist at the temple of Concord with the imprecise 'somebody'.

As is clear from the examples above, the act of non-official writing varied in terms of materials and method: we have references to notices being affixed, carved, and written. It is worth considering the differences and what they suggest about the context of these writings as 'spatial tactics' – whether spontaneous incidents or premeditated activity. The example of the non-official message on the temple of Concord is a useful starting point: it was carved beneath the inscription. Presumably this was in the entablature and therefore at a considerable height above ground level – not the easiest of surfaces on which to leave a mark. Perhaps this was achieved by making use of scaffolding associated with the temple's construction. In any case, carving is the slowest of the possible methods. Inscribing is time consuming and a key aspect of spatial tactics is that they are rapid. This is particularly important when, as in this case, the work is carried out under the (fleeting) cover of darkness. Indeed, because of this consideration I am moved to agree with Hillard's suggestion, in this volume, that the Latin inscription – whose essence but not precise formulation is recounted in Plutarch's Greek – would have erred towards brevity. Another well-known non-official text relies on extreme brevity – the *arci/arkei* pun carved on one of Domitian's many arches.[55] Its brevity furnishes an enjoyable bilingual pun, but it may also be related to the material reality of its production – when inscribing on (and defacing) a public monument, fewer characters mean it is quicker to accomplish; the quicker the better.

Affixing or writing, rather than inscribing, also has the advantage that those messages can be prepared elsewhere. Indeed, a common feature of the non-official writings discussed in this chapter is the posting/publishing/displaying of *libelli* – more like pamphlets than what we would call 'graffiti', and perhaps more like the *pasquinade*: written elsewhere and quickly stuck to the statue base.[56] These are spatial tactics that suggest some consideration of opportunity, discussed above and, recalling the *Rhetorica ad Herennium*, a consideration of whether there is enough time to carry out the act. An alternative to both inscribing and affixing graffiti on surfaces was the use of charcoal or chalk – impermanent materials but relatively easy to acquire and quick to use. Martial (12.61.7–10) associated charcoal (*carbone*) and chalk (*creta*) with an inferior type of literacy, associating the materials with dank locations and the inebriation of the writer.[57] Plautus, too, seems to imply that charcoal is the preferred medium of spontaneous 'graffitists'.[58] Horace preserves a saying which borders on the pejorative – 'are they to be marked with chalk or charcoal?' – implying, perhaps, as in Martial, that such writing represented the trivial or the inferior.[59] Yet, if these materials were considered socially and aesthetically inferior by some, they had advantages for others. They probably represented the quickest means of marking a surface, they were widely available, and – according to one source at least – they may even be legible at night. In Petronius' *Satyricon*, Giton is so afraid of losing his way in the city, even by day, that he marks all of the posts and columns with chalk. These marks guide the footsteps of Encolpius and Ascyltos, at midnight: they overcome even the darkest night.[60] As noted above, Chelidonion and Drosis planned to write on the walls in Athens using a piece of charcoal picked up on the way. The activity of non-official writing is planned in advance, but the acquisition of materials is a matter of the moment – a balance of reconnaissance and spontaneity.

Conclusions

The examples above, indicative rather than exhaustive, establish the ways in which non-official writing was produced and displayed in the Roman city. This evidence contributes to our understanding of the on-going formation of the materiality of urban space, and emphasizes the need for a temporal understanding of location-specific behaviours.[61] We can conclude by considering the ways in which non-official texts entered (and shaped) other rhythms of the Roman city – rhythms of discovery and dispersal.

These examples of non-official writing whether written on, inscribed, or affixed, are interjections in urban space – left at night to be discovered by day. They succeed in producing new associations and expectations of space, wherein their discovery and reading become part of the everyday routine of urban movement and part of the temporal structure of the Roman day (for example, movements associated with the *salutatio*; the structured movement to the forum; and the pedestrianized city prior to the ingression of vehicle traffic after the tenth hour).[62] While I have focused on the rhythms of their production, we must also give attention to the rhythms of their reproduction, whether that is through being read, or copied and taken elsewhere (at which point the message is divorced from the location-specificity of its production, and assumes a new role in the urban networks of rumour and communication).[63] This dispersal of non-official texts itself depends on movement (to the site and then away from it) and would have been associated with the morning. Livy (36.61.14) gives an example:

> Aristo [...] as soon as it was dusk hung a written tablet over the place where the magistrates daily held their sessions, in the most crowded part of the city [...] The next day, when the *sufetes* took their seats to administer justice, the tablet was seen, taken down, and read.[64]

Aristo waits until the beginning of the evening before hanging this tablet.[65] He chooses a location which is used daily (*cotidianam*).[66] This spatial tactic is evidently a successful one as the tablet is noticed (*conspicio*), taken down and read the very next day. It is a tactic that is enabled by the predictable rhythm of the city's spaces of authority and movement, and by exploiting the opportunities that are presented at certain times of the day. Although he is not anonymous, Aristo had long since departed by the time his tablet was read; the *locus celeberrimus* has been appropriated and rewritten from an official space to a non-official, spontaneous, and 'tactical' space.

Another example of the ways in which nocturnally-produced non-official texts interrupt the following morning is the graffiti-campaign associated with Brutus' tribunal seat in the forum.[67] These appeared every night and were found every day: new messages, new rhythms, and a new 'written space'. Their discovery and discussion is temporally-fixed by Appian at the time of day 'before there was to be a meeting of the Senate', i.e., in the morning at around (*before*) the third hour.[68] Given that such things attached to public monuments would have been removed, and given that many examples are in impermanent materials (chalk or charcoal) and would have been easy to erase, non-official texts have a narrow timeframe in which they might be seen, become known, be copied, or be otherwise communicated to others. One can imagine Brutus removing the things posted to his tribunal seat as soon as he saw them, which would mean that the survival of non-official texts might not be expected to routinely outlast the moment of their discovery.[69]

Livy's example, above, notes how his tablet was taken down and read, and this is an important example of the ways in which graffiti enter into other urban communications. The *pasquinade*, for example, was so successful in Rome in the sixteenth century because the Pasquino group was located close to region's printing shops, compilers, and booksellers.[70] We should consider too that the non-official texts around the Forum would have been visible to those moving through and from the *Argiletum*, well-known for its booksellers.[71] Much as the *acta diurna* would have been copied, we should expect the same for non-official writings. This copying and dispersal is an important measure of impact. All written space, whether official or non-official, to an extent imposes itself upon a moving viewer. This implies a tension between 'the assertive claim of the writer(s) and the often unwilling compulsion of a reader, who has no choice but to take in the texts that scratch across communal space'.[72] Where such written space may therefore be considered intrusive, copying and dispersal suggests adoption (and approval) of the sentiments expressed. To return to the frescoes from the *Praedia Iuliae Felicis* at Pompeii, one depicts a man sitting on a stool beside an equestrian statue, to which his gaze is directed (Figure 4.3). On his lap rests a tablet and in his right hand a stylus.[73] He may be drawing, or just as likely copying (whether an official inscription or a non-official addition). Such copying of non-official texts should be seen as another location-specific activity, associated with a particular time of the day but one that, in terms of the relationship between reading, copying, movement, and urban rhythm, gathers things together 'only to the extent that it pushes them away and disperses them'.[74]

The interpretations offered in this chapter can be summarized in three related observations. First, written space in the Roman city – its monuments and public spaces – were not static but were rewritten. Second, urban space was contested space, between different interest groups and in terms of the negotiation between official 'strategies' and non-official 'tactics'. Third, activities within the Roman city were highly temporalized; different times enabled different practices which themselves formed parts of the rhythms of the urban day. Written spaces – whether official or non-official – do not simply respond to existing patterns of movement, but generate and sustain new ones. Such spaces construct an audience which subscribe to new associations and expectations of a given place: a site is chosen as a written space because it is busy, therefore more people – an expectant crowd – go there to read, and it is busier still. This links these spontaneous and fleeting spatial tactics to the everyday. Non-official writing and the posting of official documents within paths of daily urban movement reshapes them – 'charging certain urban spaces with expectation, urgency, and conflict'.[75]

Although they may only be impermanent and easily removed from physical fabric, non-official texts play a key role in the reproduction of dynamic urban space. In terms of spatial tactics, what is most important is not the message itself but the temporal

Figure 4.3 A seated figure copying from an equestrian statue. From the *Praedia Iuliae Felicis*, Pompeii (II.4.3), *Le pitture antiche d'ercolano e contorni* III (1762), tav. XLI, p. 213

and location-specific behaviour of the production of non-official writing in the first place. Graffiti, *libelli*, and posted *tabella* on public monuments or imperial statues are the traces of spatial tactics that have already escaped by the time they are read. They were enabled by and survived because of the rhythms of movement that characterized Roman urban space.

Notes

1   I am grateful to the editors for their invitation to contribute to this volume. I thank Tom Hillard for sharing his chapter prior to submission, in the hope that we might avoid repetition. Translations are from the Loeb Classical Library with modification by the author where indicated. Figures 4.2 and 4.3 are reproduced with written permission from Special Collections, University of Birmingham.

2   *La Repubblica* – Roma, 10/3/10, p. 8.
3   Reynolds, 1985. On Pasquino and the *pasquinade* see Damianaki, Procaccioli and
    Romano, 2006. The similarity between *pasquinades* and the verse epigram of Martial
    is discussed by Spaeth Jr., 1939. See also Corbier, 2006 and in this volume.
4   Lanciani, 1901, pp. 47–50. The 2010 plans to remove the *pasquinades*, restore the
    statue, and replace the medium with a dedicated website were met with derision. The
    compromise that greets passers-by today is a plastic board beside the statue base.
5   This means not only movement *past*, but movement *to* and stopping *at*.
6   Newsome, 2008, 2010, 2011a, 2011b.
7   Newsome, 2011a, pp. 34–8; 51.
8   On the term *locus celeberrimus* see Newsome, 2011a, pp. 20–6. Corbier (2006 and in
    this volume) provides some examples, and notes the contrast with the *angustissimo
    loco* in which Caligula tried to minimize the visibility of new taxes (Suet. *Cal.* 41).
    On expectations more broadly, Corbier argues that the importance of a text can be
    judged according to the 'survival expectancy' of its support.
9   Corbier, 2006 and in this volume; Zadorojnyi, 2010, p. 123; Hillard in this volume.
10 See de Certeau, 1984, pp. xix; 29–30; 36–7.
11 De Certeau, 1984, pp. xiv–xv.
12 De Certeau, 1984, p. 37. Opportunity is considered in the broader discussion of
    (criminal) activity in, e.g. Cic. *de Inv.* 1.38; Quint. *Inst.* 1.1.47, both noting the
    importance of understanding time as well as place.
13 Lefebvre, 1996, p. 230. Lefebvre and Regulier-Lefebvre, 2004, p. 78.
14 Lucian, *Dial. meret* 10.4.
15 While Chaniotis, 2010, p. 194, is right to highlight that the premeditated nature of
    this act diminishes any sense of spontaneity, the act is still opportunistic.
16 De Certeau (1984: 18).
17 Plut. *C Gracchus* 17.6. See also App. *Bel. Civ.* 1.26 and Hillard in this volume.
18 See Newsome, 2010, pp. 66–71. Ov. *Fasti* 1.637–8 notes how the temple oversees 'the
    Latin throng'. Movement to the temple is mentioned in two texts by Cicero: *Dom.* 11,
    on the mob moving there quickly in protest during famine; *Cat.* 3.21, on movement
    through the forum in the morning.
19 Ulp. *Dig.* 43.6.1 (1); Herm. *Dig.* 43.6.2.
20 Ulp. *Dig.* 47.10.7 (8).
21 This is considered close to sacrilege: Ulp. *Dig.* 48.4.1pr. *proximum sacrilegio crimen
    est, quod maiestatis dicitur.*
22 Such material is compiled in *Dig.* 48.4. Again we see a distinction between motive
    and consequence, as in the example of stone-throwing: if someone throws a stone
    that hits an imperial statue, they are exempt from prosecution so long as the stone
    was not specifically aimed at it (Marc. *Dig.* 48.4.5). Acts against imperial statues were
    considered more serious when committed by soldiers: Mod. *Dig.* 48.4.7 (4).
23 Marc. *Dig.* 47.10.37pr. *constitutionibus principalibus cavetur ea, quae infamandi
    alterius causa in monumenta publica posita sunt, tolli de medio.*
24 Ulp. *Dig.* 47.10.5 (9–10). Also *Inst.* 4.4.1.
25 Ulp. *Dig.* 47.10.5.10. As well as this senatorial decree, Ulp. *Dig.* 47.10.15 (27)
    indicates that such publications or their oral recitation in poetry or singing, is
    prohibited by the Praetor (*vetuit praetor*).
26 The formulation '*quod vi aut clam*' reflects the manner in which violence (*violentia*)
    and clandestine (*clam*) activities were conceptually and legally related, e.g. in *Dig.*
    43.24.

27 Viv. *Dig.* 43.24.1 (5), *vi factum videri quintus mucius scripsit, si quis contra quam prohiberetur fecerit: et mihi videtur plena esse quinti mucii definitio.*

28 Ulp. *Dig.* 43.24.3 (7), *Clam facere videri cassius scribit eum, qui celavit adversarium neque ei denuntiavit, si modo timuit eius controversiam aut debuit timere.* In terms of temporality, Ulp. *Dig.* 43.24.5 (1) indicates that any notice should include the date and time. The production of non-official written space is used as a hypothetical example for the purposes of discussing things done by violence or clandestinely: Venuleius asks us to consider the legal ramifications 'if you attach a tablet to my door' (Ven. *Dig.* 43.24.22 (2), *si ad ianuam meam tabulas fixeris*).

29 Indeed, the *Instituta* (4.1.1–2) discusses the term 'theft' (*furti*) as derived from '*furvus*' – black.

30 De Certeau, 1984, p. 19.

31 The best survey of the frescoes remains Nappo (1989). This banner most likely represents a temporary addition to this space. It may have displayed public notices at the behest of the city authorities or have been related to the varied market activities that appear in the other frescoes.

32 As can be seen in Figure 4.2, the banner carried four lines of unbroken 'text', from left to right. There is an attempt here to depict a written space, but the writing itself is not legible. The fresco at the *praedia Iuliae Felicis* is 50 c.m. wide and 67 c.m. high. Other frescoes do contain legible text – as Ray Laurence reminded me, the fresco (at I.3.23) that depicts the riot around the amphitheatre includes texts on nearby walls that are clearly readable.

33 See also the posting of messages to columns (Prop. 3.23.23; Suet. *Ner.* 45.2; Plin. *Ep.* 8.8.7; Plut. *De curiositate* 520 D–E).

34 *hoce in tabolam ahenam inceideretis ita senatus aiquom censuit uteique eam figier ioubeatis ubi facilumed gnoscier potisit atque.*

35 See San Juan (2001, p. 23) on how the *bandi* in Rome 'insist on transitory and provisional conditions' and provoke passers-by to take sides.

36 Plin. *Ep.* 8.6.14. See Corbier (1997 and in this volume) on the location of this statue; Plin. *HN* 34.18. Corbier suggests that Pliny was directly citing the Senatorial decree.

37 Suet. *Iul.* 20 (*diurna acta confierent et publicarentur*). A parody of the *acta*, giving a clue as to its likely contents, appears in Pet. *Sat.* 53. See also Tac. *Ann.* 5.4.

38 *civile ius, repositum in penetralibus pontificum, euolgauit fastosque circa forum in albo proposui.* See Corbier (in this volume) on the Vespasianic edict published '*in albo*'.

39 Plin. *HN* 33.6.

40 Cic. *Mur.* 11.25; Plin. *HN* 33.6.

41 Cicero describes Flavius' actions with the verb *compilo* (to plunder/rob); Pomponius' *Libro singulari enchiridia* (recorded in the later *Digesta*, 1.2.2.7) describes how the book was stolen (*subreptum librum*).

42 I use the term 'theft' here as Ulp. *Dig.* 47.2.31 (1): 'if anyone steals or makes erasures in the acts of the Republic [...] he will be liable for the action of theft'. Flavius' actions would have been an example of peculation – the theft of publicly-owned things – as Paul. *Dig.* 48.13.9 (5): 'who, without the order of the official in charge, permitted the examination and copying of public registers'.

43 *De Rhet. ad Herennium* 2.4.7.

44 Lanciani, 1898, pp. 207–8); Plaut. *Am.* 1.1.95 (*qui hoc noctis solus ambulem*).

45 Not that the night concealed everything: both Cassius Dio (55.10.3) and Pliny (*HN* 15.20.78) refer to the antics of Julia, daughter of Augustus, who would engage in

inappropriate activities – in the forum, including on the *rostra* and at the statue of Marsyas – at night.

46 Dio Cass. 73.17.1.

47 On the increase and decrease of moonlight, see Cic. *Tusc.* 1.28.68.

48 Cic. *Nat D.* 2.69, *noctu quasi diem efficeret.* Varro states that there was a temple to *Noctiluna* on the Palatine (*LL.* 5.68).

49 *CIL* IV 3884 = *ILS* 5145, Scr(ipsit) Aemilis Celer sing(ulus) ad luna(m).

50 Indeed, in similar places. It is interesting to imagine the overlap of routes that is implied in Plut. *Brut.* 9.5 – statues of the elder Brutus and statues of Caesar, although there were no doubt many in public space, were adjacent in at least one particular place – on the Capitol at the *statuae Regum Romanorum*, where a statue to Caesar was added in 45 BC (Plin. *HN* 33.9; Dio Cass. 43.45.3–4). Suetonius (*Iul.* 80.3) also mentions writing on both the statues of L. Brutus and Caesar.

51 Such as Suet. *Iul.* 80.3, 'some wrote on the base of Lucius Brutus' statue' (*subscripsere quidam Luci Bruti statuae*).

52 Back to the *pasquinade*, in 1585, Sixtus V offered clemency and reward should the author of a *pasquinade* declare himself to the authorities, but the gallows if his or her identity was revealed by another.

53 *exercentibus plerisque per occultum atque eo procacius libidinem ingeniorum.* See also Corbier, in this volume.

54 Suet. *Ner.* 39.2–3 (*qui se dictis; auctores*). Not that their anonymity could be taken for granted – an informer reported them to the Senate (*delatos ad senatum*).

55 See Corbier, in this volume. Suet. *Dom.* 13.2.

56 Tertullian (*Ad nat.* 1.17) talked of the satirical *libelli* 'known to the statues' (*festivos libellos quod statuae sciunt*).

57 See Zadarojnyi, 2011, pp. 116–7 for discussion.

58 Plaut. *Merc.* 2.3.73 – 'my door, perhaps, will be filled with charcoal marks' (*simpleantur elogorium meae fores carbonibus*).

59 Hor. *Sat.* 2.3, *sani ut creta, an carbone notati.*

60 Pet. *Sat.* 79, *quae lineamenta evicerunt spississimam noctem.*

61 Edensor, 2010, pp. 1–3. This takes de Certeau's concepts of 'writing' the city almost literally: graffiti is not only the figurative rewriting of urban space but the physical act of writing *on* urban space – 'remaking its material fabric as text' Tonkiss 2005, p. 142.

62 Ray Laurence rightly urged me to make these points explicit.

63 On rumour and communication (the role of the *rostra* in the Forum Romanum as a locus for the formation of public opinion and its dispersal to *compita* and *vici*), see Laurence, 1994b. See Hillard, in this volume, on the *subrostrani* and the formulation of gossip within public space.

64 *Ariston* [...] *tabellas conscriptas celeberrimo loco super sedem cotidianam magistratuum prima uespera suspendit* [...] *postero die cum sufetes ad ius dicendum consedissent, conspectae tabellae demptaeque et lectae.*

65 Livy's use of *prima vespera* (dusk, the start of the evening, or literally 'the first star') does not quite place this in the same nocturnal category as other examples mentioned here, although it still implies a time after the daily business (and busyness) had finished.

66 On the notion of 'everyday' urban life see Cic. *Pis.* 26.64, *in hac cotidiana adsidua urbanaque vita.*

67 Plut. *Brut.* 9.5.

68 App. *Bel. Civ.* 2.113.
69 But as Hillard's chapter (in this volume) reminds us, they survived in other ways.
70 San Juan, 2001, p. 7.
71 Mart. 1.2.7–8; 1.117.9–12, referring to a shop with its doorposts completely covered in notices.
72 Tonkiss, 2005, p. 142. See also Corbier, in this volume, on the way in which monumental letters are imposed upon the gaze of the passer-by.
73 Nappo, 1989, p. 83.
74 San Juan, 2001, p. 6; Lefebvre, 1991, p. 386.
75 San Juan, 2001, p. 38.

5

Time in Written Spaces

Robert Hannah

Introduction

Time in written form pervades our social existence. From the daily news, whether on the web or in print, to wall calendars in our homes or offices, which tell us what day it is; from personal watches or cellphones to public clocks, which tell us what hour it is; from small change in our purses or pockets to use-by dates on our groceries, which remind us when things were made; and from personal or recreational diaries to bus and train timetables, which tell us when we did or should do things, we are constantly made aware of time and its passing in the modern world. And because of the means by which we tell the time in these contexts, it is easy to fall into the trap of thinking that the ancient world did not have such persistent reminders as well. Yet archaeology and literature combine to tell us differently. In this chapter I wish to discuss aspects of this combination, focusing on time in written forms, on the collocation of the mechanisms of time and writing, and on the spatial setting in which these are found, all of which demonstrate a politicization of time in the late Republic and early Empire.

Calendars

Let us start with calendars as written time. We may distinguish two types of monumental calendars in the Roman world, one (*Fasti Anni*) charting the days and months of the year and representing a cyclical approach to time, the other (*Fasti Consulares*) listing the eponymous magistrates of Rome and demonstrating a linear approach to the passage of time from one year to the next. A third type of *fasti* recognized nowadays, the *Fasti Triumphales*, should be separated from these first two, as they do not signal continuous time, but commemorate one-off celebrations in episodic time, with events separated by irregular interstices. Furthermore, several of the *Fasti Anni* and *Fasti Consulares* appear together in the archaeological and literary record (six of the 35 surviving consular lists are accompanied by calendrical *fasti*), and it is thought that they may always have appeared together.[1]

Of the calendars of days and months, there survive over two dozen in various states of preservation from republican and imperial Rome, and almost another two dozen from elsewhere in Italy and Gaul.[2] Only four painted versions survive. The rest are made of marble but date mostly to the Augustan-Tiberian period.[3] This association of stone calendars only with the early Principate, and the absence of bronze examples (in contrast, say, to bronze tables of laws, known from literature and archaeology) probably signify that from the republican period to Late Antiquity the standard mode of presentation of the *fasti* was as painted wall-decoration, which has largely disappeared.[4]

These *fasti* were generally public documents, insofar as they were displayed in the meeting-rooms of priestly colleges, associations and country towns,[5] but the findspots of the *Fasti Antiates Maiores* (found in a building on the site of Nero's later villa at Antium, about 57 km south of Rome),[6] and the *Fasti porticus*[7] may have been private. Even so, in both of these cases, if the buildings were private, then we are talking of domiciles on a luxury scale. The *Fasti porticus* also demonstrate a capacity for this type of calendar to be illustrated on a large scale, with (as far as can be told from the surviving parts) frescoes of appropriate seasonal activities accompanying each month.[8] Earlier surviving painted calendars happen not to demonstrate this illustrative element, but much later the Calendar of AD 354 comes as an illustrated book, a compilation of various types of calendar, and we might suppose earlier versions existed too, whether in codex or roll form.[9]

The earliest sign of a public calendar in the Republic is of *fasti* set up by M. Fulvius Nobilior, some time after his Aetolian victory, celebrated in triumph in 187 BC.[10] These *fasti* were part of the decoration of the temple of Hercules Musarum ('Hercules of the Muses', a Roman adaptation of the Greek Herakles Mousagetes) in Rome, to which Fulvius added statues of the Muses which he had taken as booty from Ambracia.[11] The Severan Marble Plan of Rome situates the temple in the vicinity of the Circus Flaminius, built some 40 years earlier in 220 BC between the western side of the Capitoline hill and the Tiber. Its podium was discovered in 1980–1. While the Circus itself provided a large space for public meetings and markets, it maintained a major military function as the point of assembly and departure for triumphal processions. The addition of the temple in its neighbourhood is therefore apt.[12] In Fulvius' company during his Aetolian campaign had been the poet Ennius, author of the *Annales*, the first history of Rome in Latin. If Fulvius' *fasti* included not only a calendar of days but also a consular list, as is supposed on the basis of the only surviving republican *fasti*, the *Fasti Antiates Maiores*,[13] then the approach to time that these represent is congruent with Ennius' sequential approach to history. In this context it is noteworthy and appropriate that the temple of Hercules Musarum may have served as the meeting place of the *collegium scribarum histrionumque*, an association identified with the later *collegium poetarum*.[14]

We have only a few fragmentary indications of the content of Fulvius' *fasti*, notably from Varro, Censorinus and Macrobius. These can be strung together to read as a preface, which may have run somewhat like this at the head of the calendrical data:[15]

> *Bello Aetolico confecto fastos posuit M. Fulvius Nobilior cos. cens.*
>   *Romulus X menses appellavit: primos in honorem patris proaviaeque; postquam populum in Maiores iunioresque diviserat, ut altera pars consilio altera armis*

rem publicam tueretur, tertium et quartum in honorem utriusque partis; ceteros a numeris. Numa II additos a Iano et dis inferis. mensis XIII lege Acilii cos. anni DLXII interkalatur.

The consul and censor M. Fulvius Nobilior set up this calendar after the conclusion of the Aetolian War:

Romulus gave names to the ten months, the first and the second he named in honour of his father and his ancestress; after he divided his people into older and younger so that one group would defend the state with their counsel, the other by force of arms, he named the third and fourth months in their honour; the rest of the months were named from their number. Numa gave names to the two months he added from Ianus and the gods of the netherworld respectively. A thirteenth month was intercalated according to a law of the consul Acilius in the year 562.

Another calendar demonstrates a more thoroughly exegetical tendency in its appendages to the calendrical data. The now fragmentary *Fasti Praenestini* (Figure 5.1) were dedicated in the forum of Praeneste probably between AD 6 and 9, with some annotations being added later between AD 10 and 22. Suetonius relates that the *fasti* were the handiwork of the grammarian M. Verrius Flaccus, the freedman teacher of Augustus' grandsons, Gaius and Lucius. A statue of Flaccus was set up in the upper part of the forum, near the hemicycle in which the calendar was displayed.[16] The physical setting of the calendar, in the civic centre of the town, is decidedly public and as such it encourages visual connections with nearby buildings, not only the forum itself but also the temples of (perhaps) Jupiter Imperator in the forum and of Fortuna Primigenia up the hill.[17] Sacred and secular structures surround the calendar, which then reflects back content related to functions in these environments, through references to public festivals and market schedules. On the other hand, however, the semi-circular form of the calendar's hemicycle would also have drawn the reader into its half-enclosed space and so enforced an individual focus on the calendar's form, content and messages. In much the same way, the hemicycles of the Forum of Augustus in Rome drew visitors into their ambit to view and consider the messages embodied in the statues of prominent Romans from the past and their association with Augustus.[18]

In Flaccus' *fasti*, the beginning of the month of March (the middle column in Figure 5.1) reads:[19]

```
MARTIUS·AB·LATINORUM·[DEO·BEL]LANDI·ITAQUE·APUD
ALBANOS·ET·PLEROSQUE·[P]OPULOS·LATI[N]OS·IDEM·FUIT·ANTE
CONDITAM·ROMAM·UT·A[U]TEM·ALII·CRE[DU]NT·QUOD·EI·SACRA
FIUNT·HOC·MENSE
D    K · MART(IAE) · NP.
        FERIAE·MARTI·IUN[O]NI·LUCINAE·EXQUILIIS
        QUOD·EO·DIE·AEDIS·EI·D[EDICA]TA·EST·PER·MATRONAS
        QUAM·VOVERAT·ALBIN[I·FILIA]·VEL·UXOR·SI·PUERUM
        [PARIENTEM]QUE·IPSA[M·FOVISSET]
E    VI    F
F    V    C
```

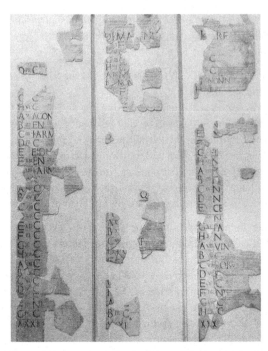

Figure 5.1 Fasti Praenestini, AD 6–9. Rome, Museo Nazionale Archeologico, Palazzo Massimo (photo R. Hannah)

March: from the god of fighting of the Latins, therefore among the Albans and most Latin peoples, it was the same before the founding of Rome; as, however, others believe, because things were sacred to him in this month.

D   Kalends of March   NP

Festivals: for Mars; for Juno Lucina on the Esquiline,

because on that day there was dedicated to her on behalf of married women a temple, which the daughter or wife of Albinus had vowed, if she favoured her while bearing a son.

E   6   F

F   5   C

This is indeed a commentary, yet not separated from but embedded within the very fabric of the calendar itself, with the exegeses appended in smaller red letters above the month and beside the day entries. We can see its particularly academic nature, as Flaccus explains in scholiast-like fashion the origin of the name of the month, emphasizing its source in Latium, perhaps in contrast to others who argued for a simple connection with Mars, the god of war: Fulvius had earlier explained that March was so named by Romulus after his father, i.e., the god Mars.[20] Etymologies follow for the other nine months of the originally ten-month Romulan year, and then Numa's two extra month names, January and February, are explained, and the introduction of the intercalary month is dated.

What these *fasti* indicate is a particular level of literacy on the part of the intended users, as the calendars are constructed in a highly compressed form, with single letters or abbreviations signalling individual days and their commemorated events. Just how distinctly literary, more than just literate, Verrius Flaccus' *fasti* are, may be gauged by comparison with its earlier republican counterpart, the *Fasti Antiates Maiores* (Figure 5.2), dated to 84–55 BC and so the only one that predates the reforms of Julius Caesar from 45 BC. It was found as more than 300 fragments of stucco, painted in black and red lettering. Complete the calendar of days measured 1.16 by 2.50m. The preserved remains cover just over half the year's days. The nature of the original building that it decorated, however, is unknown, and so we are deprived of a full appreciation of the public accessibility of this visually impressive monument.

This calendar is well-ordered into thirteen columns but packed with abbreviations. Here is the month of June, with restorations:[21]

```
E    K·IVN·N
         – MARTI·IN·CL
         IVNON·IN
F    F
[G   C]
H    C
A    NON·N
         – DI·FIDI
B    N
C    [N]
D    [N]
[E   VESTAL·N]
         [– VESTA]E
[F   N]
[G   M]ATR·NP
         [– M]ATRI·MATV
```

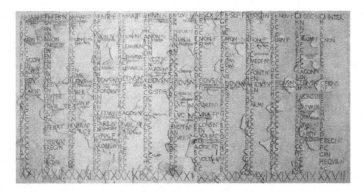

Figure 5.2 Fasti Antiates Maiores, 84–55 BC. Rome, Museo Nazionale Archeologico, Palazzo Massimo (photo R. Hannah)

```
              FORTV[N]AE
[H  N]
 A    EIDVS·N[P]
 B    N
[C]   Q·ST·D[·F]
[D]   C
[E]   C
 F    C
 G    C
              – MIN[ERVAE]
 H    [C]
 A    [C]
 B    [C]
[C   C]
[D   C]
[E   C]
[F   C]
 G    C
              – LARV[– – –]
[H]   C
 A    [C]
 X         X       I       X
```

The explanations for the abbreviations and entries for this part of the *Fasti* from Antium may serve also for the excerpt of the *Fasti Praenestini* presented earlier.

The whole calendar starts on 1 January with a column on the left, which presents a continuously repeated sequence of the eight letters, A to H. The series begins with A on 1 January and runs uninterruptedly to 29 December – recall that this is the pre-Julian calendar, with only 29 days in January, April, June (signalled by the number XXIX at the bottom of the month's column), Sextilis, September, November and December, 31 days in March, May, Quintilis, and October; the intercalary month, with 27 days, is attached after December.[22] By 29 December the eight-letter alphabetic sequence has reached C. When it gets to 1 June, the sequence has come to the letter E, and it then runs through the month until 29 June and the letter A; 1 July then follows with B.

These letters are called the nundinal letters. Ovid is assumed to be referring to them near the beginning of his poetic commentary on the Roman calendar, the *Fasti*, when he mentions the type of day 'which always returns from a cycle of nine' (*Fasti* 1.47–54). This 'cycle of nine' is presumably the *nundinae*, an eight-day week, which is marked in the public calendars by the first eight letters of the alphabet. It counts as nine days because of the Roman habit of inclusive reckoning from the last day of the previous week. The name *nundinae* came to mean 'market day', because the Romans held their markets in different towns on successive days of the cycle. Quite how the system worked, however, remains a mystery. A number of nundinal cycles survive from different localities,[23] and the fact that some share the same town names has led to attempts to correlate the separate cycles. Some of these inscriptions also provide the seven-day week named after the planets (Saturn, Sun, Moon, Mars, Mercury, Jupiter, and Venus), which is an innovation introduced in the time of Augustus,[24] but because the towns they share turn up in a different order in the week, these hebdomadal days seem to confirm that one town's nundinal cycle was not necessarily another's.[25] Timetables, however, whether of market days or buses and trains, are fluid things, subject to change with and without notice, and we know too little of the actual dates of these surviving nundinal cycles to be sure that they are actually contemporary and therefore open to correspondence. Some appear ephemeral, scratched as graffiti on plaster (e.g., the Pompeii calendar)[26] while others seem more permanent, carved on marble (e.g., the *Pausilipum parapegma*).[27] They may reflect circumstances that changed on an *ad hoc* basis, rather than schedules fixed in Roman concrete. Or perhaps people simply got their information wrong – the following graffito from AD 60 in Pompeii presents several chronological problems.[28] Its spatial setting is also curious: within a private house, the Casa delle Nozze d'Argento (V.2.i), it is scratched on the middle column of one side of the peristyle, on yellow-grey plaster, in letters almost 9mm high. We can only guess who was meant to read it.[29]

Nerone Caesare Augusto
Cosso Lentulo Cossi fil. Cos.
VIII idus Febr(u)arius
dies Solis, luna XIIIIX, nun(dinae) Cumis, V (idus Februarias) nun(dinae) Pompeis.

When Nero Caesar Augustus
And Cossus Lentulus son of Cossus were consuls
Eight days before the ides of February
Sunday, 16th day of the moon, the nundinae at Cumae, five days before the ides of February the nundinae at Pompeii.

The year is neatly provided by the consular names (the Emperor Nero and Cossus Lentulus), and *VIII idus Febr(u)arius* is 6 February. But Mau noted that the writer incorrectly made this day 'the day of the Sun' (i.e. Sunday), when it was in fact the day of Mercury (i.e. Wednesday). The lunar day is also questionable, because in AD 60 there was a full moon on 5 February, and so 6 February was the fifteenth day of the moon, not the sixteenth.[30] Finally, the nundinae would suggest that market-day in Cumae was on 6 February, and in Pompeii on 9 February, whereas the Pompeii calendar would place Pompeii's a day later in the cycle.[31]

But to return to the month of June in the *Fasti Antiates*: the second column for June starts with the letter K, followed by the abbreviation IVN. This stands for *Kalendae Iuniae*, the Kalends of June. Further down in this column will be found NON, indicating *nonae*, the Nones, on the fifth day; and EIDVS, signifying *idus*, the Ides, on the thirteenth day. These constitute the very familiar triple division of each Roman month under the Republic and the Empire: the Kalends (*kalendae*) on day 1, the Nones (*nonae*) at day 5 (in the shorter months) or 7 (in the 31-day months), and the Ides (*idus*) on day 13 (in the shorter months) or 15 (in the longer). Rüpke has suggested a fourth dividing point may be found at the end of the month, almost matching in its position the Nones at the beginning of the month. The vestiges of this last marker, he argues, are to be found in the calendars at the point of the 'double festival' of the *Tubilustrium* on 23 March and May and the day marked QRCF (*Quando Rex Comitiavit Fas*) on 24 March and May. Overall, we would be facing four 'weeks' in the month, which, importantly for our present purposes, match lunar periods: from new moon to first quarter (Kalends to Nones), from first quarter to full (Nones to Ides – *idus* may stem from a Greek word for the full moon),[32] from full to last quarter (Ides to *Tubilustrium*/QRCF), and last quarter to new (*Tubilustrium*/QRCF to Kalends).[33]

A further feature worth noting in this context takes us back to the *Fasti Praenestini*, as this aspect does not occur on the *Fasti Antiates Maiores*. In the extract from the former, there are two entries on the two days after the Kalends: the numbers VI and V. These are abbreviated references respectively for *ante diem VI nonas Martias* and *ante diem V nonas Martias* – the sixth day and the fifth day before the Nones of March, as the Romans counted 2 and 3 March. Beyond the Kalends, Nones and Ides, the remaining days of the month were numbered according to their relationship to one of these three primary divisions, using inclusive and prospective reckoning.

In so compressed a form of writing, it is remarkable that we can still discern former means of telling the time via the lunar phases, especially as these lost their strict correspondence with the moon itself at an early stage – at 29 and 31-day lengths, the Roman month on average does not equate as well as it might with a lunar month. In addition, there is a trace in the Roman calendar of an earlier oral element in the very word *kalendae*. Varro tells us that the word derived from the fact that the Nones of a month are called (*calantur*) on the Kalends.[34] The formula spoken by the priest who did the calling, Varro tells us, was '*kalo Iuno Covella*' ('I call, o Juno Covella'), which was repeated five times if the Nones were to fall on the fifth day of the month, and seven times for Nones on the seventh. Macrobius explicitly derives the word *kalendae* from the Greek verb *kalo* (I call), on the basis of the same story as Varro's.[35] He describes the event in more detail, which demonstrates the observational and oral aspects: originally a minor priestly official was delegated the task of watching for the first sign of the new moon and then reporting its appearance to the high priest. A sacrifice would then be offered, and another priest would summon the people and announce the number of days that remained between the Kalends and the Nones, 'and in fact he would proclaim the fifth day with the word *kalo* spoken five times, and the seventh day with the word repeated seven times'. The first of the days thus 'called' was named *kalendae* after *kalo*.

We see elsewhere in the second column for June in the *Fasti Antiates* the letters F, C, N and NP, the last apparently a ligature of N and P. From literary definitions[36] we know that the first three letters stand respectively for *fastus*, a 'lawcourt day'; *comitialis*, an 'assembly day'; and *nefastus*, a 'non-court day' (the first two had appeared in the excerpt of the *Fasti Praenestini* examined above). Lawcourt days (*fasti*) were technically those days on which the praetor could utter the words 'I grant, I pronounce, I award' (*do, dico, addico*), which are associated with formulae for judgement in court cases.[37] So the calendar clearly demarcates the days on which legal and political business may take place. This is a primary function of the *fasti*, a facet easily lost sight of if we approach them through the literary construct of Ovid's *Fasti*. We do not know precisely what

NP means. A common view is that the assumed underlying N and P stand for *nefastus publicus*, which indicates that the day so designated is like a *nefastus* day, on which law courts cannot do business, but is also a day on which the great public festivals, *feriae publicae*, can be held.[38] An alternative reading of the letters as meaning *nefastus purus* still has its adherents, and it too retains the notion of a day whose character changes partway through.[39] A third interpretation is that it stands for *nefas piaculum*, with *piaculum* signalling the need for an act of expiation on these days.[40]

We need not concern ourselves here with the details of all the festivals marked for June, but a glance at those on 1 June is in order, to gain a sense of what else these calendars actually marked beyond the legal-political timetable.[41] MARTI·IN·CL stands for *Marti in cliuo* ('for Mars on the hill'). The *cliuus Martis* was originally a rise in the road leading to the temple of Mars, where troops assembled on their way to war, on the Via Appia in the south-east of Rome.[42] This festival marked on the calendar may have celebrated the dedication of the temple. The inscription marking the other festival on 1 June, IVNON·IN, is incomplete. But it obviously refers to a festival in honour of Juno, and the festival and temple of Juno Moneta are mentioned by Ovid in his entry for the Kalends of June, while Macrobius records that the temple of Juno Moneta was dedicated on that day.[43] On this basis, the calendar entry may be restored as IVNON IN ARCE, which is slightly shorthand for *Iunoni in arce*, 'Juno on the Arx', a reference to the festival celebrating the dedication of the temple of Juno Moneta on the northern part of the Capitoline hill called the Arx.[44]

With the *Fasti Antiates Maiores*, and therefore undoubtedly from the republican period onwards, perhaps even from Fulvius' time, the calendars of days are sometimes, and perhaps always were originally, accompanied by a further list organizing the Roman state in time. This was a list of the consuls and other top magistrates of the state (*Fasti Consulares*) and a further list of those who gained triumphs (*Fasti Triumphales*). In the *fasti* from Antium the consuls were named for each year, arranged in paired columns, as the example from the year equivalent to 154 BC demonstrates:[45]

Θ L. Postumi(us) A[l]binu[s]	Q. [Opi]mi(us) Q. f.
suffectus M.' [Acili(us) G]labrio	
M. Valeri(us) Messal(la)	[C. Cas]si(us) Lon(ginus)-cens(ores)
	lustrum f[ecerunt]

The names of the two regular consuls, Lucius Postumius Albinus and Quintus Opimius son of Quintus, begin the entry. When a regular consul did not complete his year of office, owing to death or other circumstance, the name of his replacement, the suffect consul, was included on the following line, slightly indented and written in red in contrast to the black for standard entries. Thus, Postumius Albinus died in office – the Greek letter theta, Θ, at the beginning of the first line stands for θάνατος (*thanatos*), 'death' – and was replaced by Manius Acilius Glabrio, whose name appears underneath Albinus', and slightly indented from the left margin. Censors' names were also added in red letters, punctuating the lists eventually every five years, although six or seven years separate them early on. So here we have the names of Marcus Valerius Messalla and Gaius Cassius Longinus added underneath the consuls' names, along with the phrase *lustrum f[ecerunt]*, i.e. 'performed the lustration', the purification rite undertaken by the censors after the (ideally) five-yearly census.[46] The preserved period of the *Fasti Consulares* from Antium runs from 164 to 84 BC; with the gaps filled, from c. 173 to 67 BC.[47]

Far grander and better preserved are the marble *Fasti Capitolini* from the period of Augustus – the list of consuls runs down to 13 AD. Where the earlier lists had focused on a relatively narrow period of republican history, the *Fasti Capitolini* sought to take the record much further back in time, to the beginning of the Republic.[48] For comparison, here is the entry for 154 BC from the *Fasti Capitolini*:[49]

> Q. [Opi]mi(us) Q. f. Q. nepos   L. Postumius Sp. f. L. n. Albin(us) in m(agistratu)
>   m(ortuus) e(st). In e(ius) l(ocum) f(actus) e(st)
>   M.' Acilius M.' f. C. n. Glabrio
> cens(ores) M. Valerius M. f. M. n. Messalla, C. Cassius C. f. C. n. Longinus
> lustr(um) f(ecerunt) LV

The names of the magistrates are the same, but in greater genealogical detail – Opimius is now also 'grandson of Quintus', while Postumius is 'son of Spurius, grandson of Lucius'. The order is reversed, with Opimius placed first now, whereas his colleague Postumius is characterized explicitly now as having 'died in office'. A fuller notice tells us that 'in his place Manius Acilius Glabrio, son of Manius, grandson of Gaius was appointed' consul. Then follow the names of the censors, also embellished with their immediate family history, and the phrase 'performed the lustration'. But this time a number follows this notice: 55, i.e. this is the fifty-fifth lustration performed by the censors. Tradition held that the census and consequent lustration began under the sixth king of Rome, Servius Tullius, so, as Feeney points out, we have here a temporal rhythm in the *Fasti* which goes back beyond the time of the republican office of consul, even though this was the organizing principle of these *Fasti*.[50] Feeney also rightly questions Rüpke's suggestion that this five-yearly census-lustration period is equivalent in concept to the Olympiad system of dating by periods of four years: the five-yearly period in Rome takes a long time to become established, so if it is a dating system, it is a rough-and-ready one.[51] Illustrative of the instability of the sequence of censorships and ritual purifications are the entries for the censors in the years 93–89 BC:[52]

> ÐCLX C. Valerius C. f. L. n. Flaccus   M. Herennius M. [f. (– n.?)]
> C. Claudius Ap. f. C. n. Pulcher   M. Perpena M. [f. M. n.]
> cens(ores) Cn. Domitius Cn. f. Cn. n. Ahenobarb(us), L. Licinius L. [f. C. n.
>   Crassus abd(icarunt)]
> L. Marcius Q. f. Q. n. Philippus   Sex. Iulius C. f. [L.? n. Caesar]
>   Bellum Marsicum
> L. Iulius L. f. S[e]x. n. Caesar   P. Rutilius L. f. L. n. [Lupus in pr(oelio)
> occ(isus) e(st)?]
> Cn. Pompeiu[s S]ex. F. Cn. n. Strabo L. Porcius M. f. M. [n. Cato in pr(oelio)
> occ(isus) e(st)?]
> cens(ores) P. Licin[ius] M. f. P. n. Crassus, L. Iulius L. f. Sex. n. [Caesar lustrum
> f(ecerunt) LXVI]

We find censors in 92 BC, Cn. Domitius Ahenobarbus and L. Licinius Crassus, and then again in 89 with P. Licinius Crassus and L. Iulius Caesar, the consul of 90. The *Fasti Antiates Maiores* provide the details which support the restorations here for 92: 'the censors resigned, did not perform the lustration'.[53] The lustration took place in 89, according to the *Fasti Antiates*, although the census of the people seems not to have been undertaken, according to Cicero.[54]

Notwithstanding the unlikelihood of the censorship-lustration being used as a dating system, another chronological system does appear in this excerpt. Valerius Flaccus and Herennius were consuls for the year 93. Before their names, however, we can see the number ÐCLX, i.e. 660. This signals the six-hundred-and sixtieth year since the founding of Rome.[55] Once again, this system is set up against the fundamental organizing principle of the tables, namely the consular list, for the foundation of the city predates the Republic. More than this, Rome's 'birthday' was taken to be 21 April,[56] whereas the consular year, after 153 BC, was 1 January–31 December, so it was not coterminous with the 'foundation year'. Consistency in temporal argument, however, was not what governed these *Fasti*. It was politics. This is seen best in the section of the *Fasti* that covers the period from 1 to 13 AD. If we take just the year 12 AD as an example, we can pick out some of the underlying political emphasis:[57]

[Imp. C]aesar Divi f. Augustu[s, pont(ifex) max(imus), tr(ibunicia) pot(estate) XXXIIII]
[Ti. Caesar] Augusti f. Divi n. [trib(unicia) potest(ate) XIII]

Germanicus Ca[esar] Ti. f.	C. Fonteius C. f. C. n.
Augusti n.	Capito
ex k(alendis) Iulis	
C. Visellius C. f. C. n. Varro	

The year starts, as it has done on the surviving tablet since 1 AD, with the name of Augustus, but not as consul for the year, for he had resigned from that post in 23 BC, as the *Fasti* tell us, and accepted instead a novel annual authority, *tribunicia potestas*, 'tribunician power'. In 12 AD he holds this for the thirty-fourth time. He also has as a colleague with the same authority his adopted son, Tiberius, who holds tribunician power for the thirteenth time, but his name is added underneath, not alongside, Augustus'. Under Tiberius' name we find at last the two ordinary consuls of the year, Germanicus, the son of Tiberius, and Fonteius Capito, their names reverting to the twin column format of the republican part of the *Fasti*. A suffect consul, Visellius Varro, is listed under Germanicus as taking up office on 1 July. What matters most now, as Feeney has emphasized, is not the office of the consulship *per se*, for that is now subservient to the princeps and his colleague with tribunician power, but rather an idea of time, with the consulship serving to separate one year from the next, and one part of the year from another.[58]

One final point of interest in the entry for the years 93–89 BC is the extra notice given in the year of the consulship of L. Marcius Philippus and Sex. Iulius Caesar (91 BC). Beneath their names is added centrally *Bellum Marsicum*. Within the general framework of the *Fasti* there are placed occasional entries which reflect the beginning of major wars, and in this case we have the Marsic War, i.e., the Social War of 91–87 BC. Elsewhere we find the First Punic War and the war against Perseus of Macedon.[59] This will remain a tradition in consular *fasti*, even down to the time of the codex Chronicle of 354, where the list of consuls is punctuated by notices in the republican period of secular events – the election or omission of dictators – and then under the Empire only of Christian events, including the birth and passion of Jesus Christ.[60]

We do not know where the *Fasti Capitolini* were originally placed, but the most popular guess at present is a commemorative arch erected by Augustus in the Roman Forum.[61] They were public documents, made to be viewed, if not read, by all passers-by. In this respect they differ from the other *fasti* we have examined, the calendars of days, whose readership was likely to be limited to a household and its inhabitants and clients, or to an association or college. But then the sort of information proffered by the calendars of days is typologically different from the information presented in the *Fasti Consulares*. Although time informs the *Fasti Consulares*, it presents it in a variety of ways that do not seek mutual consistency. A calendar of days without such inherent consistency would be an oxymoron; it could not perform its primary function.

Sundials

Inscriptions help us to recognize the politicization of time elsewhere in the early Empire in monuments both small and grand, in both the small country towns and in the metropolis of Rome. In Pompeii a sundial on a column was donated by two magistrates, perhaps in the time of Augustus, in front of the Temple of Apollo near the main forum in Pompeii. An inscription on the column states:[62]

> L SEPVNIVS L F
> SANDILIANVS
> M HERENNIVS A F
> EPIDIANVS
> DVOVIR I D
> D S P F C

L. Sepunius L.f. Sandilianus, M. Herennius A. f. Epidianus duo vir(i) i(ure) d(icundo) d(e) s(ua) p(ecunia) f(aciundum) c(urarunt)

L. Sepunius Sandilianus son of Lucius, Marcus Herennius Epidianus son of Aulus, *duoviri* for administering the law, saw to it being done at their own expense.

The same *duoviri* set up near the 'Temple of Hercules', i.e., the unidentified Doric Temple in the Foro Triangolare, a semicircular bench (*schola*) with a magnificent view of the coast, and with a very similar dedication:[63]

> L SEPVNIVS L F SANDILIANVS
> M HERENNIVS A F EPIDIANVS
> DVOVIR I D SCOL ET HOROL
> D S P F C

L. Sepunius L.f. Sandilianus, M. Herennius A. f. Epidianus duovir(i) i(ure)
d(icundo) scol(am) et horol(ogium) d(e) s(ua) p(ecunia) f(aciundum) c(urarunt)

L. Sepunius Sandilianus son of Lucius, Marcus Herennius Epidianus son of Aulus,
duoviri for administering the law, saw to the *schola* and sundial being made at
their own expense.

At the temple of Apollo it makes sense to dedicate a sundial, since the god had long
been equated with Helios/Sol the Sun god, but the setting up of a sundial and bench
at the Foro Triangolare is simply municipal beneficence, or 'euergetism', which was so
strong a feature of both Greek and Roman life, and which could find expression in
the setting up of a public timepiece as an amenity. We learn of a similar benefaction
in the first century AD at Talloires in southern France, where a private tombstone
commemorates the deceased's donation of a public *horologium* (probably a water
clock) and an attendant slave to look after it, plus its own building and decorations, all
at great personal expense.[64]

In Rome, on the other hand, amenity is turned by Augustus into agitprop through
the erection of a monumental time-piece in the Campus Martius in Rome.[65] This
comprised a 30-metre high Egyptian obelisk taken from the Sun temple of Heliopolis,
and set on a base which carries an inscription commemorating the settlement of Egypt
by Augustus and dedicating the monument to the sun (Figure 5.3):[66]

IMP·CAESAR·DIVI·F·
AVGVSTVS
PONTIFEX·MAXIMVS
IMP·XII·COS·XI·TRIB·POT·XIV
AEGVPTO IN POTESTATEM
POPVLI·ROMANI·REDACTA
SOLI·DONVM·DEDIT

Imp(erator) Caesar Divi f(ilius) Augustus, pontifex maximus, imp(erator) XII,
co(n)s(ul) XI, trib(unicia) pot(estate) XIV, Aegupto in potestatem Populi Romani
redacta, Soli donum dedit

Imperator Caesar, son of the Divine [Julius], Augustus, Pontifex Maximus,
Imperator for the 12th time, consul for the 11th time, with Tribunician power for
the 14th time, with Egypt to the power of the Roman People subjected, gave this
as a gift to the Sun

The obelisk was to act as a (partial) sundial's gnomon by casting a shadow which
pointed north at midday along a bronze line, which was inlaid in the stone pavement
and marked to show the division of the year into zodiacal months and their days
(Figure 5.4). It thus told noontime, and hence provided a measure of the midday
shadow through the year, a function mentioned by Pliny,[67] although the obelisk would
seem an excessively large monument were this its only function. The excavator of the
line, Buchner, argued that the shadow would, of course, be cast elsewhere through
the day and year, and he particularly emphasized its relationship with the *Ara Pacis
Augustae* (Altar of Augustan Peace) to the north-east of the obelisk. The Altar was

Figure 5.3 Rome, Piazza di Montecitorio: obelisk of Augustus' *'horologium'* (photo R. Hannah)

Figure 5.4 Rome, Via Campo Marzio 48: part of the meridian of Augustus' *'horologium'* (photo R. Hannah)

voted in 13 BC by the Senate, to commemorate Augustus' return from the western provinces of Gaul and Spain, and stood beside the Via Flaminia, the road along which Augustus would have travelled on his way back into the city. It was completed in 9 BC, the year the obelisk was also erected. Whether or not the Altar stood at the end of a physical equinoctial line on an enormous grid, as Buchner thought, the general effect at the equinoxes would still hold, as the shadow pointed in the direction of the Altar, and may indeed have reached it. With the obelisk's shadow cast on the entrance to the Altar, Buchner saw Augustus encapsulating the two monuments in a single theme: his own cosmological import as bringer of peace to the Roman state. The correlation made sense insofar as the shadow would have hit the Altar on the autumn equinox, which coincided more or less with Augustus' birthday on 23 September.[68] On this day observers could be reminded of Augustus' prime role in restoring peace to the Roman world after a century of violence, through his settlement of Egypt (the source of the obelisk), and of the western provinces (symbolized by the Altar). This cosmological symbolism applies to his conception day too: the northern extremity of the meridian line marks the turning point of the noonday sun's shadow at the winter solstice and when the sun entered Capricorn, nine months before Augustus' birthday.

Heslin, however, has recently argued that the shadow could not have reached the Altar's entrance, and that therefore the intimate relationship perceived by Buchner between the obelisk as timepiece and the Altar is illusory.[69] Heslin's argument rests partly on criticisms of Buchner's case made earlier by Schütz, who was taken to argue that the very physics of shadow-casting precluded the shadow of the obelisk ever reaching the Altar,[70] and partly on his contention that there was nothing special about the obelisk's shadow pointing towards the Altar, since it would do this every day of the year.

The second objection is the easier to dismiss, as experience ought to suggest that the shadow of the obelisk cannot point towards the Altar every day of the year. The circuit of the sun in winter is considerably smaller than it is in summer, and since the Altar was situated effectively on the vernal/autumnal equinoctial line of the obelisk-as-gnomon, there would appear to be a good chance that the shadow would not point near the Altar in wintertime. Calculation demonstrates that this is indeed so, and that the shadow would not point towards the Altar or anything south of it between about 7 November and 5 February. Conversely, from about 5 February to 7 November the shadow would have pointed towards the Altar every day.[71]

Heslin's first objection, on the other hand, appears to be a misunderstanding of Schütz, who rightly notes that the shadow of the globe on top of the obelisk would become so diffuse as to be invisible near the Altar. But the obelisk, at almost 30 metres in height, was able to cast a shadow about 66 metres long at noon on the winter solstice, to judge from Pliny's assertion that 'a stone pavement was laid out in accordance with the height of the obelisk, equal to which was the shadow at the sixth hour on the day of the full winter solstice'.[72] By calculation, at the equinox the shadow of Augustus' obelisk would theoretically have stretched about 89.5 metres in the direction of the Altar, which was 83m away. It still remains to be demonstrated that the obelisk's shadow could not reach the Altar at that distance – the present setting of the obelisk prevents such testing, and Schütz's criticism of Buchner is focused only on the effective disappearance of the shadow of the globe on top of the obelisk, not on the obelisk itself. Tests conducted with a monument of a comparable scale suggest to me that in fact the obelisk's shadow could have reached the *Ara Pacis*.[73] Sun and time, then, *were* linked architecturally into cosmological signposts for those Romans who could read such things.

Time and writing

Roman time was distinctly oral and practical in its origins. The division of the day and the month into pockets of time not only relied initially on observation of the passage of the sun through the day, and the phases of the moon through the month, but the words used to define moments of time, such as *kalendae*, sometimes retained an element of a preliterate society, in which these moments in time had to be publicly heralded. The Greeks had begun to write their public calendrical data at least by the fifth century BC, to judge from the sacrificial calendars and *parapegmata* of the Athenians.[74] Rome took advantage of writing for similar purposes only much later, and arguably under Greek influence.

Writing provided new opportunities for the organization of knowledge, and its manipulation in the Greek world. I have argued this in the case of the Greek *parapegmata* of the fifth century BC.[75] Much the same argument may be applied to the construction of the *fasti* in Rome, even though these belong to a later period. Let us rehearse some of that argument here, and check it against the *fasti*.

A generation ago, Jack Goody argued that writing serves two principal functions: to store information, and to facilitate the process of reorganizing information.[76] Writing, he stated, insists upon 'a visual, spatial location which then becomes subject to possible rearrangement'.[77] A particularly common form of preserved early writing is the list, which permits both of the functions of storage and reorganization, and at the same time necessarily imposes a spatial arrangement of words which is left open to rearrangement. Three types of list are common: the retrospective inventory of persons, objects or events; the prospective plan, such as an itinerary; and the lexical list.[78] These types of list, Goody believed, process information in a way that is usually quite distinct from ordinary speech: they do not represent speech directly, but rather reflect a mode of thought, or a cognitive operation, that differs from that of speech, insofar as they treat verbal items in a disconnected and abstract way; they may have no oral equivalent at all.[79] A list permits the organization, and reorganization, of information which is received at various times and places, for instance, a religious calendar of sacrifices to the gods through the year. Such a list not only provides a record of an activity at a particular time, but also establishes a more formalized way of conceiving that activity.[80] The activity becomes 'decontextualized',[81] set apart from its particular context in time and space, and instead is placed into another context in which it may gain other significances as it is juxtaposed beside other activities or other classes of events. To quote Goody's summary of his theory:[82]

> Lists are seen to be characteristic of the early uses of writing, being promoted partly by the demands of complex economic and state organization, partly by the nature of scribal training, and partly by a 'play' element, which attempts to

explore the potentialities of this new medium. They represent an activity which is difficult in oral cultures and one which encourages the activities of historians and the observational sciences, as well as on a more general level, favouring the exploration and definition of classificatory schemas.

Goody argued for a position in which writing, and list-making in particular, provided the impetus for intellectual reflection on information. It is for him a facilitator of cognitive growth.[83] Of course, the very act of list-making is not the preserve of the literate alone. Oral societies were perfectly capable of creating lists which incorporated variable data. So, to this extent, he overstates his case for list-making as a peculiarly literate activity. But in the area of the development of ideas from the very act of manipulating data into lists, I think he is probably correct. In terms of cognitive skills, the ability to construct and then to recall a list – as oral poets did – is at a lower level than constructing, recalling, reflecting on, checking and adjusting the contents of a given list, which is what we find the constructers of the *fasti* doing.

Rüpke has argued that the *fasti* of Fulvius represents the spread of writing in Rome to new social contexts and types of communication:[84]

> It was a new idea for history not to be narrated orally but to be written down. Similarly novel was the phenomenon of not just participating in but of recording the celebration of festivals and the building of temples and then to have these records not simply displayed on the building but also available elsewhere. One could claim that this is not exactly the case for the wall painting of the fasti. It was tied to a particular place. But we need to keep in mind that the site where this wall painting was displayed was the meeting place of the professional writers in Rome. It was available for copying, and indeed it was, as the *Fasti Antiates Maiores* demonstrates.

He sees the systematization of the *fasti* as indicative of members of the elite class in Rome 'exploring new intellectual possibilities and new venues for organizing knowledge'.[85] The subtle yet dramatic shift in the way the *Fasti Consulares* in particular were written in the time of Augustus demonstrates the manner in which seemingly innocent, historical data could be reorganized to reflect a new political world, in which the princeps, not the consuls, now dominated with a new, unrepublican authority. The physical emphasis on Augustus' name and titles that we witness in these *Fasti* is replicated in the simple inscription on the base of the obelisk in the Campus Martius. Here, however, the relationship with time itself, which subtly underlies and is played with in the *Fasti Capitolini*, is made much more explicit, through the collocation of the obelisk with the Altar of Peace. This is indeed, to borrow Wallace-Hadrill's phrase, 'time for Augustus'.[86]

Notes

1   Feeney, 2007, pp. 167–9.
2   Rüpke, 1995b; Degrassi, 1963.
3   Rüpke, 2006, p. 492, 2011, pp. 8–9.
4   Rüpke, 2006, p. 492.

5   Rüpke, 2007, p. 187.
6   Degrassi, 1963, p. 1.
7   Reynolds, 1976, *pace* Magi, 1972.
8   E.g. September, Magi, 1972, pls. IV, XLIII–XLVII.
9   Salzman, 1990; Claridge et al., 2012, cat. nos. 1–13.
10 Dates for the dedication range from 184 to 179 BC: cf. Feeney, 2007, pp. 143–4, opting for the earlier, and Rüpke, 2006, pp. 490–1, opting for the later; Flower, 1995, p. 186 keeps an open mind.
11 Eumenius 9.7.3; Macrob. *Sat.* 1.12.16. The texts are conveniently presented at Rüpke, 2006, pp. 491 n. 7 and 499.
12 Richardson, 1992, p. 187; Claridge, 2010, pp. 250–1, 256, Figure 107 (based on the Marble Plan). Photographs of the relevant fragments of the Marble Plan are also available online at: http://formaurbis.stanford.edu/fragment.php?record=145 (last accessed 4th February 2013) and http://formaurbis.stanford.edu/plate.php?plateindex=28 (last accessed 4th February 2013).
13 Rüpke, 1995b, pp. 43–4, 331–68, esp. pp. 365–6; 2006, 509.
14 Rüpke, 2006, p. 491; Feeney, 2007, pp. 143–4, 167–70.
15 Rüpke, 2006, pp. 507–8, who calls it a dedication, although 'not a dedication that is associated with a specifically religious monument, but with a monument that commemorates history.'
16 Suet. *Gram.* 17.
17 Cf. Coarelli, 2007, p. 523. I am grateful to Peter Keegan for encouraging me to consider this aspect of the *Fasti*.
18 On the effects of spectator involvement in the *Fasti Praenestini*, see Hernández, 2005, pp. 118–9.
19 Degrassi, 1963, pp. 120–1.
20 Censorinus, *DN* 22.9–11. Rüpke, 2006, pp. 495–7.
21 Degrassi, 1963, pp. 12–3; Michels, 1967, Figure 4.
22 See Hannah, 2005, pp. 106–12 for a discussion of how the intercalary month worked.
23 Degrassi, 1963, pp. 300–6; Lehoux, 2007, pp. 198–200.
24 So we may judge from its presence on the fragmentary *Fasti Sabini* (after 19 BC), *Fasti Nolani* (early imperial) and the Augustan *Fasti Foronovani*: Degrassi, 1963, pp. 51–4, 156, 229–31, 326. Tibullus (1.3.18), in the time of Augustus, refers to 'Saturn's holy day', meaning what we call Saturday.
25 Lehoux, forthcoming.
26 *CIL* 4.8863, Degrassi, 1963, p. 305; Lehoux, 2007, pp. 173–4. One is reminded of the equally ephemeral and thoroughly domesticated wall calendar in *Satyricon* 30, where it is used to note when Cinnamus is dining out (see also Lehoux, 2007, pp. 41–2, 201).
27 Degrassi, 1963, p. 304; Lehoux, 2007, p. 174. I recall, however, my first visit as a student to Rome in the 1970s, when I encountered signs, carved in marble, stating that sites were temporarily closed.
28 *CIL* 4.4182.
29 I am grateful to Peter Keegan for drawing this issue to my attention.
30 Mau notes (*CIL* 4.4182, at p. 515), however, that if the moon had 29 days in December rather than 30, as seems to have occurred in the Calendar of Filocalus (i.e. the Calendar of 354), then 6 February would be the sixteenth day of the moon.
31 Lehoux, forthcoming, speculates that the nundinal days for any given locality, like Pompeii or Cumae, might effectively represent another type of week, so that 'the

names of cities may have been simply used as the names of the days of the nundinal week, just as the names of the gods Saturn, Sol, Luna, and so on, were used to name days in the hebdomadal week'.

32 Macrob. *Sat.* 1.15.14–17.
33 Rüpke, 1995b, pp. 209–25.
34 Varro, *Ling.* 6.27.
35 Macrob. *Sat.* 1.15.9–11.
36 See Hannah, 2005, pp. 103–4 for references.
37 Varro, *Ling.* 6.30, Macrob. *Sat.* 1.16.14.
38 Michels, 1967, p. 76; Beard et al., 1998, p. 62.
39 Brind'Amour, 1983, p. 227.
40 Rüpke, 1995b, pp. 258–60.
41 See the discussion on the remaining days and their duties or festivals in Hannah, 2005, pp. 104–6.
42 Cf. Livy 7.23.3; Ov. *Fast.* 6.191–2. Platner and Ashby, 1929, pp. 123–4, 327–8; Haselberger et al. 2002, pp. 165, 256–7.
43 Ov. *Fast.* 6.183–4; Macrob. *Sat.* 1.12.30.
44 Degrassi, 1957, p. 31; Invernizzi, 1994, pp. 64–5; Haselberger et al. 2002, p. 153.
45 Degrassi, 1947, pp. 160–1.
46 Feeney, 2007, pp. 167–83 has an excellent, illustrated discussion of the *Fasti Consulares*, focusing on the *Fasti Capitolini* with glances cast back occasionally to the *Fasti Antiates*; the seminal publication is Degrassi 1947.
47 Rüpke, 1995b, p. 43; Degrassi, 1947, pp. 159–66.
48 Rüpke, 2006, pp. 509–10.
49 Degrassi, 1947, pp. 50–1; 1954, pp. 68–9.
50 Livy 1.44.1–2.
51 Feeney, 2007, pp. 176–7, 289 n. 55; Rüpke, 1995a, pp. 192–3.
52 Degrassi, 1947, pp. 54–5; 1954, pp. 74–5.
53 Degrassi, 1947, pp. 129, 165.
54 Cic. *Arch.* 11.
55 On the meaning of the founding of Rome as a date see Feeney, 2007, pp. 86–8; Hannah, 2005, pp. 149–57. The founding of Rome is used as the starting point for the *Fasti Triumphales* associated with the *Fasti Capitolini*, starting with year I and Romulus' triumphs, and continuing with each triumph dated from this point down to the last in 19 BC, in the 734th year from the founding: Degrassi, 1947, pp. 64–87; 1954, pp. 90–110.
56 Ov. *Fast.* 4. 807–62; Plin. *HN* 18. 247.
57 Degrassi, 1947, pp. 62–3; 1954, pp. 88–9.
58 Feeney, 2007, pp. 177–80.
59 Feeney, 2007, p. 173.
60 Hannah, 2005, pp. 151–2.
61 Feeney, 2007, pp. 172, 285 n. 1; Beard, 2003, p. 24; Coarelli, 1985, pp. 269–308.
62 La Rocca et al. 1994, p. 107.
63 De Vos and de Vos, 1982, p. 32; Gibbs, 1976, p. 394 no. 8007.
64 Hannah, 2009, pp. 176–7 nn. 56–9; *CIL* 12.2522, *ILS* 5624; Harvey, 2004, p. 91, no. 58.
65 Rehak, 2006; Zanker, 1988; Wallace-Hadrill, 1987.
66 *CIL* 6.702.
67 Plin. *HN* 36.72.

68   Buchner, 1982, pp. 1993–4.
69   Heslin, 2007.
70   Schütz, 1990.
71   In the time of Augustus, Varro (*Rust.* 1.28.1–2) says that the first day of spring occurred on the twenty-third day of Aquarius, that of summer on the twenty-third day of Taurus, of autumn on the twenty-third day of Leo, and of winter on the twenty-third day of Scorpio. These dates he then computes to their equivalents in the new Julian calendar: the first day of spring is 7 February, that of summer 9 May, that of autumn 11 Sextilis (August), and that of winter 10 November. By this reckoning, the Altar of Augustan Peace may have served as a boundary marker for the change from autumn to winter in early November, and the change from winter to spring in early February. The liminality is suggestive.
72   Plin. *HN* 36.72.
73   Hannah, 2011.
74   Hannah, 2005, pp. 42–70.
75   Hannah, 2001.
76   Goody, 1977, p. 78.
77   Goody, 1977, p. 104.
78   Goody, 1977, p. 80.
79   Goody, 1977, pp. 81, 86.
80   Goody, 1977, pp. 87, 88.
81   The term is introduced, with some caution, by Goody, 1977, p. 78.
82   Goody, 1977, p. 108.
83   Goody, 1977, pp. 108–11.
84   Rüpke, 2006, p. 510.
85   Rüpke, 2006, p. 511.
86   Wallace Hadrill, 1987.

Written Space and Social Groups

6

Graffiti's Engagement. The Political Graffiti of the Late Roman Republic

Tom Hillard

This chapter will analyse the nature of forensic graffiti in terms of its authorship, content and likely impact – in so far as such an exercise can be essayed given the surviving evidence. It will in particular attempt to contextualize parietal polemic and popular political texting in the belief that context may provide a further indication of the medium's efficacy.[1]

I begin with a secondhand source (Plutarch), but one clearly drawing on close to contemporary material (and referencing primary evidence). In his *Life of Tiberius Gracchus*, Plutarch reviews the various explanations advanced as to why Gracchus (trib. pl. 133 BC) undertook his controversial reform program and pursued it so relentlessly to its disastrous end. This section of the *Life* provided the fullest ancient collection of data that we possess concerning the psychology of Gracchus. It closes:

> 'Most of all, the energy and ambition [of Tiberius Gracchus] was fired by the People (*autos ho Demos*), calling upon him through writings upon porticoes (*stoai*), walls (*toichoi*) and monuments (*mnemata*) to recover the public land for the poor.'[2]

The above item offers a number of insights. I would remark upon two of them at this point. The first is that Plutarch deemed this popular expression of political feeling to be worthy of registration within a survey of the factors motivating Tiberius Gracchus with regard to his legislative programme and then dangerous political brinksmanship when confronted by opposition.[3] This graffiti campaign is registered alongside the serious social problems with which Rome was faced at the time and the palpable need for reform; the possible influence of Greek philosophy and political thinking upon Gracchus; the traditional Roman pressures of performance anxiety; and the insistence that urgent demographic considerations obtruded. Indeed, the 'popular' graffiti campaign in the interests of social equity is entered by way of a climax (and more than a simple finale) to this survey: it is the factor that influenced Gracchus 'most of all'.

The second observation is that this factor had been *remembered* as historically significant, and had been recorded as such;[4] it had become a part of the historio-graphical debate as to what made Tiberius Gracchus tick. The Roman community took such a factor seriously. Anonymous graffiti had played its part. It had agency.[5]

I would like to take up this and two other case studies, examples drawn from highly dramatic years in the closing century of Rome's 'Free Republic' (in 133, 121 and 44). The first has been cited – and its importance underscored. The second case is, by way of contrast, a singular graffito etched into the façade of the newly renovated temple of Concord: a grim note of dissent following the violent suppression of Gaius Gracchus (the killing and/or violent executions of around 3,000 citizens). The last case study returns to another concerted graffiti campaign: the incitation of M. Iunius Brutus to take up the mantle of ancestral tyrannicide.

133 BC

Let us return to the first item and discuss (as in all three cases) authorship, content, impact and location (topographical context). The authorship was, of course, as with almost all examples of this kind of graffiti, anonymous. Nor can we know whether it was genuinely popular or orchestrated by a clique in favour of Gracchus' already formulated plans – though it is worth noting that no hint of such suspicion (as the latter) entered the historical tradition as Plutarch received it. For him, it was the voice of 'the People'.[6] The message? Plutarch tells us: the need for land redistribution. But Plutarch reports that the message was even more precise than this. It was cast as apostrophe; it targeted Gracchus – not as a victim, but as the putative addressee and potential champion. (In this, it provides a quasi-parallel to the graffiti campaign of 44 to be discussed below.) And it was, if we can trust the report in Plutarch, specific as to its aim. Gracchus was called upon to retrieve 'for the poor (*toîs pénesi*) the public land (*tèn demosían chóran*)'. The poor (I would guess that the word *pauperes* was used here) were *not* to be despised. Despite the obvious fact that the Roman citizenry was graded according to wealth (and enjoyed political rights accordingly), despite the disdain of the super-rich for the less rich and Cicero's utter contempt for the impoverished (by way of example and not by way of indicating that Cicero was idiosyncratic), *paupertas* might be taken as a badge of honour within the complex web of values that circulated (to mix the metaphor) in the public discourse of the Late Roman Republic.[7] And if we couple this with the evidence of Appian (following) and the fragment of an actual speech delivered by Gracchus at the time, Plutarch's term *penes* embraced veterans of the Roman army. The fragment is well known, the only surviving fragment in the form of *oratio recta* (though, of course, in Greek translation). It is polemic, and very effectively aimed at stirring outrage, class-consciousness and a sense of social inequity. It compares unfavourably the plight of Rome's impoverished veterans and that of the wild beasts of Italy. The latter have dens and lairs, but the ex-soldiers who have fought for the profit of others have not a clod of earth that is their own.[8] Appian's background briefing elaborates, and, in doing so, probably offers a further clue to the content of the graffiti messages. In his account of the build-up to the final crisis, he retails the general arguments put forward by both 'sides' – the rich on the one side, and the poor on the other. But in what form were these arguments delivered? He offers the two causes in the form of very loose *orationes obliquae*. From both sides came lamentation. The latter (*hoi pénetes*) complained that they had been reduced to extreme circumstances (*es penían escháten*).[9] They outlined their military service upon the back of which Rome had prospered – and complained that they were deprived of what ought to have been a fair share of common prosperity, the latter cast, in Appian, as *ta koina*. They reproached the rich with the employment of slave labour. It might be that Appian has cast here, in indirect speech, that which Plutarch reports – hardly inventing the curious fact – as graffiti.[10] What was in the original we cannot be sure, but we may have here (in Appian) the gist of the entreaties, demands and polemics that appeared on the walls: a limitation (deemed traditional) on the amount of land that an individual ought to be allowed to own; a limitation on slave numbers, which robbed the poor of their livelihood; a due recognition of war service.

Graffiti were perhaps the vehicle of choice for the expression of class-war sentiments from below – and, taking our cue from Plutarch's testimony and the absence of evidence to the contrary, it was here the medium of the impoverished and the politically disadvantaged.[11] It has to be noted, however, that in this instance these epigraphs of entreaty might not have been clandestine, nor the sole means by which the voice of defiance made itself seen. The case was perhaps *heard* also. Appian treats first the grievances of the rich (*hoi ploúsioi*).[12] Faced with the upcoming law and the probability that they faced the inevitable prospect of bowing to now-ancient legislation, they gathered together in groups and made vocal their dissatisfaction. Presumably they had the services and the voice of those who had access to the rostra. In any case, they need not closet their discontent. Then Appian introduces the contrary complaints of the poor: 'on the other side, the poor (*hoi pénetes*) again lamented ...'. Audibly? They *recounted* (κατέλεγον) their military service; they *reproached* (νείδιζόν) the rich; both sides 'calling each other out in mutual recriminations' (ἀλλήλοις ἐπικαλούντων).[13] How figurative is Appian's language? Do the walls speak for the poor? From this distance, it is impossible to tell. Appian's account seems to assume that the exchange was (eventually, at least) voluble. Both sides, exasperated by the other and emboldened by numbers found their strength augmented by those who now flocked into the city to help influence the outcome.[14]

There is no doubt, however, that wall inscriptions played a part – perhaps as an adjunct to other demonstrations of protest; perhaps as the principal medium. It cannot be ignored that Plutarch privileges the graffiti campaign. There is more. The land marked for this redistribution was *demosia chora* (public lands); the graffiti concerned itself with *ager publicus*. The distinction is important. In the light of renewed interest in the exact nature of the Gracchan legislation, it would be good to know whether the wording retailed by Plutarch can be taken as faithfully recording the original, or whether this was a gloss on the part of Plutarch and/or his source.[15] If *ager publicus*, and only *ager publicus*, was at stake, there was, in the specificity, an unexpected degree of moderation. Polemic leading up to the crisis may not have been so qualified. The Gracchan programme possibly built upon ancient legislation which aimed to limit *in toto* the amount of landholding in any individual's hands[16] – that is to say, antique laws that promoted the ideology of egalitarianism. One might then have expected slogans such as 'Land for the poor', 'Land for Rome's soldiers', 'Gracchus, give us land' or even simply 'Equity' which would have had more punch than the subtle qualification that Plutarch's text implies.[17] Demands and entreaties may have prevailed;

if Plutarch's report is correct, there was a degree of reassurance in the now-proposed package, a public acknowledgement that private property was not in danger. In terms of a graffiti campaign, this is nuanced indeed.

The above discussion has touched also upon the question of impact (which Plutarch explicitly emphasizes). This is inextricably linked to the program's apparent saturation coverage: walls, porticoes and monuments. The *toichoi* may have been those of residential sites, but were probably public walls rather than private – and almost certainly not those of the house of Gracchus. That would be in accord with Gracchus not being intended as the target *qua* victim (see below). It is more likely that the program was addressed rather to the community and not the nominal addressee. The overall effect would have been the diffusive replication of the community's engagement in a matter of social justice. Expressions of community concern (inscribed on walls or otherwise articulated) had their origins in various modes of public expression lying at the heart of primitive Roman justice and which, as a meme or cultural practice, ought not to be overlooked as an ancestor – or cousin – of graffiti:[18] *convicium* (collective shouting), *flagitatio* (a public demand for restitution), *occentatio* (an 'evocation' of infamy), verbal assaults representing community action, and even the physically aggressive action of *lapidatio* – all explored by Andrew Lintott in useful detail.[19] But the demands and/or entreaties of those who called for land in 133 might more helpfully be likened to *quiritatio*, the public imploring of assistance by those threatened or injured – thus explaining in part why ancient chroniclers would have recorded the graffiti as a significant element of the public discourse.

It was crucial then that the graffiti be not furtively placed, but be eye-catching. The anonymity which may or may not have served to protect the authors must not distract us from the public nature of this campaign. Visibility was the principal desideratum; and a passage in Plautus reminds us that this was a well-established requirement for this form of immediate and urgent communication by the post-Hannibalic war era, at least.[20] The choice of location was, of course, of the essence for graffiti prompted by anything other than sheer idleness. And unless convenience ruled, the aim must have been a message that caught the eye. The space available for purpose-designed graffiti was already, it can be imagined, crowded[21] – and not just with the quasi-official *programmata*, but with private messages seeking urgent attention. Such were the notices that promised rewards for lost goods.

> *Cubitum hercle longis litteris signabo iam usquequaque*
> *si quis perdiderit vidulum cum auro atque argento multo*
> *ad Gripum ut veniat.*[22]

By Hercules, I'll post notices everywhere, in letters a cubit high, that if anyone has lost a trunk with much gold and silver, he ought to apply to Gripus.

Cubitum longis litteris ... usquequaque. The larger the lettering, believes Gripus the fisherman, the better – and maximum exposure, saturation coverage, ubiquity.[23]

Usquequaque. Which *stoai* and monuments were targeted by this 'Gracchan' graffiti? There were the porticoes down by the Tiber and on the slopes of the Aventine. There the graffitists would have the attention of the working-day crowds, and might be thought to be preaching to the converted – but much was to be gained by alerting Rome's urban labour force to rural affairs and the need to accommodate the demands of the excrescent unemployed in the city. Other porticoes were more central.[24] And the *portico Metelli*, while lying outside the walls but well frequented, a mere 13 years old in 133, was among other things a veritable art gallery. Graffiti here would have been a visual assault – and particularly galling to the Metelli, who would prove unfriendly to Gracchus' programme.[25]

And the monuments? Almost by definition – one would think – these would have been centrally located.[26] And we know of key spots where people would congregate for news. One was the *solarium*, probably the timepiece set up close to the *rostra* by M'. Valerius Messalla in 263.[27] Here we might find much informed, if not well-informed, *subrostrani* (those who lounged by the Rostra).[28] The *rostra* were formally recognized as the *locus oculatissimus*: the place 'most-eyed'.[29] The men with the opportunity or inclination to frequent the forum had by this time, we are told, a political agency beyond that which their status might have suggested (or, according to our conservative source, beyond what that status commended).[30] The bases of the statues that cluttered the forum would have provided surfaces difficult to resist. One of those was that of the statue of Marsyas, which became a symbol of (defiant) *libertas*[31] – but given an almost sacred aura (invested by community consensus as by anything else), the statue may have been virtually sacrosanct.[32] Would such sensitivities have deterred the politically enflamed, or attracted them? The contemplation of such 'desecrations' brings to mind, by way of a contrary example, the removal by order of the censors of 159/8 of all honorific statues *circa forum* that had been erected without a resolution of the People or Senate.[33] That censorial edict represents – 25 years prior to the crisis of 133 – an attempt to control the area of the forum: the proliferation of messages was not desirable. We shall see with the next item the way in which graffiti might challenge that attempt at management.

121 BC[34]

The next item derives from a different epoch. The violence of 133, and then – before many citizens had recovered from that shock – the violence, exponentially increased (by, indeed, a factor of ten), of 121 had altered the political landscape in a way that could never be reversed. These events transformed fundamentally the mode and the means of political expression in the Roman Republic. After the declaration of what has come to be called the *senatus consultum ultimum* (a deadly new weapon in the arsenal of those who would establish senatorial authority against challenge), the posting of a reward for the heads of those deemed to be leading sedition, the killing of something like 3,000 citizens – either in quasi-battle using foreign auxiliaries or in subsequent executions – and again, as in 133, the disposal of the massed dead in the Tiber, the consul L. Opimius sought to restore order and confidence. Placatory gestures were required by the dictates of *religio* – to the gods.

> … the city was cleansed [by lustration] of the bloodshed. And the Senate ordered that a temple be built to Concord in the forum.[35]

This was the *aedes Concordiae*. The irony, and from a modern perspective it is easy to read irony into the gesture, was not lost on Augustine.[36]

> Surely this was but a mockery of the gods ...? Or perhaps Concord was to blame for this crime, because she had deserted the hearts of the citizens, and she deserved the penalty of being shut up in that shrine as it were in a prison.[37]

The exercise was, in fact, a restoration. A temple existed on this site.[38] The rebuilding, however, was substantial, and was undertaken by Opimius.[39] This, Plutarch says, was particularly vexing – that a man like this, who was the first consul to exercise the power of a dictator, should profess such a concern.[40]

> However, what vexed the people more than this [sc. the execution of the blameless son of Gaius Gracchus' confederate Fulvius Flaccus] or anything else was the erection of a temple to Concord by Opimius; for it was felt that he was priding himself and exulting and in a manner of celebrating a triumph in view of all this slaughter of citizens. Therefore at night, beneath the inscription on the temple, somebody carved this verse: 'A work of mad discord produces a temple of Concord.'[41]

Augustine, we now see, had taken his cue from an alternative Roman tradition – especially when he asks '[if] they wanted to suit the shrine to the historical background, why did they not rather erect on that spot a temple to Discord?'[42]

Authorship? This item was most definitely of anonymous composition. Protest was unsafe. The people had been 'cowed', Plutarch tells us, by the unprecedented act of repression instituted by Opimius – as well might be expected after the killing of more than 3,000 Gracchani. The graffito was the act of one (or those) who dared not speak aloud. Graffiti in this sense were the medium of the disempowered.[43] Yet a graffito was empowering; its content was precise, its purpose subversive. Its impact cannot be doubted; it became an historical item. And it is the location that most serves its purpose (and highlights one of the themes in this chapter). The location was essential; Plutarch reports that the verse was placed beneath the inscription of the temple. It did not simply convey dark irony and an exposure of the hypocrisy of those who had repressed the 'sedition' of Gaius Gracchus. The temple being, as Plutarch hints, a trophy, the graffiti diminished Opimius' monumental statement. The *aedes Concordia* was a text; and the counter enterprise was to overwrite that message – by attacking the site.[44] A *monumentum* was, of course (or was intended to be), a remembrance dictated. Roman orators assaulted a rival's pretensions with rhetoric (in a competition to establish memory) in much the same fashion that one might assault a physical monument; historians did so with the pen.[45] The temple of Concordia being Opimius' victory monument, this was a defacement.[46]

The exercise was potent; the author not only communicated via the written word, but by the appropriation of space. Within a community well attuned to visual display, the graffiti compromised the original message.[47] In this case (as in the following case-study), it appropriated the very language of the monument hijacked. (This need not be laboured here; it has already been highlighted by Morstein-Marx.) The graffiti (which Plutarch records in Greek) must have replicated the dedicatory inscription:

L. Opimius fecit.[48] It would thus have read: *Aedem Concordiae Discordia fecit.* Perhaps simply *Discordia fecit.* The verse had become an alternative proclamation. The assault on this space was not random. And it was an attack against a potent symbol.[49] Within the highly politicized landscape of the Roman forum, the *aedes Concordiae* also represented the power of the conservative forces to articulate their own reality and to bend language itself (not to mention Roman worship) to their needs. *They* would define what was concord; it was not concessional. The graffiti, however, would not allow the western end of the forum to pass for uncontested space.

Lest it be thought that there is anything strange about attacking a structure itself in this fashion, let us turn to poetry. Catullus deemed his verses a means by which he could inflict injury. When he seeks to attack the unnamed *moecha* of *carmen* 42, *hendecasyllabi* are his weapons.[50] In carmen 37, he thinks to use this violence not simply against his rivals-in-lust but against the building that houses them. This poem is only the first salvo; in the follow-through he plans to abandon altogether the elegance of verse (as obscene as he can make the latter).

Salax taberna vosque contubernales

Sleazy tavern – and you, its habitués,
Nine posts down from the capped Brethren,
do you think that you're the only ones with pricks?
the only ones fit to screw the girls, and think the rest (of us) goats?[51]

The location of this notoriously *salax* inn is nine doors down from the temple of Castor and Pollux. This quarter, the *vicus Tuscus*, had a seedy (to some, attractive) reputation, a reputation that was established by the beginning of the second century and still in place at the end of the first.[52] In the following lines (6–8), as he does from the second part of line 1 on, Catullus flays into the bar's unsavoury denizens, threatening them with sexual violence, even though there be 100 or 200 of them. (The reason becomes clear in lines 11–14; 'Lesbia', *his* 'girl', now frequents the place.)[53] The direction of lines 2–8 misleads many translators who interpret the poem as an attack on the hostelry's *contubernales.*[54] Note that the threat is addressed to the tavern itself (and only secondly to those who frequent it). It is the tavern and its face to the world that Catullus will assault. He will cover its entire façade – with graffiti.

namque totius vobis
frontem tabernae sopionibus scribam

I'll draw your peckers over the whole front of the place.[55]

The redecorated frontage of this inn of ill-repute would not go unnoticed. The place was the haunt of the Beautiful People as well as low life, the *boni beatique* alongside *omnes pusilli et semitarii moechi.*

It was not always intended so, but here, in Rome's civic centre, it is as well to think of some vandalizing graffiti as an assault on the monuments that carried them – and these monuments might be the walls of private houses. The *domus* might in itself be a message to the people.[56] Let us contemplate the important symbolic function of the house among Rome's social and political elite (and those who would join them).[57]

A building was a political ally. In Cicero's injunction that the owner ought to bring *dignitas* to the house, rather than the house to its owner, we see the inverse expectation in the thoughts of many. The house spoke to the *praetereuntes* (those passing by), whom Cicero imagines in conversation with it.[58] And the aristocratic house was a thoroughfare.[59] It was judged by the quality (for good or ill) of those who thronged it. Thus its message was constantly monitored.[60]

So it was that Catullus did not want simply to convey a public message in the tart phrases of his squib. The attack he forecast was aimed at a particular wall. That private walls were targeted by those conveying political messages must remain speculation, but I underline here that such messaging was conveyed not in words alone but by the contestation of space.

Let us return to the *aedes Concordiae*. In the end, the conservative forces won the battle for the site's identification, in that the temple became a symbol for the restoration of order: an inspiration to conservative thinking.[61] *They*, as noted above, would define Concord. That might suggest that the message of indignation did not prevail – and, in a sense, it did not. But, for a moment, the graffiti challenged the aristocratic episteme of republican Rome, and reduced Opimius' monument to the overwritten text on a palimpsest. And the lone but effective voice of dissent in 121 was not forgotten – the memory kept alive by historians, the guardians of a communal memory in an increasingly hostile environment. Augustine may witness to the efficacy of that memory bank.[62]

44 BC

In 44 BC, sometime between 26 January and 15 February, Caesar had been declared Dictator Perpetuus, yet the excessive honours kept being proffered. There was even talk of *regnum*. A senatorial conspiracy to end Caesar's life was in train, Cassius its instigator, but a more public movement – we are told – fixed its attention on Cassius' brother-in-law and political rival, Brutus.

> Those ... who were eager for change and upon [Brutus] first and foremost fixed their eyes, not daring to approach him directly, covered the praetor's tribunal and his chair by night with writings which were mostly of this sort: 'Do you sleep, Brutus?' and 'You are not Brutus'. Cassius, seeing that these things stirred his (sc. Brutus') ambition was more pressing with him than before ... [63]

So, Plutarch in his *Caesar*. In his *Brutus*, Plutarch is characteristically more sympathetic to Brutus, and augments the account in ways we shall discuss below. Brutus, as opposed to Cassius:

> was urged on and roused to the deed on the one hand by many arguments from those with whom he was close and, on the other by the many messages and writings emanating from his fellow citizens.[64]

But, among much else, he records essentially the same two items of graffiti (it being of passing note that one of the items gains in urgency by the addition of an adverb).

'Brutus, do you sleep?' 'You are not truly Brutus.'

We shall return to this fuller account in a moment. Here, it may first be noted that Plutarch accords graffiti the same agency with Brutus as it had with Tiberius Gracchus. A similar report is offered in the parallel account of Appian. As Plutarch had canvassed the various motivations of Gracchus, Appian does for Brutus. He closes with:

> whether he was such a lover of freedom that he preferred his country over all, or whether it was because he was descended from that Brutus of old who had expelled the kings, he was provoked to this deed foremost by the people through their censure (for frequently were inscribed on the images of the elder Brutus and on his [own] tribunal such messages as):
>   'Brutus, have you received a "gift"?'
>   'Brutus, are you dead?'
>   'You should be living now!'
>   'Your posterity is unworthy of you!'
>   'You are not his descendant.'
> These and many similar fired the youth to the deed in imitation of his ancestor.[65]

Only the first two and the last are addressed here to the contemporary Brutus, with the first suggesting that he had in some fashion been 'bribed' to lose his political conscience and to forget, as the last item takes up, his noble ancestry. We shall return to the third and fourth items shortly.

The message is clear. The authorship? Again, we cannot know. The messages appeared at night (as Plutarch tells us) and were clandestine (as Appian).[66] Appian has Cassius insist to Brutus that these scribblings were *not* written *asémōs* (i.e., in a manner indistinct, obscure and without dignity), not by those of no social standing, but by Rome's finest[67] – not by the 'artisans and sellers', says Appian's Cassius, but by 'the best of the Romans'; in Plutarch, not 'the weavers and sellers', but the foremost and most powerful (the *prótoi* and *kratístoi*). Appian and Plutarch, in this entire section of their work (and not just at this point), give every impression of following a common source; their different choice of vocabulary would be explained if they were following a Latin source (and by their respective grasps of its text). In any case, Plutarch's choice of *kratístos* would seem particularly inappropriate. These furtive scribblers might have been well born; they were hardly 'powerful'. The circumstances underlined that. The Latin is likely to have been *principes* or *optimates*.

But of more interest to us here are those to whom Plutarch and Appian have Cassius refer as the individuals who under normal circumstances it would be assumed had recourse to this medium – the artisans, weavers and *kapeloi*. (Are the *kapeloi* who appear in both the versions small businessmen [shopkeepers] or hawkers and pedlars? Probably the former, and that is why *populares* could expect to flood the forum on days when businesses were shut down and shutters went up.)[68] This is an invaluable piece of evidence with regard to the customary authorship of graffiti (usually allowed to pass unnoticed);[69] it preserves the default assumption. Graffiti were the preserve of shopkeepers and artisans – and in this fashion the lowly had a political voice.[70] We note also that the campaign was aggressive. Brutus felt effectively shamed and reproached.

It is, however, the location of these graffiti upon which I wish to conclude. It is clear, as observed above, that Brutus was in some ways a victim of these graffiti and that he was not simply a would-be champion to whom 'the people' called. His formal seat of justice was targeted – and his honour was questioned, if not impugned. But his curule chair and praetorian tribunal were not the only targets, as daring as was that assault on the public domain. Appian's reference to the statues of the elder Brutus obscures the most audacious of reclamations of public space. Let us return to Plutarch's fuller account in the *Brutus* and observe that Plutarch was talking about one particular statue – and saw Brutus' tribunal in the forum as an *additional* target, the messages inscribed or daubed there being thrown into sharp relief and made crystal clear by the first.

> [Brutus] was urged on and roused to the deed on the one hand by many arguments from those with whom he was close and, on the other by the many messages and writings emanating from his fellow citizens. For on the statue of his ancestor, the Brutus who overthrew the rule of the kings was written:
>   'Would that you were (here) now', and
>   'Would that you lived, Brutus'
> On the praetor's tribunal of Brutus himself were found, daily, writings to the effect:
>   'Brutus, do you sleep?', and
>   'You are not truly a Brutus'.[71]

Suetonius places the former for us – and provides the Latin for at least one graffito on the statue of the elder Brutus.

> On the statue of Lucius Brutus, some wrote (on the base of the pedestal):
>   'Would that you lived! (*Utinam viveres*)'
> and on that of Caesar himself:
>   'Brutus, who threw out the kings, was made first consul
>   This one, who threw out the consuls, is finally made king.'[72]

The proximity is implied and was real. The location was highly charged, and this act of vandalism parallels that which adorned the temple of Concord. L. Brutus' statue stood with those of the seven kings of Rome (the seven included Tatius): on the Capitol, in front of the temple of Jupiter.[73] The statue of Brutus probably took the place of Tarquinius Superbus.[74] Where could a more appropriate location be found for protest? Yet there is more.[75] The eight statues had been joined in 45 BC by a ninth. Dio reports that a statue of Caesar was erected there.[76] And Dio adds that this extraordinary placement was no small cause in arousing M. Brutus' wrath against Caesar. Small wonder. Caesar's image usurped the elder Brutus' crowning glory (and negated it). It was ideologically provocative, to say the least. Was, then, Dio's notion (that this provoked M. Brutus more than anything else) born of a tradition that the statue became a flashpoint? This is the context in which we should imagine the graffiti: 'We need a Brutus now'.

Concluding remarks

We have seen that graffiti were typically the weapon of those politically less empowered in institutional terms: shopkeepers, tradespeople and those involved in craft. Not always, perhaps. The graffiti evoking Brutus emanated – we are told – from the politically dispossessed; it implicitly took up the discourse of *res publica* and *libertas*. These were the slogans of the political elite. We might have picked this up even without the advice of Appian's Cassius. Yet the latter provides us with what ought to be our default presumption. Graffiti were customarily the work of those whom the likes of Cicero, in his more candid works, despised.[77] Their collective voices had become increasingly audible and effective in assemblies as the Republic was politically transformed from the mid-second century,[78] but that massed sound was likely to lapse on many occasions into incomprehensibility, in all but its general tenor. Graffiti offered its membership a distinct voice. As much as Roman politicians appreciated 'sensational optics' during electoral campaigns, there would be something *infra dignitatem* about politicians arranging their own campaign in this manner.[79] The medium, it seems, was beneath them.[80] They might get their message across in a *salutatio*, and leave it to the enthusiasm of those who took the political cue.[81] This proposition, I think, is strengthened by the *omission* of any reference to this medium in the *Commentariolum Petitionis*. Although all options are reviewed and the campaign is to be intense, graffiti, it would appear, were not the most acceptable form of expression.[82]

Yet the language we have encountered above was not crude.[83] Graffiti and the other media of 'popular' *rumores* were transmitted in the language of the street – the language of the every day (*infimus et cotidianus sermo*),[84] yet it generally did not make its impact by being harsher (*petulans atque acerba*): the type of language to make even the common person blush?[85] Certainly, obscene language appears in surviving examples of graffiti, but political graffiti did not automatically stoop to those depths.[86] Indeed, embarrassing language was *not* the type of talk heard *ad solarium*, according to the author of the *ad Herennium* (or one of the orators he cites) – the *solarium* being one of the forum's sundials near the *rostra*, where people gathered for news and gossip.[87]

Political graffiti served both the dissemination and the creation of political opinions. They could seed ideas and give the impression that those ideas were current. They had agency. Most readers of graffiti will have met and digested items accidentally and in passing. Graffiti, like other inscribed messages, had to grab attention quickly and more vigorously than current billboards (given the opportunities for mass-dissemination which service the latter).[88] The same was certainly true of so many *monumenta*. 'Reader, stop and read.' Thus the grave entreaties encountered along the roadside. Yet taking into consideration the thoughtful comments of Giancarlo Susini on the 'place' of inscriptions in scholarship, one is struck by the differences that mark the political graffiti at which we have been looking and the usual objects of an epigrapher's gaze. Susini contemplates the need for modern scholars to 'go to the place where [an inscription] is located' and act almost as accomplice in aiding the latter to 'reach beyond the limits of its original environment, cultural and social'.[89] The items that have interested us here *went* to the intended readers and undermined the assumptions of the space in which the graffiti spoke; there was nothing accidental about the reception. And the graffiti were transmitted to modern scholarship by intermediaries who accepted their immediacy and relevance. There were places where people might congregate in expectation;[90] but the examples of political graffiti discussed above were aimed, I have argued, at those who would be affected by the location. Public space was contested. Thus the political graffiti of Rome did not simply offer the (superficial) message but might represent, in so many cases, a diminution of the integrity of the space in terms of that location's original intent.[91]

It was this precise locational engagement that gave force to the items here studied and ensured their historical significance. The writers of graffiti punched above their (expected) weight. Their voice was heard beyond the confines of their humble station, and collectively they added momentum to a cause or, as in 121 BC, checked – in memorable ways – the pretensions of the victorious.

Notes

1   The chapter has its origins in a wider study still in progress: an examination of the expression of popular discontent in the 70s BC – and of the force which Cicero characterized as a *ventus popularis*.
I would like to thank Dr Lea Beness for her comments on an earlier draft, saving me from many a slip.
This chapter had been submitted to the editors when there came into my hands Morstein-Marx, 2012. Not surprisingly it covers the same ground covered here and in much the same detail. Indeed, it pre-empts some of the points made in this chapter. The principal concern of Morstein-Marx's paper is with the extent to which this 'communication across status-lines' represents an 'authentic, autonomous voice of the *plebs*' (for which proposition he finds in the positive). The principal interest in this chapter is in the placement of graffiti (a topic with which Morstein-Marx also inevitably deals). I have endeavoured, in the following notes, to provide cross-references to his valuable study.

2   Plut. *Ti. Gracch.* 8.7. On this item, see also Morstein-Marx, 2012, pp. 201–2. Morstein-Marx makes the suggestion that *mnémata* are to be read as 'tombs' (201, n. 34).

3   Plut. *Ti. Gracch.* 8 *passim*.

4   Nor should this surprise us. If a graffiti campaign is sufficiently distributed, it will have an impact on the public mind, and be remembered; cf. Keegan, 2011, p. 165, offering a classic example of how a single practitioner of graffiti-writing can 'speak' to a vast number of the simple and sophisticated alike – and how the message might endure.

5   For observations of the extent to which this 'communicative agency' might counterbalance what Gramsci conceived of as 'cultural hegemony', see Morstein-Marx, 2012, p. 192.

6   There is a parallel with Aulus Gellius' report of some defamatory graffiti in 43 (*NA* 15.4.3). (This item will be discussed below.)

7   Cicero stands as a useful source because of the quantity of evidence he supplies. He

should not be taken as solely representative, but nor should his views be regarded as singular. For his disdain for the less wealthy, *maculosi senatores* and *nudi equites* (all of them sitting on property evaluations that placed them in the first class of Rome's census ratings), see Cic. *Att.* 1.16.3; for Cicero's contempt for the masses, Cic. *Att.* 1.16.11. Yet in the rich vocabulary for expressing social disdain, *paupertas* remained immune. Even the word *proletarius* was coined, we are asked to believe, in an attempt to give those who were virtually without property a degree of respect; Gell. *NA* 16.10.12–13. For the veritable celebration of *paupertas*, see Val. Max. 4.4.11. For the complexities of addressing poverty, see Kavita Ayer, 'Measuring Worth', a forthcoming Macquarie University doctoral dissertation. *Exempla* of honourable poverty are well known, but I would point to the case of the famous Aelii Tuberones; Val. Max. 4.4.9. The poor who were the subject of this graffiti belonged, of course, to another class altogether.

8 Ti. Gracch., *Suasio legis agrariae*, frg. 13 Malcovati [= Plut. *Ti. Gracch.* 9.4].

9 App. *BCiv.* 1.10.40.

10 Plutarch concentrates on one aspect of the issue only – but the nub.

11 But note that the poor are not casting themselves as on the fringe. They are the Roman citizenry who have won Rome its empire and its wealth. They want what should be common profit. They want property. Slogans are easy enough to imagine.

12 App. *BCiv.* 1.10.38–9.

13 App. *BCiv.* 41.

14 App. *BCiv.* 41–2.

15 For the debate, see Rich, 2008 (an exciting reopening of the way in which the evidence should be read).

16 See again Rich, 2008.

17 Whether the word *aequitas* would have been used in this context is open to debate, but cf. Wirszubski, 1968, pp. 44–6. There seems to be an echo of Gracchan arguments in Florus 2.1[3.13].2–4.

18 I thank Ann-Marie Barrett-Brown for drawing my attention to this important aspect of Roman popular expression.

19 Lintott, 1968, pp. 6–21. Some of this traduction was conveyed in song, drawing upon the potentially magical quality of that medium. An earlier draft carried a more elaborate discussion on this score, excised for reasons of space. On song as a means of popular political expression, however, see Plut. *Sull.* 6.10 [= Livy 77, frg. 15 Weissenborn] and Suet. *Caes.* 80.2; the anti-Caesarian verses reported by Suetonius 'were sung everywhere'. The parallel is clear. Cf., on the medium, Horsfall, 2003, esp. pp. 11–17; 23; 36–47; Habinek, 2005, pp. 77; 220–56.

20 Possibly by 192 BC, to be more precise. For the date of Plautus' *Rudens* (cited below), see Buck, 1940, pp. 96–8, questioning the strength of the argument for 192, but acquiescing in a date in the late 190s.

21 This does not require too much an exercise of imagination. We have confirmation in the repeated mock prediction that a given wall would collapse from the weight of text thereupon. Apparently popular with Pompeian scribblers, it is popular too with modern commentators; see, e.g., Beard, 2008, p. 59.

22 Plaut. *Rud.* 1293–5.

23 Cf. Corbier (this volume). On size mattering, calligraphically, see also Plaut. *Poen.* 837 (which item I owe to Sonnenschein, 1901, p. 148.). Cf. Propertius 3.23 for the poet's urgent search for his lost (highly valuable) *tabellae*: 'Go, boy, and post this

on some column – quickly!' See also *Dig.* 47.2.43 (a reference I owe to Becker, 1873, Sc. IV n. 8 (p. 45)): *solent plerique* (who want to advertise) *hoc etiam facere ut libellum proponant.*

24   An earlier draft carried a register of possible sites. It is omitted here for reasons of space.

25   On the *portico Metelli*, see *LTUR* 4, 130–2. On the opposition of Q. Metellus Macedonicus (the portico's founder) to Tiberius Gracchus, see Plut. *Ti. Gracch.* 14.3. A complete speech of Macedonicus against Tiberius Gracchus was retailed in the *annales* of C. Fannius (Cic. *Brut.* 81). If Filippo Coarelli is right, this was exactly the place that would attract hostile attention (and the desire to compromise Metellan self-advertisement); 1978, pp. 13–28 (= 1996, pp. 280–99).

26   As noted above, Morstein-Marx suggests that the *mnémata* were tombs (201, n. 34). And for a useful discussion of 'sites of memory', see Morstein-Marx 2004, pp. 104–5, n. 168, citing Sehlmeyer, 1999, pp. 68–74.

27   For which, see Plin. *HN* 7.213—or that set up by Q. Marcius Philippus in 164; cf. *LTUR* 4, 336. For gatherings *ad solarium*, Cic. *Quinct.* 59; cf. [Auct.] *ad Herenn.* 4.14.

28   We meet them in a letter of M. Caelius Rufus, *apud* Cic. *ad fam.* 8.1.4. Whether or not the term was in use in the second century, the classification was. (See the following note.)

29   Plin. *HN* 34.24.

30   Plut. *Aem.* 38.4 (an item dated to 142 BC).

31   On this statue and its associations, see Torelli, 1982, pp. 89–118; Coarelli, 1985, pp. 91–119; Richardson, 1992, pp. 370–1; *LTUR* 4, 364–5. For the continuing significance of this site (relevant here), see Sanderson and Keegan, 2011.

32   One thinks also in this regard of the statue group set of Romulus, Remus and the wolf. Set up by the Ogulnii in 296 BC and commemorating as it did the *twin* founders of Rome, it might fairly be called a *popularis* monument, even if the term would be anachronistic. On the statue, see Wiseman, 1995, pp. 72–6.

33   L. Calpurnius Piso, *Annales* frg. 37 Peter [= frg. 40 Chassignet] (= Plin. *HN* 34.30).

34   For a full discussion of this incident, see Morstein-Marx, 2012, pp. 197–201. It is a discussion with which I am in full accord. It underwrites Morstein-Marx's theme of the 'hidden transcript'.

35   App. *BCiv.* 1.26.120.

36   For an attempt (which does not underplay the force and terror deployed) to appreciate Opimius' 'efforts to bring acceptable closure to political strife and civil conflict' and an interpretation of '[Opimius'] honouring of this deity' (sc. Concord) as 'a pious hope for a return to a renewed sense of political harmony within the civic community', see Flower, 2010, p. 87.

37   August. *De Civ. D.*, 3.25 (trans. G. E. McCracken [modified]). Cf. Littlewood, 2006, p. 29 ('Cults of Concordia invariably indicated political disunity'[!]). As Bispham (2000) says commenting on Curti, 2000, pp. 77–91: 'One man's *concordia* is another man's capitulation' (p. 11).

38   Richardson, 1992, 'Concordia, Aedicula' (p. 100). Further, on the history of the site, see Curti, 2000.

39   On this temple, Richardson, 1992, 'Concordia, Aedes (2)' (pp. 98–9); *LTUR* 1, 316–20.

40   Plut. *C. Gracch.* 18.1.

41   Plut. *C. Gracch.* 17.6 (trans. B. Perrin).

42   August. *De Civ. D.* 3.25.

43 A fuller discussion of the licence traditionally afforded to Italic 'vinegar' needs more space than is here available. Such freedom, in any case, was not to be found in 121.

44 Opimius would not have shrugged off the vandalizing of his *monumentum*; cf. Meadows and Williams, 2001, pp. 27–49, for the place of *monumenta*.

45 Wiseman, 1986, pp. 87–101 (= 1994, pp. 37–48), see esp. p. 101 (48). Wiseman sees annalists attacking with variant historical traditions as the equivalent of defacing or destroying a physical monument of a rival *triumphator*.

46 Cf. Morstein-Marx, 2004, p. 102. On the extent to which a temple might carry the name of its builder, see Wiseman, 1987, pp. 395–413 (= 1994, pp. 98–115, see esp. pp. 395–6 [98–100, and 156 nn. 14–16]). The adjoining Basilica Opimia, probably built at the same time, doubly trumpeted Opimius' name (even if only an annex to the temple). On the basilica, Richardson, 1992; Bonnefond-Coudry, 1989, pp. 108–12.

47 For this understanding of the function of Roman *monumenta* (with the suggestion that Livy saw his *History* cast in that role), see Feldherr, 1998, pp. 12–13; cf. Miles, 1995, p. 17, on which Feldherr usefully draws here. Miles defines *monumentum* as 'something that makes one think'. Both Miles and Feldherr are concerned with Livy's text, but their appreciation of the figurative use of *monumentum* serves to remind us of one of the primary functions of Roman building. 'For the Romans, the fundamental task of a *monumentum* was to act as a prompt to memory, to remind' (Feldherr, 1998, p. 12, n. 30).
An important reference point here is Hölkeskamp, 2006, pp. 478–95, see esp. pp. 482–92.

48 As Morstein-Marx has already noted (2004, pp. 102–3, n. 159).

49 It was not, of course, comparable to the storming of the Bastille in 1789 which, it has been suggested, should be understood as representing the animosity of the people to monuments which were in themselves dominating (Georges Bataille, *Dictionnaire Critique – Architecture* Documents 1 [1929], 117, cited by Smith, 2003, p. 6). But it illustrates a similar instinct. (I thank Mary-Jane Cuyler for drawing this item to my attention.)

50 This is a comic *flagitio*; cf. Green, 2005, pp. 225–6.

51 Catull. 37.1–5.

52 Plaut. *Curc.* 481–3; Hor. *Sat.* 2.3.228. Cf. on the district, *LTUR* 5, 195–7; and on its reputation, see esp. 196.

53 Further on the tavern, see *LTUR* 5, 12–13. The idea that this metaphorically referred to the house of Lesbia herself does not convince me.

54 In fact, the attack on the habitués might be shorter by a line. It has been suggested that line 5 be excised; cf. Trappes-Lomax, 2007, pp. 104–5.

55 Catull. 37.9–10. Here I come closest to the translation of Myers and Ormsby, 1972. Most translations rest content with Catullus scrawling verbal obscenities over the frontage. The Latin, I think, is clear. *Sopio*, unless referring technically to a (presumably elongated) red fish, was a figurative label for penis. Thus, Plotius, *Art. Gramm.* 1.153–4 (*GL* VI. 461, 30–462, 3). Adams (1982, pp. 34; 64–5) is cautious here. The style, and the offence it might cause, is manifest from at least one graffito from Pompeii (*CIL* 4.1700): VT MERDAS EDATIS <QUI> SCRIPSERAS SOPIONIS.

56 The public walls of a Roman house, as bland as might be the exterior of many a *domus* (an inviting space), might speak on special occasions to the pretensions of those within. Decorations, sometimes triumphal *ornamenta*, were in those cases a public *declaration* of worth. The *locus classicus* is Plin. *HN* 35.7.

57 Cic. *Off.* 1.138. The house of the *novus*, Cn. Octavius (cos. 165), was *praeclara* and *plena dignitatis*. The commonality went to see it (*vulgo viseretur*); it was thought to have won him votes.

58 Cic. *Off.* 1.139. Cf. von Hesberg, 2005, pp. 19–52 (on the social and political functions of the Roman *domus*); 33, citing Wiseman, 1985, p. 21ff.; Wiseman, 1987, p. 393ff.; Wallace-Hadrill, 1988, p. 43ff.; and Clarke, 1991.

59 So Cic. *Off.* 1.138–9; cf. Vitr. 6.5.2.

60 See also on the function of the house in aristocratic 'messaging', Stein-Hölkeskamp and Hölkeskamp, 2006, pp. 300–20. See 300–10, n. 1 for a bibliography of earlier scholarship. Highly relevant here is Roller, 2010, pp. 117–80, arguing that demolition of a house, rather than effacing the memory of the owner, dishonours his memory, commemorating him as a negative *exemplum*, 'stitching the owner's misdeeds into the topographical and monumental fabric of the city'. I thank Lea Beness for bringing this to my attention.

61 This could be argued at length, but I must content myself here with reference to Bonnefond-Coudry, 1989, pp. 63 (and note 52); 90–112, esp. 97–102 (on the relationship of the temple with the ideology of concord). Also essential reading in this regard is Clark, 2007, particularly her fourth chapter, 'Capitolizing on Divine Qualities', esp. pp. 121–3; and 133–4; 170–1. (I am grateful to Evan Jewell for first bringing these references to my attention.) Cf. Morstein-Marx, 2004, pp. 101–2). For possible resonances in the Augustan period, see Levick, 1972, pp. 779–813, at 803–5; and 1978, pp. 217–33. Rich, 1990, p. 226 is unconvinced; cf. Fears, 1981, pp. 828–946; Littlewood, 2006, p. 30.

62 See also, here, the discussion of Morstein-Marx, 2004, pp. 54–6, suggesting 'the sense of permeable and shifting boundaries at an ideologically fraught meeting-point between *senatus* and *populus*' (i.e., the area contained by the rostra, *curia* and temple). Popular space or senatorial space, Morstein-Marx appropriately asks. Cf. Morstein-Marx, 2004, pp. 101–4.

63 Plut. *Caes.* 62.4. This episode is also dealt with in detail by Morstein-Marx, 2012, pp. 204–13.

64 Plut. *Brut.* 9.5.

65 App. *BCiv.* 2.112.

66 In passing we may note that these are not the only clandestine messages produced in this volatile situation. Those who wanted to see Caesar's elevation accelerated placed diadems on his statues at night (Plut. *Brut.* 9.8). The nocturnal debate was two-way.

67 App. *BCiv.* 2.113; cf. Plut. *Brut.* 10.6.

68 *Pace* Mouritsen, 2001, p. 42 (in whose work I find much to admire).

69 I was not surprised, however, to see that Morstein-Marx, 2012, pp. 207–9, has made the same observation.

70 Furthermore, Appian gives us an indication of their customary messages. From other praetors, they demanded (says Appian's Cassius) 'spectacles of horses and wild beasts' (sc. *ludi, circenses, venationes*); to Brutus, they called out for *libertas*. This was presumably the way in which Sulla expected the readers of his *commentarii* to assume that he knew the negative mood of the less-privileged populace when he was canvassing for the praetorship (Plut. *Sull.* 5.1).

71 Plut. *Brut.* 9.5–7.

72 Suet. *Caes.* 80.3.

73 The precise position is sometimes debated (as is the date of erection). See App. *BCiv.* 1.16; cf. *LTUR* 4 368–9 (for discussion, source references and a modern

bibliography). For the date (not relevant to the current discussion), see Jane DeRose Evans, 1990, pp. 99–105.

74 Coarelli understandably doubts the presence of Tarquinius Superbus. Dio (43.45.3–4) tells us there were eight statues, seven of kings. One was of Tatius (Ascon. 29C; Plin. *HN* 33.23).

75 Morstein-Marx also spots the significance of this plausible location 2012, pp. 205–6.

76 Dio 43.45.3–4.

77 Contrast Cic. *Off.* 1.150–1 (with its disdain for fishmongers, cooks and butchers) with *Sest.* 97 (which, for political reasons, is socially inclusive – and tendentious in the extreme; cf. Kaster, 2006, pp. 35; 320–1). Cf. Wood, 1988, pp. 97–100.

78 See Plut. *Aem.* 38.4. (Their station is rhetorically diminished for political purposes.) Cf. Beness and Hillard, 2012, esp. pp. 7; 9–12. On the impact of these people on more formal assemblies, see Yakobson, 1999, esp. pp. 13–19.

79 I adopt the phrase 'sensational optics' from Jeff Tatum, discussing the 'leading' map display of L. Hostilius Mancinus in 147/146 (Plin. *HN* 35.23) – a tactic that won him, the consulship at the next election, reports Pliny. ('No stump speeches? Campaign rhetoric in the late Roman republic', a paper delivered to the *Culture, Identity and Politics in the Ancient Mediterranean World Conference* (held in honour of Professor Erich Gruen), Australian National University, 24/9/11. It will appear as a chapter in a collection edited by Catherine Steel and based upon the conference 'Oratory and Politics in the Roman Republic', 1–3 September 2010, at the Ioannou Centre for Classical and Byzantine Studies, University of Oxford).

80 As a medium, it excited a degree of distaste that contemporary examples excite in those who have effective access to more 'elevated' forms of discourse, or aversion in those who feel threatened by the exercise. (Some rejoiced in the medium. Mary Beard observes that those driven to 'decry' the habit of wall-desecration simply added to the phenomenon they deplored (2008, p. 59). I take it she is being tongue in cheek.)

81 On the use of *salutationes* for broadcasting political messages, see Laurence, 1994b, pp. 62–74, esp. 64–7; cf. Goldbeck, 2010, pp. 74–5 and 229–46 (with regard to canvassing rituals). I thank Jeff Tatum for the latter reference.

82 All means of securing victory are canvassed. It was now or never (*Comm. Pet.* 4; 38). He had recourse, it would seem, to (something approaching) an electioneering slogan: a vote for Cicero was a vote that thwarted an almost unthinkable alternative. It was cast in the negative: ['Can there be a citizen so vile as to want to unsheathe, with one vote, two daggers against the State?' (*Comm. Pet.* 12; trans. Shackleton Bailey)]. (The slogan is echoed at Asconius 93C.) You could have put this, Jeff Tatum (cited three notes above) remarked, on a bumper sticker – a very long bumper sticker. The interesting point is that there is no evidence that such a slogan bedaubed walls (though it may have); and, more to the point, Quintus Cicero, if the author of this handbook, did not suggest it.

83 We might note, in passing and by way of contrast, the graffiti aimed against P. Ventidius P.f. Bassus (praet., cos. suff. 43 BC). (Catullus 52, aimed at other 'unworthy' occupants of curule office, comes to mind – reminding us that the discourse was served by many media.) 'Assemble, all augurs and haruspices! An omen unaccustomed has but recently occurred. For he who used to rub down mules, has been made consul (*nam mulas qui fricabat, consul factus est*).' (Gell. *NA* 15.4.3) For the sexual undertones of *frico*, see Adams, 1982, p. 184; 208. There seems to be little doubt that the suggestion was that the consul used to 'jerk-off' mules – or

perhaps engaged in something more bestial. Horsfall (2003, p. 141, n. 42) mistakenly thinks that this was inscribed under a statue. These *versiculi* were inscribed 'everywhere' (*vulgo*) along the streets of the city. As noted above, Gellius professes no doubts as to the authorship: the *populus Romanus* (15.4.3).

84   On which, see [Cic.] *ad Herenn.* 1.14.

85   On this, *loc.cit.*, a valuable passage for illustrating strata of language. The author refers to the type of language found 'backstage and in similar places' as an example of the worst. Popular gossip (see the text following) was of a different sort.

86   The item encountered three footnotes previously is, then, the exception rather the rule in this company.

87   *LTUR* 4, 336, for references.

88   Those who wished to communicate in such a fashion were instinctively aware of the medium's limitations. Hence, recourse to *libelli*. They were more mobile, where dissemination was of the essence.

89   Susini, 1973, pp. 62–3. See also Keegan (this volume).

90   This is covered in more detail in this volume by David Newsome. I have discussed in passing above where people might congregate in search of pasquinades – and for news. We have a melancholy instance in the case of Q. Aurelius, 'a stranger to politics', who came into the forum merely to read the proscription lists – and found himself on them (Plut. *Sull.* 31.6). His was a dangerous curiosity. Nothing is known of this otherwise inoffensive but perilously wealthy individual; cf. Hinard, 1985, pp. 334–5 [no. 7].
For a public avid for news and gossip, see Champlin, 1991, p. 5, drawing so effectively on August. *Enarr. in ps.* 21, 2.30) on the public reading of wills; and the *subrostrani* (mentioned above).

91   It was not, in a sense, so different from any other social reclamation or architectural interference with a given site or location. People will often use a site 'in ways that need not coincide with the intentions of its creators' (Laurence, 1994a, p. 135).

7

Writing in Public Space from Child to Adult: The Meaning of Graffiti[1]

Renata Senna Garraffoni and Ray Laurence

The Roman city was a place for the public display of writing in a variety of mediums. Writing was visible in parts most of public and private space and Pompeii was not an exception. In considering this, we would like to focus on the walls of Pompeii. The walls that withstood the earthquake and the volcanic eruptions became a unique archaeological *corpus*: wall decoration (frescoes) and a variety of inscriptions reveal to us heterogeneous data that allows us to gain a greater insight into the lives of inhabitants of a city in the first century AD. The wall inscriptions can be divided in two major groups; the *tituli picti*, comprising different types of announcements that were painted on external walls by professionals and could be read from a long distance, and the graffiti.[2] The research for this chapter focused on graffiti within their spatial context to answer four key questions:

a) whether particular forms of graffiti were confined to certain types of public space;
b) whether parts of the city of Pompeii were more strongly associated with distinct subject matter;
c) whether the pattern of representation of graffiti as opposed to imagery was distinctive (here we address the relationship of the verbal and the visual with a view to seeking out a spatial pattern of representation);
d) whether there is another logic that produces the patterns of graffiti found in Pompeii.

In dealing with these questions, we have chosen to focus on the differentiation of age in Pompeii drawing on the evidence of alphabets (that were located at a low level on walls and columns in Pompeii) that place the learning or practice of writing in public space.[3] This opens the whole question of literacy in Pompeii and how learning of the ability to produce graffiti was achieved. The problem put simply is that we have trouble identifying a material culture that should be associated with childhood. What is striking about the evidence for Pompeii is this: although there may have been no public provision of schools in the city, language acquisition did occur for some or many depending on where a scholar stands on the literacy debate.[4] Our approach is rather different from that taken in the recent work on Roman literacy, which has for the most part looked at literacy as a useful acquisition – for example if you could learn to write your name, you would be able to witness documents, such as those found in the Jucundus and Sulpicii archives.[5] We see an intrinsic pleasure in gaining the ability to write your name, and a greater pleasure in using another person's name and connecting it to another word to insult that person. If you had this skill, you could name people as *fellators* and *cinaedi*. The use of verb forms permitted boasts about your sexual prowess in the brothel or elsewhere. Moving up a level, the ability to reproduce the most famous lines of Virgil can be found on the walls of Pompeii. To create a better understanding of alphabets of children and as evidence for learning, we contrast this pattern in the evidence with that of the drawing of pictures on walls (termed pictorial graffiti) and then contrast these two patterns with the more adult graffiti form that can be seen in the various sexual insults directed at others. This allows us to see children as far from marginal in the ancient city – a conclusion that then informs a study of gladiators in graffiti – a group within Roman society that were termed *infames* yet have a prominence in both textual and pictorial graffiti. What we find is that gladiators are represented in private and public space in a similar way to other groups. Importantly this would suggest that concentrations of graffiti do not locate gladiators in the House of the Gladiators in the form of a *ludus*, but instead defines that building as part of public space.

Approaches to graffiti in Pompeii

These questions and the approach adopted here respond to recent research on Pompeii that has developed a new understanding of graffiti and their context.

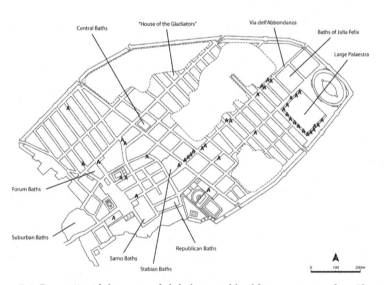

Figure 7.1 Pompeii with location of alphabets and buildings mentioned in Chapters 7 and 11

The number of graffiti recorded, according to Feitosa,[6] totals nearly 11,000. These objects have been a matter of speculation or curiosity for more than two centuries from the discovery of Pompeii in the 1760s but this is not to say that they have been approached or studied with the objective of explanation of the phenomenon of graffiti writing. There has also been little discussion of graffiti as material culture in theoretical archaeology. Instead, graffiti are utilized as evidence for daily life.[7] Part of the problem stems from graffiti being categorized as vulgar and, at the best, a fragmentary record when compared to other forms of evidence.[8] Where systematic study has occurred it has focused on linguistic variation and sexual vocabulary.[9] It should also be added that within the field of onomastics and the study of the uses of names, the graffiti of Pompeii, due to their number and dated context (pre-AD 79), take on a prominence within the systematic study of linguistic adaptations.[10] Cooley has also stated that archaeological evidence can suggest alternative frameworks to understand the spread of Latin and to provide balanced interpretative models on how different groups adopted the Latin language.[11] The other tradition is for the graffiti to inform writers of the nature of the common experience of living in Pompeii that detaches the graffiti from the culture of the elite found in literary texts.[12] However, this seems less than compelling because there would seem to have been a convergence between the two types of writing, and the fact that sections of literary texts appear in graffiti points to a relationship between the two very different forms of textual preservation.[13]

This chapter engages with recent developments that have transformed the study of graffiti, not least Langner's cataloguing of the figurative graffiti that appear across the site and also in Stabiae and Herculaneum.[14] There is a new interest in graffiti, both in the context of Anglo-American scholarship and within that of the southern hemisphere – notably in Brazil and Australia. A conference at the University of Leicester in 2008 provided a window into the development of the subject matter.[15] Scholars had shifted their focus away from graffiti as indicators of names or mistaken Latin to an understanding of graffiti as an essential element of the everyday culture and of spoken language. Keegan stresses the link between graffiti and speech, emphasizing that unlike speech graffiti provide a temporal longevity to the words of a person.[16] At the same time, Milnor has stressed that there is an importance to understanding graffiti not as just a text to be read, but as an act of text making in a particular place, which means that graffiti become evidence for an activity, rather than as simply being a text to be read.[17] This is a theme pursued by Newsome, in this volume, who argues that graffiti act as a *pasquinade* and, to an extent, require a written response. This feature causes graffiti to become concentrated together, rather than isolated from one another. This causes a variation in density of graffiti and a notable concentration of graffiti types in particular locales – for example Craig Williams locates a concentration of sexually explicit graffiti in the Casa dell Nozze di Argento.[18] There were also certain limitations to the placement of graffiti – interestingly, the baths were not spaces for much graffiti – since presumably writing instruments were left with clothes while bathing. The process of writing an individual graffito was often a response to existing graffiti that causes these texts to have a relationship that could be described as a conversation in a written format.[19] The conversation is in many ways in an abbreviated format, and can appear like a modern graffiti tag; but like the modern tagging, for the writers there is an engagement with each other.[20] The graffiti mark the writers' identity in space and in dialogue with each other. The result of these written conversations is a clustering of graffiti in groups that suggests writing on walls was not a uniform phenomenon and does not display a random pattern. Indeed, Keegan argues that the location of graffiti can be related to a social logic of space as defined through space syntax.[21]

Brazilian scholarship on graffiti has sought to bring to the fore the identities of the marginalized within Roman society, who have also remained obscure in mainstream scholarship on classical antiquity. Pedro Paulo Funari pioneered the study of these groups in a series of publications in the 1980s and 1990s and it is his students who have developed a fusion between traditional classics and perspectives drawn from archaeological theory to reveal new work on violence, gladiators and sexuality.[22] Our chapter brings this Brazilian perspective on antiquity into juxtaposition with an Anglophone emphasis on the study of space in Pompeii to seek a better understanding of how graffiti can be understood as a spatial phenomenon.

Children and literacy

The basis for language acquisition was the alphabet and a series of complicated memory exercises known from literary texts. An extreme example of this is Herodes Atticus' scheme for his son's education: he employed 24 slaves each with a name beginning with a different letter of the alphabet, who were to accompany his son at all times – presumably rearranging themselves into different combinations and orders.[23] Less extreme were the provision of children with wooden letters and maybe depending on the reading of texts even cakes shaped as letters – an alternative might be that cakes were given as rewards.[24] These items obviously do not survive in the archaeological record, but what do are examples of the alphabet written from its beginning forwards, from its end backwards and a combination of both of these to form AXBYCV and so on. The height at which these alphabets were written is significant. It coincides with the height at which Huntley identified childlike figurative graffiti to show that these were produced by children, cross-referencing height off the ground with analysis of the drawings based on developmental psychology to demonstrate these were produced by children.[25] This causes us to associate alphabet graffiti with children rather than adults – a feature that is discussed in more detail by Baldwin, Moulden and Laurence in their chapter in this volume. It is worth noting that age-related graffiti have also been identified in the Forum of Julius Caesar in Rome.[26]

There are 102 alphabets recorded and published from Pompeii. We find examples of alphabets in the famous houses such as the Villa of the Mysteries, and the House of the Menander, where both Latin and Greek alphabets are located (see Figure 7.1).[27] It is relatively well known that a graffito identifies the Large Palaestra, next to the amphi-theatre, as a location for teaching; what is perhaps less well known is that on 18 of its 118 columns were written alphabets.[28] There is a tendency for these written alphabets to cluster in the corners of the portico of the palaestra. These inscriptions therefore locate children at the earliest age of learning in public space among the columns, in a manner that is familiar from the famous scene of punishment found on a fresco in the Praedia of Julia Felix.[29] What we need to bear in mind is that the onlookers are watching not the punishment, but are instead looking to see what the children are reading or writing.[30]

There are few alphabets on public buildings more generally (Table 7.1): there is a record of an alphabet from the Eumachia building, another was found in the Macellum, another in the corridor leading to the theatre, and also another from the Temple of Fortuna Augusta.[31] Another location needs to be mentioned – the portico of the Stabian Baths to the right of the entrance, in which was written AXBVCTDSER – a combination of a forwards and backwards alphabet, an exercise that is referred to by Jerome.[32] The baths would not seem to have been a place of graffiti, generally, perhaps due to the difficulty of carrying a stylus when naked or semi-naked.

On the other hand, 21 alphabets have been recorded in the streets of Pompeii. When looking at this distribution we should be aware that recording of this material massively improved in the twentieth century and this accounts for the apparent concentration in Via dell'Abbondanza. What we are looking at is a clustering of examples at certain points in the street. The street was the place associated with teachers and their pupils in Latin literary texts.[33] However, we are not just finding them in the locations imagined in literature – e.g. Horace's *extremis in vicis* that Bonner suggests means 'at the end of the street' or 'the side street' of the city.[34] The five examples outside the Porta Marina with a further example inside the gateway itself exist in just such a location as are those found in Vicolo del Labirinto and Vicolo del Modesto in Regio VI of Pompeii. These locations and others in Pompeii coincide with Quintilian's assertion that a child picked up its letters at the street-corner.[35] A place also populated by others from beggars upwards in literature.[36] Yet, this is revealing of the place of children in public space. They are at the street corner learning the alphabet from dawn until midday, when children may have visited the baths.[37]

The distribution pattern of alphabets needs discussion in the context of Katherine Huntley's full study of pictorial graffiti that may be attributed, on the basis of developmental cognition, to children (Table 7.1).[38] There is a degree of convergence and

Table 7.1 Distribution of graffiti by type

Location	Alphabets (%)	Pictorial Images (%)	Sexual Insult (%)	Gladiators (%)
Domestic Spaces/ houses	41	40.9	44	37
On façades	32	13.7	43	27
Theatre and theatre corridor	0	26.1	0	3
Large Palaestra	21	10.6	4	15
Baths	1	7.5	0	0
Public Buildings	5	0	9	15
Other	0	1.8	0	3

divergence in the placement of the two types of graffiti with the ABCs appearing more commonly in streets on the façades of houses and in the Large Palaestra. The divergence may be caused by the nature of the two types of actions – ABCs are part of instruction and learning within Roman culture, whereas the drawn images may be seen as not so much instruction but as a leisure pursuit and, therefore, have a wider distribution. Hence, what we are seeing with the alphabets is the positioning of children in the city with respect to instruction and practice of their letter forms.

Within the body of graffiti known from Pompeii, there exist quotations from known Latin texts.[39] Developmentally, the ability to rewrite quotations and texts shows a degree of knowledge of literature. These can provide a contrast to the placement of alphabets. The replication of quotations from literature might be described as our more literate, and thus more adult, comparator for the graffiti. The most frequent text quoted is that of Virgil's *Aeneid*. There are 36 graffiti explicitly quoting lines from this text. Fifteen of these are found in private houses, 18 are scratched on the façades of shops or on columns in the streets, three examples are located in public buildings associated with the circulation of people: the basilica, the Large Palaestra and the House of the Gladiators. The overall pattern does not show a great divergence from that found for alphabets, apart from the appearance of the *Aeneid* in shops and bars – spaces in which alphabets are absent.

If we are to assume that alphabets should be associated with the early learning of literacy, which contrast to distribution of the drawings of human form, we need to see if it might be possible to see a contrast between these patterns and those of an adult form of graffito – the sexual insult.[40] These, we may assume, were post-pubescent forms of communication and involved an understanding of sex and/or sexual maturity. When we wish to examine what might be described as sexual insults or the discourse on sex and sexuality, there needs to be a realization that the graphic representation of sex in graffiti is a rare phenomenon – if compared to that of ships, gladiators, birds, or any other category. However, the characterization of others as cocksuckers, *cinaedi*, etc., was a more common phenomenon in the linguistic graffiti.[41] Where graphic caricature does appear, the phallus that penetrates the fellator need not be present, which reminds us of a phenomenon of graffiti that they can allude to an image, through a text, without actually describing the image. Thus, the use of sexual language based on human anatomy – penis, anus, mouth etc., or verbs associated with penetration of the body by a penis – creates a mental image of sex. This is a feature that Funari has emphasized in order to view a linkage between words and images in the form of an iconographic discourse within which are the expression and embodiment of the *ethos* and world-views of the authors – in the case of the graffiti often unnamed and unknown.[42]

Graffiti are also shorthand and an abbreviated form that enable the reader to understand a range of meanings from them, for example, a whole list of sexual practices was associated with the *cinaedus*. There was little need to state them unless specific reference was needed as to why that person was a *cinaedus*, as in the example: 'Vesbinus cinedus, Vitalio has buggered you', found on a façade of a building in Vicolo del Panettiere.[43] This type of graffiti has a distinct pattern to it. In general this coincides with the overall pattern of graffiti in Pompeii that associates words with the façades of buildings and internal spaces of houses (see Table 7.1).[44] However, when compared to the distribution of alphabets in the city, we do find differences – most notably the relative absence of sexual insults from the Large Palaestra. What this indicates is that the learning of letters, in public, is a very specific action that has its own locales – most prominently the Large Palaestra. Indeed, it would seem that the learning of letters produced its own pattern that cannot be mapped onto other patterns of graffiti – such as drawing of humans by children or sexual insults.

Gladiators: image and text

The one type of graphic graffiti that is associated with a single professional group is that of the gladiator. Their distinctive weaponry causes them to be recognized more easily than other images that represent the faces of other groups of people in profile who are today unknown to us. What the representation of gladiators demonstrates is that the pattern of graffiti in Pompeii remains pretty similar regardless of type of gladiator. Writing about gladiators in graffiti was an action to be found in public and private contexts; there seems to be little deviation from the overall pattern for other types of graffiti. However, the association between the images of gladiators and texts naming gladiators, their weaponry (a Thracian, a Murmillo, etc.) and to a lesser extent their number of combats, causes these graffiti to be of a different type.

There is a huge diversity of gladiatorial graffiti. Some are simple drawings of gladiators' distinctive weapons and helmets without a single written word, while others represent the image of a single gladiator or pairs of gladiators and can mention names or details of their previous fights. There are also graffiti that are composed only of inscriptions with no drawings. This heterogeneity presents us with a different type of information that is rarely explored by scholars who study gladiatorial games. The image of a single gladiator shows us the ability of the author as he/she draws details of the gladiator's weapons and clothes, and most of them include their names. They are always dressed with their weapons and standing ready to attack, perhaps at the start of a contest. In contrast, the images of pairs of gladiators represent a very specific part of the combat: its conclusion with a victor and a vanquished gladiator represented. Most of these images inform us of the winner and the loser through words or symbols; generally when there is no word the loser is represented on his knees or with his weapons on the ground and the winner is surrounded by palms and carries his weapons. Many of these graffiti also indicate whether the loser was killed or forgiven, and it is interesting to note that most of them were not killed.

The fusion of text and image to convey an understanding of prowess or qualities associated with the arena causes such graffiti to share much in common with statuary and their associated inscriptions. Of course, commemorative inscriptions and statuary were not set up to gladiators – due perhaps to their categorization as *infames*,[45] but as with the subjects of other categories of graffiti the gladiator was written into private as well as public space. Façades of buildings and the interior spaces of houses are the dominant locations for the writing and visualization of gladiators and their prowess (see Table 7.1). However, there were some locations that attracted a greater number of written graffiti with regard to gladiators. The first of these is the palaestra of the theatre where ten written and one graphic graffito were found – it is also the place where, famously, the armour of gladiators was found. The Large Palaestra, adjacent to the amphitheatre was another location featuring ten written examples mostly graphic visualizations of the individual gladiators referred to. The temples of Jupiter and Asclepius were associated with five examples. The location with the greatest concentration of graffiti referring to gladiators, and which needs further discussion is the so called 'House of the Gladiators'.

The discovery in the 1890s of a building in the north of the city on Via di Nola (V.5.3) that was unlike any other house in Pompeii would have been discussed for its architectural arrangement primarily, were it not for the discovery of a number of graffiti referring to gladiators and its subsequent naming as the House of the Gladiators (Figure 7.2).[46] The interpretation that gladiators lived at this place is based on the graffito *CIL* IV 4220 that states that 'Samus the *Murmillo* lives here'.[47] However, this graffito is found in a dining room next to another listing the prices and the wine drunk and therefore does not imply that Samus literally lived in the building, instead a joke is being made that Samus 'lived' there in the sense that he spent much time in this dining room.[48] In total 27 of the 145 graffiti from the house can be explicitly associated with gladiators:[49] Ten named individuals are each described as an *Essedarius*; ten more named individuals as Thracians; five identified as a *Murmillo*, one of whom was also an *Eques*, and two *Retiarii*. Their presence led the building to be regarded as a forerunner of the *ludus* in the palaestra of the theatre (that had been identified by a find of gladiatorial equipment) which had fallen out of use after the earthquake of AD 62.[50] This interpretation involves a number of conceptual leaps and conflates the evidence needlessly. The structure requires a re-assessment that pays greater attention to the architecture and the context of the graffiti.

The architecture of the building is formed from a peristyle approached by eight steps from Via di Nola, it contains two dining rooms but little else in terms of space for accommodation. It should be noted that tree roots were found in the central area of

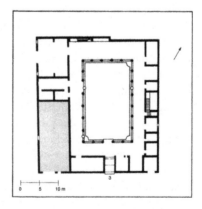

Figure 7.2 House of the Gladiators

the peristyle.[51] If we were looking for an architectural parallel, ignoring the graffiti for a moment, we would regard this structure as perhaps a headquarters of a guild – such as those found in Ostia.[52] Turning to the graffiti, 145 examples from a single structure is fairly unusual. These include a whole range of subject matter, including: alphabets, quotations from the *Aeneid*, and sexual insults alongside a preponderance of gladiator related examples. These were not accompanied by similar examples of pictorial graffiti. Langner identifies one helmet of a gladiator, a caricature of a face in profile, and for the most part geometrical designs from the *triclinium*.[53] The emphasis in this building is upon writing and some 121 examples of graffiti (83 per cent of graffiti in the building) were recovered from the 24 columns of the peristyle. This reflects a preference for writing on columns that is found in other parts of Pompeii: 300 examples of graffiti were recovered from the columns of the Large Palaestra. What is different though is that the 'House of the Gladiators' has a large concentration of graffiti referring to gladiators, unlike the Large Palaestra. Yet, we can also find other types of graffiti in the so-called House of the Gladiators that would suggest that it need not be a *ludus* for gladiators. The graffiti and structure of the building would, instead, suggest that this was a public space, which should not be associated with any one particular group of people – the presence of alphabets points to a possibility of children learning their ABC here. In any case, gladiators need not leave behind graffiti of their fights – few graffiti have been located in the Palaestra of the Large Theatre – a location that produced gladiatorial weapons and armour.

The large number of graffiti found in the House of the Gladiators should also be explained with reference to the nature of its architecture. When looking at the position of graffiti in the houses of Pompeii, it is the spaces with columns that tend to yield the highest numbers of examples: the peristyle, the *viridarium*, and the *atrium*,[54] and it is the columns and façades of shops that appear in literature as the locations of written space.[55] These are all spaces of circulation and point to graffiti as both something to be written (the action of creation) and to be placed in a location to be read by others.[56] This causes the written space of the graffito to align itself both with columns, seen as markers of status, and with spaces that had large numbers of people moving through them.[57] This phenomenon, of itself, shifts our perceptual frame of ancient architecture – the column was an individuated surface on which the gaze might dwell, as much as on the fancy paintings glimpsed in the distance across a peristyle.

Conclusion

For decades scholars based their research on the elite's material culture and the common peoples' daily lives had not always been discussed. Often they were described as a homogeneous and apolitical mass: free and poor men, women, the elderly, children, gladiators, slaves and freedmen had been labelled together 'the Roman people'.[58] Pompeii's graffiti constitute important evidence to rethink the concept of non-elites as an idle mob, as it helps us to capture some ephemeral moments of Roman existence. The graffiti allow us to understand the common people's points of view and they also throw some light on this particular form of written communication. This allows us to view this aspect of Roman epigraphic culture not just as a written message or text, but as an action of writing and reading that was located in a specific social environment and had a spatial aspect to it. Graffiti were written for public display and could be read in different forms and if we consider the contextual situation, they can be understood as archaeological artefacts.

However, graffiti are an outcome of writing and it is the action of writing that we are in fact studying. The writer of a graffito was making a choice within a range of options that were limited by his/her understanding of the use of writing, knowledge of words in a written form and the available surface on which to scratch the letters. It is difficult to pick out a reason why one person might write their name and another chose to boast of their sexual virility, or to insult another person. Yet, there is a pattern to the production of graffiti that: places children in public space, separates the distribution pattern of alphabets from other distributions of graffiti, and locates the drawings of the textually under-represented. These marginal figures, regulated by legal taboo (*infames*), were written and drawn into the fabric of the city that identifies their centrality for those who wrote and drew these images.

In terms of space and graffiti there is an absence of any clear and absolute division between graffiti writing in public and private space – nearly every type of graffiti can be found in both contexts. Equally, although we have identified categories of texts in this chapter, spatially there is no absolute delineation of where any particular type of graffiti should or should not occur. The act of writing graffiti is a social one in which there is anticipation of the text being read and, for that to be achieved, places through which others circulated predominate. This would suggest that learning to write or to read was an action that allowed a person to have a quite different relationship with their city, when compared to others unable to read or write. The action of writing (and subsequently reading) was a public phenomenon that was an aspect of spatial practice at Pompeii and an aspect of urban living in antiquity. However ephemeral we may feel graffiti are there is significance to them as a form of communication that creates through writing – an identity in space.

Notes

1 This chapter is based on a dialogue between the two authors between December 2008 through to March 2009, during which time Renata Garraffoni held a British Academy Visiting Research Fellowship at the University of Birmingham. Both authors are grateful to and wish to acknowledge the roles of the British Academy and the University of Birmingham in facilitating this piece of research and also acknowledge additional support from the Federal University of Paraná (Brazil), Fundação Araucária and the University of Birmingham (UK). The ideas expressed here are our own and we are solely responsible for them and any errors.

2 Giordano and Casale, 1991 for an account of the discoveries made in the period 1954–78.

3 Given the problem, authors seem to have a default setting a male *paterfamilias* with *familia* that can occupy the buildings of the city. Such a situation is as preposterous as imagining every *atrium* house in the city owned by a grieving widow celebrating the fact that she was a *univira*.

4   Harris, 1983, pp. 102–11; 1989, pp. 9, 200–1; compare with Franklin, 1991; also
    Corbier, 1987a, translated in this volume, develops the concept of a basic literacy,
    see now Kruschwitz, 2010. For earlier identifications of schools in Pompeii based on
    graffiti, see Della Corte, 1959a, 1959b.
5   E.g. Cribiore, 2001, pp. 167–8; Harris, 1983, pp. 102–11, 1989, pp. 261–2 notes there
    is no survey of the evidence for literacy, but most authors utilize the Jucundus and
    Sulpicii archives as proxy data.
6   Feitosa, 2005, p. 61.
7   Varone, 2002; Cooley and Cooley, 2004, see comments of Baird and Taylor, 2011,
    pp. 11–2.
8   E.g. Cèbe, 1966, p. 372 referring to wall drawings.
9   E.g. Adams, 2007; 1982.
10 Solin, 1970, 1973.
11 Cooley, 2002b, pp. 9–11.
12 E.g. Tanzer, 1939.
13 See e.g. Williams, 2010 for discussion of the relationship and the usage of the two
    types of textual evidence together, also Milnor, 2009.
14 Langner, 2001.
15 Published as Baird and Taylor, 2011.
16 Keegan, 2011.
17 Milnor, 2009, p. 293.
18 Williams, 2010, pp. 299–301.
19 Baird and Taylor, 2011, pp. 7–8; Benefiel, 2010a, 2011.
20 Keegan, 2011.
21 Keegan, 2011, pp. 184–5.
22 Funari, 1986, 1989, 1993; and work by his former students: Feitosa, 2005; Feitosa and
    Garraffoni, 2010; Garraffoni, 2008; Garraffoni and Funari, 2009.
23 Philostratus, *VS*, 558; Cribiore, 2001, pp. 164–7 for discussion.
24 Quint. 1.1.26–7; Jerome, *Ep.* 107.4; Hor. *Sat.* 1.1.25–6; Jerome, *Ep.* 128.1.
25 Huntley, 2011.
26 Della Corte, 1933, nos. 7, 126, 139; Marrou, 1932.
27 *CIL* 4.9311–12 for Villa of the Mysteries and 9271–6 for the House of the Menander.
28 *CIL* 4.9279–96; Della Corte 1939, 1947; Ray, forthcoming.
29 Harris, 1989, pp. 34–5 for discussion.
30 Bonner, 1972, p. 527.
31 Respectively: *CIL* 4.9299; *CIL* 4.2548; *CIL* 4.2547.
32 *CIL* 4.2541; Hieron. *Ep.* 25.26.
33 Bonner 1972, pp. 515; Harris 1989, pp. 236, based on Mart. *Ep.* 9.68, Dio.Chrys. 20.9,
    Hor. *Epist.* 1.20.18.
34 Bonner, 1972, pp. 516–7 for parallels; see Castrén, 2000; Wallace-Hadrill, 2003;
    Laurence, 2007a, 2008 on meaning of *vicus*.
35 Quint. 1.4.27.
36 Hor. *Epist.* 1.17.58–9; Bonner, 1972, pp. 517–8.
37 Ovid, *Amores*, 1.13.17–18; Mart. *Ep.* 9.68.1–4; 12.57.4–5; 14.223; Apul. *Met.* 10.5.
38 Huntley, 2011.
39 See discussion by Milnor, 2009.
40 Williams, 2010, pp. 290–301 specifically and passim throughout his book.
41 Williams, 2010, pp. 292–5.
42 Funari, 1993.

43 *CIL* 4.2319b.

44 Compare examples of houses discussed in Williams, 2010, pp. 295–301.

45 Hope, 2000 on epitaphs of gladiators, but note that the actor Norbanus Sorex was commemorated by two statues at Pompeii.

46 See Sogliano, 1899 for description of structures and paintings on excavation.

47 More than 100 years on from excavation the original connection between this graffito and the notion (Mau, 1893) that this was where gladiators lived still persists, if guardedly, e.g. in Berry 2007, pp. 142–3.

48 *CIL* 4.4222.

49 *CIL* 4.4280, 4281, 4291, 4295, 4296, 4333, 4334, 4386, 4393, 4413 = *essedarius*; 4286, 4290, 4308, 4309, 4335, 4342, 4345, 4349, 4356 = *Thraex*; 4327, 4329, 4336, 4407, 4420 = *Murmillo*; 4420 = *Eques*; 4353 and 4356 = *Retiarius*.

50 Sabbatini Tumolesi, 1980, pp. 148–9.

51 Jashemski, 1993, p. 118.

52 Hermansen, 1982, pp. 55–90.

53 Langner, 2001.

54 A pattern also found by Williams, 2010, pp. 299–301 with reference to Casa dell Nozze di Argento – 39 of 68 graffiti found in the peristyle.

55 Mart. *Ep.* 1.117; Hor. *Serm.* 1.4.71, *Ars Poetica*, 372–3; see also Catull. 37 on sex and writing obscenity on the front of *tabernae*; White, 2009.

56 Grahame, 2000, pp. 56–73.

57 Wallace-Hadrill, 1994, pp. 20–3.

58 Beard, 2008: pp. 105–10 reflects on the place of the poor, which illustrates how far our knowledge has reached on the topic. Yet much more is to be written on this subject.

8

Inscribed in the City: How Did Women Enter 'Written Space'?*

Emily Hemelrijk

To Indelvia Varilla, daughter of Titus, perpetual priestess of the imperial cult, who in return for the honour <of being appointed as a priestess> set up a silver statue with its base costing 50,000 sesterces in the basilica. Because of her munificence, the most sanctified council decreed that a statue should be set up for her at public expense. Gratified by the honour, she reimbursed the expenses.[1]

Iunia Rustica, daughter of Decimus, first and perpetual priestess in the *municipium* of Cartima, restored the public porticos that had decayed due to old age, gave land for a bathhouse, reimbursed the public taxes, set up a bronze statue of Mars in the forum, gave at her own cost porticos next to the bathhouse on her own land, with a pool and a statue of Cupid, and dedicated them after giving a feast and public shows. Having remitted the expense, she made and dedicated the statues that were decreed by the council of Cartima for herself and her son, Gaius Fabius Iunianus, and she likewise made and dedicated at her own cost the statue for Gaius Fabius Fabianus, her husband.[2]

When entering a Roman town, an ancient visitor would meet a bewildering number of written texts vying for his attention: epitaphs on tombs lining the streets towards the city, inscriptions on public buildings in the city centre recording the generosity of benefactors, inscribed bases of portrait statues drawing attention to the achievements and virtues of (local) notables, rows of inscribed altars in sanctuaries testifying to the piety of the dedicators, and graffiti and painted texts conveying all sorts of messages. The red paint and the habit of highlighting the most important part of the message by using larger letters – picking out particularly the name of the donor, honorand or dedicator – drew the attention of the passers-by and presented the text in such a way that even the semi-literate would roughly understand its meaning.[3] Of course, there are huge differences in 'epigraphic density' across the Empire and over time,[4] but any self-respecting Roman city had at least three 'written spaces': the monumental centre, the precincts of the sanctuaries, and the graveyards outside the cities.

When we consider urban public writing with an eye to gender, the predominance of men is striking, especially in the monumental centre of the cities. Male councillors and magistrates ruled the city and decided on the erection of public buildings and honorific statues in public locations. Consequently, it is the names of male notables – together with those of deities and emperors – that are most often recorded on public monuments in the city centre. Women are also underrepresented in funerary and votive inscriptions,[5] but their names and portraits are especially rare in the public areas in the centre of the towns, where references to women arrived on the scene late and remained a minority throughout antiquity. In the course of the first centuries of the Empire, however, we find a growing number of women among the donors of public buildings and among the dedicators and, to a lesser degree, honorands of public statues in the cities of the Latin West. Through the inscriptions on such buildings and statue bases women entered the 'written space' of the city. This chapter addresses women's share in public writing in the most prestigious 'written space' of Roman cities: the urban centre, which despite numerous modern studies on Roman women is an under-examined area.[6] Restricting my discussion to women outside the imperial family, I focus on the presence of non-imperial women in the monumental inscriptions on public buildings and in inscriptions on the bases of public statues. What roles did women play in these inscriptions and how were they presented? Why was there such a discrepancy between cities and regions as regards the number and variety of these inscriptions? Finally, what did this official, written record mean for the women in question and for the city?

Some examples

Let us start with the most prestigious inscriptions: on public buildings financed by women and on public statuary set up for them. In the cities of Italy, such inscriptions are found from the mid- first century BC onwards.[7] One of the earliest examples is that of Mineia, a woman of senatorial rank in Paestum, who built the basilica, and perhaps the temple of Mens Bona opposite it, at the local forum in the first century BC. A statue was erected in her honour by the *magistri* of Mens Bona, probably in the vicinity of the temple of this deity. Moreover, in the niches along the inside walls of the basilica, Mineia set up six statues portraying herself and her male relatives (her two brothers, her husband, her son and her grandson), thus transforming this public building into a monument celebrating her family. In this monument, her own name stands out: not only did she place her own portrait statue in the central niche (flanked by those of her brothers and opposite the statue of her husband), but her name is recorded as the dedicator in all inscriptions of her relatives. To crown it all, her name and benefactions were inscribed in large letters in the marble plaque over the entrance of the basilica.[8] Thus, apart from meeting her inscribed portrait statue on their way to the basilica, visitors came across her name at least seven times. Finally, the local senate of Paestum minted small bronze coins with her portrait and the legend *Mineia M(arci) f(ilia)*, displaying the basilica on the reverse (see Figure 8.1).[9]

Highly placed benefactresses such as Mineia enjoyed great renown and, because of their high rank and the early date of their donations, they may have inspired the empresses rather than the other way round.[10] Yet, women of families whose

Figure 8.1 Small bronze coin (*semis*), British Museum, London. Obverse: *Mineia M(arci) f(ilia)* with the head of Mineia; reverse: a three-storey building, which must be the *basilica* she donated, with the legend *P(aestum) s(emis) S(enatus) C(onsulto)*

importance was merely local could also achieve public recognition by having their names and portraits displayed in the city; their less elevated background and the later date of the inscriptions suggest that some of these women may have followed imperial examples. In the Augustan or early Tiberian period, for instance, Salvia Postuma, a woman of decurial rank, erected an honorific arch over ten metres high adorning the southeast gate of Pola (modern Pula in Istria, see Figure 8.2). It commemorated her deceased son, who had attained equestrian rank and whose over life-size bronze statue crowned the arch, flanked by statues of his father and uncle (or another male relative).

Figure 8.2 Upper part of the arch of Salvia Postuma: winged Victories in the corners above the arched doorway (author's photo)

All the statues have been lost; only their inscribed bases survive. Among the statues, a (posthumous?) statue of Salvia Postuma herself may once have stood (oddly causing the family group to become somewhat asymmetrical), since her name was inscribed between the statue bases of her husband and son. The arch of monumental proportions and standing in a prominent location was adorned with motifs symbolizing triumph (winged Victories) and perhaps even apotheosis (eagle with snake; Figure 8.3); it must have lent the family an almost regal status. As she was the sole donor *and* one of the honorands, Salvia Postuma's name appeared twice: in the central dedication recording her donation 'from her own resources' (*de sua pecunia*) and under what was probably her statue.[11]

A third example are the eight statues (four each) that were erected for the *flaminica perpetua* Cornelia Valentina Tucciana and her husband Marcus Plotius Faustus, a *flamen perpetuus* of equestrian rank, inside and in front of the *macellum* built by the couple in Thamugadi in Numidia in the early third century (only the inscribed bases have been preserved).[12] We may assume that Cornelia Valentina's four statues – some of which were posthumous – depicted her in different dress and poses, perhaps with attributes matching the various roles that were recorded in the inscriptions (wife, mother, priestess, patron). One other statue base of Cornelia Valentina Tucciana has been found outside the city; its original location is unknown.[13] Since Cornelia

Figure 8.3 Relief in the doorway: eagle with snake (author's photo)

Valentina Tucciana also dedicated one of the statues of her husband *and* had her name, together with that of her husband, inscribed over the entrance of the *macellum:* her name is met at least six, or perhaps seven, times in Thamugadi. The multiple statuary of Cornelia Valentina Tucciana and her husband seems an extreme case of self-promotion. Yet, the other examples make clear that such visual prominence may have been less uncommon for women of local upper-class families than we are inclined to think.[14]

Distribution and location

When we turn from these individual examples to the question of how common it was for women to be publicly recorded in the centre of Roman towns in the Latin West, we find great differences from place to place and over time. As can be seen in Figures 8.4 and 8.5, the largest group of the 408 inscriptions on the bases of public honorific statues for women in my corpus stem from Italy (46 per cent), especially central Italy, and from those provinces that were the most densely urbanized and Romanized: Africa Proconsularis and Numidia (27 per cent), and Hispania Baetica and Tarraconensis (20 per cent).[15] By contrast, very few public statues of women have been found in the other provinces listed in Figure 8.4, and none at all in the north-western provinces, such as Gallia Belgica, Germania Inferior and Britannia.[16]

When we compare the 216 inscriptions recording public buildings financed by women as sole donor or in cooperation with a single co-donor (Figures 8.6 and 7), we find a similar percentage for Africa Proconsularis and Numidia (27 per cent), and the

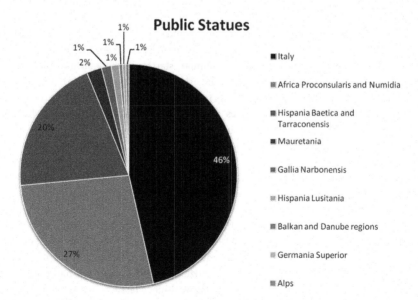

Figure 8.4 Public statues for non-imperial women (n = 408): geographical distribution

Public Statues

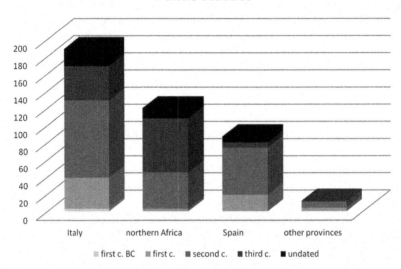

Figure 8.5 Public statues for non-imperial women (n = 408): geographical and chronological distribution

even greater predominance of Italy (51 per cent).[17] However, here southern and eastern Spain (8 per cent) are less well-represented and there is slightly more evidence from the provinces north of Italy (central and northern Gaul, the Germaniae) and from the Balkan and Danubian provinces. Despite these differences, the general pattern is remarkably consistent: the overwhelming majority of women's public statues and buildings are found in the most densely urbanized and Romanized Mediterranean regions. Moreover, their chronological spread is also very similar: starting in Italy around the mid-first century BC, the numbers rise steeply in the first and second centuries AD and drop – in Spain sharply – in the early third. Only in northern Africa does the evidence for women's public buildings and honorific statues continue into the mid-third century, which is in line with the sustained prosperity of urban life in these regions.[18]

Thus, there appear to be marked regional differences in the written presence of women in Roman cities. Whereas in the northern and northwestern provinces women's names are virtually only found on tombs and on votive altars,[19] the cities of the Mediterranean areas feature, in addition, the names and public portrait statues of women in the urban centres. This difference cannot be explained solely by the 'epigraphic habit' or by variations in the density and survival of inscriptions.[20] Saliently, there is a marked connection with the spread of urbanization and Romanization in the Latin West, and specifically with the spread of Roman citizenship and the introduction of Roman civil law. Particularly Roman citizenship and Roman law had great consequences for Roman citizen-women of the wealthier classes – many of whom were from prominent indigenous families – since this allowed virtually all of them to own and control property in their own right, at least at some stage of their lives.[21] By using

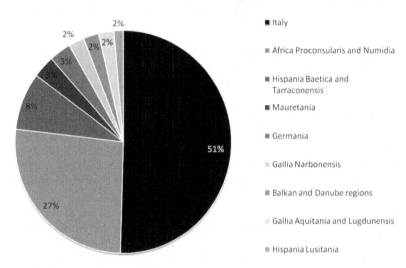

Figure 8.6 Public building (n = 216): geographical distribution

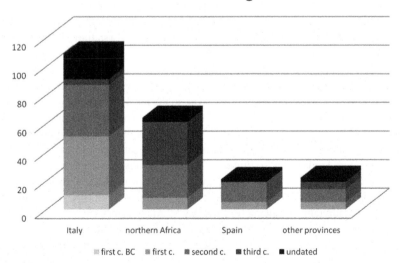

Figure 8.7 Public building (n = 216): geographical and chronological distribution

their wealth for the benefit of their cities, some of these women entered the written space of the urban centres.

Dedicators and honorands

Though high rank and civic merit were important requirements, there were no fixed rules as to who was granted a public statue in what place and for what reason. Decisions about the award of a public statue – and its location, material, format and size – must have taken up a great part of the deliberations of the local council.[22] This provided opportunities for private individuals (relatives, friends, dependants or even the prospective honorand) and civic groups (such as the *plebs* or a civic association) to try and persuade the local council to grant a public statue for a local worthy or, at least, to assign a location for it. Women participated in these negotiations both as dedicators and as honorands. The inscriptions quoted at the beginning of this chapter record the successful negotiations between two priestesses, Indelvia Varilla and Iunia Rustica, and the local councils of their towns, which are presented as a polite exchange of gift and counter gift. Both women were granted public statues as a reward for their munificence. Pleased with the honour, they offered to bear the costs themselves, thus surely quickening the erection of the statues.[23] On her own initiative, Iunia Rustica added a statue of her husband to the statues granted to her and her son. In all likelihood, she also had a say in the text of the inscriptions; the base of her own statue records her name (in the nominative) at the head of the text summing up all her benefactions to the city, and she probably added her name as the dedicator of the other statues (both bases and statues are lost). Thus, apart from an unknown number of inscriptions recording her generosity on her public buildings, her name featured at least three times on statue bases in the city centre.

Unfortunately, due to the transfer and reuse of statues (and their bases) from antiquity onwards, the original location of honorific statues of women and their relation to neighbouring statues and buildings are mostly unknown. Together with its size and material, and the social rank of its dedicator(s), the location of a statue and its relation to other statues and buildings expressed differences in social standing.[24] As a rule, public honours for women are less prominent than those for men. Not only are honorific statues of women much rarer, but women (with the exception of those of imperial rank) were less often granted a statue in the forum or 'in the most frequented place' (*frequentissimo loco or loco celeberrimo*). Moreover, their statues were usually somewhat smaller than those of males.[25] Yet, just as for men (though less often), several statues might be granted to a single woman of rank or merit within the same city. Five public statues were granted to Annia Aelia Restituta, for instance, because of her promise to build a theatre in her hometown of Calama in Numidia, and at least two statues were erected in the local forum for Fabia Bira, first priestess of the imperial cult (*flaminica prima*) of Volubilis in Mauretania Tingitana (present-day Morocco). Since Fabia Bira also set up statues for others, her name was attested at least six times in her town.[26]

This brings us to women's contribution to the dedication of public statues. In contrast to the award of a public statue (which was restricted to the most wealthy, high-ranking or meritorious citizens of a town), setting up a statue for others was also open to people of more modest social standing. Though less prestigious than receiving one, dedicating a public statue brought honour by association; the names of the honorand and dedicator featured together in the same inscription, though, obviously, the name of the honorand took pride of place. As we have seen, women participated in the Roman 'statuary habit', setting up public statues for themselves and for relatives. Thus, visitors to Roman towns in Italy and the Mediterranean areas were confronted with the names of women much more frequently than their rare honorific statues suggest. To gain some idea of women's written presence in the urban centres in comparison with that of men, I have examined the statue bases of two regions studied by Geza Alföldy: Venetia and Istria (*regio* 10) in northern Italy, and the *conventus Tarraconensis* in Spain.[27] In both regions, women appear to have been a minority in public writing: only 14 (*regio* 10) to 20 (*conventus Tarraconensis*) per cent of the names of non-imperial persons on public statue bases are female. Moreover, women more often set up a statue than received one (whereas the inverse holds for men): 23 (*regio* 10) to 31 (*conventus Tarraconensis*) per cent of the dedicators of public statues were female, as opposed to 3 to 12 per cent of the honorands.

As regards the recipients of their statues, relatives predominate, followed at some distance by deities.[28] Male dedicators show a wider range and a more even spread of beneficiaries, who also comprise patrons, friends, and members of the imperial family. Thus, the public profile of women is more restricted, both as regards the number of their statues (set up or received) and in the range of their dedicatees. Their virtual confinement to relatives and deities – with its implication of religious piety and devotion to their families – accords with Roman notions of female propriety, but it also shows that the social esteem of women was lower than that of men. In contrast to statues for the emperor, for instance, statues for relatives and deities were open to the widest range of dedicators. Nevertheless, the public presence of women in the written space of the urban centres in these regions should not be underestimated. To generalize from the number of women recorded on public statue bases in *regio* 10 and in the *conventus Tarraconensis* to Italy and the Mediterranean regions of the Latin West, roughly one in every five or six names of non-imperial individuals on public statue bases was that of a woman. Though much more often mentioned as dedicators than as honorands – and therefore usually carved in smaller letters – the names of women could not be overlooked in the public inscriptions of a Roman town. By erecting statues for deities and relatives, women not only conformed to Roman rules of propriety, but also preserved their names in the public domain.

Responsible citizens and virtuous matrons

This brings us to the representation and, to a lesser extent, self-representation, of women in public writing. In descending order of frequency, women were honoured in public inscriptions by referring to their high rank and the careers of their male relatives, their civic merits and, rarely, their traditional female virtues. As we see in Figure 8.8, women of families of the elite are greatly over-represented: sixty-one per cent of the public statues of non-imperial women were erected for women of decurial, equestrian and senatorial families, which formed only a tiny percentage of the population. Thirty-nine per cent of the statues were set up for wealthy and deserving women of (probably) non-elite rank, including three per cent for women who were freed or related to freedmen. The wording of the inscriptions shows a marked connection with (high) rank. As a rule, the higher the rank and family of the honorand, the less often personal merits are recorded.[29] Thus, honorific inscriptions for women of consular, or more generally senatorial, rank stress their elevated status, the careers of their male relatives, and their awe-inspiring pedigree, but often omit benefactions or other civic merits.[30] In this respect, their statues resemble those of the empresses, which needed no justification. Of course, this does not mean that these women had no civic merits, nor does it imply that all women of senatorial rank received a public statue in their hometowns. Yet, it does show that high rank and family connections were a socially accepted reason for a public statue. For the city, setting up a statue to a high-ranking woman was not without self-interest. Since a public statue was regarded as a gift, the honorand (and her family) were encouraged to reciprocate with benefactions or other services to the city. Moreover, by publicly associating itself with a female compatriot of the highest rank, the city shared in her glory.

Lower down the social scale, civic merits, such as lavish benefactions or the exemplary fulfilment of an expensive priesthood, are more often recorded as the reason for a public statue. Apparently, the lower down we get, the greater the effort a woman had to make to achieve, and justify, the honour of a public statue. With some exceptions, a public statue was beyond the expectations of almost all women of modest social standing or unfree birth; they had to content themselves with setting

Social Status

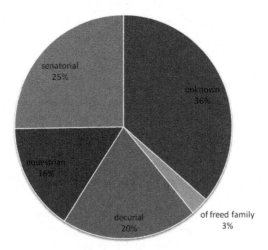

Figure 8.8 Social status of female recipients of public statues (n = 408)

Figure 8.9 Cassia Victoria and her husband in the pediment of the temple of the Augustales in Misenum (photo courtesy of Paola Miniero, 2000, 40)

up statues for others, or with portrait statues in, or on, their tombs.[31] However, by lavish benefactions a wealthy woman of non-elite family could compensate for her modest social background and publicize her name and achievements in the urban centre. Cassia Victoria, for example, priestess of the Augustales of Misenum around 165, embellished the temple of the Augustales near the local forum in her own name and that of her husband with a marble *pronaos*, giving a banquet and a handout to celebrate its dedication.[32] Her name and priesthood are recorded prominently in the first words of the monumental inscription on the frieze of the *pronaos*. Moreover, in the two-metre high pediment above the inscription, her portrait and that of her husband are displayed, encircled by a wreath of oak leaves held by two winged Victories (possibly a word-play on her *cognomen*, Victoria; Figure 8.9). The portraits follow imperial models: that of her (deceased?) husband resembles the traits and hairstyle of the late Antoninus Pius, whereas her own portrait is inspired by contemporaneous portraits of his daughter, Faustina Minor.[33] The choice of such self-representation in the pediment of a temple devoted to the imperial cult seems an instance of self-glorification but, at the same time, it expressed the couple's loyalty to the imperial family. The inscription emphasizes the generosity of Cassia Victoria, her priesthood *and* her familial devotion, since she includes her husband's portrait and name (carved below hers) in her donation. Thus, she presents herself not only as a woman of great wealth and civic merit, but also as a loyal wife.

Similar forms of public representation and self-representation as a responsible citizen are found in the inscriptions on the bases of public statues of women that praise their munificence, civic priesthood or, more generally, their 'merits' (*merita*), or 'love' (*amor*) for the city.[34] In exceptional cases, deserving women were honoured as the patroness (*patrona*) or mother (*mater*) of a city.[35] Thus, they are presented first and foremost as benevolent and responsible female citizens. Public praise of traditional feminine virtues, such as chastity and modesty, is rarer but, of course, these virtues were displayed by the modest dress and comportment of the portrait statues.[36] Thus, statue and inscription complement each other. The fact that statues of women were often part of a family group and that their statue bases record the careers of their male relatives accords with the Roman ideal of female devotion to the family, but it does not mean that these statues were set up solely *because* of their families. To my mind, the modern distinction between individual honour and the honouring of the family is too rigid: the wealth, munificence, priesthoods and achievements of both its male and female members reflected on the family as a whole. Just as women were honoured for the merits of a male relative, so men might occasionally be praised for those of a female relative.[37] In sum, women's public image in the urban centre shows a combination of high rank, prominent family, civic merits, traditional female virtuousness, and familial devotion. It is this blending of family connections and female virtuousness, on the one hand, and individual wealth and achievement, on the other, that must have eased women's entry into the written space of the urban centre.

Women in the written space of Roman cities

Though dominated by the names and achievements of men, the public areas of the Roman cities of Italy and the Mediterranean regions of the Latin West exhibited a distinct minority of statues set up by and – less frequently – for women, thus allowing them a permanent presence in the most important written space of their towns. Moreover, the public buildings they donated kept their names and generosity alive – in some cases, such as Eumachia's building at the Forum of Pompeii and Ummidia Quadratilla's amphitheatre in Casinum – even to the present day.[38] In contrast to the broader social range of women setting up votive altars in sanctuaries or commemorated in funerary inscriptions, most of the women recorded in the public areas of Roman towns were from high-ranking families or wealthy families that aspired to elite status. Having one's name inscribed in stone or bronze in the urban centre meant public recognition and perpetual remembrance, which was of the utmost importance for the honorands *and* for their families and descendants. In presenting the honorand as an exemplary woman, the honorific statues and inscriptions formed a model for other women who aspired to public prestige. Thus, the erection of public statues for women was probably a self-reinforcing process: the more statues were set up for highly placed women, the more a similar honour was sought after by others. As a result, Roman cities of Italy and the Latin-speaking provinces in the first three centuries of the Empire showed a small but growing number of public statues for women. Together with women's more frequent dedications of statues and their donations of public buildings, these statues and inscriptions enriched the written space of the urban centre.

Contrary to the conventional praise for female virtues in the funerary inscriptions of women on the outskirts of Roman towns, their public image in the urban centre combined the ideal of the distinguished and responsible female citizen with that of the exemplary Roman *matrona*.[39] Moreover, the women whose names we meet in the public areas of Roman towns are the most prominent and ambitious, for whom Pliny's almost regal characterization of Ummidia Quadratilla as *princeps femina* (leading lady) seems an apt description.[40] Of course, neither the statues nor the inscriptions should be taken at face value; they highlight what was successful and socially desirable, while concealing complicated behind-the-scenes negotiations and failures. Thus, they illustrate social ideals rather than the everyday reality of Roman towns. Yet, these inscriptions show how, and to what extent, women were able to make their mark in the 'written space' of Roman cities; at the same time, such representations broadened the traditional ideals of femininity to include the figure of the highly placed and responsible female citizen.

Notes

* This chapter is based on a chapter of my forthcoming book *Hidden Lives – Public Personae. Women and Civic Life in Italy and the Latin West during the Roman Principate*. I thank the Netherlands Organization for Scientific Research (NWO) for their financial support of this research project.
1 *AE* 1982, 682 (Nemausus, Gallia Narbonensis, AD 161–200): *Indelviae T(iti) fil(iae)/ Valerillae/flaminicae/perpetuae/quae pro eo honore/statuam argenteam cum/basi ex HS L M N(quinquaginta milibus nummum)/in basilica posuit/ob quam munificentiam/ ordo sanctissimus/statuam ei ponendam/de publico decrevit/quae honore contenta/ inpendium remisit*. Unless otherwise stated, the English translations of the inscriptions are my own.
2 *CIL* 2.1956 = *ILS* 5512 = *ILMMalaga* 6 (Cartima, Hispania Baetica, late first century AD): *Iunia D(ecimi) f(ilia) Rustica sacerdos/perpetua et prima in municipio Cartimitan[o]/porticus public(as) vetustate corruptas refecit solum/balinei dedit vectigalia publica vindicavit signum/aereum Martis in foro posuit porticus ad balineum/solo suo cum piscina et signo Cupidinis epulo dato/et spectaculis editis d(e) p(ecunia) s(ua) d(edit) d(edicavit) statuas sibi et C(aio) Fabio/Iuniano f(ilio) suo ab ordine Cartimitanorum decretas/remissa impensa item statuam C(aio) Fabio Fabiano viro suo/d(e) p(ecunia) s(ua) f(actas) d(edit)*.
3 For ancient literacy, see Harris, 1989; Beard et al., 1991; and Johnson and Parker, 2009. Though full literacy was restricted to a small group, many people were able to read brief formulaic inscriptions (cf. Petronius, *Sat.*, 58.7: *lapidarias litteras scio*) or at least the name of the honorand of a public statue or that of the donor of a public building; many more must have known his or her name and deeds from hearsay.
4 For 'epigraphic density', see Harris, 1989, pp. 265–8; Woolf, 1996, pp. 36–7 and 1998, pp. 82–105; Laurence, Esmonde Cleary and Sears, 2011, pp. 310–1. For regional differentiation, see Cooley, 2002a.
5 Eck, forthcoming, 2013.
6 Eck, forthcoming, 2013 on women's public presence in Italy (on the basis of two cities); similarly, on their presence in two cities in northern Africa, Witschel, forthcoming, 2013.
7 See Hemelrijk, 2005 on the introduction of public statues for women in the Latin West. In Italy in the third and second centuries BC, virtually all benefactors were local magistrates and city patrons and thus invariably male, Jouffroy, 1986, pp. 59–61; see also Pobjoy, 2000 on the construction of public buildings as part of the duties of local magistrates and other civic officials.
8 *ILPaestum* 163, a very damaged inscription suggesting that she also donated the *porticus* and pavement in front of the basilica. Torelli, 1996 believes that she also

built the temple of Mens Bona, but apart from the statue erected for her by the *magistri Mentis Bonae* (*ILPaestum* 18) there is no evidence to support this. For the statues she erected for herself and her relatives in the basilica: *ILPaestum* 81–5 and *AE* 1975, 248–50; both sides of the basilica had three niches for statues: on one side the statue of Mineia was flanked by statues of her brothers, on the other her husband was portrayed, flanked by statues of their son and grandson.

9   For the bronze coins of Mineia (*semis* and *quadrans*), see Crawford, 1973, pp. 52–5 (who assumes – to my mind mistakenly in view of the legend *P(aestum) s(emis) S(enatus) C(onsulto)* – that the coins were struck by Mineia herself as a gift to her fellow citizens) and 97–9, no. 38a–c with pl. XI.
Other bronze coins: a *quadrans* of Mineia, 15mm, 2.8g: http://www.wildwinds. com/coins/greece/lucania/poseidonia/i.html (last accessed 4th February 2013) and http://www.vcoins.com/ancient/romanumismatics/store/viewItem. asp?idProduct=6615 (last accessed 4th February 2013) (3.04g, 16mm) and, for several coins of Mineia (between 15 and 18mm): http://www.acsearch.info/search. html?search=similar%3A273066 (last accessed 4th February 2013). Weiss, 2005, p. 63 mentions her coinage together with coin issues funded by benefactors, which are found mainly in the Greek East. However, Mineia's coinage does not show any indication (such as *d(e) s(ua) p(ecunia)*), which would support this.

10   The same holds for Octavia, who improved and decorated the Bona Dea temple in Ostia in 70–60 BC: *CIL* 1.3025 = *AE* 2004, +361 = *AE* 1973, 127.

11   *CIL* 5.50 = *ILS* 2229 = *Inscr.Ital.* 10.1.72 (Pola, Italia, *regio* 10), see Letzner, 2005, pp. 25–32 (early Tiberian period); Woodhull, 2004, pp. 82–90 (Augustan); and von Hesberg, 1992, pp. 277–9.

12   See also Sears in this volume.

13   Statues of Cornelia Valentina Tucciana: *CIL* 8.17905, 2396–8, *AE* 1987, 1072 = *AE* 1992, 1833 (Thamugadi, Numidia; early third century); statues of Marcus Plotius Faustus: *CIL* 8.2399, 2394/5, 17904; building inscription of the couple: *AE* 1980, 956; see Zimmer, 1992, pp. 312–13; Witschel, 1995, p. 344; and Wilson, 2007, pp. 313–4.

14   Of course, this was restricted to the topmost families; men of such families received even more statues, see Eck, 2010, p. 101: 25 statues for a male honorand in Pergamon. The custom of multiple statues may have been more widespread in the Greek East, see van Bremen, 1996, Chapter 6, and Trimble, 2011, Chapters 4 and 5 on women's visual prominence.

15   Despite valid criticisms of the use of the concept, summarized by Mattingly, 2011, pp. 38–40 and 204–7, I shall here retain the term 'Romanization', for want of a better term for the participation in a way of life, customs and values, which, despite local and regional differences, were recognized as 'Roman', see Hemelrijk, forthcoming, Chapter1.

16   This distribution is roughly similar to the general distribution of my corpus of inscriptions for women's civic roles in the Latin West. For a more detailed treatment, see Hemelrijk, forthcoming in 2013.

17   Almost 30 per cent of the public buildings funded by women are joint donations by a couple or by a woman together with her father or son. I here exclude the more common family donations (by husband, wife and children). For a more detailed treatment, see Hemelrijk, forthcoming.

18   For the economic prosperity of the North African cities in the second and third centuries, see Duncan-Jones, 2004; Laurence, Esmonde Cleary, and Sears, 2011, pp. 301–3, 307 and 316.

19 Spickermann, 1994, see also Hemelrijk, forthcoming in 2013.

20 The spread of my corpus of inscriptions differs from that of the 'epigraphic habit' in several respects, for instance in the virtual absence of evidence from the city of Rome, where public building and honorific statues were increasingly reserved for members of the imperial family, see Hemelrijk, forthcoming in 2013; Eck, 1984 and 1992; and Lahusen, 1983, pp. 97–107.

21 Hemelrijk, 2012. For the legal capacity of Roman women *sui iuris* as property owners under the Empire, see Gardner, 1990, 1993, pp. 85–109 and 1995; see also Treggiari, 1991. For the spread of Roman citizenship and Roman law, also among *civitates* who were not compelled to use Roman law, see Lintott, 1993, pp. 129–45 and 154–60, and Fear, 1996, 152–6 and 162–9. Municipal charters, like that of Irni, also stimulated non-Roman citizens to live according to Roman law, *inter alia* by dealing with them *as if* they were Roman citizens, see Gardner, 1993, pp. 188–90 and 2001.

22 See n. 25; cf. van Nijf, 2011, p. 235 on Termessos in the Greek East.

23 Eck, 1997, p. 317 suggests that the costs were negotiated before a statue was awarded and that in many cases the willingness of honorands or relatives to pay for the statue was decisive for the grant. I have counted 22 women in my corpus who bore the costs of their own statue; a much larger number bore the costs of public statues granted to (mainly male) relatives. Some examples: for husbands: *CIL* 2.1342 = *IRPCadiz* 507 (Lacilbula, Hispania Baetica), *CIL* 2.7.799 = *CIL* 2.2344 = *AE* 1987, 539 = *AE* 1992, 982 = *AE* 1999, 901 (Mellaria, Hispania Baetica); for sons: *CIL* 2, 3252 = *CILA* 3, 1, 48 (Baesucci, Hisp. Baet.), *CIL* 2.1065 = *CILA* 2.1.225 (Arva, Hispania Baetica), *CIL* 2.5.49 = *CILA* 3, 1, 20 = *AE* 1990, 635 (Aurgi, Hispania Baetica), *AE* 1958, 4 = *CILA* 3.1.101 (Castulo, Hispania Tarraconensis).

24 On the finely graded hierarchy of statuary honours, see Alföldy, 1979 and 1984; Zimmer, 1992, pp. 308–9; and Witschel, 1995. For the relocation of female statues, see Murer, 2013.

25 In a few cases, the location is mentioned in the inscription; for instance, Grattia Paulla, the wife and mother of local *duumviri* of Catina in Sicily, was granted a public funeral and a (posthumous) statue in the local forum by decurial decree: *AE* 1989, 341m = *ILSicilia* 43 (Catina, Sicily, first half of the first c. AD): *funere publico elata et lo[co]/publico sepulta et sta[tua]/data in foro d(ecurionum) d(ecreto)*. *AE* 1910, 203 = *AE* 2003, +352 (Brindisium, Italia *regio* 2; AD 144): a statue in memory of Clodia Anthianilla *frequentis/ simo loco*. *CIL* 10.1784 = *ILS* 6334 (Puteoli, Italia *regio* 1; AD 187): three statues in memory of Gavia Marciana to be erected in locations of her relatives' choice: *locisq(ue)/ tribus concedendis / quae ipsi elegerint*. *CIL* 8.15880 = *ILTun* 1593 (Sicca Veneria, Africa Proconsularis): a statue for Licinia Severa 'in the most beautiful and busiest place' *([loco] pulcherrimo atque celeberrimo)*. All statues were decreed in connection with public funerals. For differences in size between male and female portrait statues, see Fejfer, 2008, pp. 285–305 and 331–69, and Smith, 1998, p. 63: portrait statues of non-imperial women (without base) are roughly between 1.75 and 2 metres high – but taller statues occur – whereas statues of non-imperial men are usually 2.10– 2.20 metres in height.

26 Annia Aelia Restituta (Calama, Numidia; AD 161–9): *ILAlg.* 1.287 = *CIL* 8.5366: *ordo univer/sus statua[s] n(umero) quinq(ue) de pu[bl(ico)] faciend[as]/decrevit*; *ILAlg.* 1, 286 = *CIL* 8.5365 = *CIL* 8.17495: *or/do ob eam causam sta/tuas quinque de pu/ blico pon[i] censuis/set*. Fabia Bira: *IAM* 2.439 = *ILAfr.* 630 = *ILM* 129 (Volubilis, Maururetania Tingitana, c. AD 54) and *IAM* 2.440 = *ILAfr.* 631 = *ILM* 130. The bases are found *in situ*. *IAM* 2.368, found in the forum, also seems to have belonged to a statue in honour of her. Her name is recorded in several other inscriptions in the city: *IAM* 2.342, 448 and 449.

27　Alföldy 1979: 453 statue bases and 1984: 275 bases; I have excluded statue bases without a name of a non-imperial individual (mainly statues set up by the city in honour of members of the imperial family or deities) and statue bases that may more plausibly be called funerary. This reduces the number of bases used for my calculations to 330 (with 385 names of men and 98 of women) and 188 (with 207 names of men and 34 of women), respectively. However, in many cases public (or private) display cannot be established with certainty. For a more detailed treatment, see Hemelrijk, forthcoming.

28　Cf. also Navarro Caballero, 2001 and 2004 on statues set up by women in the Spanish provinces.

29　Apart from senatorial women, women had no formal claim to elite (equestrian or decurial) rank. Yet, since they were in practice included in the dignity (and constraints) of the rank of their father or husband, I refer to them as women of equestrian or decurial rank, see Hemelrijk, 1999, pp. 11–2.

30　A typical example is Acilia Manliola, who was honoured with a statue in Allifae in central Italy in the early third century, as the daughter, granddaughter and great-granddaughter of consuls, see *CIL* 9.2333 = *ILS* 1133 (Alifae, Italia *regio* 4).

31　See Hemelrijk (2008) on the difference in public honour for patronesses and 'mothers' of civic associations. On the importance of funerary statuary for non-elite groups see, among others, D'Ambra, 2002. For regional differentiation, cf. the difference between Tarraconensis and northern Italy in the number of statues for Augustales, Alföldy, 1979 and 1984.

32　*AE* 1993, 477 (Misenum, Italia regio 1; AD 165): *Cassia C(ai) fil(ia) Victoria, sacerdos Augustalium, pronaum cum columnis et epistyliis, nomine suo et / L(uci) Laecanii Primitivi, mariti sui, ob eximiam eorum erga se benivolentiam, cuius dedic(atione) epulum et sing(ulis) HS XII n(ummum) dedit* ('Cassia Victoria, daughter of Gaius, priestess of the Augustales, donated the pronaos with its columns and epistyle in her own name and that of her husband, Lucius Laecanius Primitivus, because of their [i.e. the Augustales] extraordinary benevolence towards herself [or themselves]. To celebrate its dedication she gave a banquet and a handout of twelve sesterces each').

33　See Adamo Muscettola, 2000, pp. 39–42 and Hemelrijk, 2012.

34　Some examples: Cassia Cornelia Prisca, *sacerdos Augustae et patriae* in Formiae (Italia *regio* 1, after AD 199), was honoured with a public statue *pro splendore/ munificentiae eius* (*AE* 1971, 79) and Licinia Rufina, *sacerdos perpetua* in three cities of Baetica in the late second–early third century, was honoured as *amantissima civium suorum* and *ob merita eius* (*CIL* 2, 5, 387 = *ILS* 6909 = *CIL* 2, 1572 = *ILPGranada* 127; Ipsca, Hisp.Baet.).

35　Nicols, 1989; Hemelrijk, 2004, 2008 and 2012.

36　Some examples: *CIL* 10.483 = *ILPaestum* 99 = *ILS* 6448 (Paestum, Italia *regio* 3; ca. AD 240): *Digitiae L(uci) f(iliae) Rufinae/ob eximiam castitatem ei/dem(!) verecundiamque/eius* ("because of her extraordinary chastity and modesty") and Gavia Marciana, an 'honourable matron of incomparable moral discipline', was praised for 'her extraordinary decency and admirable chastity': *CIL* 10.1784 = *ILS* 6334 (Puteoli, Italia *regio* 1; AD 187): *Gaviae M(arci) fil(iae)/Marcianae/honestae et incompara/bilis sectae matron(ae) ..... ob eximi[u]m pu/dorem et admirabilem cas[tit]a/tem. CIL* 11.4660 = *AE* 1985, 363 (Tuder, Italia *regio* 6; AD 270–75): Publicia Honesta is praised as a *matrona castissima*.

37　Some examples: *CIL* 9.698 (Sipontum, Italia *regio* 2; second century AD): Magia Severina was awarded a public statue by the decurions and the people 'because of the merits of her father' (*ob merita/Q(uinti) Magi Seve/ri patris eius*), and the merits of a son are recorded in *ILS* 6471 (Petelia, Italia, *regio* 3; AD 138–61): *ob merita ... fili eius.* Conversely, some male statues were set up because of the munificence of a female relative, see, for instance, *AE* 1917/18, 23 = *ILAfr.* 280 (Thuburbo Maius, Africa Proconsularis; late second century AD): the equestrian Publius Attius Extricatianus was honoured with a public statue recording his career 'because of the honourable munificence of his mother Iulia Bassilia' (*ob honestam munificentiam Iuliae Bassiliae ... matris eius*). *AE* 1958, 4 = *CILA* 3. 1.101 (Castulo, Hispania Tarraconensis; first half of the second century AD): a statue was set up for L. Cornelius Marullus 'because of the liberality of Cornelia Marullina, his mother' (*pro liberalitate Cor(neliae)/ Marullinae matris/eius*).

38   Public buildings were called after the donor as long as the building was in use, Wesch-Klein, 1989, pp. 187–8. The Eumachia building in Pompeii (*CIL* 10.810/1 = *ILS* 3785 = *AE* 2001, +793) and the amphitheatre of Ummidia Quadratilla in Casinum (*CIL* 10.5183 = *ILS* 5628 = *EAOR* 4.46 = *AE* 1991, +326) are still referred to by the names of the original donors.

39   For the difference between women's public image in honorary and funerary inscriptions from Italy, see Forbis, 1990.

40   Plin. *Ep.* 7.24.

9

Slaves and Children in a Roman Villa: Writing and Space in the Villa San Marco at Stabiae

Eamonn Baldwin, Helen Moulden and Ray Laurence

There is an awareness of the limitations of exploring graffiti in their published print-media formats. The principal one being that it is difficult and often impossible to relate the text to the physical location where it was originally written.[1] It is with this in mind, that we explore, in this chapter, the possibilities of combining the use of desk-based spatial analysis and a field-based application of 3D laser scanning in the study of Roman graffiti. The Villa San Marco was chosen as a case study[2] with a focus on using these techniques to understand the role of children and slaves in the production of graffiti. Importantly, service areas with associated graffiti have been identified in the villa[3] and have already been documented and published in a traditional format. As the villa is partially excavated, and was, at the time of the fieldwork, undergoing restoration, the study area was limited to 43 rooms of the villa, 20 of which contain documented examples of graffiti (see Figures 9.1 and 9.2). The primary platform for the spatial analysis was a schematic plan of the Villa San Marco which was derived digitally from a plan published in Barbet and Miniero.[4]

Previous studies

Studies of graffiti traditionally revolved around a rather basic rationale of transcription and publication without a full record of their precise position and those undertaken previously at Villa San Marco are of this nature. In 1999, Antonio Varone identified, visually, the areas of graffiti and specific instances of graffiti.[5] He also identified three separate classes of ancient graffiti: textual, numerical and pictorial. By comparison, Martin Langner's more recent study, *Antike Graffitizeichnungen* placed a much greater emphasis on pictorial graffiti.[6] His collection of pictorial graffiti from the Villa San Marco supplements that completed by Varone, and includes many examples that are absent in the initial work. While the study by Langner is invaluable when researching pictorial graffiti, the emphasis on one particular type of evidence still maintains the dichotomy between pictorial, textual and numerical graffiti. Methodologically, these two studies do not relate the graffiti to the persons who created them. In the case of

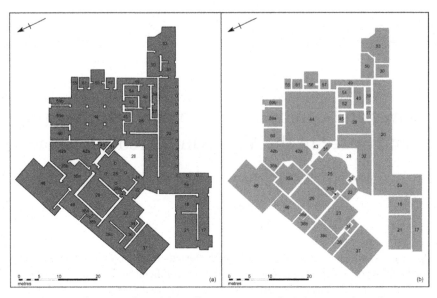

Figure 9.1a Schematic plan of the Villa San Marco

Figure 9.1b Schematic plan of space within the villa

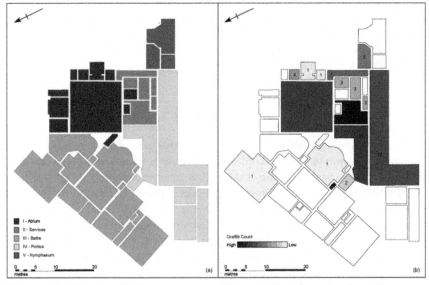

Figure 9.2a Division of villa into domestic areas

Figure 9.2b Schematic plan with quantity of documented graffiti per room

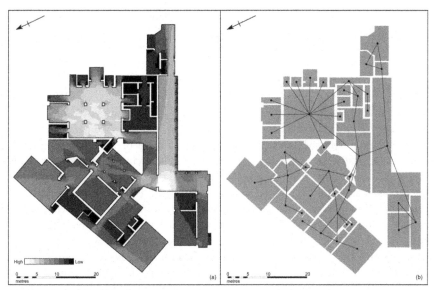

Figure 9.3a Visibility analysis graph displaying connectivity within the villa based on the schematic plan presented in Figure 9.1a

Figure 9.3b Convex map analysis graph displaying linkages within the villa based on Figure 9.1b

children, we may see them as a group that is somewhat marginal – yet, did produce graffiti.[7] The work of Katherine Huntley, drawing on the discipline of developmental psychology, looks at the patterns of pictorial graffiti and their height above floor level to identify a presence of children in the corpus of graffiti from Pompeii.[8] Unlike adults, children tend to draw to characterize rather than replicate (for example a human figure walking in profile will have both eyes, both legs and both arms visible even though certain aspects should be hidden).[9] This work shifts discussion away from subjective perceptions of 'primitive execution' or 'simple design' to associate graffiti with children and allows us to see into the mentality of childhood.[10] Like children, slaves were a ubiquitous part of Roman households, but there is a view that they contributed little to the material record from which archaeologists might be able to identify them.[11] Henrik Mouritsen's analysis of the graffiti from the Insula of the Menander in Pompeii suggests a way forward. He examines the spatial context of the graffiti, which identified clusters in the latrines and kitchen[12] that might have been produced specifically by slaves and/or freedmen. It is the spatial awareness that allows him to present an understanding of who produced specific graffiti in the household, a principle that underpins the current work undertaken at Villa San Marco.

Mention should be made here of Rebecca Benefiel's work that has attempted to account for the position of graffiti in the House of the Four Styles, the House of Maius Castricius in Pompeii, and graffiti within the wider context of Pompeii.[13] Her research has attempted to move away from traditional recording by transcription and to a fuller understanding of the spatial location or visual effect of graffiti.[14] Underpinning this approach has been the use of a Geographical Information System (GIS) database of the wall inscriptions.[15]

Quantitative analysis

The initial step was amalgamating the two previous graffiti studies of Varone (1999) and Langner (2001) to create a working dataset of all graffiti previously documented at the Villa San Marco.[16] This provided a pool of more or less 100 examples of documented graffiti for spatial analysis. The 100 graffiti documented across 20 rooms at the Villa San Marco may be grouped into three types (pictorial, numerical and textual) as in standard in similar discussions, and their distribution can be explored across the study area (summarized in Table 9.1a–c) on the basis of household areas as defined in Barbet and Miniero, or less coarsely, across individual rooms (summarized in Table 9.2).[17] For the analysis, the external area[18] is treated as a room, as is the double-portal 25a.[19] One graffito survives on the door lintel between rooms 40 and 26 (the kitchen) and is treated in this section as belonging in neither. This raises the interesting question of whether or not these two rooms were screened or divided from each other, or perhaps open plan.

While each type is well represented throughout the study area, the pictorial type is dominant at 44 per cent of total graffiti, three-quarters of which are distributed throughout the bath and portico areas (Table 9.1a), with Room 25a, a double-door into the baths and the smallest room in the villa, containing 36 per cent of all pictorial-type graffiti (Table 9.2). It is interesting that of the 18 graffiti recorded in the baths area, a household quarter frequented by slaves, masters and guests and one where a range of graffiti types may have been expected, 100 per cent are pictorial (Table 9.1a). Just over a third of these were identified (as mentioned above) in one of the most confined spaces of the baths area, and indeed the villa – Room 25a, which measures less than 1.3m^2 in area (Table 9.2). This portal room is currently thought to have functioned (in contrast or in tandem to corresponding room 24) as a double door air-lock controlling temperature and access between the baths and the corridor.[20] The presence of graffiti may be a by-product of a person/slave waiting to open the doors to alter the temperature within the baths. If so, we may assume that the person(s) preferred to draw images to textual expression. The presence of these drawings at a height of 120–180 c.m. suggests that they cannot be attributed to a younger child.

In contrast, nearly three-quarters of all numerical graffiti, which comprises 30 per cent of all graffiti recorded in the villa, is concentrated in the service area (Table 9.1a). Over half of these examples are in the kitchen, equating to 19 per cent of all total graffiti recorded throughout the villa (Table 9.2). The kitchen, with its associated service rooms, is associated with slave-based household production of food for their owners and guests. It is here that we find examples of the use of numbers on walls, whereas the elite may have used other media (wax-tablets) to perform calculations.

Two-thirds of all types of graffiti are more or less evenly shared between the service area and the portico area; however, where the service area is dominated by numerical graffiti (58 per cent of numerical total), the portico area displays an even spread of pictorial (47 per cent of pictorial total) and textual (47 per cent of textual total) types (Table 9.1a). It would seem therefore, that numerical examples are obviously functional and explicit in terms of location within the villa; other examples being confined specifically to room 61 in the Atrium area and room 50 in the Nymphaeum area (Table 9.1a). Although Barbet and Miniero designate the latter as belonging to the Nymphaeum area,[21] this room is accessible only from the peristyle via Rooms 30 and 53; its small window aperture overlooks only the forecourt and entrance, and could well be described as a private back room of some status judging from the wall paintings.

However, considering the more transitory nature of the portico areas which connect various destinations within the household, it could be fair to suggest that their even mix of pictorial and textual graffiti was intended for display. Interestingly, if the portico areas are considered another crossover zone shared by all members of the household, it becomes harder to attribute authorship (even broadly) to various graffiti. What is clear though is a spatial relationship between rooms and graffiti: the atrium (the second largest room) has relatively few graffiti; whereas other larger rooms have a greater number (Table 9.2).

Height and age of the writer

There is logic in the concept of using height as a defining factor in identifying children's graffiti – children are typically shorter than adults. The attribution of child graffiti is conventionally governed by the equation of the height-above-floor level with the eye level of the graffitist, where 110 cm is the generally accepted approximation of eye level for young children.[22] The heights of graffiti associated with children in Huntley's study were found no lower than 55 cm, and no higher than 110 cm.[23] It cannot be the sole identifier however, as the height does not take into account the furniture that would have existed within a household and the ability of children to climb, or seated adults. For example, a height of 80 cm would be consistent with the low couches found in *triclinia*.[24] If we accept, for simplicity and for the purpose of preliminary quantitative analysis, the conventional approximation of 'child' graffiti at 110 cm or below, it is interesting that one-fifth of surviving graffiti occurs under 110 cm. This figure is to a greater or lesser extent consistent across various areas within the villa (Table 9.1b and 9.1c). Of the examples surviving below 110 cm, only two are of numerical type, with no numerals surviving below 82 cm. Perhaps contrary to expectation, the surviving examples of graffiti at the lowest height above the floor are textual – where we may have expected (child-like) pictorial graffiti. Elsewhere, an 'alphabet' graffito (often associated with early learning i.e., children) occurs at a height of 126.5 cm in Corridor 22 but it could represent the presence of a teacher or an adult slave.[25] There would seem to be patterns to the graffiti, but these are not necessarily answered via the basic quantification by room type, partly because graffiti are a visual medium that need not be functionally determined in their placement and that this placement may only be understood via a more precise understanding of their location.[26]

Space syntax

Space syntax theory was developed in the late 1970s and has become a tool for the analysis of the built environment of Pompeii and the Vesuvian sites.[27] Its resurgence in the twenty-first century is based on the premise that social relations are structured by space; for example, Newsome applies space syntax analysis to investigate the change and control of movement through, and around, focal points in the urban layout of Pompeii. Earlier work by Grahame applied these techniques to the ordering of internal space in Pompeian houses.[28] These space syntax studies typically utilized access map analysis to emphasize the relationship between all spaces within a system;[29] this involved a straightforward conversion of architectural ground plans to abstract 'access' maps comprising nodes and linkages from which to calculate the space syntax measure of *mean depth* (MD), the shortest path through any given system to each other space or node. This value, is normally translated further into the related measures of *relative asymmetry* (RA), a generalized measure of integration to allow theoretical comparison of how deep any given space should be within a system, and *real relative asymmetry* (RRA) to allow comparison between systems (buildings, streets, etc.) of different sizes. Based on the success of these studies, the application of space syntax to the spatial distribution of graffiti throughout the Villa San Marco was initiated.

Unlike many studies the aim of the present assessment was to focus on relationships within one system (the villa) rather than between systems (a range of villas). This was facilitated by freely available space syntax software[30] developed at the Bartlett School of Architecture at University College London. It allowed for a similar but more sophisticated analysis of space than the by-now traditional access map. In essence, this software tool can swiftly calculate the various measures of space syntax of a system (such as the ground or floor plan of a structure), visualize the results, and provide a platform for statistical and other analyses. Drawing on recent research and in order[31] to integrate visibility studies into the application of space syntax studies, we set out to develop an understanding of the visibility of graffiti at Villa San Marco via visibility graph analyses (VGA).[32] This incorporated a visual element to the analysis of a location which focuses on the visual connectivity between spaces rather than direct connections between neighbouring spaces, and is based in essence on viewsheds or isovists (see Figure 9.3a). The result is a cumulative graph (plan) of inter-visibility representing the viewsheds of all known locations within that system, providing a further platform for the calculation and analysis of space syntax measures and to allow for the movement of people through space.[33]

Convex map analysis

The conversion of a ground floor plan of the villa into a convex map, much like the creation of the more conventional (paper-based) access map described above, entailed the re-definition of each room into a polygon (i.e. a space or node) from which to establish connections (or linkages) between communicating spaces (i.e. through doors) (see Figure 9.3b). The result (a convex map) would form the basis for an initial calculation of various space syntax measures:

Connectivity – a measure of the number of immediate neighbours that are directly connected to any given location.

Control – a measure of locations that dominate neighbouring locations in terms of connectivity.

Controllability – a measure of locations easily dominated by a neighbour in terms of connectivity.

Entropy – the path of least disorder from a point to all other points within a system; gauged by the level of orderliness of surrounding locations (low disorder equates with ease, high disorder equates with difficulty).

Integration – the normalized measure of the mean shortest path from a point to all other points in the system; ranked from the most integrated to the most segregated.

Mean depth – the shortest path through the graph to each other node then summed and divided by total number minus one.

Relativized entropy – expected (theoretical) distribution of locations in terms of orderliness surrounding a space which would affect the path of least disorder between it and any other given location within a system (low disorder equates with ease, high disorder equates with difficulty).

Visibility graph analysis

For the purpose of producing a visibility graph or map, the schematic ground floor plan of the villa was overlain with a matrix of points, effectively dividing all openly available space into a series of approximate standpoint locations (or nodes) and consequently, potential viewpoints. A graph linked, graded and visualized all inter-visible locations within the system (i.e. the villa). The result is a boundary map of the visual inter-connectivity of all locations along the schematic walls of the villa, and provides the platform to perform the calculations of various (visual) measures of space syntax. This is not based on direct connectivity as the above measures, but rather on the extent of the visual field (viewshed) surrounding any given location. Included here are:

Visual connectivity – how many locations each node can see from any given point.

Visual control – locations which are visually dominant over more visually constrained areas.

Visual controllability – locations more easily dominated visually (and tend to have smaller visual fields).

Visual entropy – the path of least visual disorder between two locations within a system; gauged by the level of orderliness of surrounding locations (low disorder equates with ease, high disorder equates with difficulty).

Visual integration: a measure of how deep each location is to all others visually, counted in terms of visual steps between points within the system.

Visual mean depth – the shortest visual path through a system to each other node then summed and divided by total number minus one.

Visual relativized entropy – expected (theoretical) distribution of locations in terms of orderliness surrounding a space which would affect the path of least visual disorder between it and any other given location within a system (low disorder equates with ease, high disorder equates with difficulty).

The calculated values from both analyses (convex map and visibility graph) were subsequently merged into one tabular dataset. Five relevant attributes, concerning graffiti, were manually appended as five additional fields to the record of each of the 43 rooms contained in this dataset; these were: the quantity of graffiti found in each room,[34] the quantity of graffiti found in each room according to three types (pictorial, numeric and textual), and the quantity of graffiti found in each room equal to, or less than a wall height of 110 c.m. These values could now be subsequently displayed and explored statistically in relation to all the space syntax measures generated above, with a view to identifying positive or negative associations between them using statistical scatter plots.

These statistical scatter plots offered a swift visual check by displaying the various calculated measures of space syntax as a function of observed examples of graffiti as recorded per room. Any positive or negative trends would then be quantified with a correlation co-efficient value (R^2) ranging between –1 and +1. The closer an R^2 value is to one, the better the positive correlation, while the closer to minus one it is, the better the negative correlation. An R^2 value of zero indicates no correlation.

As tests for linear correlation assume variables that are evenly distributed (which the space syntax measures approximately are) all values in the five fields concerning the quantification of graffiti were translated to a logarithmic scale for the purpose of statistical analysis; with both scales (space syntax measures and graffiti values) distributed approximately evenly, comparison was possible.

Statistical analysis – results

Each of the five graffiti fields were tested against 16 measures of space syntax described above – the majority of either positive or negative associations were so weak as to be of no significance when quantified. Some positive correspondence (listed here with increasing strength) was noted between:

rooms with textual graffiti and connectivity ($R^2 = 0.38$);
rooms with textual graffiti and visual connectivity ($R^2 = 0.45$);
rooms with pictorial graffiti and harmonic mean depth ($R^2 = 0.39$);
rooms with graffiti ≤ 110cm and visual controllability ($R^2 = 0.49$);
rooms with graffiti ≤ 110cm and visual mean depth ($R^2 = 0.56$);
rooms with graffiti ≤ 110cm and visual relativized entropy ($R^2 = 0.56$).

The strongest correspondence evident was between:
rooms with textual graffiti and visual control ($R^2 = 0.63$).

Some negative correlations were also noted – the strongest of which was between:
rooms with textual graffiti and entropy ($R^2 = -0.44$).

The strong correlation found in rooms with textual graffiti is certainly significant. Indeed, this trend supports the view that textual graffiti within the villa intentionally target visually dominant spaces within the household. It also correlates well with spaces of high visual connectivity (see above). It could also be observed that Corridor 32, the room with the most examples of textual graffiti, is the most integrated and most visually integrated, room within the study area.

Shifting the analysis towards children writing, we identified those graffiti below 110 cm in height to establish if their distribution pattern was convergent or divergent from the overall pattern, so far discussed. Intriguingly, the rooms with the highest values for visual controllability, visual mean depth and visual relativized entropy occur in the areas classified here as belonging to the service area – rooms 27, 40 and 54 which between them contain 35 per cent of all recorded examples of graffiti equal to or less than 110 cm in height. Perhaps, this is the first indication that rooms 27, 40 and 54 were used by children and contain evidence of their activities. Some caution is needed as the published graffiti from Villa San Marco is incomplete, as any examination of the so-called Palaestra shows (represented by Langner and Varone by only one published example). The full publication of an objective record of all graffiti (1) would affect the statistical outcomes greatly, and (2) complete and enhance the overall accuracy, confidence, result and interpretation of all analyses described here.

Terrestrial laser scanning (TLS) pilot study

The desk-based study set out above was undertaken in parallel to an investigation of field-based techniques for the data-capture of graffiti at Villa San Marco. The availability of high-precision and high-speed 3D laser scanners capable of swiftly recording objects, structures and landscapes in high resolution as clouds of individual Cartesian co-ordinates, creating not only a point-in-time record of the intended survey target, but also a digital platform for further modelling, manipulation and analysis using appropriate computing and software. The swift, objective and total documentation of graffiti and associated structures which could then be explored in a 3-Dimensional (3D) environment became an attractive option.

Such technological approaches to the recording of graffiti are not entirely new – in 2008, Varone employed a more technological approach to enhance and objectify the reading of Pompeian inscriptions (both painted and incised) involving the manipulation of colour photographs to separate inscriptions from background noise (scuffs for example) using image processing software.[35] Recent advances in technology have the potential to allow a viewer today to see the graffiti in context as a virtual 3D dataset.[36] This need for the enhanced recording of graffiti, and a greater spatial accountability of graffiti[37] led to a trial application of non-contact 3D terrestrial laser scanning within the Villa San Marco in locations associated with graffiti in earlier publications.[38]

In practice, the 3D scan data proved invaluable with the swift spatial mapping of graffiti previously identified in the catalogues of Varone or Langner. The 3D point cloud data was exported into a Computer Aided Design (CAD) environment and generated into accurate plans and elevations, which is a significant development from the text-based and picture-based assessments of the Villa San Marco. Langner produced similar elevation plans within his study of Roman graffiti, though none of these were for the Villa San Marco. Included in these plans are any notable wall markings or features (such as decoration, plaster variation, scuffs, chips) that could serve as navigational aids for others. Unfortunately, the capacity of the scanner to pick up indiscriminate surface detail resulted in a confusing variety of colours and markings within the intensity returns.

While it was possible to locate the graffiti identified by Varone and Langner, it was virtually impossible to indicate any new instances of ancient graffiti. Until there is a method for filtering extraneous surface noise, it would be difficult to see such graffiti clearly in the captured dataset of a single wall. Only one instance of previously unrecorded graffiti was identified – a bird-like etching (formed from a series of substantial etchings) on the wall of Room 25a. A range of other technical issues were also identified as contributing to the degradation of optimum point resolution, loss of detail, or lack of contrast in intensity readings. These issues, especially the problems with irrelevant surface noise, could be overcome in future through the use of terrestrial and object laser scanners in combination. An object scanner with flexible mounting head-system would ensure orthogonal scan angles and control of proximity to scanning target, as well as permitting work close up and in confined spaces. It follows that, where possible, laser scanning should occur soon after excavation or cleaning/conservation; laser-scanning of all newly exposed graffiti to ensure precise recording of their spatial position is an obvious recommendation before surfaces are degraded through exposure to climate and visitors. This is particularly relevant since recent excavations in a villa neighbouring San Marco, seen during scanning fieldwork in 2010, have exposed walls with numerous graffiti inscriptions.

Conclusion

Examining the available graffiti data from the Villa San Marco with regard to their distribution according to type, household area and room (with additional regard to its height occurrence), this exploratory case study has noted at a basic level that textual graffiti are recorded predominantly in the portico area and in particular the peristyle, while numerical graffiti are chiefly evident within the service area and most evident in room 26, the kitchen. Furthermore, pictorial graffiti were, it seems, exclusively favoured by those using rooms associated with the baths, where one of the smallest occupied spaces of the villa, room 25a, not only holds the largest count for any room of pictorial graffiti, but also second largest count of all graffiti per room; this points to the suitability of the wall's texture in the villa for incising graffiti. As a written space, the villa is segmented into the practical space of the kitchen where functional writing (mathematics) associated with food preparation occurs. The most spatially integrated parts of the villa were the location for texts and the use of language to communicate with other members of the household. The baths, on the other hand, have drawn pictures – perhaps their creators had long periods of waiting to serve the bathers. It is precisely in parts of the house associated with work or waiting to work that have the highest concentrations of graffiti (Table 9.1a) especially rooms 25a and 26. The preliminary findings of this study have revealed (as discussed above) possible evidence for the presence of children (perhaps associated with slaves) in service rooms 27, 40 and 54, which significantly, are rooms that have been also demonstrated to be among the most controlled, hidden, and marginalized spaces within the study area of the Villa San Marco, pointing to neither the seclusion nor the overall control of children by adults – but, instead, that children inhabit the villa alongside adults. Both children and adults produced the writing, drawing and the use of numbers that can be found today in publications of the texts and images. However, it is only by relating these texts to space that we can begin to understand the dynamics of houses and villas and question who may have written them and who was likely to have read them.

Table 9.1a Summary of Graffiti distribution classified by area within the villa and type (P = Pictorial, N = Numerical, T = Textual)

Area*[39]			Graffiti type				Percentage			
Area	Area m²	Floor %	P	N	T	Total	P	N	T	Total
I (Atrium)	176.9	25	1	4	3	8	2	13	12	8
II (Service)	80.5	11	9	21	6	36	20	70	23	36
III (Bath)	163.2	23	18	0	0	18	41	0	0	18
IV (Portico)	237.6	33	15	2	15	32	34	7	58	32
V (Nymphaeum)	60.3	8	1	3	2	6	2	10	8	6
Total/Check	718.5	100	44	30	26	100	100	100	100	100

Table 9.1b Summary of graffiti distribution classified by area within the villa and height

	<110 c.m.	% <110 c.m.	c.m. min	c.m. max	c.m. range
I (Atrium)	1	14	55	182	127
II (Service)	8	22	41	181	140
III (Bath)	2	11	96	180	84
IV (Portico)	8	25	67	186	119
V (Nymphaeum)	1	17	80	170	90

Table 9.1c Graffiti classified by type and height

	%	<110 c.m.	% <110 c.m.	c.m. min	c.m. max	c.m. range
Pictorial	44	12	27	67	186	119
Numerical	30	2	7	82	182	100
Textual	26	6	23	41	181	140
Total	100	20	20	41	186	145

Table 9.2 Summary of graffiti distribution classified by type and room[40]

Rooms		Location	Graffiti type				% of type		
Room No.	Room name	Area	P	N	T	Total	P	N	T
25	Frigidarium	III: Baths	1	0	0	1	2.3	0	0
44	Atrium	I: Atrium	0	1	0	1	0	3.3	0
48	Palaestra	III: Baths	1	0	0	1	2.3	0	0
51	Forecourt	0: Forecourt	1	0	0	1	2.3	0	0
53	Cubiculum	V: Nymphaeum	1	0	0	1	2.3	0	0
56	Vestibule	I: Atrium	0	0	1	1	0	0	3.8
57	Cubiculum	I: Atrium	0	0	1	1	0	0	3.8
26a	portal kitchen	II: Service	0	0	1	1	0	0	3.8
22	Corridor	IV: Portico	0	1	1	2	0	3.3	3.8
27	Cubiculum	II: Service	0	0	3	3	0	0	12
40	Cubiculum	II: Service	2	1	0	3	4.5	3.3	0
54	Cubiculum	II: Service	2	1	0	3	4.5	3.3	0
5	NE Peristyle (W)	IV: Portico	0	0	4	4	0	0	15
61	Cubiculum	I: Atrium	0	3	1	4	0	10	3.8
3	SE Peristyle	IV: Portico	3	1	1	5	6.8	3.3	3.8
50	Cubiculum	V: Nymphaeum	0	3	2	5	0	10	7.7
49	Corridor	II: Service	3	2	2	7	6.8	6.7	7.7
20	NE Peristyle (E)	IV: Portico	8	0	2	10	18	0	7.7
32	Corridor	IV: Portico	4	0	7	11	9.1	0	27
25a	Portal bath	III: Bath	16	0	0	16	36	0	0
26	kitchen	II: Service	2	17	0	19	4.5	57	0
		Total check	44	30	26	100	100	100	100

Notes

1 Benefiel, 2010a, p. 65.
2 The authors would like to acknowledge their debt to the British Academy for the British Academy Small Grant that was awarded to them, facilitating the fieldwork element of this case study at the Villa San Marco, Castellamare. They would further like to thank the staff of *La Soprintendenza Speciale per i Beni Archeologici di Napoli e Pompei* at the Villa San Marco and in particular Enzo Sabini for their support; as well as to the Co-ordinator General of the *Restoring Ancient Stabiae* foundation (RAS), Professor Thomas Howe and Paolo Gardelli.
3 See Allison, 2004, pp. 62–123; villa plan in Barbet and Miniero, 1999, p. 343; Clarke, 1991; Wallace-Hadrill, 1994, p. 38.
4 Barbet and Miniero, 1999, Figure 1.
5 Varone, 1999, p. 345.
6 Langner, 2001, p. 1.
7 As observed by Baxter, 2005, p. 20; Golden, 2011, pp. 262–75; Rawson, 2003, pp. 211–14. See also Garraffoni and Laurence this volume.
8 Huntley, 2011, pp. 69–89.
9 Huntley, 2011, p. 76.
10 For examples of subjective attribution of graffiti to children see Beard, 2008, p. 15; Vivolo, 1993, p. 77.
11 For more on slavery see Allison, 2004, p. 155; Clarke, 2003; George, 1997a, 1997b, p. 15; 2007; Mouritsen, 2011, pp. 129–44; F. H. Thompson, 2002; Webster, 2008, p. 115.
12 Mouritsen, forthcoming, p. 20.
13 Benefiel, 2010a, pp. 69–101, 2010b, pp. 45–75, 2011, pp. 20–48.
14 Benefiel, 2011, p. 24, pp. 45–75; Keegan, 2011, pp. 184–5; Milnor, 2009, p. 293.
15 Benefiel, 2010b.
16 It is worth pointing out that there are discrepancies between the two studies of graffiti from Villa San Marco by Varone and Langner. For example, Langner records more pictorial examples of graffiti than Varone. Other inconsistencies may reflect different sampling strategies, classification criteria, lighting conditions, interpretation of chronology, and time constraints among others; e.g. Corridor 42 where Langner records two items separately, in contrast to Varone, who records them as one group scene. An examination of room 48 in the bath area (sometimes referred to as the Palaestra), the north-east wall is perhaps the most graffitied surface in the villa; however, both Varone and Langner only record a single example of graffiti from this room in their publications.
17 Barbet and Miniero, 1999.
18 Numbered 51 in Barbet and Miniero, 1999, p. 343.
19 Again following Barbet and Miniero, 1999, p. 343.
20 Enzo Sabini – personal communication.
21 Barbet and Miniero, 1999, p. 343.
22 Huntley 2011, pp. 72–3, 77; Langner 2001, p. 143. Huntley's research identified some 161 examples of children's graffiti across the sites of Pompeii, Herculaneum, and the villas of San Marco and Arianna at Stabiae.
23 Huntley, 2011, p. 77.
24 Benefiel, 2011, p. 28; Ellis, 1997, p. 43.

25 See Laurence and Garraffoni's chapter in the present volume for a complementary discussion of graffiti associated with child development.

26 Benefiel, 2011, p. 23.

27 Hillier et al., 1976; Hillier and Hanson, 1984. For archaeological applications, see Leach, 1978. For Pompeii Grahame, 1997, 2000; Laurence, 1997, 2007a; Newsome 2009, 2011b; Wallace-Hadrill, 1997. Compare for prehistory, Foster, 1989.

28 Newsome, 2009; Grahame, 2000.

29 For example see Foster, 1989; Grahame, 2000; Laurence, 2007a, pp. 102–16.

30 Called UCL Depthmap, this software is distributed for free academic use courtesy of Space Syntax Limited http://www.spacesyntax.net/software/ucl-depthmap/ (last accessed 8 January 2013).

31 Documented in Penn and Turner, 2002; Turner et al., 2001.

32 Turner, 2001; Turner, 2004, pp. 1–4.

33 Royal Festival Hall in Doxa, 2001; London Department Store in Penn and Turner, 2002; Tate Gallery in Turner et al., 2001.

34 For the purpose of the spatial analysis, the single occurrence of a portal graffito (between rooms 26 and 40) is quantified as belonging to the room with the greater number of graffiti, in this case room 26 (the kitchen). Similarly, the sole example of external graffiti (documented close to the main entrance) is included as belonging to the room 56 (the vestibule).

35 Varone, 2008, p. 125.

36 Santopuoli et al., 2007, p. 177.

37 As identified by Benefiel, 2011; Santopouli et al., 2007; Varone, 2008.

38 Varone, 1999, p. 355.

39 Single forecourt graffito counted as atrium area here as forecourt is only partially excavated.

40 See Figure 9.2.

Written Space and Building Type

10

Text, Space, and the Urban Community: A Study of the Platea as Written Space

Francesco Trifilò

Introduction

Among all sources of evidence for the description of Roman urban space, inscriptions are unique in providing a direct link between buildings, the spoken language, and an audience's perception of urban space itself. This link allows us to approach the study of inscriptions as one aimed at understanding collective experiences of urban space and their role in shaping the space itself. The example of the *locus celeberrimus* as evidence for a collective spatial hierarchy regulating the display of honorific statues represents the first instance in which this new approach has been tested.[1] With the epigraphy of the *platea*, a term applying to a space rather than a statue, comes the study of a different instance in which word meaning and spatial setting combine in an inextricable but dynamic way. Where *locus celeberrimus* applied to objects that would be located within the urban environment, the word *platea* concerns features which comprise the urban environment's very makeup.[2] The term is of particular significance, as it was used equally to define broad monumental streets and open public spaces. This duality has resulted in a degree of 'fuzziness' in the way the *platea* is understood in contemporary scholarship. There are ambiguities over its definition, the understanding of its material appearance, and of the nature of its generative forces.[3]

While this may cause issues with typological approaches to the building blocks of the Roman city it does offer unparalleled opportunities to research intent on scrutinizing spaces one would assign to the realm of the 'becoming', already qualified by Gros as '*lieux de la convergence*' (places of convergence).[4] We have no real understanding of how the meaning of the term *platea* maintained this sort of duplicity or, eventually, how this duplicity may have consolidated into a single meaning recognized by a collectivity.

The relationship between duality and single meaning is an issue which invests with particular force the transfer of the word *platea* onto stone, as part of a dedicatory inscription. Epigraphy, more directly than literature, expresses and educates a collective understanding of something.[5] Its makeup and appearance are both intended to absolve this function. Therefore, setting, quite literally, in stone a word or a name generates or consolidates the identification between the word and the object represented by that word. An enduring awareness and memory of the correspondence between the two will depend on their continued existence, as loss of memory of this correspondence will set in motion the transformative powers of the collective and individual re-elaborations of the names of things.

This particular property outlines a key connection between our understanding of the term *platea* and its mention on inscriptions. In particular, if we identify the term as displaying a particular meaning we should try and work out how we relate this to instances in which the meaning itself is substituted by another. This is particularly important, in a Roman context, where terms indicating public buildings (*forum*, *amphiteatrum*, *theatrum*) appear to maintain a constant and long-lasting identity of name and appearance.

Here, a study of the *platea* in inscriptions is therefore modelled as a study of how epigraphy conveys variations and mutations in the collective understanding of space within the Roman city. Through an analysis of available evidence I will draw attention to key features and practices connected with the definition and use of the word *platea* in inscriptions. The result will be to emphasize the role of written space as a descriptor of that continuous process of transformation that characterizes every living community of people.

The epigraphy of the *platea*: chronological characteristics

A survey of dedicatory inscriptions mentioning work concerning a *platea* amounts to 36 instances located in Numidia, Africa Proconsularis, the southern *regiones* of Italy, Germania Superior and Galatia.[6] The dating of these inscriptions suggests that they were dedicated with particular intensity in the second century AD and, although less so, in the third and first. The dedication of inscriptions mentioning the term *platea* appears to decline later on, with three dedications dated to the fourth century AD and one in the fifth (Figure 10.1). This chronological distribution should not be taken at face value for two reasons: the low number of examples affects its statistical significance, as does the fact that some inscriptions (eminently those dedicated in the second century AD) are repeated commemorations of the same act of euergetism. In fact, the reduction of repeat texts to one affects second century dedications from Timgad, Lambaesis, and Ammaedara, thus reducing the second century majority and emphasizing a more gradual image of increase and decrease in popularity in the dedications mentioning this word.

Notwithstanding these limitations, some general considerations on the chronology of the use of the term *platea* on inscriptions can be made. This mainly concerns its popularity, which appears to be connected with a particular period in the history of the Roman city, the period following the reign of Hadrian, during which the city is the object of significant building activity.[7] The gradual increase in inscriptions recording *plateae* from the first century AD to the second, followed by a gradual decrease from the second century all the way to the fifth, may be a sign of the combined influence of the popularity of a certain type of urban space (called a *platea*), of its possible association

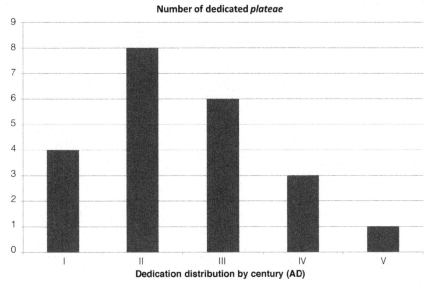

Figure 10.1 Chronological spread of inscriptions mentioning the term *platea*. Quantities are adjusted as expressions of one single act of euergetism or altar dedication, rather than representing every single inscription found

with cities in expansion, and with the consequential link between urban space and wider social and economic factors connected with the history of the Roman Empire. Given this chronological pattern, it is reasonable to speculate that the flourishing of the term *platea* in inscriptions is eminently connected with towns in expansion (or change), rather than with new urban foundations. The following analysis will help us determine this more accurately.

The *platea* as a broad street

The majority of inscriptions in this sample refer to the *platea* as a broad street. In a few of these cases the nature of the *platea* is explicit, while in others it has to be concluded on the basis of collateral evidence found in the text. A first reference to *plateae* as a street type comes from Cagliari, in Sardinia, and dates from 83 AD. Here, the commemoration of a *procurator Augusti*'s management of the working infrastructure of *Municipium Caralitanorum* includes the description of '*plateas et c[3] itinera sternenda*' which refers quite clearly to the surfacing of roadways within the *municipium*.

The connection between a *platea* and roadworks is not only present in the procurator's intervention in Sardinia but extends to a substantial part of the sample in which the work undertaken constitutes our best descriptor of the nature of the space. We

Table 10.1 The inscription from Cagliari

*Imp(eratori) Caesari div[i Aug(usti)] / Vespasiani f(ilio) Do[mitiano] / Aug(usto)
pont(ifici) max(imo) / tr(ibunicia) pot(estate) II imp(eratori) III p(atri) p(atriae)
[c]o(n)s(uli) / VIIII des(ignato) X Sex(tus) Laecanius Labeo pro[c(urator)] /
Aug(usti) praef(ectus) provinci[ae] / Sardin(iae) plateas et c[3] / itinera municipii
C[aralit(anorum)] / sternenda et cloa[cas] / [f]aciendas et t[e]g[endas] / p(ecunia)
p(ublica) et privata [curavit]*[8]

To the emperor Caesar Domitian Augustus, son of the *divus* Augustus Vespasian,
Pontifex Maximus, holding the Tribunician Potestas for the second time, acclaimed
Imperator for the third time, Father of the Country, Consul for the ninth time,
designated Consul for the tenth time, Sextus Laecanius Labeo, imperial procurator,
prefect of the province of Sardinia took care of the laying down of plateas and ...
pathways of the municipium of the Caralitanii and (took care of) the construction
and covering of the sewers which were undertaken with the use of public and private
money.

Table 10.2 Inscriptions relating to roadworks

*Segesta: L(ucio) Iulio C(ai) f(ilio) Agrippae / euergetae / hic plateam a Sosia / usque ad
    fanum*[9]
To Lucius Iulius Agrippa, son of Caius, benefactor, this platea from Sosia up-to the
    temple

*Saepinum: C(aius) Coesius / Tertius Aug(ustalis) / plateam stravit / a tervio ad /
    tervium ped(um) / [3]os p(osuit?)*[10]

Caius Coesius Tertius Augustalis surfaced the *platea* from the third to the third foot
(?) ... (?)

*Aquilonia: L(ucius) Percennius / L(uci) l(ibertus) Epicadus Aug(ustalis) / plateam
    stravit / pedes DCCC*[11]

Lucius Percennius Epicadus Augustalis and freedman of Lucius surfaced 800 feet of
the platea

*Ammaedara: [Imp(eratore) C]aesa[re] M(arco) Aurelio [Antonino Augusto pont(ifice)]
    / [max(imo) trib(unicia) p]ot(estate) XXV im[p(eratore) V] co(n)s(ule) III p(atre)
    p(atriae) divi An[tonini Pii fil(io) divi Veri fratre] / [divi Hadria]ni nepoti [di]vi
    Traiani Parth[ici pronepote divi Nervae abne]/[pote opus pla]teae novae [de]recta a
    porta milit[ari*[12]

To the emperor Caesar Marcus Aurelius Antoninus Augustus Pontifex Maximus
at his twenty fifth *tribunicia potestas*, acclaimed emperor for the fifth, consul for
the third time, father of the country, son of the *divus* Antoninus Pius and brother
of the *divus* Verus, grandson of the *divus* Hadrian, great-grandson of the *divus*
Trajan, victorious over the Parthians, great-great nephew of Nerva, is dedicated the
construction of the new *platea* straight from the military gate.

have this in four inscriptions found in Segesta, Saepinum, Aquilonia, and Ammaedara in Africa Proconsularis (Table 10.2).

In these examples work is recorded as having been undertaken within markers that have much to tell us about the nature and location of the spaces described. In Segesta the work is undertaken '*usque ad fanum*', in Saepinum '*a tervio ad tervium pedum*'. In Aquilonia the worked sections of *platea* are recorded in feet (DCCC). These all suggest that the *plateae* in question, all roads, were already there at the time of their partial paving and that they could therefore possess that specific denomination even before acquiring a formalized appearance. In Ammaedara, what appears to be a double copy of the same inscription records the actual construction of a *platea* undertaken in a straight line '*a porta militari*'. By taking into account the military origin of Ammaedara and its early foundation, it would appear logical to suppose that this construction does not refer to a street which forms part of the internal articulation of the town, but one which projects outside of the military gate mentioned in the text.[13] It would appear that we have examples of *plateae* as paths, which are only paved in a second moment, and *plateae* as monuments, inserted in the landscape anew. The site of the city of Timgad offers a richer collection of inscriptions describing *plateae* in comparable settings.

The *plateae* at Timgad

The site of Timgad has produced nine inscriptions referring to four separate acts of euergetism (A, B, C, and D) which mention the word *platea* (see Figure 10.2 for find-spots). The comparison between them, their findspots, and likely date, offers us the key to determining that in the Numidian town, the word *platea* was unequivocally used to describe a broad colonnaded street. In this group, the inscriptions of group A[14] have a very similar text referring to an act of euergetism dedicated by Marcus Valerius Etruscus in AD 151–152, and refer to the *platea* as paved (*stratam*). Of very similar content, but different date, are inscriptions commemorating benefactions C (AD 143–46),[15] and D (AD 169).[16] In C the *platea* is referred to as paved (*stratam*), while in D it is referred to without further specifications. Inscription D was found reused in the construction of an absidal building located next to the 'porte nord' of the town.[17] Group B[18] is a different inscription from the others, as it refers to a *platea* which we can locate with some confidence between the southern entrance to the town and the Byzantine fort, which is built on the site of a temple complex called the *Aqua Septimiana Felix*.[19] The inscription, dated to AD 213, refers to the construction (*opus*) of a *platea* extending from the bath house (*a thermis*) to the entrance (*usque ad introitum perfectum*) of the temple site. Four inscriptions referring to this particular benefaction were found close to the Western Gate, reused in the rebuilding of the *capitolium*, and around the site of the *Aqua Septimiana Felix*.

The findspots of the other *platea* inscriptions from Timgad should also be noted. Inscriptions of group A were found in the *porticus* of the court of the temple to the *genius coloniae*, now dated to around AD 169,[20] and reused as flagstones for the *forum*'s *basilica* and for the building of the external *capitolium*.[21] It has been argued that these inscriptions could refer to work undertaken in the *forum*.[22] If that were the case, the fact that one of these has been found used as a flagstone for the *basilica* floor would suggest that this pavement belonged to an earlier phase of the life of the public space.[23] This hypothesis, however, is unconvincing for three reasons: first, these inscriptions have been found reused in the *forum* and may not necessarily belong there. Second, as the later inscription B appears to refer to a large road, it is unlikely that the inhabitants of Timgad also used this term to indicate their *forum*. Moreover, the presence of three identical copies of this dedication raises the question of why would the commemoration of the paving of a *forum* be repeated so many times in a single open space. In order to understand why so many copies were produced and how to interpret the inscriptions' findspots it is worth looking at the location of all of them on a single plan of the city (Figure 10.2).

In light of the terminology, date, and location of these it is possible to make the following argument: the presence of three inscriptions referring to work undertaken in the *forum* is unlikely. The fact that another work on a *platea* is undertaken six years after the first should further discount the idea that reference is made to the space of the *forum*. Furthermore, the fact that B provides a clear reference to a *platea* as a street suggests that we associate the other inscriptions with streets. The answer, I suggest, is that all four sets of inscriptions (A, B, C, D) refer only to the *plateae*, which we know existed in more than one example (as opposed to the *forum*): the broad streets of the *decumanus maximus*, the *cardo maximus*, the western *decumanus*, and the southern *platea* connecting the Aqua Septimiana Felix complex to the *colonia*. This appears to be confirmed by the plan, which locates their find-spots in broad conformity to this interpretation. All these elements help confirm the fact that multiple copies of the same dedication referring to work undertaken in a *platea* all refer necessarily to a space which is a broad street.

The criteria that have helped us determine the form of Timgad's *plateae* can also help us determine the form of *plateae* on similar dedications as well. Two inscriptions from nearby Lambaesis,[24] for example, point incontrovertibly to the interpretation of these *plateae* as a single street. The two inscriptions, which reproduce the same text, are dated to AD 172–73, sometime after the establishment of a civilian settlement around the fort. The repetition of the text suggests that the work refers to a large street dedicated by the municipality through the imperial legate Marcus Aemilius Macer Saturninus. Another, much later (AD 315) inscription from Lambaesis,[25] refers to the decoration of a *platea* (*ad exornandam plateam*) possibly by the insertion of arches.[26] On the basis of a similar repetition in the number of inscriptions and of the close connection between Lambaesis and Timgad it is reasonable to accept that these inscriptions refer to broad streets rather than plazas.

Four remaining inscriptions mention construction work. One is from Sétif and appears to refer to a *platea strata*.[27] Two are from Lilybaeum, in Sicily, and describe the paving of two separate *plateae*. The first is the *platea Cererum sacra*, paved between AD 169 and 172, while the second is a *platea vici Septizodi*, the paving and completion of which was commemorated between AD 200 and 250. The last of the four is an inscription from Sulci, in Sardinia, dating to circa AD 115 and commemorating the paving of a *platea*.[28] Of these four inscriptions, the one from Sulci contains

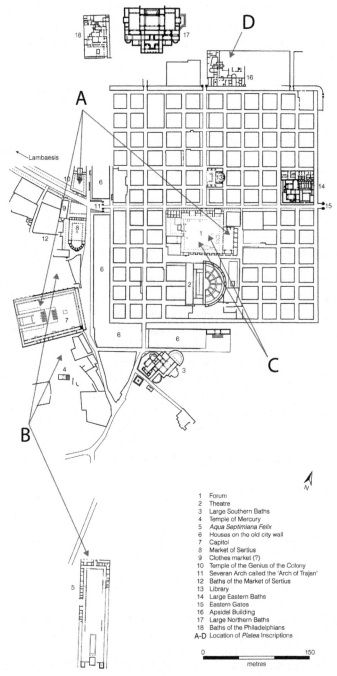

Figure 10.2 Map of Timgad showing the discovery sites of all known inscriptions concerning *plateae*. Only the public buildings are picked out in detail. After Ballu, 1897: pl. 12 and 31; 1903: pl. 18 and 1911, main map.

the least information. All we know is that a *proconsul* paved a *platea* that was previously unpaved. The Sétif inscription gives us only one more possible piece of information; the reference to a *vicus* expressed in the ablative singular case. However, the fragmentary state of this inscription does not allow us to venture into trying to determine the nature of the described space.

A reference to a *vicus* is certainly present on one of the inscriptions from Lilybaeum. This, however, refers explicitly to the fact that the commemorated paving is of the *platea vici Septizodi*. One could be tempted to claim, in this case, that the link between a *platea* and a *septizodium* mirrors references to the Severan *septizodium* in Rome, which is likely to have been placed in a large open space.[29] However, the inscription tells us explicitly that this is the *platea vici*, rather than a *platea septizodi*, thus suggesting a more direct connection with a portion (a *vicus?*) of ancient Lilybaeum which was connected with one such monument.

The matter is not made easier when we focus on the earlier inscription which mentions a *platea Cererum sacra*. Like the former, this inscription describes only the paving of a *platea*, with no further indication as to its appearance. However, both inscriptions present the *platea* in a very similar way. Both refer to a *platea* which is qualified by its connection with another feature of the town and which must have existed before the time when it was paved. Unlike the *plateae* at Timgad, these examples appear as spaces which acquire an identity in connection with town features which viewed as more remarkable. Their later paving may suggest that these *plateae* exist only in as far as their associated town features do, and that their paving is witness to a continued and prosperous association. As a note, the reference to the Cereres should not only be associated to a cult with its roots in Africa, but also to the production, storage, and distribution of cereal, which may have had an impact on the topography of Lilybaeum itself.[30] A suspended judgement on the interpretation of the actual nature of these spaces should not distract from the fact that both convey a strong sense that informal activity (such as stall-based commerce) occurring on the edges of a town is closely connected to their existence. A link between *platea*, informal activity and religion, as exemplified by the connection with the Cereres, is certainly confirmed by our examples in Germania Superior.

Statue dedication and the *platea*

Five inscriptions from Germania Superior contribute greatly to our knowledge of *plateae*. All of these inscriptions belong to dedicatory bases. Three of these are from Mogontiacum[31] and the remaining two from Nida.[32] All share a fundamental military nature as they originated as forts and because, with the exception of one (*CIL* 13.7263), all are dedications of statues or altars by members or veterans of the military which mention *plateae* as the spaces in which they were set: In Mogontiacum '*post portam praetoriam*'[33] and '*plateae dextrae*',[34] and in Nida '*plateae novi vici*'[35] and '*plateae praetoriae*'.[36] None describes the provision of infrastructure at any level. All were located outside the forts.

The term *platea* does not belong, as far as we know, to a strictly military environment. In the case of Nida the two dedicatory inscriptions mentioning *plateae* can be linked to their associated context, the two large axes projecting from the fort's *Porta Praetoria*, the key streets of the *novus vicus* mentioned in the dedications. Moreover, in the case of the inscriptions from Mogontiacum, the dedicatory inscriptions are reported by the *Corpus Inscriptionum Latinarum* as belonging rather to the nearby *Castellum Mattiacorum*, a bridgehead fortress of Flavian date which was built on the opposite side of the Rhine and was located between the bridge itself and a triumphal arch of Germanicus. In both cases the term *platea* appears to be linked to peripheral conurbations. Also of note is the declared occupational (and therefore economic) status of the dedicators of three of these monuments, *CIL* 13.7261, 7264, 7335, who are listed as *milites* (one of whom in 7335 is an *immunis consularis*) and/or *veterani*. The remaining two, *CIL* 13.7263 and 7337, do not mention the occupation of their dedicators. Taken together, the peripheral position and non-elite dedicator status lead us to picture these *plateae* as locations for social display and, in this respect, as *loci celeberrimi* of second choice,[37] in which non-elite members of the urban community, with no access to prime *loci celeberrimi* such as *fora*, could choose to dedicate monuments.

One interesting aspect concerning inscriptions from both Nida and Mogontiacum is the mention of a *genius plateae*.[38] This connects these inscriptions with the spatial and religious aspects connected to the *genius loci*, and more specifically with *compitalia*.[39] This association between *genius plateae* and *genius loci* also helps determine the likely appearance of the *platea* mentioned on these dedicatory bases. The term *genius loci*,[40] with its topographic connotations, identifies this *platea* as an aggregative place (perhaps even connected to a crossroad) rather than a street. In this respect one should also take into account the way statues interact with urban space and how they affect it. These dedications contain all the elements that are typical of the *locus celeberrimus* and should be noted as the features that signal change in the nature of this portion of urban space as a space for display.

Commerce in the platea

Two inscriptions in the sample refer explicitly to commercial activity and, more specifically, the regulation of commercial activity. The first of these is Pisidian Antioch's so called edict of Antistius (AD 93) which, following a famine, forbids the hoarding of grain and sets a maximum price (one *denarius* per *modius*) for its sale to *emptores* (buyers).[41] The importance of this inscription for us resides in the fact that it was set in the 'Tiberia platea', a space commonly identified with a very broad colonnaded street (or a square) opening onto the south eastern end of the *cardo maximus* of the city (Figure 10.3).[42]

Other mentions of *plateae* recorded in Pisidian Antioch encourage us to interpret the *Tiberia Platea* as a square. These are two fragmentary inscriptions which mention a *curator plateae et vicorum*, which we should translate as magistrate in charge of *plateae* (as squares) and precincts.[43] The epigraphy helps better comprehend the

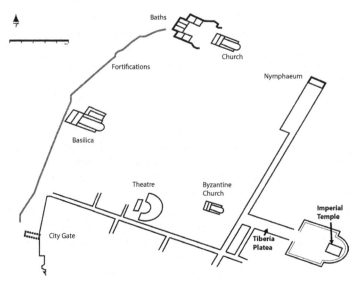

Figure 10.3 Schematic plan of Antioch of Pisidia showing the location of the Tiberia Platea (after Ossi and Harrington, 2011)

context in which the edict of Antistius was found, a stretch of road that is significantly wider than the main arteries of the city, and which leads only to a sanctuary (the Imperial Sanctuary), thus not offering any real through-route which a road would offer.[44] The parallel between the sale of grain at Antioch and the *platea Cererum sacra* of Lilybaeum should be remarked upon as a possible clue to the role of commerce in this type of space. Although the identification of a link can only be suggested, it raises questions about the seasonality of grain commerce and the impact that this may have had on the spaces dedicated to its sale.

Another reference to a *platea* on an inscription concerning the regulation of commerce comes from Utica in Africa Proconsularis (AD 362). This inscription mentions the existence of a *vectigal plateae ex sacra dispositione nundinandi*, a '*platea*-tax' issued by sacred rule and having commercial exchange as its object.[45] All translations of the inscriptions follow the original interpretation of the *vectigal plateae* as a '*taxe de plaçage*',[46] where the genitive case is used to express a generic association between the term and activity taking place within it. This would easily translate in English as 'placement tax' or 'location tax'. There is, however, no reason why *vectigal plateae* should not be translated more literally, especially in the light of the association of taxation and the space of the *area*.[47] The implications of translating more literally '*plateae*' pose the problem of identifying what kind of space the inscription is referring to. Although we do not know exactly where the inscription was found, we do know that Utica's street system included a very large colonnaded street ('*la grande avenue à portiques*') flanked by shops and some 32 metres in width.[48] Regardless of the identification of this space, the inscription conveys an important idea by setting apart a specific spatial denomination as requiring the payment of a commercial tax. This is a tax concerning *plateae* which implies that the reader, the seller, and the authority in charge of implementing the tax will all agree on how this space is delimited; an operation that is achieved with difficulty on a long stretch of road. Finally, the comparison between this *platea*-specific legislation and law more generally dedicated to streets and roads shows one fundamental element of distinction: while this law concerns being on the space of the *platea*, law on streets and roads are concerned exclusively with transit.[49] It would be unreasonable, at this point, to identify a univocal connection between commerce and the *platea* as a square. Commerce was a practice typical of streets as it was of large open spaces. What these examples do, though, is show us the verbal identification of a space as a function. Whatever its formal appearance, the *platea* in these commerce-related inscriptions is expressed in writing as a meeting place.

The *platea* as a square

An inscription discovered during excavations in 1994 takes the verbal portrayal of the *platea* to a formal level, by describing it explicitly as a monument. The inscription, broken into two parts, had been re-employed in the construction of the tomb of a man called Felix, located in the so-called Basilica I in the town if Sidi Jdidi, in Tunisia.[50] The inscription itself commemorates an act of euergetism undertaken by Titus Flavius Dyscolius Therapius between AD 402 and 408 and concerns work connected with a *platea*:

> *Beatissimis florentissimisq(ue) [temp]orib(us) ddd(ominorum) nnn(ostrorum)*
> *Arcadi Honori et Theodosi / ppp(erpetuorum) Auggg(ustorum) administrante*
> *M[an]lio Crepereio Scipione Vincentio v(iro) c(larissimo) / consulare p(rovinciae)*
> *Fl(aviae) Valeriae Byz(acenae) plateam quae splendori est civita/ti et huic natura*
> *loci denecabat ornatum aegestis ruderib(us) inaequalitate silicib(us) coequa/*
> *ta{m} additis quoq(ue) columnis arcib(us) circumclusis in meliorem faciem T(itus)*
> *F(lavius) Dyscolius / Therapius ex t(ribuno) fl(amen) p(er)p(etuus) c(urator) r(ei)*
> *p(ublicae) liberalitatem ob amorem civicum patriae inpendens proprio / sumptu*
> *excoluit perfecit et ludos scenicos praemiales edidit et cum splend/dissimo ordine*
> *feliciter dedicavit*

In the most blessed and prosperous times of our lords, Arcadius, Honorius and Theodosius, *Augusti* in perpetuity, under the administration of the highly regarded Manlius Crepereius Scipio Vincentius, *consularis* of the province Flavia Valeria Byzacena. Titus Flavius Dyscolius Therapius, ex-tribune, *flamen perpetuus*, curator of the *res publica*, with prodigality born out of his civic love for the fatherland, independently and with his own funds improved the *platea*, which is the lustre of the town and which was deprived, because of the nature of the place, of ornament. (He) had it cleared of debris and its unevenness levelled with (paving) stones, and also had it better enclosed with colonnaded arches and also gave theatrical plays with rewards and dedicated this auspiciously with the most splendid *ordo* of the town.

In this, which is probably the most detailed description of a *platea*, several important points should be noted:

1. The *platea* is described as *splendor civitatis*, splendour of the town. This space is therefore perceived as high (or highest) in ranking among the public spaces of late Roman Sidi Jdidi.
2. The *platea* is identified with a portion of the *civitas* possessing a *natura loci*, a set of 'natural' properties that is so prominent as to form part of its description.
3. This *natura loci* is described as one that 'denied it elegance' (*denecabat ornatum*).
4. This *platea* is not built: debris is eliminated, its irregular surface flattened with stone, and colonnaded arches are added (*aegestis ruderib(us) inaequalitate silicib(us) coequa/ta{m} additis quoq(ue) columnis arcib(us) circumclusis*).
5. The last verb, *circumclusum*, describes the appearance in plan of this space. It is a space enclosed with arches on each side. It is a square.[51]

This is perhaps the most informative piece of written evidence we possess on the appearance and composition of a space identified as a *platea*. The description points to a space identifiable as a square, not planned and built in a town, but a natural space that was generally identified as a *platea* and which we can presume to have gained its name through a consolidation of its use. Furthermore this space appears to have acquired a particularly important status among the monuments of late Roman Sidi Jdidi, although it is unclear whether this was before or after its monumentalization.

The cultural and chronological contexts of this inscription should be taken into account when evaluating how we define the term *platea* in Roman language and town planning. This inscription describes a variation in the collective understanding of how its appearance and expression in language coincide at this time and in this place.

Conclusion

In epigraphy, as in archaeology and literature, '*platea*' is a word connected with mutation. As is the case for its investigation in literature,[52] one may decide that this term is too generic to associate with the normative definitions of architectural disciplines. However, from the point of view of built-space as a process, few terms are more effective descriptors of the becoming of architectural space. In epigraphy, as well as in other sources of evidence, the *platea* illustrates the re-birth of the central square.

In the majority of examples referring clearly to *plateae* as streets, we recognize an urban setting in the course of being monumentalized, with large axes that are provided with monumental *dignitas* as part of those piecemeal actions of euergetism that consolidate social hierarchy, as well as embellishing a town. It has clearly emerged that although it can be inserted anew into the landscape through a larger funding and building effort, the *platea* appears as a function before it does as a monument. It is always a connection between existing buildings before it acquires its own, individual, characterization. Even when it is dedicated as a building, rather than as a paving example, a *platea* exists only inasmuch as a connection between other buildings. All inscriptions, through their text, place of discovery and estimated date, illustrate a space that exists in an expanding town, which sees the development of areas outside its planned limits.

The recognition of these basic qualities helps us understand how to read the other events recorded in association with *plateae*. In the examples from Germania, the association of *plateae* with statue dedication appears as a collective strategy in the determination of *loci celeberrimi*. The association of the *platea* with a *genius* reinforces the fact that statue dedication, whether with the purpose of honouring a single individual or a divinity, has transformed a place of linear movement (a street) into a place where people converge. In these examples the erection of statues in the *platea* is part of a stratification of social and religious practices taking place in expanding towns. In erecting statues in a malleable public space, the dedicators were taking advantage of the occurrence of key connections within the city, such as those produced by other streets that crossed the *platea*.

This transformation of linear space into a central square is also revealed in key references to regulation, referring either specifically to a 'place' in which to set an inscription or to *platea*-specific regulation. Both are examples of place-making actions which give a street, however broad, the property of attracting people. In addition, regulation raises the issue of the development of specialist activity, such as the commerce of grain, which may be also behind the naming of a *platea* as the *platea Cererum*. If we accept the possibility of one such connection, we should recognize behind it a series of complex processes connecting central-square formation, specialized activity and religious practice, all contributing to the construction of this organic public space.

The final inscription that was examined, from Sidi Jdidi, which describes in detail the gradual emergence of a *platea* as *splendor civitatis*, confirms what could be, and was, the outcome of the processes which establish the *platea* as a square in an urban landscape. This variety of practices can only take place in a space that is not architecturally and symbolically codified.

Epigraphy does not just inform our understanding of the *platea* as an urban process. The *platea* as written space describes an internal logic which connects town dwelling, euergetic practices, and the names of things. An abstract narrative of the interconnections of the three will illustrate this clearly. The foundation of a town, as well as its expansion, includes the formation of paths, sometimes planned, sometimes spontaneously generated. These become, formally, roads, once the act of paving has equipped them with the accessories that will allow a common consensus on their name. In the case of *plateae* the typical accessory may be viewed as being two lines of columns. Before this act takes place, however, a common understanding of the features of a town may evoke an identification of form that relates to function, not to monumental appearance. In the case of some paths, their widths may suggest a common agreement on one type of definition, that of *platea*. In time we can see two things happening to these 'informal' *plateae*: They can be monumentalized quite quickly or they can be monumentalized slowly or very slowly (or not at all!). Whether this happens or not does not change what these spaces are called by their users but may result in a change in their shape that better suits their use. If, for example, these become major *foci* for commercial exchange, their shape will tend to change to one resembling an open space or square (this depends on available space).

The act of euergetism, whether it happens early in the history of the space or at a later date, fossilizes a space which, in the case of *platea,* is evolving. The addition of a dedicatory inscription labelling the space, as a *platea,* seals the connection between the collective knowledge of that space and its appearance at the moment it is monumentalized. In this case, written space witnesses to the diachronic process that leads to different agreements on the nature of a *platea.*

Written space, however, has an even greater role to play. In fact, once the first *platea* has been identified, through an inscription, as being a square or a broad street, other *plateae* emerging as written spaces in that city will be affected by that very first association between name and object and thus perpetuate that first association through memory and history; for this reason Sidi Jdidi may have never had more than one *platea.* This *platea,* described in the entirety of its becoming rather than as a *fait accompli,* was born as a street, but died, once monumentalized, as a square.

Notes

1 Trifilò, 2008 and Newsome, 2011a, pp. 20–6.
2 Trifilò, forthcoming 2013.
3 Gros, 1986; Segal, 1997, pp. 67–79; Thomas, 2007, p. 118. For an overview see Trifilò, forthcoming, 2013.
4 Gros, 2005, pp. 191–214.
5 Woolf, 1996, pp. 25–9.
6 *AE* 1899, 3; *AE* 1914, 39; *AE* 1920, 77; *AE* 1925, 126 = *AE* 1926, +1 = *AE* 1926, +58 = *AE* 1926, +78 = *AE* 1927, +53 = *AE* 1927, +93 = *AE* 1927, +96 = *AE* 1997, 1482; *AE* 1931, 74; *AE* 1948, 111; *AE* 1964, 182; *AE* 1967, 565; *AE* 1985, 876a; *AE* 1989, 891; *AE* 1995, 1551; *AE* 1997, 740 = *AE* 2000, +640; *AE* 2004, 1798; *BCTH* 1902, 313; *CIL* 8.304 = *CIL* 8.11529; *CIL* 8.2723 = *CIL* 8.18120 = *ILS* 5568 = *AE* 1987, 1061, *CIL* 8.4878 = *ILAlg.*1.1273 = *ILS* 2943 = *AE* 1903, 97; *CIL* 8.10935 = *CIL* 8.20367; *CIL* 8.11530 (p. 2359); *CIL* 8.23291 = *AE* 1898, 48; *CIL* 8.23880 = *ILTun.* 666; *CIL* 8.24609 = *AE* 1893, 56 = *AE* 1968, 559b = *AE* 1980, 903; *CIL* 9.968; *CIL* 9.2476 = *ILS* 5353; *CIL* 9.6259; *CIL* 10.7516 (p. 995) = *ILS* 5352; *CIL* 13.7261 (4, p. 123) = *ILS* 7088; *CIL* 13.7263 (4, p. 123) = *ILS* 7089a; *CIL* 13.7264 (4, p. 123) = *ILS* 7089; *CIL* 13.7335 (4, p. 125) = *ILS* 7096 = *AE* 1998, +996; *CIL* 13.7337 = *ILS* 7097; *EAOR* 03.12 = *AE* 1964, 181 = *AE* 1965, 219; *IK* 67, 201, *ILSard.* 1.50 = *ILS* 5250 = *AE* 1897, 133; *IMCCatania* 42; Tourrenc, 1968, p. 219 (Data source: Clauss-Slaby Epigraphik-Datenbank: http://www.manfredclauss.de/gb/index.html (last accessed 3 June 2011).
7 Duncan-Jones, 1990, pp. 59–67.
8 *ILSard.* 1.50 = *ILS* 5250 = *AE* 1897, 133.
9 *AE* 1997, 740 = *AE* 2000, +640.
10 *CIL* 9.2476 = *ILS* 5353.
11 *CIL* 9.6259, 968.
12 *CIL* 8.304 = *CIL* 8.11529 and *CIL* 8.11530.
13 Ben Abdallah, 1992, p. 12.
14 *AE* 1899, 33; *AE* 1985, 876a; *AE* 1989, 891.
15 *BCTH* 1902, 313 and *AE* 1902, 146. The inscription has been recognized in multiple

copies (*AE* 1954, 150). Two of them were found in the forum (*CIL* 8.17851, 17860). See also Leglay and Tourrenc, 1985, p. 112.

16 Tourrenc, 1968, p. 219.
17 Tourrenc, 1968, p. 219.
18 *AE* 1948, 111; plus *CIL* 8.2369 and 2370 and another which is unpublished.
19 Leschi, 1947, pp. 87–99.
20 Tourrenc, 1968, pp. 197–209.
21 Tourrenc, 1968, p. 208.
22 Leglay and Tourrenc, 1985, p. 112.
23 Leglay and Tourrenc, 1985, p. 116.
24 *AE* 1967, 00565; *AE* 1914, 39.
25 *CIL* 8.2723 = *CIL* 8.18120 = *ILS* 5568.
26 The fragmentary state of the inscription does not allow us to demonstrate incontrovertibly that this is, in fact, the case.
27 *CIL* 8.10935 = *CIL* 8.20367.
28 *CIL* 10.7516= *ILS* 5352.
29 Lusnia, 2004, pp. 518–23.
30 Naddari, 2008, pp. 935–50.
31 *CIL* 13.7261, 7263, 7264.
32 *CIL* 13.7335, 7337.
33 *CIL* 13.7261.
34 *CIL* 13.7263, 7264.
35 *CIL* 13.7335.
36 *CIL* 13.7337.
37 On which see Trifilò, 2008.
38 *CIL* 13.7261, 7335, and 7337.
39 Gesemann, 1998, pp. 95–8. On *vici* and *compita* in Ancient Rome see Lott, 2004, pp. 13–18. On *compita* see also Laurence, 2011, pp. 388–90. We should also add a note about the *platiodanni vici novi*, mentioned on an inscription from Germania and interpreted by Zeller as figures corresponding to a Latin-Celtic hybrid corresponding to *magistri vicorum* (Zeller, 1906, pp. 312–15).
40 *Thesaurus Linguae Latinae* VI.2.3, p. 1835.
41 *AE* 1925, 126 = *AE* 1926, 1 = *AE* 1926, +58 = *AE* 1926, +78 = *AE* 1927, +53 = *AE* 1927, +93 = *AE* 1927, +96 = *AE* 1997, 1482; Johnson et al., 1961, n. 168.
42 Mitchell, and Waelkens, 1998, pp. 147–54.
43 *AE* 1931, 74; *IK* 67, 201; Harsh, 1937, pp. 51–2.
44 Ossi and Harrington, 2011, pp. 11–32.
45 *CIL* 8.24609 = *AE* 1893, 56 = *AE* 1968, 559b = *AE* 1980, 903.
46 Callu, J.-P., 1980, p. 281.
47 Piganiol, 1962, pp. 343–6.
48 Lèzine, 1968, pp. 83–6.
49 Saliou, 2008, pp. 63–8.
50 Ben Abed-Ben Khader et al., 2004, pp. 24–30. See also *AE* 2004, 1798 and Lepelley, 2011, pp. 286–7.
51 Lepelley is also convinced that this is the nature of Sidi Jdidi's *platea* (Lepelley, 2011, p. 287). The original excavators leave the question open (Ben Abed-Ben Khader et al., 2004, p. 27).
52 See note 3, above.

11

Writing Up the Baths: Reading Monumental Inscriptions in Roman Baths[1]

Alison E. Cooley

Along with other types of urban space in Roman cities, such as *fora* and theatres, baths could be transformed into written spaces by the display of inscriptions. This chapter explores the functions of inscriptions associated with baths in cities of the Roman West, focusing in particular upon Italy and North Africa, and considers the extent to which baths developed distinctive characteristics as written spaces, through an analysis of monumental inscriptions, leaving graffiti to one side. It offers an alternative perspective on understanding written spaces in Roman cities, one which is distinct from the more usual focus on themes such as identity and status. Although, as the first part of this chapter will explore, some inscriptions in baths *were* akin to those found in other public spaces, the rest of the chapter will examine how other inscriptions appear to have performed functions distinctive to bath buildings, in advertising their amenities and encouraging passers-by to appreciate their attractive environment. Monumental inscriptions associated with the baths complemented literary descriptions, with both types of texts promoting the expectation that visitors to the baths would have an enjoyable experience. The same thematic motifs are found, albeit on different scales, in Lucian's praise for the design of a set of baths by Hippias and in inscriptions. Lucian highlighted the fact that the baths were not just functional, but were of generous dimensions, brightly lit, attractively decorated with statues and marble, and offered convenience and variety to their users in terms of the number of pools and access routes.[2] As we shall see, epigraphy at the baths echoed the same language. Whether or not the expectations raised by such texts were in fact fulfilled for visitors to the baths is perhaps another question.

Benefactors at the baths

Before turning to distinctive types of writing at the baths, we should first consider the extent to which baths did also share characteristics with other written spaces, analysing first building-inscriptions and then the inscribed bases that originally accompanied portrait-statues. Baths, like other public buildings, could be built and repaired by private individuals (both male and female), public officials, or emperors. Their acts of generosity might be recorded in building-inscriptions, and the baths might be named after them. At Ostia, for example, the complex which we now know as the Forum Baths (I.xii.6) was still known after its Antonine founder as the 'Baths of Gavius Maximus' in the late fourth century AD, when it was restored by Ragonius Vincentius Celsus.[3] As elsewhere, the right that a donor's name be publicized in this way was an important mechanism for encouraging others to make similar donations to a town: a legal ruling protected a benefactor's name from being erased from a building precisely in order not to discourage future benefactors.[4]

Portrait statues of members of the imperial family or of the local elite might appear in the baths, some of which reflected the building history of the baths. At Ostia, the imperial statues of members of the Trajanic, Hadrianic, and Antonine dynasties found in the Baths of Neptune (II.iv.2) and Baths outside the Porta Marina (IV.x.1) probably reflected imperial investment in building those baths, both of which were on a grand scale.[5] A building-inscription believed to relate to the Baths of Neptune records that Hadrian had promised a sum of money to fund baths which were then completed by his successor Antoninus Pius.[6] A statue of Hadrian's wife, Sabina in the guise of Ceres, was found next to an *exedra* (niche) in the baths' *palaestra* (exercise-area), while the size of the base – big enough to accommodate two statues – suggests that her statue was probably originally accompanied by one of Hadrian himself.[7] Colossal portrait-heads of Trajan, his sister Marciana, and Sabina from the Baths outside the Porta Marina, along with a long-lost Trajanic inscription, are likewise suggestive of imperial sponsorship.[8] As the architectural scale of bath-buildings grew, so it seems did the scope to include increasingly lavish statues within them. The infiltration of the emperor and his family into public spaces in the form of portrait-statues, however, did not always entail imperial financial input into those spaces, but might reflect their dominant socio-political position.[9]

Demonstrating such a connection between a particular honorific statue and a set of baths for certain is often problematic, because of the reuse of inscribed material: fragments of inscriptions honouring Gavius Maximus found in various contexts around Ostia could equally well have been displayed either in his baths or in the forum or in some other public space.[10] Furthermore, the large quantity of marble sculpture together with inscriptions and fragments of architecture found in the Baths of Neptune bears no relationship to the original display of sculpture there (in contrast to the statue of Sabina mentioned above, which was found *in situ*), but is rather explained by the insertion of a lime-kiln into the baths during the medieval period, and perhaps also of another lime-kiln in the nearby Caseggiato delle Fornaci (II.vi.7).[11] By contrast, at Bulla Regia (Tunisia), the inscription upon a statue base honouring Julia Memmia, found in the vestibule to the baths, specifically praised her 'on account of the exceptional splendour of her work, the baths, by which she both adorned her place of origin and thought it right to care for the citizens' public(?) health'. Her statue's spatial context and location upon a tall base must have grabbed the attention of any visitor to the baths.[12] Furthermore, the inscription was engraved upon both the front and right faces of the base, ensuring that it could be seen from different angles. In this case, the text of the inscription itself points to a connection between honorand and baths.

Baths could also be an extension of civic space more generally, with some individuals being honoured with statues even though they had no obvious connection to the baths where their statues were located. At Timgad, for example, a series of imperial statues for members of Gallienus' dynasty were set up in the Large South Baths in the AD 250s (see Figure 10.2).[13] Of course, it is not always possible to be certain whether or not an honorand had some connection with the baths since statues are often found divorced from their inscribed bases, while inscriptions are not always explicit in revealing the motivation for granting honours. A benefactor at Ureu in Africa Proconsularis was decreed a statue by the local council and people of the town of the Uruenses (*ordo et populus municipii Uruensium*) after he had repaired the town's baths possibly in the second half of the third century AD.[14] Although it would seem likely that this statue was set up in the baths, another urban setting cannot be ruled out since it was found in a reused context. Nevertheless, it seems likely that baths became places where the local elite might assert its status in honouring members of the imperial family, Roman officials, and local dignitaries; the fact that they were used daily and were highly frequented made them suitable spaces in which to set up honorific statues. Baths, along with other public spaces such as *fora*, theatres, and temples, displayed honorific statues; we cannot now calculate whether particular spaces attracted particular types of statue-honours, nor is it clear whether there was a hierarchical division among civic space, with some places being perceived as more prestigious than others, nor whether decisions about where to erect statues were largely based upon pragmatic reasons. In the case of imperial statues, for instance, it would seem rash to suggest that an emperor's statue in the baths would somehow appear a lesser honour than one set up in the forum. Instead, emperors simply pervaded civic space as a whole. In this respect, therefore, epigraphic display within the baths belonged to the broader context of civic epigraphy.

Pleasures of the baths

balnea, vina, Venus corrumpunt corpora nostra set vitam faciunt.[15]

Baths, wine, and sex ruin our bodies, but make life worth living.

Visiting the baths was one of life's pleasures, an excuse for relaxation and self-indulgence. As various epigrams suggest, drinking, sex, and bathing were arguably the ultimate joys of Roman life, and the baths might accommodate all three activities at once.[16] There are striking similarities between inscriptions and literary epigrams giving an impression of the ethos of the baths. Various Greek epigrams in the *Palatine Anthology*, which purported to be copies of inscribed texts on buildings, illustrate how closely associated the baths were with Venus and the Graces. When these mention how deities are present at the baths, the epigrams are not just metaphorical in tone, but allude to their presence in the form of statues, which, appropriately enough, might depict the immortals as they bathed.[17]

Towns in the Latin West commonly contained multiple bath buildings. Although it might at first be tempting to consider a set of baths as a neighbourhood facility serving an individual district within a town, it seems more likely that individuals would choose which set of baths to patronize, given that different establishments had different facilities on offer. Monumental writing had a particular role to play both in publicizing these facilities and in helping to generate great expectations among potential visitors that a specific set of baths would offer them a pleasurable experience. As Fagan has explored,[18] Martial's epigrams give a vivid impression that individuals might patronize different establishments, even though they might have a particular favourite. We should, of course, be wary of reading Martial's poems straightforwardly as a reflection of society, but even so the epigrams do still use monuments in the city of Rome for constructing an image of the author.[19] In 3.36, addressed to Fabianus, Martial complains that, as his *amicus*, he has to accompany him to the Baths of Agrippa even though his personal preference is for the Baths of Titus: '(you order me) when I am exhausted to follow you at the tenth hour or later to the Baths of Agrippa, although I myself am bathing at those of Titus'.[20] In another epigram that begins with an echo of Catullus' invitation-poem to Fabullus,[21] Martial declares his intention of bathing at the Baths of Stephanus since they are near his house, as a prelude to entertaining friends for dinner: 'You will dine nicely, Julius Cerialis, at my place; if you have no better offer, come. You will be able to observe the eighth hour; we shall bathe together: you know how Stephanus' baths are adjacent to me'.[22] Martial mentions differences between the baths available in Rome in terms of their décor, size, and water-temperature (for instance, Nero's baths could be excessively hot),[23] praising the Baths of Claudius Etruscus in extravagant terms: 'Unless you bathe in the lovely little Baths of Etruscus, you will die unbathed, Oppianus. No waters will so charm you ... Nowhere is there an emptiness so gleaming and clear; the light itself is longer there, and from no place does day withdraw more slowly. There the quarries of Taygetus are green, and the rocks which the Phrygian and Libyan have cut out more deeply vie with multi-coloured beauty. Dense onyx exhales dry heat, and serpentine stones are warm with a faint flame. If Laconian practices please you, content with dry heat you will be able to take a dip in the vigorous Virgin or Marcia; these waters shine so bright and clear that you would not suspect any water there, and you would think that the Lygdian marble gleams empty'.[24]

Martial's depiction of customer choice is further supported by Seneca, who commented upon the way in which particular baths could go out of fashion: 'And so, the baths which had enjoyed throngs of admirers when they were dedicated, are avoided and jettisoned into the category of antiques when luxury has imagined up something new, by which luxury smothers itself'.[25]

The architectural layout of a set of baths was designed to attract customers, by showing consideration for the bather's enjoyment, creating variety in the routes through the baths that were available to bathers. At Ostia, for example, the Forum Baths – comprising 20 different rooms covering a surface area of c. 3,200 square metres – conformed to the half-axial ring design, with a symmetrical cold section to its north and asymmetrical heated section to the south (see Figure 11.1). A careful sequential layout of rooms enabled bathers to follow a circular route through these baths, avoiding having to double back through rooms already used.[26] The rooms themselves, identified as a *heliocaminus* (sun-room), *laconicum* (sweating-room), two *tepidaria* (warm-rooms), and a *caldarium* (hot-room), were different geometrical shapes, offering a range of humidity and temperatures. In this way, the innovative architectural design contributed to creating variety in the bathers' experience, and complemented the way in which inscriptions tried to direct and enhance this experience as well, as discussed later.[27]

Nor is the literary picture of the choice available to bathers relevant only to the city of Rome and nearby Ostia. At Pompeii, for example, eight different bathing establishments have so far been identified (see map of Pompeii): Stabian Baths (VII.i.8), Republican Baths (VII.v.36), Forum Baths (VII.v), Central Baths (IX.iv), Sarno Baths (VIII.ii.17, 22–4), Suburban Baths, Baths of Julia Felix (II.iv.3), and Baths of Crassus Frugi.[28] Six of these may have been operational simultaneously at the time of the eruption in AD 79, with the Republican Baths having fallen out of use before the Augustan era and the Central Baths being as yet unfinished. The archaeological evidence suggests ways in which the complexes offered distinctive user experiences. The Stabian Baths differed from other baths in the town by offering a spacious *palaestra* (porticoed exercise-area) with a swimming-pool and *sphaeristerium* (court for ball-games).[29] Bathing in segregated male and female sections was available in the Forum, Stabian, and Sarno Baths.[30] The Suburban Baths were of a modern design (like the incomplete Central Baths), being roomier, lighter, and more luxurious than the pre-existing facilities at Pompeii, even including a heated swimming pool.[31] This complex also included a *laconicum* (sweating-room), a facility which had been replaced by a *frigidarium* (cold-room) in both the Stabian and Forum Baths. Both the

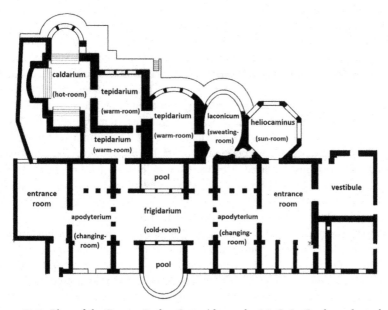

Figure 11.1 Plan of the Forum Baths, Ostia (drawn by M. G. L. Cooley, adapted from Nielsen, 1993, vol. 2, Figure 69)

Sarno Baths and the Suburban Baths had less space for physical exercise than the other baths and more spaces for socializing.[32] It is likely, therefore, that bathers would have chosen to frequent a particular set of baths because of the distinctive facilities on offer there.

Inscriptions had a specific role to play in drawing to people's attention what was on offer in individual bathing establishments. Building – and rebuilding – inscriptions belonging to baths might mention the attractiveness, elegance, and luxury of the facilities on offer.[33] The proverbial *voluptas* of bathing was even promoted in building inscriptions: a fourth-century inscription from Ocriculum (Umbria) records the refurbishing of the 'pleasure of the winter baths' (*voluptatem thermarum hiemalium*).[34] Several of these inscriptions belong to the wider context of an emphasis during Late Antiquity upon improving the townscape and a tendency towards including more detail in epigraphic texts. Nevertheless, the idea that the decoration of the baths was a key component earlier too is clearly reflected by the way in which Pliny the Younger bequeathed a sum of money specifically for decorating the baths which he had sponsored.[35] Inscriptions might list specific improvements made to bath-buildings, such as adding new facilities and repairing old,[36] or improving the quality and quantity of the water-supply.[37] Benefactors took pains to enumerate not just the improvements made to the architecture and design of the bath-buildings, but also their contribution to enhancing the elegance of the baths:[38] at Municipium Aurelium Commodianum in Africa Proconsularis during the late third century AD, for example, Q. Vetulenius Urbanus Herennianus recorded the fact that he had created a new changing-room and two pools, had restored everything else, and had also added ornamentation in the form of marble statues and paintings.[39] In roughly the same period, at Thibursicum Bure, also in Africa Proconsularis, four marble statues were added to the changing room to increase its attractiveness and splendour.[40]

While words such as *cultus*, *splendor*, and *ornamenta* were not exclusively used in inscriptions describing baths, the contribution of these factors to making a visit to the baths a fundamentally pleasurable experience was a defining characteristic of bathing complexes, and the language of inscriptions reflected this. Some inscriptions also evoked the ultimate in bathing experiences, as measured by two yardsticks, namely the city of Rome and Baiae. Rome, with its grandiose imperial *thermae*, became synonymous with luxury and sophistication, while the thermo-mineral springs at the allegedly louche resort of Baiae on the Bay of Naples, became proverbial for pleasure seeking.[41] Inscriptions displayed at baths many miles from Italy might evoke these distant epitomes of luxury and pleasure, wishing for those who read their words as they visited the baths just as much pleasure and relaxation as might be sought at these famous establishments. Claims to be offering a fleeting taste of Baiae could appear in appropriately sophisticated format, in Virgilian-sounding dactylic hexameter verses: *en perfecta cito Baiaru(m) grata voluptas/undantesque fluunt aq(uae) saxi de rupe sub ima/nisibus hic nostris prostratus libor anhelat/quisquis amat fratrum veniat mecumq(ue) laetetur* ('Behold the delightful pleasure of Baiae swiftly completed, and gushing waters flow from beneath the rock. Laid prostrate here through our efforts, envy breathes its last. Whoever of my brothers loves me, let him come and be glad with me.').[42] This third-century text appeared in the coastal baths at Sullecthum (Tunisia) in a *tabula ansata*, at the steps leading to the pool of the *frigidarium* (cold-room). Likewise, promises of 'city-style' bathing (*urbico more*) were made in inscriptions which might be presented in the form of a public announcement, within a *tabula ansata*, as at Equizetum in Mauretania Caesariensis: *in his praediis Cominiorum/ Montani et Feliciani Iun(ioris)/et Feliciani patris eorum/balneum [et] omnis humani-/ tas urbico more praebetur* ('In this estate of the Cominii, of Montanus and Felicianus Junior and of their father Felicianus, a bath and everything civilized will be supplied, city-style').[43] In these cases, the inscribed texts could promote the expectation among visitors to the baths that they were about to enjoy a first-class bathing experience; it would probably not be anachronistic even to see them as serving an advertising function. Concern for advertising the quality of privately-owned baths emerges from a painted inscription from the estate of Julia Felix at Pompeii, offering her property for rent: one of the aspects of her estate listed individually was the *balneum venerium et nongentum*, which may be roughly translated as 'elegant baths for the discerning user'.[44] Clearly this feature of the estate was listed with the intention of persuading a potential lessee to invest in real-estate that was likely to attract customers, and thereby profit.

Other inscriptions contributed to the attractiveness and distinctiveness of individual sets of baths, but not in the form of words alone.[45] Mosaics in the baths often juxtaposed words and images. Mosaic inscriptions hailed bathers at their entry to and exit from the baths in order to wish them pleasurable bathing.[46] Bathers entering the *frigidarium* (cold-room) in the Theatre Baths (V.1) at Sabratha were met with the greeting 'Wash well' (*bene laba*), and were sent upon their way by the comment 'It is healthy to have washed' (*salvom lavisse*).[47] These texts were accompanied by images of strigils, sandals, and oil-flask. Katherine Dunbabin has argued that such expressions were not just polite messages, but might also reflect a perception that baths were not just places of beauty, pleasure, and well-being, but might have a more sinister side. Quite apart from potential physical accidents such as drowning, there was a sense that too much beauty could be a bad thing, attracting jealousy and the Evil Eye. These texts, therefore, were also intended to provide protection to visitors to the baths.[48] Apotropaic inscriptions might be displayed in vulnerable spaces at the baths in order to protect owner and users alike. Ostia was particularly well provided with around 20 privately-owned baths, many of which included memorable black-and-white mosaics of this type. Several of the modern names for the various baths derive from these mosaics, and it seems likely that they would have contributed something to their individuality in antiquity too. In the 'Baths of Buticosus' (I.xiv.8), for example, a naked male figure is depicted in a room leading to the hot rooms, holding a bucket in his left hand, accompanied by the label 'Epictetus Buticosus'.[49] On one interpretation, he simply represents the overseer of the baths, and the image implies that the needs of customers will be met by him, one of his tasks possibly being to pour warm water over them.[50] In this way, the mosaic perhaps advertised one of the attractions provided by these baths. This interpretation, however, does not adequately account for the figure's ithyphallic representation, something which has led Katherine Dunbabin to suggest that the mosaic may equally well have served an apotropaic function as much as one of welcoming bathers.[51]

Figure 11.2 Mosaic from the Baths of Buticosus, Ostia (author's photo).

Other mosaics encouraged visitors to the baths to associate the idea of visiting the baths with the idea of enjoying healthy relaxation and exercise. Mosaics of athletes invited viewers to regard themselves as participating in similar activities in the *palaestra* (exercise-area) of baths; some of these may have been generalized depictions of training, while other figures depicted upon the mosaics can be identified in some cases by their *cirrus* (hair worn in a top-knot) and spiked gloves as professional athletes rather than as casual visitors to the baths.[52] Commemoration of specific athletes is also implied by a mosaic paving in the baths along the Via Severiana at Ostia, which depicts framed portraits of four athletes and one trainer/umpire, each labelled with what look like nicknames.[53] In this way, bathers who chose to train while visiting the baths were perhaps encouraged to regard the athletes depicted on the various mosaics as role models to some extent.[54]

More unusual is a sizeable marble plaque at Pompeii, which displayed an inscription designed to generate custom for the privately-owned baths of Crassus Frugi. The precise location of these baths is unknown, since the plaque was found reused outside the Herculaneum Gate. This inscription advertised the distinctive attractive qualities of the baths owned by Crassus Frugi, but was set up by a freedman who was probably in charge of the business: 'Baths of Marcus Crassus Frugi with seawater and baths with freshwater. Ianuarius, freedman.'[55] The baths must have been located near the sea since their distinctive claim was to combine different types of seawater and freshwater. The owner may have been M. Licinius Crassus Frugi, consul of AD 64, of whom Pliny the Elder records that he exploited the health-giving properties of seawater in a bathing establishment near Baiae: 'In the sea itself too, steam rises from the water that belonged to Licinius Crassus, and there comes something valuable to health in the very midst of the waves'.[56] Pliny's comment relates to baths at Baiae, not at Pompeii, so what this inscription demonstrates is the way in which Crassus Frugi may have developed a particular marketing strategy in establishing baths of a particular character – with both seawater and freshwater – both at Baiae and at Pompeii, and how his freedman agent then took pains to commission a plaque for publicity for the less famous establishment. In this case, it is not so much pleasure that seems to be at stake as claims for health-giving properties from bathing.

Healthy bathing

The multifaceted properties of the baths were illustrated through statues on display in them, designs on mosaics, and inscribed texts. Statues abounded in the baths, with the overwhelming majority of them representing divine figures.[57] Deities associated with themes appropriate to the baths were especially common. Asclepius and Hygeia, Venus and Cupid, Bacchus, and Hercules variously recalled cleanliness, hygiene, and health, love, wine, and athletic prowess. Baths were not just places where pleasure might be sought, but were, equally importantly, somewhere to refresh the body and pursue good health. An acrostic verse inscription composed by centurion Q. Avidius Quintianus and

Figure 11.3 Greek epigram from the Forum Baths, Ostia (A. E. Cooley, by kind permission of the Soprintendenza Speciale per i Beni Archeologici di Roma e Ostia)

displayed in the baths of the army camp at Bu Njem in Tripolitania, on the fringes of the Sahara desert, praised the health-giving properties of the *frigidarium* (cold-room), in relieving the soldiers from the oppressive Saharan winds, dedicating the complex to *Salus* (health): 'I have given to all the genuine waters of Health amid such great fiery temperatures, in the midst of those unending sand-dunes of the south wind that stirs up the burning flames of the sun, so that they might soothe their bodies by bathing in tranquillity'.[58] Admittedly, one can appreciate that the extreme climate of the North African desert may well have strengthened considerably the soldiers' appreciation of their bath building, but this link between well-being and bathing was not unknown elsewhere too. Bath owners were eager to remind visitors to their baths of the link between bathing and health, especially in the sense that good health was not just a result of medical treatment: the baths were regarded as a place of escape from life's hardships.[59]

The Forum Baths at Ostia offer an interesting case study of the role of inscriptions in promoting the perception that visiting the baths could promote a sense of well-being among those who frequented them. A Greek verse epigram in the form of an elegiac couplet was inscribed during the early fourth century upon an architrave, which was displayed in the *frigidarium* (cold-room): 'Victor, the noble leader of Ausonia, offered bathing to soothe troubles' (λουτρὸν ἀλεξίπον[ον – – δε]ιξεν Βίκτωρ ἀρχὸς ἐὼν κύδιμος Αὐσονίης).[60] The Victor named here is most likely to have been Fl. Octavius Victor, prefect of the *annona* (grain-supply) during the reign of Constantine.[61] A number of fragmentary inscriptions bearing his name have been found in various parts of Ostia, one of which may originally have been associated with the Greek epigram.[62] It has a distinctly watery theme: 'A horse carries Glauce, going across the waters by swimming, seeing that no opportunity for being rowed across presents itself' (*Glauce[n v]ectat equ(u)s tra[mi]ttens aequora [n]ando, quippe v[ehi remis] copia nu[lla datur] Fl(avius) Octabi[us Victor] v(ir) c(larissimus) praef(ectus) a[nn(onae)] curavi[t]*). Fausto Zevi has made the attractive suggestion that this inscription accompanied a sculptural group, which was originally displayed in the baths.[63] The choice of Greek language for the verse epigram reassuring bathers of the soothing properties of bathing is no coincidence, but allowed linguistic resonances of a type that can also be seen in contemporary literary sources. One of the epigrams in the *Palatine Anthology*, from a bath complex in Constantinople, puns on the verbal similarity between the lotus (λωτὸν) and baths (λουτρον), and the capacity of both to free the mind from all thoughts: 'The old story of the lotus-eaters is no falsehood. This bath confirms its truth. For if a man once bathes in these pure waters he does not regret his country or desire his parents'.[64] St Augustine, too, related how, on hearing of his mother's death, his thoughts turned to bathing: 'for I had heard that the bath owes its Greek name to the fact that it drives anxieties from the mind'.[65] Isidore of Seville refers to the same idea, that the Latin word *balnea* was derived from the Greek *balaneion* ('bath'), because baths give relief from worries and sorrow, and this rather dubious etymology is more explicitly articulated in a grammatical text, which suggests that *dicitur balneum* ἀπὸ τοῦ βάλλειν νόον ('*balneum* is named after the act of casting aside thinking').[66] Returning to the Greek epigram at Ostia once more, we now appreciate that a decision to compose and inscribe the couplet in Greek reflected such etymological hypotheses and must potentially have enhanced the enjoyment of the baths for at least some of its well-educated users. The very use of Greek supported the inscription's claim that these baths would soothe their bathers. The juxtaposition of the inscribed epigram with statues of the health-giving deities Hygeia and Asclepius, which were displayed alongside it in niches in the *frigidarium* (cold-room), complemented each other to support the claim that bathers would benefit from their visit to these baths.[67]

Conclusions

Inscriptions in baths could serve a range of functions, some of which they shared with other urban spaces, but others of which appear to have been distinctive to the baths as written space. Many of the texts on display in bath-buildings in different formats – as building-inscriptions, on statue bases, as part of mosaics – shared the same purpose. The display of writing had particular functions in the context of baths that distinguished it from writing on display elsewhere in towns, namely, to attract visitors and to contribute in a positive way to their enjoyment of the baths. Both epigraphic and literary texts – notably the epigrams of Martial – shared common themes, anticipating the readers' pleasure in particular baths, focusing upon the qualities of individual sets of baths, and perhaps even advertising them at times. This helped to shape baths as written spaces in a way that was distinctive from other types of public space, by promoting the impression that an aesthetic response was what was appropriate to the baths on the part of viewers. Texts helped to direct responses to bathing-spaces, writing them up in a positive way.

Reading inscriptions is not a straightforward task, however: both in Roman times and nowadays different interpretations are possible of a single inscription. To understand the baths as written spaces, it is crucial to examine as far as possible inscriptions as they were displayed within their spatial contexts. Inscriptions combined closely with sculptural and mosaic decoration in order to evoke an atmosphere of relaxation, beauty, and pleasure to match the avowed aims of providing social and cultural refreshment for their users. In this way, texts and images complemented each other in promoting the pleasures and benefits of bathing and exercising at the baths. One distinctive function of the writing associated with baths was its use for advertisement, something which makes sense within the context of customer-choice, as individuals would choose which set of baths to patronize, but as well as extending promises of self-indulgence and pleasure, some inscriptions were designed to persuade visitors to the baths that their experience there was going to be not just pleasurable, but also salutary.

Notes

1   I am grateful to Gareth Sears and Ray Laurence for their insightful feedback on this chapter.
2   Lucian, *Hippias*, 4–8.
3   Bloch, 1953; Meiggs, 1973, p. 415; Fagan, 1999a, p. 239; Cicerchia and Marinucci, 1992, p. 216 C106 = *CIL* 14.4718 = *AE* 1955, 287; cf. Cicerchia and Marinucci, 1992,

p. 222 C109a = *AE* 1995, 246a; Cicerchia and Marinucci, 1992, p. 220 C107bis = *AE* 1984, 150 = *CIL* 6.29769.

4   Cf. *Digest* 50.10.2.2 (Ulpian): *ne eius nomine, cuius liberalitate opus exstructum est, eraso aliorum nomina inscribantur et propterea revocentur similes civium in patrias liberalitates, praeses provinciae auctoritatem suam interponat.*

5   Baths of Neptune: Pavolini, 2006, p. 58; Baths outside Porta Marina: Pavolini, 2006, p. 180.

6   *CIL* 14.98 = Fagan, 1999a, p. 234, no. 6.

7   Statue of Sabina: Manderscheid, 1981, pp. 37, 78, no. 90.

8   Trajanic inscription – Meiggs, 1973, p. 408. Statue fragments: Manderscheid, 1981, p. 79, nos. 99–101.

9   Cooley (in press).

10 *AE* 1955, 176; *CIL* 14.191 + 4471; Cicerchia and Marinucci, 1992, p. 217; Zevi, 1971.

11 Turchetti, 1994, p. 100; Lenzi, 1998, p. 256, nos. 5–6.

12 Broise and Thébert, 1993, pp. 347–51: *ILAfr* 454: *...ob/[praecipu]am operis sui thermarum / [magnifi]centiam qua et patriam/[suam e]xornavit et saluti civium/ [publ?]ico consulere/[dignata] est/...*; AD 220/40; Fagan, 1999a, pp. 296–7.

13 Thébert, 2003, pp. 517–18.

14 *AE* 1975, 880: Thébert, 2003, p. 499; Fagan, 1999a, p. 267, no. 110.

15 *CIL* 6.15258.

16 Dunbabin, 1989; Fagan, 1999a, pp. 30–6.

17 *Palatine Anthology* 9.606–10, 616, 619–20, 623, 625–6, 637–9; discussed by Dunbabin, 1989, pp. 12–14.

18 Fagan, 1999a, pp. 19–21.

19 Laurence, 2011.

20 Martial, *Ep.* 3.36, vv.5–6: *lassus ut in thermas decuma vel serius hora/te sequar Agrippae, cum laver ipse Titi.*

21 Catullus 13.

22 Martial, *Ep.* 11.52: *cenabis belle, Iuli Cerialis, apud me;/condicio est melior si tibi nulla, veni./ octavam poteris servare; lavabimur una:/scis quam sint Stephani balnea iuncta mihi.*

23 Martial, *Ep.* 10.48.3–4.

24 Martial, *Ep.* 6.42.1–3 *Etrusci nisi thermulis lavaris,/inlotus morieris, Oppiane./nullae sic tibi blanientur undae,/...ll7–* nusquam tam nitidum vacat serenum:/lux ipsa est ibi longior, diesque/nullo tardius a loco recedit./illic Taygeti virent metalla/et certant vario decore saxa,/quae Phryx et Libys altius cecidit;/siccos pinguis onyx anhelat aestus/ et flamma tenui calent ophitae. ritus si placeant tibi Laconum,/contentus potes arido vapore/cruda Virgine Marciave mergi;/quae tam candida, tam serena lucet/ut nullas ibi suspiceris undas/et credas vacuam nitere lygdon.

25 Seneca, *Ep.* 86.8: *itaque quae concursum et admirationem habuerant, cum dedicarentur, devitantur et in antiquorum numerum reiciuntur, cum aliquid novi luxuria commenta est, quo ipsa se obrueret.*

26 Cicerchia and Marinucci, 1992, p. 20.

27 Cicerchia and Marinucci, 1992, pp. 29–38; Nielsen, 1993a, p. 52.

28 Pesando and Guidobaldi, 2006, pp. 77–90; Nielsen, 1993b, pp. 7–8.

29 Pesando and Guidobaldi, 2006, p. 79.

30 Both Forum and Sarno Baths were partly being redesigned in 79, however: Pesando and Guidobaldi, 2006, pp. 83, 87; Koloski Ostrow, 1990, pp. 50–3.

31 Jacobelli, 1995, p. 18.

32 Pesando and Guidobaldi, 2006, p. 78; Koloski Ostrow, 1990, pp. 81–105.
33 *CIL* 14.98 Ostia (*Regio* I) = Fagan, 1999a, p. 234 no. 6; *CIL* 14.3594 Tibur (*Regio* I) =
    Fagan, 1999a, p. 241 no. 30, fourth century; *AE* 1987, 307 Canusium (*Regio* II); *CIL*
    10.212 Grumentum (*Regio* III) = Fagan, 1999a, p. 246 no.45, fourth to fifth centuries;
    CIL 11.7285 Volsinii (*Regio* VII); *CIL* 8.1297 Membressa (Africa Proconsularis); *AE*
    1975, 873 Abbir Maius, Africa Proconsularis; *AE* 1913, 227 Regium Iulium = Fagan,
    1999a, p. 237 no.18, AD 374; *CIL* 10.6656 Antium = Fagan, 1999a, p. 244 no.37, late
    fourth century.
34 *CIL* 11.4095 Ocriculum, fourth century= Fagan, 1999a, p. 274, no. 124.
35 *CIL* 5.5262.
36 *AE* 1928, 2 Cyrene (*balineum cum porticibus et sphaeristeris*) = Fagan, 1999a,
    p. 234 no. 5, Hadrianic; *CIL* 8.24106 Carpis (*assa, destrictarium solariumque*)
    = Fagan, 1999a, p. 238, no. 21, 43/42 BC; *CIL* 14.2121 Lanuvium (*balnea virilia
    utraque et muliebre*) = Fagan, 1999a, p. 246 no. 46; *CIL* 11.6040 Pitinum Pisaurense
    (*pavimentum tepidari ... tubu[los ... la]cus piscinamque*) = Fagan, 1999a, p. 247,
    no.50; *CIL* 14.2119 Lanuvium (*apodyterium [ope]re tectorio ... piscinam ... labrum
    [ae]num cum salientibus [r]ostris navalibus tr[ibu]s*) = Fagan, 1999a, p. 249, no. 59;
    CIL 3.7342 Philippi (*cella natatori[a...]*) = Fagan, 1999a, p. 250 no. 60; *CIL* 10.829
    Pompeii (*laconicum et destrictarium ... porticus et palaestr(am)*) = Fagan, 1999a,
    p. 250, no. 61 mid-first century BC; *ILAlg.* 1.2102 Madaurus (*piscinalem ... et soliarem
    cellam ... exquisitis diversorum co[lorum marmoribus ... splen]dentes novoque omnino
    opera tes(s)ellatas*) = Fagan, 1999a, p. 278, no.131 mid-fourth century; *ILAfr.* 285
    Thuburbo Maius (*[cellam s]oliarem cum solis omni etiam refuso instrumento aeris
    et plumbi firma...piscinam novam nomine cochleam redditis veteribus exceptoriis*) =
    Fagan, 1999a, pp. 280–1 no. 137 late fourth century.
37 *CIL* 12.2494 Vicus Albinnensis (Gallia Narbonensis) second century AD = Fagan, 1999a,
    p. 256 no. 82; *CIL* 8.5335 Calama (Numidia) AD 366–8 = Fagan, 1999a, p. 278, no. 131.
38 Dunbabin, 1989, p. 9.
39 *CIL* 8.23964: Q(uintus) Vetulenius Urbanus Herennianus ... *apodyterium novum/in
    dextera cellis exeuntibus/a solo constructum piscinas duas/cetera restaurata adq(ue)
    statuis/marmoribus tabulis pictis/columnis ingressu cellaru[m]/alisq(ue) rebus ornata
    sumtu proprio ...perfecit adq(ue) dedicavit* = Fagan, 1999a, p. 269, no. 114.
40 *CIL* 8.25998, AD 260–305: Thébert, 2003, pp. 496–7 = Fagan, 1999a, p. 269 no. 115;
    cf. *AE* 1987, 307 Canusium third century = Fagan, 1999a, p. 270, no. 116: *omni
    cultu restituit*; *IRT* 601b Lepcis Magna, third century= Fagan, 1999a, p. 270 no.
    117: *cellam thermar(um) marmorib(us) Numidicis et opera musaeo exornavit*; *CIL*
    10.5348 Interamna Lirenas ?third century = Fagan, 1999a, p. 271, no. 118: *restituit
    exornavitque*; *AE* 1937, 119/20 Amiternum, fourth century= Fagan, 1999a, p. 272,
    no. 121: *omni ornamento at pulcritudinem restauravit statuisque decoravit*; *CIL*
    11. 4095 Ocriculum, fourth century= Fagan, 1999a, p. 274, no. 124: *ad meliorem
    pulcritudinem*; *CIL* 9.3677 Marruvium Marsorum ?late Republic = Fagan, 1999a,
    p. 284 no. 151 [*balneum muliebre ...fecit, eadem lapide va[rio ex]ornavit*; *CIL* 11.7285
    Volsinii first century = Fagan, 1999a, p. 286, no. 159: *balneum cum omn[i ornatu]*.
41 Yegül, 1996; Dunbabin, 1989, pp. 14–15.
42 *AE* 1968, 610 Sullecthum = Thébert, 2003, p. 494, third and fourth centuries. Cf. *CIL*
    8.25362 for a sixth-century continuation of this idea = Thébert, 2003, p. 498: *cerne
    salutiferas sp[lendent]i marmore Baias,/qui calidos aestu[s tin]gere quaeris aquis,/hic
    ubi Vulcno Ne[rine] certat amore,/nec necat unda f[ocum? n]ec nocet ignis aquas./
    gaude operi Gebam[unde t]uo regalis origo, deliciis sospes ute[re cu]m populo.*

43 *AE* 1933, 49 = Thébert, 2003, p. 506. Cf. *CIL* 14.4015 Ficulea; *CIL* 11.721 Bologna.
44 *CIL* 4.1136.
45 Dunbabin, 1989, pp. 16–18.
46 Dunbabin, 1989, pp. 18–19.
47 *IRT2009* 170–1 (with photographs online).
48 Dunbabin, 1989, pp. 33–45, esp. 42.
49 Becatti, 1961, Tav. CIX no. 51; Pavolini, 2006, p. 124.
50 Nielsen, 1993a, p. 129.
51 Dunbabin, 1989, p. 43.
52 Newby, 2002, p. 181.
53 Floriani Squarciapino, 1987 = *AE* 1989, 131; Newby, 2002, pp. 194–6.
54 Newby, 2002, p. 200.
55 *CIL* 10.1063: *thermae/M(arci) Crassi Frugi/aqua marina et baln(ea)/aqua dulci Ianuarius l(ibertus)*; Fagan, 1999a, p. 62.
56 Plin. *HN* 31.2.5: *vaporant et in mari ipso quae Licinii Crassi fuere, mediosque inter fluctus existit aliquid valetudini salutare*; D'Arms, 1970, pp. 214–15.
57 Manderscheid, 1981, p. 28.
58 *IRT2009* 918, ll.18–25: *cunctis dedi/veras salutis lymphas/tantis ignibus/in istis semper ha/renacis collibus/nutantis Austri solis/flammas feruidas/tranquille ut nando/ delenirent corpora*; Rebuffat, 1987.
59 Fagan, 1999a, pp. 85–103.
60 Inv 7100a/b = Cicerchia and Marinucci, 1992, p. 219 C107; Zevi, 1971, pp. 450–67; Lazzarini, 1983, 1996.
61 *PLRE* I, Fl. Octavius.
62 Cicerchia and Marinucci, 1992, p. 216 C105.
63 Zevi, 1971, p. 466.
64 *Palatine Anthology* 9.618: λωτὸν ἐρεπτομένους προτέρων οὐ ψεύσατο μῦθος·/πίστιν ἀληθείης τοῦτο τὸ λουτρὸν ἔχει./εἰ γὰρ ἅπαξ καθαροῖσι λοέσσεται ὕδασιν ἀνήρ,/οὐ ποθέει πάτρην, οὐκ ἐθέλει γενέτας.
65 August, *Conf.* 9.12.32: *quod audieram inde balneis nomen inditum, quia Graeci* βαλανεῖον *dixerint, quod anxietatem pellat ex animo.*
66 Isidore, *Etym.* 15.2.40: *balneis vero nomen inditum a levatione maeroris; nam Graeci* BALANEION *dixerunt, quod anxietatem animi tollat*; Gramm. Suppl. 237.5.
67 Hygeia: inv. 1252; Asclepius: inv. 1253 = Cicerchia and Marinucci, 1992, p. 147 A3 + A4; Manderscheid, 1981, p. 76, nos 71, 73.

Regional Written Spaces?

12

A New Era? Severan Inscriptions in Africa

Gareth Sears

Introduction

Examine *l'Année Épigraphique* and the frequency of dedications, statues and public buildings erected in Severan-era Africa will become immediately apparent. The density of inscriptions or uptake of the 'epigraphic habit'[1] under the Severans in African cities has been linked with the obvious dynastic links between the Severans and the African provinces,[2] Severus and his family's probable presence in Africa in 202–3[3] and the need for cities across the Empire to assert their loyalty to them.[4] The Severan connection with Africa, as an explanatory framework, is perhaps confirmed by the development of some new public spaces, often coupled with dynastic monuments, as replacements or additions to the existing urban landscape, and authors can point to the example of the structures constructed under the Severans at Lepcis Magna.[5] True, the relationship of the Severans with Africa may have been important, but, as I shall argue, other factors need to be considered in the explanation of 'written space' within the African city under the Severans. Indeed, rather than being a phenomenon exclusive to the period of the Severan dynasty centred on the replication of the development of Lepcis in other cities, the development of urbanism and the 'epigraphic habit' in Africa has a wider context over a longer period of time that cannot be exclusively associated with the Severans. In order to contextualize the development of written space under the dynasty, I will examine the production of written space in Latin Africa, its context within African urbanism and the creation and form of new urban spaces, particularly monuments that were explicitly connected with the family, onto which the Severans and others could be inscribed. I will also explore how these Severan era complexes and inscriptions might have interacted with movement through the city and how it constrained and created written space for the rest of antiquity. It is not my aim here to list Severan-era building work but to explore the interrelationship and development of space and written text in Severan- period Africa.[6]

The African context

The importance of the Severan era is well known in terms of the production of the monumental African city and its written space and for the promotion of many cities.[7] Here it is important to examine how the Severan period fits into building trends across the African provinces and what the consequences of that are for the production of written spaces. A methodological approach that examines the creation or transformation of written space through the prism of imperial dynasties might be questioned; urban development cannot be neatly tied to individual imperial dynasties. For instance, although we think of Rome's imperial *fora* as belonging to a particular reign we are also well aware that they underwent regular rebuilding.[8] However, the nature of epigraphy, with the dedication (if not construction) of monuments being dated to specific reigns or years allows us to closely analyse the initial formation of a written space and, with the accretion of new texts, the intensification or alteration, of that space.

There are several factors behind the preponderance of Severan-era inscriptions in the epigraphic record; some are more quantifiable than others. An important element is that the Severan era comes at the end of a phase when the number of building projects documented and being undertaken in African cities increased reign after reign (see Table 12.1). It is important when analysing the data to compensate for the varying length of reigns; a calculation of number of inscriptions divided by years ruled allows for sensible comparison. Such an analysis demonstrates more building work being commemorated in inscriptions under Septimius Severus and Caracalla per year than in any earlier reign. So, under Antoninus Pius 1.26 buildings per year are recorded as having work undertaken on them, under Marcus Aurelius 3.5, Commodus 1.8 and Septimius Severus/Caracalla 3.64. Even under Severus Alexander there were more building inscriptions being erected per year (2.38) in the African cities than there had been under any emperor before Marcus Aurelius; across the whole Severan period (AD 193–235) the ratio is 2.98 building inscriptions per year. Importantly, the Severan period, as the Augustan or Antonine periods before it, is long enough to mitigate against distortions caused by the actions of individuals. A long-term analysis helps, for instance, to reduce the effect of an imperial wall building programme in Mauretania Caesarensis under Severus Alexander and Gordian III.[9]

The trajectory of ever increasing documented building projects during the second century does not just reflect the growth of a few urban economies and/or the deepening of the 'epigraphic habit' among a few elites. This was an era when growing numbers of communities were erecting buildings with inscriptions (see Table 12.2). Under the Antonines, African cities became increasingly inscribed spaces; existing public spaces became inscribed in a denser fashion than in the previous century and the plethora of new spaces incorporated inscriptions from the outset. This method of elite self-presentation, through a public writing culture, also broadened geographically during the course of the second century AD as many Numidian and Mauretanian communities began to set up building inscriptions and honorific statuary. One consequence of this gradual evolution of monumental space in Africa was that Severan-era building took

Table 12.1 Building/rebuilding work in African communities attested by inscriptions[10]

	Africa	Numidia[11]	Mauretania C.
Augustus	5	–	–
Tiberius	12[12]	–	–
Gaius	–	–	–
Claudius	5	–	–
Nero	3	–	–
Vespasian	5	2	–
Titus	–	–	–
Domitian	5	–	–
Nerva	1	–	–
Trajan	14	2	–
Hadrian	23	6	1
A. Pius	23	12	4
M. Aurelius	41	24	2
Commodus	17	5	–
Severus	35	17	9
Caracalla	22	8	1
Macrinus	1	1	–
Elagabalus[13]	–	–	1
S. Alexander	13	7	11
M. Thrax	1	–	–
Gordian III	5	1	6

Table 12.2 Number of African communities erecting public buildings by century

	Africa	Numidia	Mauretania C.
First century BC	7	–	–
First century AD	20	3	2
Second century (not inc. Severans)	78	16	8
Third century (inc. Severans)	74	20	24

place on a larger prepared canvas than had been the case in any of their predecessors' reigns. On this perspective Severan period activity is perhaps less notable.

The consequences of Severan building

The activity undertaken under the Severan dynasty would have major consequences for the urban topography and the prevalence of writing within cities. As has been demonstrated above, more cities were monumentalized (by which I mean these cities had constructed, multiple substantial public buildings incorporating dedicatory inscriptions) by the end of Severus Alexander's reign than they had been in 193. The broadening of urban culture produced a growing network of cities on to which loyalty to members of the Severan dynasty could be inscribed; considerable numbers of cities that cannot be demonstrated as building structures or erecting official inscriptions in the second or fourth centuries did so in the third century, many under the Severans.[14] The scale of the work is both a declaration of continuity with the past and confidence in the dynasty.[15] The building work of the early third century would have resulted in some urban landscapes being dominated by written expressions of loyalty and devotion to the Severans and by new buildings on which those dedications were located. In these centres Severan-period building inscriptions would have formed the base against which all later inscriptions could be measured and, given the lack of documented building work at many sites following the Severan period, Severan inscriptions would have dominated at many sites until Late Antiquity. An extreme case can be seen at Lepcis Magna where over 34 per cent of the dated inscriptions from antiquity were from the Severan period.[16] While Lepcis was atypical in the scale of its dedications it is not unusual for the dynasty to be disproportionately represented in a city's epigraphy. The urban form, and its written space was then codified in the Severan period and would only be substantially altered towards the end of the fourth century.

Lepcis Magna

Developments at Lepcis Magna are important in any assessment of Severan written space.[17] Under Septimius Severus and Caracalla, a series of constructions were erected. An arch was built on the main crossroads where the coastal road crossed the main route into Lepcis' hinterland to the south.[18] Severus and Caracalla appear to be directly responsible for the complex of structures near the Wadi Lebda including: a colonnaded road, a new forum and basilica, nymphaea, a plaza at the southern end of the colonnaded street and the large new port facilities at its northern end (see Figure 12.1).[19] These structures were built between 203/205 and 216 with the original plan of a double forum arranged around the basilica being abandoned when imperial funding ran out.[20]

One consequence of the Severan building campaign was that dedications to the family on buildings and statue bases came to dominate many public spaces in the city, particularly, as Condron demonstrated, the theatre and the *forum vetus*, which had been key loci for the commemoration of emperors and the local elite from the reign of Tiberius onwards.[21] The Severan forum had some dedications to the family at the outset (and a temple dedicated to the family) but it only became the primary venue for imperial dedications during the course of the third century as the theatre and *forum vetus* declined in popularity.[22] Some locations on the *forum* were more prestigious than others. The Temple of Liber Pater for instance has been recognized by Wilson as containing many dedications to the Severans,[23] but it is important to note that it was not only chosen for special attention because Liber Pater was a patron deity of the city; his temple was a location where earlier emperors had been honoured.[24]

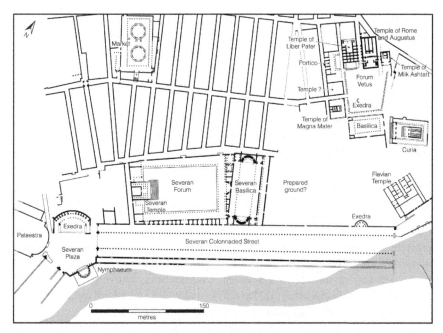

Figure 12.1 Lepcis Magna: the area of the *forum vetus* and the Severan forum, after Ward-Perkins 1995, Figures 4, 39 and Mattingly 1995, Figure 6.1

Despite the continuity of place, the Severan inscriptions were a considerable innovation in scale. Dedications relating to honorific monuments and statuary peaked under the Severi, with Severus, Geta and Caracalla all having more dedications to them than have been found for any other emperor. Even Julia Domna had as many dedicatory inscriptions to her as Antoninus Pius, who received the next largest number.[25] As an individual moved through the city they would have been left in little doubt that the Severans were the focus of a level of veneration that previous emperors had not received.

Severan written space at Lepcis was the product of long-term trends of elite expression and veneration of emperors. However the Severans were privileged compared to previous emperors. First, the sheer number of statues and inscriptions in their honour meant that the dynasty dominated the city until Late Antiquity. The conscious and sub-conscious gaze of citizens and travellers alike would have taken in countless reminders of the family as they moved through the city and particularly when they gathered in the *fora* or the theatre;[26] the success of one of their fellow citizens could not be far from their minds. Second, they were privileged by the location of inscriptions to them; dedications to the family were given pride of place in the traditional written spaces of the *Lepcitani*. Finally, the construction of the Severan forum created a dynastic monument where, unsurprisingly, the Severan family had no real competitors, even when the forum became an important place for statue erection during the course of the third century. It is also notable that the arch and Severan complex effectively changed the articulation of the city creating or recreating monumental road axes.

New written spaces

A number of African cities had new or expanded public spaces that have been dated to the Severan era. It is tempting to see these spaces as a response to the constructions at Lepcis but the dating of many of these structures does not allow for such a connection. Some 'Severan *fora*' are labouring under a misnomer with the Severan period only seeing the culmination and final monumentalization of spaces that were initially laid out in the course of the second century. At Volubilis, for instance, the quarter of the 'Severan' forum was monumentalized over an extended period from the mid-second century to the mid-Severan period and the Capitol, which was dedicated in AD 217, was only the final element in a wider building programme.[27] This is similar to the process at Thubursicum Numidarum where the *forum novum* probably dates from 161–69 but it was further monumentalized during the Severan period with an arch, some baths and possibly a basilica being constructed in and around the space.[28] Similarly at Mactar, the 'Trajanic forum', itself an additional space to the first century AD 'Numidian forum', was expanded in the Severan period.[29]

Even where substantial public spaces and dynastic monuments were solely constructed under the Severans, they cannot always be regarded as a response to the works at Lepcis. At Bulla Regia a series of constructions were built under the Severans along the main east-west road along the upper Bagradas valley, including a monumental esplanade that housed a temple with three *cellae*.[30] Around this temple were statues of the imperial family erected between 198 and 201 that mention *sedes* of the emperors.[31] The complex pre-dates the constructions at Lepcis Magna but its position on the road dominating movement through the town is similar to the development at Lepcis, it was to be seen by the traveller as well as the local.

These examples suggest that Severan Lepcis might be seen as a response to a tendency to monumentalization and multiplication of public spaces in Africa during the mid-second century AD, or a reflection of monumental space at Rome rather than being in and of itself a trigger for a new aesthetic of monumental space (although that does not mean that other elites would not have seen it as a complex to be emulated). For the Lepcitani Carthage's Antonine complex on the Byrsa hill may have been *the* space to compete with but unfortunately the actual written space of these monuments is very imperfectly known (although there is little definitively Severan epigraphy from the complex).[32] In order to assess Lepcis' place more clearly in the development of Severan era written space I will now examine Cuicul and Thamugadi as comparators.

Cuicul

At Cuicul, a new forum was created immediately to the south of the original colony around this period (see Figure 12.2). The exact date of the plaza and its porticos on the northern and eastern sides is not clear but: an honorific arch to Caracalla was erected on the west of the space in 216; the probably pre-existing temple of Saturn Frugifer on the forum's southern side appears to have had a colonnaded vestibule added under the Severans; and the Temple of the *Gens Septimia* was dedicated in 229.[33] Although the space may have existed before the Severan era it was only now fully articulated and integrated with the earlier town plan. The Severan era monuments dominated the plaza, particularly as the southern side of the forum with the two major temples was on higher ground than the northern.[34]

Inscriptions do not *seem* to have been equally distributed within the forum although the vagaries of preservation and the reuse of inscriptions (few bases were *in situ* at the time of excavation) mean that we can hardly be sure that other inscriptions were not removed in antiquity.[35] The greatest concentration of texts – milestones, some of which recorded work on the roads of the city's territory – can be found at the north-western and eastern gates of the forum; at least 19 milestones from the reigns of

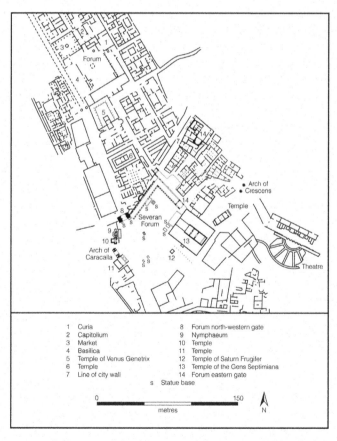

1	Curia	8	Forum north-western gate
2	Capitolium	9	Nymphaeum
3	Market	10	Temple
4	Basilica	11	Temple
5	Temple of Venus Genetrix	12	Temple of Saturn Frugifer
6	Temple	13	Temple of the Gens Septimiana
7	Line of city wall	14	Forum eastern gate
		s	Statue base

0   150   metres   N

Figure 12.2 Cuicul: the area of the *forum vetus* and the Severan forum, after Février, 1968, Figure 21a, Février, 1964, Figure 11 and Pensabene, 1992, Figure 1

Caracalla to Arcadius, Honorius and Theodosius II come from these locations; 13 from the north-west gate.[36] Salama has suggested that they were located at the former as the starting point for the road to Sitifis; the gate had been the southern gate of the old colony and the regularization of the space, and the southwards expansion of the city, did not change that conception.[37] While it may be striking that it is only following the establishment of the Severan forum that inscribed milestones start appearing at these gates – the first in the series, found to the north of the Temple of the *Gens Septimia*, dates from the reign of Caracalla – this is not a situation where a monumental space draws texts to it that were previously being erected elsewhere.[38] In part the appearance of these texts at these locations is due to wider patterns of imperial commemoration, road building and road repair in Numidia. Salama is clearly correct to suggest that the absence of milestones appertaining to earlier reigns is not a product of preservation; in general there are relatively few pre-Severan milestones west of Proconsularis.[39]

The appearance of milestones at the entrances to the Severan forum can then be interpreted as the conjunction of several phenomena – the increase of the epigraphic habit during the second century in Africa, the systematic adoption of a underused method of praising emperors, and the creation of a monumental space following contemporary practice across Africa – but the accretion of milestones at these places was not automatic and was a conscious decision about where to put official texts to maximize viewers.[40] The traveller moving between the old and new quarters had few potential choices; they were pushed through the gates out of the Severan forum and therefore past the milestones. The emperors were unavoidable at these arches, psychological break-points despite their penetrability,[41] and that, and the milestones' relatively inexpensive nature, made them a cost-effective way for the community to demonstrate their loyalty and their activity. The effectiveness of this form of dedication can be seen in its maintenance into the fourth century.

While the entrances of the plaza may have been important written spaces it does not appear that the Severan forum as a whole was a key location for the erection of texts. Obviously there were the dedications of the Arch of Caracalla and the Temple of the *Gens Septimia* and within the Temple of Saturn Frugifer dedications and stelae relating to that cult, but statues and their bases are not found on the same scale as in Cuicul's *forum vetus*. Only a few statue bases and dedications are known to have been on the 'Severan' forum in antiquity whereas many dedications are known from the old forum and its annexes.[42] As might be expected on the Severan plaza, most of the bases were placed around its edge. There do not appear to have been any particular concentrations of these texts, although again caution is needed given the problems of preservation.[43] The surviving evidence does suggest, however, that the two *fora* were apparently not regarded as equal spaces when it came to the positioning of statues and their inscriptions in the long term.[44] The Severan forum was used as a place to erect some statues and other dedications from the reign of Severus onwards,[45] but only a few imperial figures can be said with any certainty to have been honoured here: Septimius Severus, Caracalla, Julia Mammea, and Valerian and Gallienus all had bases dedicated to them and a plaque dating to the reign of Probus records the erection of porticoes.[46] A small number of bases and altars in the forum and its buildings were also dedicated to dignitaries and gods.[47] During the reign of Valentinian I, Valens and

Gratian a clutch of dedications connected to the construction of a civil basilica and a *basilica vestiaria* were erected.[48] Otherwise the main series of texts from the space were the milestones analysed above. The *forum vetus*, however, remained a locus for statues and other dedications in the Severan era and afterwards with at least ten to emperors and related deities being erected between Severus and Severus Alexander and three to private individuals or officials.[49] Over 20 statue bases to third and fourth century emperors, empresses and officials were erected there.[50]

Pensabene has argued that the new forum at Cuicul, as that of Lepcis, was a monument where: '*la memoria dei Severi, della respublica Cuiculitanorum e della sua classe dirigente*' was perpetuated.[51] To some extent this is correct. An analysis of the inscriptions, although problematic, suggests that the Severan forum remained a dynastic monument throughout its history with only Saturn challenging them. Other emperors were apparently restricted to its margins (however important those spaces were) and rarely intruded into the actual space until the mid-fourth century. The *forum vetus* on the other hand remained the prime venue for the commemoration of emperors and their collaterals into the mid-fourth century. However, Pensabene's comparison of Cuicul to Lepcis is not entirely appropriate. The Severan forum at Cuicul was not divided off from the city in the same way as the space at Lepcis. Pensabene argues that the forum could not be closed off on all sides because of unspecified topographical considerations but this is not convincing.[52] A portico running north-south along the edge of the *cardo maximus* would have closed off the majority of the space and have focused the complex on the imperial family and Saturn Frugifer. Ready movement between the junction of the old town, the eastern quarter including the theatre, and the southern quarters, was more important than creating a hallowed monument that would have slowed or limited penetration.

Thamugadi

Unlike Cuicul, Thamugadi does not display the same duplication of *fora* so an exact comparison with the organization of those spaces at Lepics or Cuicul cannot be made (see Figure 10.2). However, some of the same relationships between physical space, movement, the use of writing and urban development, can be seen in the plaza outside the original colony and the complex of the *Aqua Septimiana Felix*. These structures also show the difficulties in reading a written space when it has been disturbed in antiquity. As at Cuicul, the forum of Thamugadi continued to be used for imperial dedications until at least the reign of Julian;[53] Caracalla was honoured twice there with statues and another was erected to the divine Severus.[54]

The area between the Triumphal Arch, the Temple of the Genius of the Colony and the Market of Sertius was small (and not a forum) but the conjunction of road and plaza is close in nature to the space at Cuicul. The area was being developed from at least the reign of Marcus Aurelius but as the city developed westwards it would have become an increasingly important node of communication. In AD 169 the Temple of the Genius of the Colony was built on the northern side of the *decumanus maximus*.[55] From the Severan period the plaza also became an important written space. The arch between the old town and the new quarter may have been Severan, constructed as part of the re-development of the wall area by M. Plotius Faustus 'Sertius';[56] Doisy hypothesized that *CIL* 8.17872 might be the arch's dedication.[57] However, we should not accept this un-critically.[58] Other arches around the old city are pre-Severan, and *CIL* 8.17872 was found in fragments spread throughout the city (none near the gate).[59] The arch is, however, Severan at the latest. Its central passage was framed by statues on large hexagonal bases honouring them and dedicated to Mars Augustus and Concordia Augusta.[60] These would have overshadowed the traveller as they moved into the heart of the city, at a moment when the traveller's awareness of their environment would have been heightened by their passage through the gate (the intensity of Severan visual dominance would have been substantially increased if *CIL* 8.17872 is from here), emphasizing the importance of the Severans to the city's elites. As at the gates in Cuicul's Severan Forum, the arch became the location for milestones during the course of the third century with the earliest, damaged example, possibly dating from the reign of Severus Alexander; the latest is to Valentinian II, Theodosius and Arcadius.[61] The area is also likely to have been the location for a set of statues to the protective deities of the first tetrarchs.[62]

The other major building that faced on to the plaza was the market of the Sertii which was constructed for Sertius, almost certainly during the Severan period.[63] None of the surviving inscriptions mention when the building was erected. At least eight statue bases to Sertius and his family 'peopled' the building. Six bases to Sertius and his wife Cornelia Valentina Tucciana framed the main entrance on both the inside and outside and occupied the centre at the other end of the central *area* of the building. Other bases honoured Sertius' parents.[64] A small inscription records that: *sertii macellum et aream eius patriae siae fecerunt* but presumably there was a full building inscription honouring the emperors. Otherwise, as Wilson notes, the emperors appear not to have been incorporated into the building.[65] Just as the Severans dominated at the nearby arch, the visitor to the market or plaza could not escape Sertius and his family and the inscriptions on the outside of the building would have proclaimed their importance to people in the plaza and potentially on the *decumanus maximus*.

The overall effect of the constructions and writing around the plaza and crossroads is more mixed than at the fora of Lepcis or Cuicul or the plaza at Bulla Regia. As with other squares we have considered, this space was fully defined during the period and honorific inscriptions to the Severans dominated it. The Severan inscriptions began a trend for honouring the emperors in this space that lasted until the late fourth century. However, the Severans had competition from the Sertii whose gift of the market allowed them to dominate written space within and around it; although, of course, the family also gained prestige from their proximity to the Severan statues (and arch).

The complex of the *Aqua Septimiana Felix* on the southern fringe of the city was substantially remodelled in this period.[66] The complex was located where it was because of the spring it captured but any movement southwards into the Aurès Mountains would have been past the structure. Movement between the centre and its periphery was now past an expression of the power and wealth of the city in which the Severans were repeatedly memorialized. The improvements of the Severan era appear to be defined in dedicatory inscriptions of AD 213.[67] The three temples at the southern end of the complex, constructed on podia with individual staircases, are not mentioned in the inscriptions, which suggests that they pre-date the Severan building work, but the bronze balustrades around the spring, a *virid(i)arium* with a portico decorated by paintings, gates, a *pronaos* and a *platea* from the baths (the Southern Baths?) to the complex's entrance are detailed and indicate a considerable programme of monumentalization. It is difficult to assess how the Severans were incorporated into this space because of its reuse for a Byzantine fort.[68] Dedications to Severus and Caracalla found here that date to 199 may have belonged to the complex but this cannot be confirmed as the Byzantines reused material from across Thamugadi and part of one of these inscriptions was found nearby in a 'Byzantine' house at Henchir Terfas.[69] If the inscriptions are not at the fort because of Byzantine translocation of material, then they must come from the pre-Caracallan complex. Other inscriptions do suggest that the family were written into all aspects of the complex's decoration. Statues to Diana, probably Serapis, and the *dea patria* salute the Severans.[70] Even taking into account the vagaries of preservation there is a significant body of Severan material here.

What is unclear is if the complex remained a focus for imperial dedications after the Severan period. Relatively few post-Severan imperial dedications have been found there and the majority, including milestones and a statue base for Jupiter Optimus Maximus as protector of Diocletian have clearly been imported from other locations as building material for the Byzantine fortress.[71] While it is difficult to be certain, as with the Severan *fora* at Lepcis Magna and Cuicul, the complex of the *Aqua Septimiana Felix* appears to have been a dynastic monument incorporating a large plaza which the Severans dominated long after their deaths.

At Thamugadi then the old forum remained important for the location of dedications to the emperors but the new dynastic complex of the *Aqua Septimiana Felix* created a locus where the Severans could be honoured. The plaza and junction outside the original of the colony became a location where the city's loyalty to the emperors could be displayed; Severan-era inscriptions dominated the space and those moving through it throughout Antiquity.

Conclusion

Severan written space was the product of trajectories of African urban development whereby public space was multiplied rather than being a radical re-articulation of space.[72] In part these new spaces can be seen as the product of urban expansion and increased wealth which provided the framework in which new spaces could be created and the ability to do so but of course they were still the product of active choices about what public space should look like. The influence of developments at Lepcis Magna in these changes is not clear and, of course, the intensity of the reaction to the Severans at Lepcis is unparalleled. The building projects might have provided an additional impetus to the construction of new spaces at other cities as elites sought to emulate and better their peers but the nature of the evidence makes it difficult to be certain. Certainly the old *fora* of some of these cities remained key areas for the reiteration of loyalty to reigning emperors during the Severan period, although this chapter has pointed to important problems associated with the analysis of written space. New spaces also provided a locus where emperors and municipal dignitaries could be honoured but they did not usually take over from the pre-Severan public spaces either in this period or later. This suggests that the elites who set up the monuments and their inscriptions expected the population's interaction with space and text to remain fundamentally unchanged from earlier periods.

Continuity does not mean ossification. Some forms of commemoration intensified in the Severan period and others appeared. Wilson has suggested that there was a focus on gates or honorific arches as a means of public display of loyalty and on Blonce's figures it is possible to calculate that under Severus and Caracalla 0.68 of an arch was dedicated every year compared to only 0.29 under the Antonines.[73] However, these dynastic statistics mask a gradual upswing in the construction of arches during the second century; Severan arches were a consequence of long-term trends.[74] An element of these trends can be seen in the fact that at Cuicul and Thamugadi major gates were associated with an important monumental space. This is more than a coincidence. It reflects the process of urban development and the imperative to memorialize the city, individuals and the emperors at important nodes within the urban landscape.[75] What appears to be new is the use of these arches as a locus for concentrations of milestones as the communities fully realized the potential of the interaction between movement, space and writing. This is a pattern that persists into the fourth century and could be understood as marking a new domination of the emperors over movement within and outside the city as the erection of milestones were used both to mark work undertaken on the roads but more importantly to honour the emperors.

While the building forms are not new, and the trajectories of urban development are a continuation of earlier trends, there were novel effects on urban written spaces. The result of the multiplication of texts in honour of the Severans meant that some spaces – both fora at Lepcis, the Severan forum at Cuicul and the *Aqua Septimiana Felix* at Thamugadi – appear to have been dominated by buildings, statues and texts related to them; some of these spaces essentially remained dynastic monuments. This codification, albeit subject to alteration and repair, of the Romano-African city led to texts in honour of the family being over-represented at key nodes in the city, compared to other imperial families, throughout the rest of antiquity given the reduction in the erection of building inscriptions and honorific statuary during the third century. The visual and psychological dominance of Severan emperors in the cities of Africa will, of course, have been replicated with regard to a variety of different emperors/dynasties at different cities across the empire although it is unlikely that many populations were as physically overwhelmed by visual and written reminders of one imperial group as the *Lepcitani* were.

Setting aside a very few examples – for instance Lepcis or Thysdrus under Gordian III – we may doubt that emperors' relationships with cities or regions led directly to dramatic changes in urban development, the way in which emperors were inscribed into the city or the way that populations reacted to these written spaces.[76] However, largely coincidentally, in Africa, the construction of monuments to the Severans would have had an impact on the relationship between population, monumental inscriptions and civic space in the long-term, creating a norm against which later interventions in the urban fabric could be set.

Notes

1 MacMullen, 1982.
2 Bénabou, 1976, p. 165.
3 Birley (1988, p. 251) argues for the reality of the visit to Africa; see also Strocka 1972; Mayer 2010. Others have doubts: e.g. Romanelli, 1959, pp. 413–7; Kotula, 1985, pp. 156–7.
4 Wilson, 2007, p. 309. Clodius Albinus and Didius Julianus were from Hadrumetum and we should not expect the reaction to a Severan victory as being uniformly positive in Africa.
5 E.g. Pensabene, 1992, p. 777.
6 For Severan building work see Jouffroy, 1986 or Wilson, 2007.
7 Jouffroy, 1986 catalogues archaeologically attested building and epigraphic evidence; Duncan-Jones (2004) analyses construction not reconstruction work; Wilson, 2007; García, 2008. See also Mastino, 1999.
8 Meneghini and Santangeli Valenzani, 2007, pp. 37–8.
9 Sears, 2011, pp. 99–101.
10 Tables are based on dated inscriptions in Jouffroy, 1986 and *AE* 1982-present. Where it is possible to identify multiple buildings on one inscription then these have been counted separately.
11 Numidia became a province in the reign of Septimius Severus. Before that date inscriptions from its area are assigned to a notional Numidia.
12 This figure is largely the consequence of building work at Lepcis Magna and Thugga.
13 Duncan-Jones (2004, p. 35, n. 64) suggests that the lack of building inscriptions under Elagabalus might be due to *damnatio memoriae* but it would be strange for the process to be so effective.
14 Twenty-one African, six Numidian and 11 Mauretanian settlements only have known building inscriptions from the Severan period. See note 10 for sources for these figures.
15 The dynasty's confidence in Africa can be seen by their creation of the province of Numidia and the movement of Roman control southwards across Africa (Picard, 1944; Bénabou, 1976, pp. 167–75; Mattingly, 1995, pp. 54–5; Mastino, 1999, pp. 382–97).
16 Tantillo, 2010, p. 182 (Figure 5.3). Tantillo has grouped antiquity into periods of 30 years and the 'Severan period' essentially corresponds to the group AD 190–219 (72/212) and half of 220–49 (8/212); for ease I have only given the percentage for the years AD 190–219.
17 See: Di Vita, 1995; Ward-Perkins, 1993; Wilson, 2007, pp. 295–307; Sears, 2011, pp. 81–8.
18 An associated inscription has not been located but the dynasty is well-represented in the friezes. Bianchi Bandinelli et al., 1964, pp. 67–70; Sears, 2011, p. 82.
19 Ward-Perkins, 1993; Di Vita, 1995.
20 Di Vita, 1995, p. 71; Ward-Perkins, 1993, p. 107; Sears, 2011, pp. 112–13.

21   Condron, 1998, p. 47; Mastino, 1999, p. 363; Wilson, 2007, pp. 301–6. Kuhoff
     suggests that: 'La tradizione epigrafica dimostra che gli abitanti di *Lepcis Magna*
     avevano dopo l'uscita dalle case davanti agli occhi in ogni luogo un numero infinito
     di statue dei Severi.' Obviously this is a slight exaggeration but it must have appeared
     like that to Lepcitanians. Kuhoff, 1990, p. 952.
22   Condron, 1998, pp. 45–8.
23   Wilson, 2007, pp. 301–5.
24   Dedications to Trajan, Hadrian, Antinoös, Antoninus Pius and Faustina have all
     been found in the temple *IRT* 279, 355, 362, 369, 371, 380. The Temple was also next
     to the Temple of Rome and Augustus a foci for imperial dedications from Tiberius
     onwards. Sets of imperial portraits are common see for instance those of Verecunda
     (Faustina the Younger, Lucius Verus, Commodus, Septimius Severus, Julia Domna
     and Caracalla) near Lambaesis (Baratte, 1983; Gros, 1995, pp. 50–1).
25   Tantillo, 2010, p. 186.
26   Corbier, 2006, p. 60.
27   Euzennat and Hallier, 1986, pp. 73–103; *IAM* 2.355. A building inscription dedicated
     to Jupiter Optimus Maximus and Juno Regina dates from the reign of Severus,
     Caracalla and Geta, which may mean that the AD 217 dedication reflects the
     remodelling of an earlier structure (*AE* 1987, 1105).
28   Sassy, 1953, pp. 109–14; *ILAlg.* I.1255.
29   Picard, 1957, pp. 62–4; *CIL* 8.11800.
30   *ILAfr.* 453–4; *CIL* 8.25515; Beschaouch et al., 1977, pp. 108–13; Broise and Thébert,
     1993, pp. 384–5. For other Severan spaces see: the forum at Thibilis (Gsell and Joly,
     1914, p. 73) and the forum at Iol-Caesarea (Potter, 1995, p. 32); Many old *fora* were
     substantially improved in the Severan period or had the finishing touches put to its
     architecture (e.g. Gigthis: Constans, 1916, p. 58).
31   *AE* 2004, 1874–6; Khanoussi and Mastino, 2004.
32   Severus certainly saw Carthage and Utica as being rivals of Lepcis; he granted the *ius
     italicum* to the three cities (*Digest* 50, 15, 8, 11); Deneauve, 1990; Gros, 1995; Ladjimi
     Sebaï, 2005, pp. 105–223. City competition: Laurence et al., 2011, pp. 122–3, 279–82.
     From the area of the Byrsa Hill only *ILAfr.* 355 + *ILTun.* 1047, an altar to Magna
     Mater for the Severans, and *AE* 1998, 1538, to Caelestis and Severus Alexander, are
     definitely Severan.
33   *CIL* 8.8321; *ILAlg.* 2.3.7648; Leglay, 1966, pp. 201–8; Février, 1964, pp. 10–11; *AE*
     1913, 120; Gros, 1996, p. 196.
34   There is roughly 5 metres difference between the two ends of the forum.
35   Allais, 1938, p. 50. Lefebvre make a similar point about the old forum (2006, p. 2127).
36   See Salama, 1951.
37   Salama, 1951, p. 262. Although fora appear to be more usual as a starting point for
     roads.
38   *AE* 1911, 101.
39   Salama, 1951, pp. 269–70. On African roads see for Proconsularis: Salama, 2010,
     pp. 39–47. As examples of the change, in *ILAlg.* 1, covering Algerian Proconsularis,
     only ten out of 116 milestones are pre-Caracallan. To the east on the Ammaedara-
     Capsa-Tacapae road only 22.5 per cent are pre-Caracallan (all are Tiberian and are
     connected to the road's construction; Salama, 2004, p. 254) and in Tripolitania only
     one milestone in *IRT* dates to before the reign of Caracalla – *IRT* 930 (Chevallier,
     1997, p. 260).
40   Corbier, 2006, p. 65 and in this volume.

41 See Lynch, 1960, pp. 72–8; MacDonald, 1986, p. 75.

42 Zimmer records 68 statue bases but there are also dedicatory plaques and bases in the Capitol basement (clearly moved from their original location) and Curia that he does not count. In total there might be 90 dedications in the area.

43 Ballu, 1921, pp. 242–53; Pensabene, 1992, pp. 774–7

44 A propensity to use 'forum' without distinction in some publications makes it difficult to work out inscription find-spots. For reuse see Ballu, 1921, p. 219; Allais, 1971, p. 118; Salama, 1951, p. 230. See also Eck (2010, p. 96) on the problems of reuse for the spatial analysis of statue bases.

45 Some inscriptions pre-date the forum e.g. *ILAlg.* 2.3.7895 which may be mid-second century in date (p. 820) and 7910, to a suffect consul of AD 128.

46 *ILAlg.* 2.3.7809, 7816, 7825, 7837, 7808 a fragmentary inscription to the Severans may also come from here. An altar for Valerian, Gallienus and Valerian or Salonian was found next to the arch (*ILAlg.* 2.3.7839). *ILAlg.* 2.3.7841. A badly mutilated inscription to Philip *ILAlg.* 2.3.7836a was found to the north of the Temple of the *Gens Septimiana*. The Temple of the *Gens Septimiana* also appears to have contained a colossal statue of Septimius Severus.

47 *ILAlg.* 2.3.7678, 7714 (see Leglay, 1966, p. 209), 7693, 7637, 7895, 7907, 7910, 7912, 7917–8.

48 *ILAlg.* 2.3.7758, 7876–8, 7881, 7914.

49 *ILAlg.* 2.3.7645, 7674, 7760–1, 7666, 7807, 7811, 7813, 7817, 7819, 7898, 7911, 7944; Zimmer, 1989, pp. 54–69; Briand-Ponsart, 2008, pp. 117–9.

50 *ILAlg.* 2.3.7827, 7829–33, 7856–8, 7860–6 (latter is a milestone – Salama, 1951, p. 249 and is the same as *AE* 1982, 963 = *AE* 2001, + 2065?), 7868, 7870–5, 7900; Zimmer, 1989, pp. 54–69; Briand-Ponsart, 2008, pp. 117–9; Allais, 1971, p. 118.

51 Pensabene, 1992, p. 802 see also 777.

52 Pensabene, 1992, p. 797.

53 See Zimmer, 1989 for the forum and Fentress, 1984 for the culture of inscribing at Thamugadi more generally; *CIL* 8.2387.

54 *CIL* 8.17870–1, 17873; Ballu, 1897, p. 128.

55 Some dedications to the *Genius* found elsewhere in the city are likely to have originated at the temple but have been moved by the Byzantines. Boeswillwald et al., 1892–1904, pp. 308–10; Ballu, 1903, pp. 68–72; *BCTH* 1893, 160; Tourrenc, 1968; *AE* 1968, 647; Doisy 1953, pp. 8–9. Other dedications at the temple: Jupiter, Juno, Minerva, Liber Pater, Silvanus and Saturn: *BCTH* 1898, 157, 1901, 312.

56 Wilson, 2007, p. 314.

57 *CIL* 8.17872 + *AE* 1954, 153. Doisy, 1953, p. 130 '*on peut émettre l'hypothèse que nous sommes en presence de la dédicace de l'Arc*', followed sensibly by *AE* 2007, 51: '*qui pourrait être*'. The arch is not listed as Severan in Blonce, 2008 but that does not appear to be a comprehensive list.

58 Wilson, 2007, p. 314 appears to accept the 203 date unequivocally. Jouffroy appears to accept the attribution '*pourrait bien être*' but does present variant arguments in a footnote 1986, pp. 263–8. Corbier (2009, p. 188) argues that the arch was '*peu antérieure à la pose des statues*'.

59 Doisy, 1953, pp. 125–6.

60 *CIL* 8.17829, 17835; cf. Corbier, 2006, p. 60.

61 *CIL* 8.17872, 22313–5, 22321–4; *AE* 1936, 135; *BCTH* 1951/52: 231–3; Boeswillwald et al., 1896–7: 183–215. Some of the milestones may have come from elsewhere and have been '*rangé méthodiquement*' at the gate by excavators Salama, 1951–2, p. 226.

62   *CIL* 8.2345–7. Bases to Hercules Augustus for Maximian and Genius Virtutum Mars
      Augustus for Galerius were found nearby. A base to Jupiter Optimus Maximus, the
      protector of Diocletian, was reused in the Byzantine fort.
63   Ballu, 1897, 209–21; Boeswillwald et al., 1892–1904, pp. 308–9; De Ruyt, 1983,
      pp. 193–8; Wilson, 2007, pp. 313–4.
64   *CIL* 8.2394–9, 17904–5; *ILS* 5579. See Hemelrijk in this volume on Cornelia
      Valentina Tucciana. Also Wilson, 2007, p. 314.
65   Wilson, 2007, p. 314.
66   See Leschi, 1947, pp. 92–3; Tourrenc, 1968; Leglay, 1968, p. 262; Lassus, 1981,
      pp. 50–1. The spring appears to have been captured in AD 146; *AE* 1948, 113, 1985:
      875a and b.
67   Although none of these inscriptions are *in situ*: *AE* 1948, 111; *CIL* 8.2369, 2370 =
      17818.
68   See Lassus, 1981 and Durliat, 1981, pp. 47–53 nos. 19–21.
69   *AE* 1981, 881 a and b; *CIL* 8.2437 = 17940.
70   Following Leschi, 1947, pp. 92–9; *AE* 1982, 958, 1948, 112, 1972, 701, 1987, 1078;
      Doisy, 1953, n.6. There is also a statue base of Victoria Victrix in honour of Severus
      and Caracalla from the fortress *AE* 1941, 49. See *AE* 1979, 669 and 2008, 1697 for
      gifts to the goddess.
71   *AE* 1946, 67, 1948, 117; *BCTH* 1951/52, 233; *CIL* 8.2347; Leschi, 1957, p. 239; *AE*
      1949, 134 – only this last, to Julian, has not clearly been moved from elsewhere.
72   Laurence and Trifilò, forthcoming 2013.
73   Blonce, 2008.
74   Laurence and Trifilò, forthcoming 2013; Hurlet, 2001, p. 280. For instance at Lepcis
      there were at least six arches that pre-dated the Severan period.
75   See Trifilò in this volume.
76   Sears, 2011, p. 110.

13

The City as Preferred Written Space: The Case of Aquitania

Simon Esmonde Cleary

Introduction

Cities have long been regarded as the most diagnostic feature of the Roman period in the western provinces (Spain, Gaul, Germany, Britain) because of their layout, and their suites of distinctive public buildings and monuments along with a range of private buildings (cf. Laurence, Esmonde Cleary, Sears: *The City in the Roman West 200 BC–AD 200*, 2011). One feature of this ensemble that has been less commented on is the presence in these provincial cities of quantities of inscriptions, surviving on stone above all, but also originally in other mediums too. It will be the argument of this chapter that this epigraphic preference was one of the defining features of these places; cities were a distinctive experience because in part of the display in their public spaces of various forms of writing, something which seems also to have carried over into the private sphere. Anyone entering these cities and passing through their public spaces would thus have encountered writing on a variety of materials, in various locations and conveying a range of messages in a way that simply did not happen at any other type of site between the Pillars of Hercules and the Hadrian's Wall, except at the military bases of the Rhine and Britain. One has only to look at the distribution maps of inscriptions across Gaul under the high empire, for instance as published by Woolf[1] to notice their bias towards the cities, though there are other biases at play too, particularly favouring the cities of Narbonensis and those on the long-distance axis up the Rhône-Rhine corridor. It is one thing to observe the bias towards cities, but that bias needs explaining insofar as is possible and its effects on the physical texture and psychological impact of the city need consideration. The urban bias also needs to be factored into the long-running debate about the 'epigraphic habit', which has proceeded largely along the axes of 'when', 'who' and 'why', but more rarely 'where', starting with Ramsey MacMullen's classic treatment of the incidence of epigraphy largely in chronological terms,[2] and moving on to treatments that emphasize social and/or legal factors.[3]

In order to approach this question, the inscriptions of a single province will be examined as a case study. The province selected is Aquitania, in the south-west of

Gaul. The reasons for this selection are partly that it lies away from the Rhône-Rhine axis and any possible distortion introduced by that privileged axis; partly because it comprises a variety of different physiographic regions; partly because it encompasses two of the major ethnic groupings of Gaul noted by Caesar (*BGall* I.1); partly because it has a manageable quantity of inscriptions, many of which have been the subject of recent publication. It is also a province with which the author is familiar. In what follows, the evidence from Aquitania will be laid out and considered. There will then be a Discussion section assessing the contribution of written space to the cities of Aquitania and more widely and the contribution of cities to our understanding of the 'epigraphic habit' in the West.

Figure 13.1 Map of Aquitania showing the *civitates* and their main cities (after the map in *ILA* re-drawn by L. Bosworth)

Aquitania

The province of Aquitania was created in c. 16 BC by amalgamating Caesar's Aquitani south of the Garonne with a number of tribes Caesar described as Celts between the Garonne and the Loire, and as far inland as the western slopes of the Massif Central and the Cévennes, thus creating a province of the 'right' size (Figure 13.1). South of the Garonne, the southernmost peoples of the Aquitani inhabited the valleys along the northern face of the Pyrenees and the *civitates* created from them were generally small; other, larger units occupied the plains of Gascony to the north. North of the Garonne was a series of large tribal areas in the western lowlands, with two *civitates* in the upland eastern part of the province again covering relatively smaller areas. This descriptive order, from the south of the province northwards and then eastwards is followed in the bar-chart of the incidence of urban and rural inscriptions (Figure 13.2). Aquitania's inscriptions on stone were originally catalogued in *CIL* XIII supplemented by the inclusion of more recent discoveries in *Inscriptions Latines des Trois Gaules* (*IL3G*),[4] with individual discoveries reported in the pages of *L'Année Épigraphique*. A comprehensive catalogue of all Latin inscriptions on whatever medium in the province is currently being compiled to consistent norms in the *Inscriptions Latines d'Aquitaine* (*ILA*), of which the volumes covering the *civitates* of the Arverni,[5] Petrucorii (Bost and Fabre 2001),[6] Santones[7] and Vellavi[8] and the cities of Bordeaux (Bituriges Vivisci)[9] and Lectoure (Lactorates) have appeared.[10] In the bar and pie charts accompanying this chapter the numbers are derived only from *CIL* and *IL3G* in order to ensure consistency, though inscriptions on other materials published in *ILA* are referred to where they broaden our knowledge.

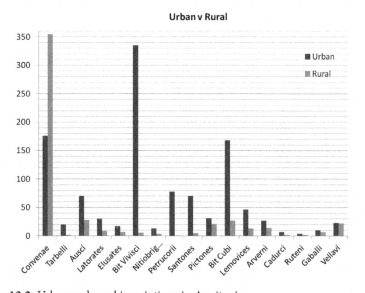

Figure 13.2 Urban and rural inscriptions in Aquitania

A particular circumstance relating to the survival of inscriptions in the cities needs to be considered and the possible biases it introduces discussed. At Bordeaux, Bourges, Périgueux, Poitiers and Saintes inscriptions survive in relatively large numbers because they were built into the late Roman walls in these cities and have subsequently been recovered from them. Since such defences do not occur at other types of site in the province, it could reasonably be objected that this alone means we are not comparing like with like. Some counter-arguments may be advanced. First of all, the pattern does show itself at some other *civitates* which do not have massive late Roman walls particularly the Convenae where the late walls at St-Bertrand-de-Comminges were not built with large blocks of reused *spolia*, often inscribed, in their lower parts; nevertheless the city has produced large numbers of inscriptions. The pattern is also reproduced, albeit with much smaller numbers of inscriptions in the Aquitani area in *civitates* such as the Ausci and Elusates, and to the north of the Garonne among the Arverni. Second, a number of secondary centres, *agglomérations secondaires*, in some of the *civitates* have been the focus of intensive survey and excavation and have yielded very little or no epigraphic material, for instance Barzan in the territory of the Santones or Angoulême in the same *civitas*, Néris and St-Marcel/*Argentomagus* for the Bituriges Cubi (Figures 13.3 and 13.4). Of course all these sites have been extensively robbed, but even so much has been uncovered and inscriptions are very few and far between, suggesting they were never common. Third and finally, one might note that for inscriptions to be reused in quantity in late Roman walls in cities such as Bordeaux they would have had to have been there in the first place, suggesting that they were a common feature of these places (there is no plausible evidence that they were derived from elsewhere). So in conclusion, though the argument that the presence of late Roman walls with *spolia* introduces an important difference has merit, it is argued here that this represents not a distortion of the evidence so radical as to make it unusable but rather a bias towards these particular sites that needs to be borne in mind.

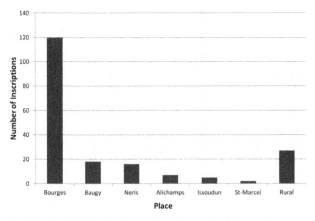

Figure 13.3 Inscriptions by site in the *civitas* of the Bituriges Cubi

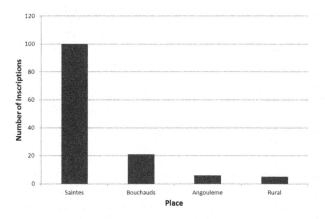

Figure 13.4 Inscriptions by site in the *civitas* of the Santones

In order to determine the comparative incidence of inscriptions in cities and at other sites within each *civitas* of Aquitania, the numbers in *CIL* and in *IL3G* were added up and are presented graphically in Figure 13.2 as 'urban' and 'rural', the latter subsuming secondary centres. There is a consistent pattern; in all cases bar one the urban figure exceeds the rural, though the absolute numbers are in many cases very low and thus statistically unreliable. The one exception, the Convenae, is discussed further below, as is the case of the Arverni where the *ILA* volume has changed the picture. So, *prima facie* the argument that cities were preferred locations for public writing is maintained. To break this down further, two of the *civitates* covered in *ILA*, the Bituriges Cubi and the Santones had their numbers for their main city (Bourges and Saintes respectively) compared with those from the secondary centres (by name) and all other rural sites (aggregated) within their territories (Figures 13.3 and 13.4). Since these figures were derived from *CIL* and *IL3G*, the major Santones site of Barzan does not figure; but examination of the recent publications shows no inscriptions have been recovered,[11] reinforcing the pattern from elsewhere in the *civitas*. These more detailed analyses maintain the dominance of the main city, but nevertheless both also show that secondary centres outnumber all other sites put together, showing that these centres to a limited extent show an epigraphic practice whereas there is very little in the way of an epigraphic presence in the countryside.

As noted above, there is one exception to the pattern of a preference for the siting of inscriptions on stone at the main city of a *civitas* and that is the Convenae in southern Aquitania in the central Pyrenees. This anomaly now needs to be considered. As also noted, despite the late Roman walls of the main city, St-Bertrand, not being of the type of Bordeaux or Saintes and thus not containing large numbers of reused inscriptions, the city has yielded some 170 inscriptions, a high figure in absolute terms for Aquitania, though this must be set against the fact that there are twice as many inscriptions as this from the rest of the territory of the *civitas*. In part this relatively large number must be because of the extensive excavations in the centre of the city over the last century or so.[12] Nevertheless, in absolute terms the Convenae were also the *civitas* with far and away the largest incidence of inscriptions on stone from the entire province, some 500, with the next most numerous set of inscriptions totalling 350 at a *civitas* being the Bituriges Vivisci (overwhelmingly from Bordeaux). It has been argued that the reason for this epigraphic visibility lies in a natural resource of the Convenae and in their response to this. The major marble quarries of the upper Garonne valley were included in the *civitas*, notably around St-Béat, producing good-quality white marble suitable for architectural stonework, statuary, inscriptions and other uses. In itself such a resource is a contributory but not a sufficient factor to explain the efflorescence of inscribing among the Convenae. If one looks at the nature of the inscriptions from locations other than St-Bertrand, then the great majority turn out to be votive altars, typologically derived from standard, Roman-style examples but very often much smaller than is usual and dedicated to a range of deities, for the most part local ones. It should be noted that they are present at Saint-Bertrand also, so this is not an exclusively 'rural' practice. The distribution of this type of altar is almost exclusively limited to what can be approximated as the territory of the Convenae,[13] so they seem to be bound up with the identity of this people. This distribution is almost identical to that of another class of objects carved out of St-Béat marble, the 'auges' or marble urns to receive the ashes of the dead and often carved with schematic human representations, which again scarcely stray beyond what we believe to be the confines of the Convenae.[14] It would seem that we have here a very particular response to the availability of an unusual local resource, one that came to be integral to defining and displaying the identity of the Convenae as a 'people of marble'.[15] The anomaly of the Convenae can therefore be explained in terms which relate solely to that people and which have no wider ramifications for epigraphic practice in Aquitania.

The publication of *ILA Arvernes* covering Clermont-Ferrand and its territory has updated the picture derived from *CIL* and *IL3G*, there being 30 inscriptions from Clermont itself as opposed to 65 from the rest of the *civitas* (excluding 13 milestones). Of these 65, just over half, 33, came from the single site of the major temple of Mercury on the Puy-de-Dôme (commune of Orcines) and a further 11 (including four on materials other than stone) from the spa of Vichy. Clearly here the urban to rural ratios have been distorted in part by the important sanctuary site where epigraphy on stone was an important element of the way cultic practice developed and which currently is not paralleled at any of the other major sanctuary sites in the province such as Barzan or Sanxay. Why this site demonstrates this particular practice is at present unknown. Moreover, the Puy-de-Dôme site has been extensively investigated whereas Roman Clermont itself remains under-investigated and also did not have an inscription-rich set of late defences in the manner of Bordeaux or Saintes, so the disparity between Clermont and the Puy-de-Dôme is in large measure a product of the conditions of modern recovery.

One of the drawbacks of so many high-empire inscriptions from the major cities such as Bordeaux and Saintes having been reused in the later walls, is that they have been divorced from their original settings. In order to attempt partly to counter this problem, the inscriptions from three urban centres with a detailed *ILA* catalogue, Bordeaux, Périgueux and Saintes, were apportioned to some basic categories to try to

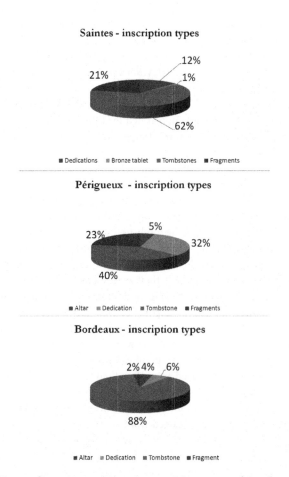

Figure 13.5 Types of inscription (%) at Saintes, Périgueux and Bordeaux

get some sense of their original functions and thus what sorts of spaces they might have lain in. These categories were: altars; dedications (there can be some overlap between these categories, in this case the physical form of the inscription has been the determining criterion, so a dedication on an altar is regarded as an altar); tombstones; fragments; along with one other inscription type from Saintes, to which we shall return (see Figure 13.5). At all three the largest category was tombstones, 88 per cent, 40 per cent and 64 per cent respectively. Thereafter there is a certain amount of divergence: Périgueux has 32 per cent dedications compared with 22 per cent at Saintes and 6 per cent at Bordeaux, and Saintes has no altars compared with 5 per cent at Périgueux and 4 per cent at Bordeaux. The dominance (occasionally overwhelming) of tombstones will be returned to below. In the meantime, a little more needs to be said about dedications. Some of these are clearly all or part of the dedication of a public building or monument, particularly good examples being the inscriptions from Bordeaux relating to the public water-supply (*ILA Bordeaux* 38, 39, 40, 41), the inscription from Périgueux commemorating the dedication of the amphitheatre (*ILA Pétrucores* 27), or of course the arch at Saintes (*ILA Santons* 7). Others equally clearly are statue-bases, be it to deities (e.g. *ILA Bordeaux* 17 to the *Tutela Augusta*), or to emperors (e.g., the series supporting statues of members of the Julio-Claudian dynasty from a monument in Bordeaux, *ILA Bordeaux* 32, 33, 34). So far no proven statue base to a local notable has been demonstrated for the areas covered in *ILA*, but there are several other inscriptions, not tombstones and therefore presumably from public buildings and spaces, mentioning such worthies.

The classes of inscription and their frequencies adduced in the preceding paragraph may start to give us some sense of where public writing occurred in the cities of Aquitania. Clearly, consistently the largest group was tombstones. Why they form such a major part of the epigraphic corpus from these cities is worth considering. At all three of the cities discussed above, the tombstones survive in number because of their later incorporation into the city walls, but why were they preferentially recovered? It may in part be simply because there were more of them in the first place. Or it may in part be simply a functional matter; they were small and portable relative to large blocks from major public buildings and monuments. Nevertheless, the evidence of architectural stonework from the ramparts of cities such as Périgueux[16] or Saintes shows that such structures were also being dismantled. Possibly, despite a tomb being a *locus religiosus* (at least in strict Roman law, provincial practice may have varied) with the passage of the generations the families whose members were commemorated by these epitaphs had died or moved away. If so, then at the time of the commissioning of major public works such as the walls, public need and power could override private commemoration, as it could also for the dismantling of major civic complexes. The funerary inscriptions themselves ranged from simple small stones with a minimum of information, to longer and more impressive epitaphs detailing the career and/or family of the deceased, to inscriptions that formed part of large tomb monuments or mausolea. But even if the term 'tombstones' comprises a wide range of types, what they all shared is that they lay outside the inhabited areas of the city, lining the approach roads. This feature of Roman provincial cities is so widespread as to be almost commonplace,[17] with all the modes and degrees of self-identification, age, gender and status patterning, family and kin structures, or occupation that the monuments convey through their size, shape and sculpture as well as their written text. Clearly this was a practice of the metropolis itself and of Italy more widely that had been assidu-ously taken up by the populations of the cities of Aquitania, the more modest as well as the wealthy, whether the latter were from established aristocratic families or were freedmen making their mark. But in terms of 'written space' it means that the traveller approaching one of these Aquitanian cities would be introduced to it by a specific type of written space; one which ringed the city with its ancestors, proclaiming their continuing presence in the fabric of the city in a way which simply did not happen either at secondary centres or in the countryside. Equally, for a traveller leaving one of these cities, the dead would be the last group of citizens encountered as they passed from the urban to the rural. To adumbrate a theme to which we shall return, over time the accumulation of these monuments and the writing upon them would have become a significant feature of the urban landscape, with hundreds, perhaps at a major city such as Bordeaux thousands, of them grouped together in the major burial-grounds.

The smaller numbers of inscriptions on stone at these cities that derived from public buildings and monuments and their appurtenances such as statues, suggest a familiar litany of such structures: fora, temples, amphitheatres, arches, water supply to other monuments such as baths and fountains. But very few, if any, of them can be securely linked back to domestic space, though evidently some altars or statue-bases could belong there as much as in public spaces. Nevertheless, the great majority of such inscriptions suggest they adorned public spaces. If so, then one of the distinguishing marks of these buildings and the spaces they enclosed must have been that monumentalized and durable writing formed part of the experience, and in this they differed from other spaces within the city. What survives for us is essentially writing engraved in stone, but there are two inscriptions from the *civitas* of the Santones which give a glimpse of other possibilities. One is from the secondary centre of Angoulême (*ILA Santons* 100), a block of limestone on to which was painted an inscription, of which the sole certain word is *veteranus*. This of course raises the question of how many other such painted inscriptions there were, and indeed of inscriptions painted or written on to other media such as wood or papyrus and publicly displayed, perhaps in the manner of the *alba* at Rome.

The other inscription that raises a wider question is from Saintes itself (*ILA Santons* 13) and consists of eight fragments of an inscription engraved on bronze, six fragments bearing writing, the other two being parts of the frame of the inscription. The text is very fragmentary, but the editors note that the repeated occurrence of the subjunctive mood and of the suffix -*ve* suggests a series of regulations. This of course would fit well with a whole area of Roman epigraphic practice attested both by surviving examples and by textual references, the inscribing of statutes and other public documents on to bronze and their display in public places. For the Western Provinces well-known examples of such documents are the laws and decrees engraved on bronze and recovered from Spain such as the *lex Irnitana*, *lex Ursonensis* or *tabula Contrebiensis*, and the many so-called 'diplomas' or military discharge-certificates on bronze, which announce themselves copies of originals posted publicly in Rome. It is clear that in Rome certain types of legal documents were routinely engraved on bronze rather than carved on stone: statutes, decrees, treaties, edicts, and then displayed in public.[18] The use of bronze went far back into the Republic and pertained to the sacred nature of the texts inscribed on them,[19] either what we would call 'religious' texts or laws and treaties, which partook of a sacred nature. This sacred nature was further emphasized by their traditional location in temples and temple precincts rather than in other types of public buildings or spaces. Though we must be wary of simply transferring practice in Rome and its significance to the provinces, nevertheless the material of the inscription along with its language and probable subject matter show that the Santones had adopted a practice of clearly Roman (in the sense of metropolitan) origin. In this case it is reasonable to argue that they followed metropolitan practice, even if they did not appreciate all the nuances. If so, we may envisage this tablet or tablets hung within the precinct of one of the major temples of the city, presumably along with others of the same type. Along with the painted inscription from Angoulême, the Saintes bronze tablet reminds us to be aware of other mediums for inscriptions alongside the ones of stone with which we are most familiar because of their survival.

Discussion

How then does the evidence for epigraphic practice in the cities and *civitates* of Aquitania illuminate our understanding both of the role of epigraphy in constituting a city and of the role of the city as a *locus* for the practice of the epigraphic habit? And what does it tell us about the ways in which the experience of the city was different from that of other types of settlement?

Let us answerthe last question first. It is clear that publicly displayed writing was one of the features that set cities apart from other types of settlement in Aquitania, apart from the special cases of the *civitas* of the Convenae and the temple of Mercury on the Puy-de-Dôme. The inhabitant of or visitor to such a city would expect inscriptions and other writings as part of the normal experience of the public buildings and spaces of the city. In this these provincial cities seem to be taking their lead from Rome itself.[20] Starting at the centre of the city, there is evidence on stone from Aquitania for the embellishment of public spaces with inscriptions dedicating particular buildings and monuments and at the same time publicizing and commemorating the donor(s). There are inscriptions recording individuals and their euergetistic actions, some of which may have been bases for statues of emperors, members of the imperial family or other benefactors (though as yet none for patrons of the cities). There are altars which can also commemorate emperors or members of their families or again local worthies. The evidence of better-preserved fora at cities such as Pompeii in Italy or *Baelo* in Spain show clearly that many such inscriptions were placed where they were either at eye level or could be read without difficulty, such as statue-bases or inscriptions carved into the paving of the forum. It may be that some inscriptions were set within buildings and monuments where they were designed to be legible. Others, though, such as inscriptions carved into the entablatures of temples and other structures may well have been placed too high to be easily visible (unless the lettering was particularly large); nevertheless, that such buildings should carry inscriptions was an expected part of their decoration and significance, even if the inscription itself was hard to decipher. The fragments of bronze tablets from Saintes raise other questions which take us away from the simple equation of inscription with text to be read and comprehended. In her discussion of inscriptions on bronze tablets, Williamson cogently and rightly challenges some modern assumptions about the place and function of such inscriptions, in particular that they were 'definitive texts' and that they were designed to be read as such, indeed to be read at all.[21] As she notes, on the one hand the placing of the inscriptions might well have rendered them illegible to anyone not owning a ladder; on the other hand, the size of the lettering, the layout of the texts and their language were not designed to be what we would call 'user-friendly'; in addition, it is clear that at Rome the documents expressed in bronze were also available in more portable forms such as, probably, papyrus, as when Vespasian had copies made of the texts on bronze from the Capitol destroyed in the fire of AD 69 (cf. Corbier this volume).

Williamson argues that what was important was not the individual words, sentences or sections of text, but their overall effect, large polished slabs of writing of religious significance, and, where placed in sunlight, shining brightly.[22] These bronze tablets, and by extension other forms of monumentalized and publicly displayed writing, expressed power and meaning in themselves by their existence, not dependent on the precise subject matter and formulas of the documents they bore.

Another related topic is: Who would or could read such texts, and how should this affect our perception of their use and meaning? What was the intended audience for such messages and how were they meant to experience them? Clearly our assumptions of near-universal literacy and thus the ability (let alone the desire) to read inscriptions must be set aside. Without wishing to embark on the vexed question of literacy rates in the Roman world, it is likely that in a province such as Aquitania, even by the end of the second century AD full literacy would have been the preserve of an elite (largely male) minority, though others such as merchants and tradesmen would have needed competence in areas that touched on their livelihoods, but it is likely that the majority of the inhabitants of a city and its *civitas* were totally illiterate or only possessed the rudiments of literacy. So we must envisage a spectrum of possible audiences for this writing, based on class and literacy. To other literate aristocrats and to literate 'professionals' such as *grammatici* or lawyers, the messages of dedications, statue-bases and the like were clearly and literally spelt out: worship of particular deities; loyalty to the emperors; devotion to their *numina* and other characteristics or to imperial families; in particular the careers, honours and benefactions of local magistrates. In such cases, and particularly for the elites of a city, what was on display was both intra-*civitas* emulation and competition as well as inter-*civitas* competition through the buildings, monuments and statues to which the inscriptions were attached. This was the audience which most closely resembled our modern perception of the function of such inscriptions. But for audiences elsewhere on the spectrum of literacy the precise message of the texts on stone, bronze or whatever was far less accessible and probably mattered less; what was important was that monuments, statues and so on of the usual types were present in the city and had attached to them the expected types of writing. Again it was writing as a nexus of symbolic expression that mattered, not necessarily the exact content.

The approach taken above is to consider the matter purely through what is essentially a status perspective, since literacy was so closely tied to class. Continuing this perspective, one might note that Aquitania has produced a number of inscriptions dedicated by or to freedmen, as the Indices to the various volumes of *ILA* attest, though not on the scale of their compatriots in Narbonensis. Therefore the discussions of epigraphy as a way in which a socially marginal and insecure group might seek to claim a position for themselves could be as relevant for Aquitania as for the more lavishly documented case of Narbonensis.[23] It would be equally possible to take a gendered perspective. The great majority of the inscriptions other than tombstones surviving from Aquitania were put up by men for men and record elite masculine activities; the intended audience seems to have been other (elite) males. The one place where women figure prominently in the epigraphy of Aquitania is tombstones, though most tombstones to women were set up by their menfolk and may therefore reflect stereotypical views of the 'good wife' as well as those which seem to display real affection in their formulation. By and large, inscriptions set up by women and perhaps giving us an insight into their concerns are rare from Aquitania, with one remarkable exception. This is the series of altars from Lectoure (*ILA Lactorates* 3–6, 8–12, 15, 18–24) commemorating the performance of the *taurobolium* to the Magna Mater and set up by a series of women of the Lactorates (probably elite women to judge by the quality of the carving of and lettering on the altars) in the later second and earlier third centuries.

This series raises most interesting questions about the ways in which this succession of women clearly used devotion to and performance of a particular cult as a means of self-expression (individual and group) and as a means to present themselves in the public sphere (sadly since the altars were found reused in, quite probably, the late Roman walls, we do not know where they were originally set up) and sometimes to associate themselves with male members of the elite such as magistrates (possibily their menfolk). It also raises interesting questions about the degree to which this monumentalized writing reflects levels of female literacy and/or the appropriation of an essentially male means of self-representation because these were the established vehicles for such representation. Moreover, two other altars (*ILA Lactorates* 7, 16) recording the performance of a *taurobolium* were set up by the *ordo* of the Lactorates, so this originally female devotion had been taken up as a suitable public, written expression of the male-organized identity of the *civitas*.

One feature of some of these inscriptions from Aquitaine is their association with statuary, whether members of the imperial family as in a lost monument from Bordeaux with statues of the family of Augustus, or whether members of the local elites commemorated by statues in the public places of their cities. At one level this association is purely functional; inscribed statue-bases supported statues in stone, marble or bronze. But at another level the association is again indicative of particular functions of the city and particular aspects of the experience of it. Recent work on the place (literal and metaphorical) of statues in the Roman cityscape has demonstrated aspects of their deployment that merit consideration as much for inscriptions as for the statues some of them supported. It is clear that in the Roman world statuary was predominantly an urban phenomenon, whether in public or in private spaces.[24] In his study of statuary from the province of Britain, Stewart demonstrates this to hold good out on the periphery of the Empire as much as at its centre (though in Britain the army again provides another *locus* for this form as it does with inscriptions).[25] The subject-matter of the civil statuary from the provinces is again largely deities, emperors and members of the imperial family, local notables. So both inscriptions and statues were a distinctive part of the texture of public spaces in provincial cities, and indeed this public space itself was distinctive because of its monumentality, enclosed nature and play of light and shade as has been demonstrated for the most extensively excavated city of Aquitania, St-Bertrand in a recent article on this topic.[26] Another approach to statuary that has been discussed recently is the effect of its accumulation over time and how that impacted on the physical appearance and mental landscape of the city. In his consideration of the incomparably richer statuary and epigraphic corpus from Aphrodisias, Smith makes just this point.[27] Modern intellectual tradition has privileged a diachronic perspective concerned with typology and its arrangement in a chronological sequence, with a tendency to consider statues singly or in small, tightly-defined dated groups. The ancient experience, particularly once some time depth was established, was a synchronic one; statues and inscriptions accumulated, were juxta-posed and co-existed; a magistrate of the late first century might stand alongside one of the early third in the same architectural framing and to much the same purpose.

This being so, the argument that I would wish to advance in consequence is that the accumulation of inscriptions, statues and the spaces and monuments that they inhabited over time came to create a *lieu de mémoire* for the identity of the community, imbuing it with a time depth and thus a historical continuity. Though devised by Pierre Nora in his publication of three volumes on *Les Lieux de Mémoire* between 1984 and 1992 in a very different context (rethinking modern France), many of his general points hold good for what is being considered here. He argued, first, that what is being memorialized is the community rather than the family or lineage. He then went on to argue that this collective memory could be materialized not just in deposits created to that end such as archives or museums but in the material world of the building, monument or also the natural place such as a mountain or a landscape which came to be imbued with meaning as an expression of the collectivity not just in the present but in the past. Of course, this memory was and is infinitely manipulable; it does not have to be a 'true' memory of personalities and events as they were, indeed for the construction of communal identities it can be argued that an idealized and self-serving form of memory is better suited. If we combine the premises of Nora with the arguments of Smith then we can construct a vision whereby the erection of statues and inscriptions in the public spaces of a city cumulatively acquired the character of a *lieu de mémoire* for the city and its surrounding *civitas* and thereby helped perpetuate a sense of the rootedness of the community and of the life of the individual, whatever the vicissitudes of the present and the threats and promises of the future. Of course, this argument can also be extended to cover the other privileged area of epigraphic activity in the cities of Aquitania, the cemeteries, where even though tombstones were created to commemorate the individual, or the individual within the family, collectively and over time these objects could also become imbued with the character of the communal and the individuals and their monuments subsumed into a more undifferentiated expression of the collective. If then we look forward to where so many of these inscriptions and other stonework ended up, in the substructures of the late Roman walls of Bordeaux, Périgueux or Saintes, then we get some sense of the impact of the construction of these monuments, not just on the physical landscape of these cities as their historic fabric was replaced but also one the mental landscape as not only the monuments but also the statues, inscriptions and tombstones which over time had contributed so much to the history and identity of the community were ruthlessly cleared and built into the new defining monument of these cities, and incorporated so that no trace of their carving or inscriptions remained visible: the past and its meanings no longer mattered in the new order of things; were indeed to be suppressed.

Finally, what do these arguments mean for wider discussions of reasons for the creation and display of inscriptions in the Roman world, particularly the Western

Provinces? As noted at the beginning of this chapter, this debate has tended to be conducted in terms of 'who', 'when' and 'why', with much less consideration of 'where'. But what the discussion above shows clearly is that there were preferred places for the display of epigraphy and those places were cities. But the type of epigraphy to be displayed in the cities of provinces such as Aquitania was circumscribed and dictated by the spaces and places in which the inscriptions were to be displayed and thus their subject-matter, as we have seen above. So when we debate the reasons for the temporal and social patternings of inscriptions in the first to third centuries AD in the West, we ought also to factor in the type of site at which they were displayed, since this has a critical importance for what sorts of inscription might be set up and for what purposes, and thus who is likely to be recorded in such testimonies, for what reasons and at what times.

Notes

1   Woolf, 1998, Figure 4.5.
2   MacMullen, 1982.
3   Meyer, 1990; Saller and Shaw, 1984; Woolf 1998, pp. 98–105.
4   Wuilleumier, 1963.
5   Rémy, 1996.
6   Bost and Fabre, 2001.
7   Maurin, 1994.
8   Rémy, 1995.
9   Maurin and Navarro Caballero, 2010.
10   Fabre and Sillières, 2000.
11   Bouet, 2003, 2011.
12   Sablayrolles and Beyrie, 2006, pp. 50–4.
13   Esmonde Cleary, 2008, Figure 4.3.
14   Sablayrolles and Beyrie, 2006, pp. 82–92; Esmonde Cleary, 2008, pp. 109–13, Figure 4.5.
15   Cf. Esmonde Cleary, 2008, pp. 113–15.
16   Tardy, 2005.
17   E.g. Carroll, 2006, esp. pp. 30–58.
18   Williamson, 1987.
19   Williamson, 1987, p. 178.
20   Corbier, 1987.
21   Williamson, 1987.
22   Williamson, 1987, pp. 166–70.
23   Woolf, 1998, pp. 98–105.
24   Stewart, 2003, esp. Chapter 5.
25   Stewart, 2010.
26   Sablayrolles, 2006.
27   Smith, 2007.

14

The Written City: Political Inscriptions from Roman Baetica

Louise Revell

Introduction

The impulse to display a permanent message is seen again and again within the material remains of past societies. Whether Palaeolithic cave art or the modern phenomenon of highly ornate graffiti, this desire to communicate in a non-verbal fashion can be documented in multiple societies over time and space. For the population of the Roman empire, one form this took was to set up monumental inscriptions, on stone and bronze, in the public spaces of the town. This is a tradition which has passed down to modern western society, the use of Latin continuing even once it was no longer the vernacular language, forming part of the perceived continuity from the Roman to the modern. However, not all societies inscribed the same messages, or for the same reasons, or with the same social consequences. This raises the question for any society of why inscribe: what is written, under what types of circumstances, and what are the results of the act of writing.[1] We are more hesitant in asking such questions of the Classical world, possibly due to the apparent maintenance of the tradition through to the modern West, making it seem a 'natural' characteristic of literate societies.

The inevitability of the act of writing on stone was questioned some 30 years ago by MacMullen, and since then, a series of articles have gone some way to account for this phenomenon.[2] Similarly, work on the idea of an epigraphic landscape has demonstrated that the choice of where to position inscriptions was structured by social norms, as well as the relationship between inscriptions and urbanism.[3] In this chapter I shall focus on the forum, the symbolic centre of the Roman town, to demonstrate how the display of political inscriptions within the forum formed part of the ongoing maintenance of a Roman mentality of urbanism. The inscriptions will be analysed as both product and producer of a specific ideological subtext. I shall also argue that these acted as a means of negotiating certain social relations: a means for sponsor and passers-by to understand and claim their place within the wider community. To do so, I will concentrate on three particular towns from Baetica: Baelo Claudia, Munigua and Singilia Barba. None of these can be described as imperial showcases, as was the case for towns such as Cordoba, Seville or Gades (Cadiz). Instead, all were rather unremarkable, workaday towns, all mid-first century AD *municipia*, constructed on the site of pre-Roman settlements. In this, they present a contrast to the towns more usually invoked in discussions of the relationship between written text and urban space, such the capitals of the three Iberian provinces. They potentially present a more typical picture (if such a thing can be said to exist) of the contribution of inscriptions to urban ideology in southern Iberia.

The Roman ideology of urbanism

Urbanism is a feature closely associated with the Classical world, whether the polis of Classical Greece, or the new urban foundations of the Roman provinces. Furthermore, its association with modernity can make it seem both inevitable and unchanging: an ahistorical process, with a series of characteristics which are constant across space-time. However, urbanism is a product of a specific social impulse, and varies across cultural groups. Thus the town is created as the result of a specific series of beliefs and values, and its material form is the expression of that ideology. The concept of the town as imbued with ideological belief has long been accepted for classical Greece and the polis. However, there has been a tendency to see Roman urbanism in more pragmatic terms, as a response to the problems of ruling an empire.[4] This view has increasingly been challenged, and elsewhere I have argued that urbanism formed one of the shared ideological structures of Roman imperialism.[5]

Locating a coherent ideology of urbanism within the Roman textual sources can be difficult, but perhaps this is because we expect too much of a consistent discourse. Instead, we should view the city as a subject of contention and debate.[6] It was intimately connected with the Roman concept of civilized living which included the organization of the community through political bodies based within the town. This connection between social organization and urbanization underpins Roman views of how their society developed, as recounted by Cicero in *de Inventione Rhetorica* (2.1–3). Here Cicero argues that prior to urbanization, there were none of the social institutions fundamental to the ideal society, such as organized religious worship, codified law and formalized family relationships. These came with the development of cities. Thus we can see how the idea of the correctly organized society was dependent upon the town, and that the two together formed the basis of a civilized society. The ideal town included a physical aspect: it was an organized, nucleated settlement, with a range of public buildings. These expressed both the wealth of the community, but also its adherence to Roman forms of behaviour, most especially, the participation of the urban community in large-scale political and religious events. Thus the citizens of the town formed a communal body and were expected to play an active role in its running. However, the nature of that participation depended upon social rank, with difference roles for different types of people. Consequently social rank was in part expressed and internalized through urban participation and political activity. Furthermore, there was the ideal of the harmonious community, and that the individual elements of the community would come together for the common good. The town had an independent political existence, but within the context of wider imperial networks, and ultimately with Rome itself. The town was organized through a series of laws, part of which remain, allowing us to trace the urban ideology enshrined within them.[7] They were publically displayed within the forum, proclaiming the new constitution for the town.

It is within this specific ideology of urbanism that we should locate the Roman impulse to write on stone. The public display of text was tied up in the maintenance of the ideal of the town. Such ideals need to be continually recreated through the everyday activities which are almost taken for granted, for example, a visit to the baths or the purchase of a new cooking pot. Any ideology relies on representing social structures which are particular to that society as being natural and unchallengeable.[8] It produces a normative consensus, representing partial perspectives as those of the whole community, and seeming to justify the inequalities between the various groups within that society. Public displays of writing were part of the material conditions used to reproduce that ideology: they formed part of the daily conditions through which the members of the urban community encountered a specifically Roman form of urbanism. The texts of the inscriptions, which present a limited range of messages, emphasized certain values connected with this ideology, such as popular participation, the authority of the magistrates, and the naming of the urban, citizen body. The decision of what to include in the text and the act of inscribing formed a restatement of the adherence to the legal structures of the town. Over time, these were internalized by the viewer through the act of reading, the permanency of the text taking it beyond the moment of its creation.

When dealing with these inscriptions, it is very easy to concentrate on the people responsible for their production, or being honoured in their texts. However, such inscriptions were meant for an audience of the wider community. The question of how many people could interpret these has been hampered by questions of levels of literacy, with Harris' estimate of 10 per cent literacy casting a long shadow over the debate.[9] However, it would be inaccurate to think of encounters with different types of text as being identical, or relying on the same levels of literacy. Reading an inscription is very different from reading a work of literature: the reader's comprehension of the text relies on different literacy or interpretation skills. Repetitive patterning across individual inscriptions can be seen in the limited messages conveyed, as well as the restricted vocabulary and frequent abbreviations used. This is reinforced by the materiality of the inscription, often topped by a statue of some form, and its position and public display. We can question how far reading the inscription actually relies upon reading the text, as opposed to recognizing what kind of things it might be referring to.[10] Furthermore, as we shall see, the dedication of an inscription could be part of a series of celebrations involving the rest of the community, and so seeing the inscription was bound up with a memory of previous events when information about the inscription was gained through other means, such as gossiping with another participant.

Within the Roman town, particular emphasis was placed on the public spaces, and above all, the forum.[11] From the end of the first century BC, it became a key feature of provincial towns, both in position and in decoration. Its architectural elaboration added significance to the activities carried out there, and in particular, the political activities, such as the annual election of the magistrates.[12] Thus the forum can be seen as ideological space, where public political activity was carried out, and the power of the elite judged on a regular basis.[13] An important element in the privileging of the forum was its role as the preferred location for certain forms of inscriptions, specifically honorific dedications, records of benefaction, or legal texts. In certain cases, these formed the base for statues of emperors or important individuals, creating a dual message between image and text.[14] As well as these permanent inscriptions, we know of other, more temporary forms of public writing within the forum. For example, in the annual election of the urban magistrates, the municipal law stipulated that the names of the candidates were to be written up in the forum so that they could be read from ground level.[15] The same instruction was given in the *lex Repetundarum* for the publication of the names of jurors. It is likely that these were written up on more temporary media, but there is still the emphasis on their visibility and the expectation that the citizens would read them. Thus, the forum was a space with writing as an integral element, whether temporary or permanent.

Baelo Claudia

While we can paint a broad picture of the display of inscriptions in the urban setting, it is only through focusing on to the detail of specific case studies that we can reconstruct how inscriptions would have been encountered on a daily basis by any particular community, and therefore how the accumulation of individual inscriptions upheld a particular ideology of urbanism through both the text, but also the relationship between text and space. I want to start with the town of Baelo Claudia in order to demonstrate how the space of the forum could be used for the display of a wealth of inscriptions in a variety of media.[16] In the publication of the inscriptions from the town, 94 could be allocated an approximate location, and of these 48 came from the area of the forum and its associated buildings. Although their relatively fragmentary nature makes it difficult to reconstruct complete texts, they do demonstrate the importance of the forum in the display of inscriptions. It is possible that this distribution is skewed by the extent of excavation on the centre of the town. Nevertheless, this concentration contrasts with the paucity of inscriptions from the theatre, the other known public space within the town. Similarly, the concentration on the forum at the centre of the town also contrasts with the relative lack of inscriptions in the cemetery areas on the approaches to the town.

    The extensive excavations in the area of the forum have produced a full plan of its layout and the varying zones within it (Figure 14.1). The forum dates from the Augustan period, and was part of the wider restructuring and monumentalization of the town. At the northern end was a temple terrace, above the general area of the forum, and consisting of four temples in total. Aligned with the forum plaza were three temples (A–C), which are usually identified as a Capitolium. To the east of this was the temple to Isis. Below this was the forum square, with a nymphaeum at the north side, shops to the east and freestanding buildings, possibly the *curia* and *tabularium*, to the west side. The southern end of the forum was closed by a basilica, with the macellum beside it and in front was a square on to the main route through the town. The ability to recontextualize many of the inscriptions to a relatively precise location means we can begin to build up a picture of the relationship between architecture and text, and how the physical space of the political heart of the town was manipulated to increase the impact of the inscriptions themselves.

The porticoes surrounding the forum seem to have been a key area for the display of texts. The west portico has produced the remains of seven inscriptions. An altar set up to the *duovir* Q. Pupius Urbicos, a *piisimus filius*, by his parents with permission of the *ordo* (*IRBaelo* 14) was found in the northern part of the portico, in front of room 9. A second inscription, although very fragmentary, seems to record the completion of an act of benefaction stipulated by a priest of the imperial cult in his will (*IRBaelo* 17). Both adhere to the expected pattern of the forum dominated by local magistrates. Other forms of inscription which may also have adorned the west portico were a bronze plaque, presumably some form of legal document, and an inscription set into the building itself, judging by the monumental size of the letters (*IRBaelo* 10, 54). Fragments of five inscriptions were found in the east portico, of which one consisted

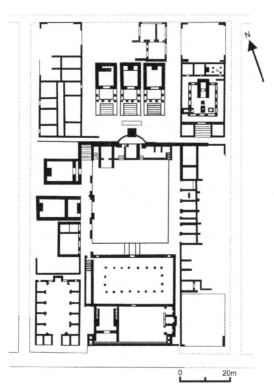

Figure 14.1 Plan of the forum and associated buildings at Baelo Claudia (adapted from Sillières, 1995, Figure 33)

of bronze letters, and a sixth found in the adjoining east shops may have originally stood within the portico. Four inscriptions were found in or around the fountain to the north of the forum square. One of these may refer to the donation of the fountain, as it contains the phrase *dedicavit* (*IRBaelo* 50). A fragment of an imperial dedication, possibly to Nero or Trajan, and two further fragments of inscribed bronze plaques were among the finds in the forum square.

The western side of the forum seems to have been a focus for the display of bronze plaques. As well as the bronze plaque from the western portico, two inscribed and 12 anepigraphic fragments were found in the western part of the forum itself. These plaques were usually used for the display of legal texts, such as urban charters, provincial laws, or even the decrees of the senate at Rome. The Iberian Peninsula has produced a range of these, most notably a number of copies of the Flavian municipal law.[17] It is possible that some of the plaques from the forum were engraved with the municipal law granted to the town by Claudius. As well as a practical legal role, the public display of these documents had a symbolic role, in calling attention to the importance of laws within the ordering of the urban community. They were to be inscribed on bronze tablets and displayed in a prominent position.[18] The remains of the tablets themselves show the remains of holes and brackets, used to fix them to walls, such as the tablets from the *lex de Gallia Cisalpina* with two sets of nail holes, presumably from being taken down and put back up again.[19] It has been suggested that these legal plaques were protected by laws of sacrilege, although this is controversial.[20] If some or all of these plaques from Baelo Claudia formed part of the municipal law, they would have occupied a substantial length of wall: the editors of the *lex Irnitana* estimate that it would have taken up approximately 9 metres of wall.[21] Their placement in the forum created a statement about the importance of the legal framework for urban living, whether the charter itself, or some other form of legal document. The possession of a collection of buildings was not enough to create a Roman town: the community also required a legal code.

To the south of the forum square stood the basilica, one of the most imposing buildings in the town. Ten fragments of inscriptions were found in it, including another fragment of a bronze plaque. These inscriptions would have been overshadowed by the statues set within the building.[22] Two bases for statues were discovered, and traces of up to four others, as well as part of a colossal togate statue of Trajan which, complete, would have stood more than 2.5m high. Excavations nearly have also produced two female statues, one a larger-than life imperial statue, which may also have been from the basilica.[23] This allows two of the inscription fragments from the basilica to be reinterpreted as possible statue bases. One, which contains only a masculine name in the nominative, may refer to the dedicator of a statue (*IRBaelo* 18), while a second may be a series of titles from the inscription for an imperial statue (*IRBaelo* 57).

The temple terrace was arguably less of a focus for epigraphic display than the actual forum square. Ten inscriptions in total were found in this area, which includes three in the area to the west of the terrace. An imperial dedication to Claudius or his son Britannicus accords with the suggestion that the central one of the triple shrines may have been dedicated to the imperial cult (*IRBaelo* 5).[24] Three inscriptions were found in association with the Temple of Isis, and these reinforce the variability in forms of epigraphic display. Two were *plantae pedum* inscriptions to the goddess. These were plaques, both bearing the carved outline of a pair of feet, and both recording the fulfilment of a vow on the part of different men. As was customary for such inscriptions, they were set into the floor, at the base of the steps to the temple (*IRBaelo* 2, 3).[25] Unusually, these were then covered with a layer of mortar, obscuring them from view. This mortar formed the floor of the temple courtyard, suggesting that this took place early in the temple's history, possibly as part of its inauguration. A second form of dedication from the temple was a *defixio*, also to Isis (*IRBaelo* 1). It took the usual form of the dedicant requesting that the goddess exact retribution on the perpetrator of the theft of several items of bedding. Such curse tablets were usually folded and then buried, concealing them from view.[26] The example from Baelo Claudia does not show the characteristic folding, and it may have been displayed within the sanctuary and concealed in a pit at a later date. Both *plantae pedum* and the *defixio* are relatively unusual forms of religious dedications, and the way which they have been incorporated into the space points to local interpretations of the form. They reveal dynamism in decisions taken about how to use epigraphy in contrast to the stereotypical image of inscriptions as a monotonous rank of stone statue bases and altars.[27]

The inscriptions from Baelo Claudia demonstrate the way inscriptions of varying media adorned the public spaces of the town. The forum was filled with the public display of texts, in particular, in the forum porticoes and the basilica. Someone walking through the various buildings and open areas was continually confronted by a series of different types of message about local and imperial power, and the forms of reverence due to the gods. At Baelo Claudia we see the range of types of inscription which might be set up in the forum: as well as the statue bases and plaques there were the *plantae pedum* and curse tablets which contrasted in size and monumentality. Some inscriptions were carved into the stonework of the building, and bronze letters may have been fixed to it (for example, *IRBaelo* 56, 62). These differences in materiality and the style of writing produced different reading experiences, and called upon different forms of literacy.

Munigua

While Baelo Claudia establishes the sheer abundance of written text which could be on display within the forum, the next two case studies demonstrate the social role these inscriptions might have had. In the case of the Flavian municipium of Munigua, excavations of the forum during the 1960s and the 1980s allow many of the inscriptions to be recontextualized with varying degrees of accuracy, allowing us to consider the relationship between message and location.[28] The layout of the town was dictated by its hilltop setting: it was built on an ascending series of terraces, linked by monumental ramps and staircases.[29] The sanctuary terrace was located at the top of the hill and the forum lay on a lower terrace. It was constructed in an atypical form of a square, substantially filled by a temple, and surrounded by porticoes on three sides (Figure 14.2).[30] Two adjoining rooms were part of the original construction, and later other rooms and a basilica were added. Although the hill-top sanctuary was the focus

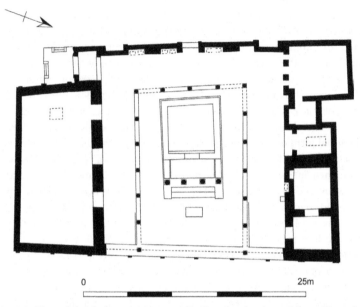

0   25m

Figure 14.2 Plan of the forum at Munigua (P. Copeland; adapted from Hauschild, 1991, Figure 5)

of the layout and architecture of the town, the inscriptions were concentrated on the forum.

As at Baelo Claudia, the porticoes formed the focal area for epigraphic display. There were four niches set in the wall of the west portico, and at least two of these were occupied by statues and their dedicatory bases to members of the Quintii family, Rufinus and his son Rufus (*CILA* 2.1074, 1075). Further inscriptions were displayed along the north portico over the forum. In a niche set into the outside wall of room 7, L. Valerius Aelius Severinus set up a dedication to Bonus Eventus on a base which probably carried a statue of the god, although it could have been of Severinus himself (*CILA* 2.1054). L. Aelius Fronto set up the bronze statue of a horse to Dis Pater in an exedra purpose-built into the northern portico, which he described as a stable for the horse (*CILA* 2.1956). The statue and its base probably stood more than 4 metres high, dominating the space. Room 7, probably the *tabularium*, yielded two further types of inscription: an imperial letter from Titus and a *tessera* recording an agreement of *hospitium*. Both of these were bronze plaques, and the imperial letter was originally affixed to the wall, as demonstrated by the nail holes still visible in the plaque. This letter contained the emperor's arbitration in a dispute between the townspeople and the provincial governor (*CILA* 2.1052).[31] Although he ruled against the townspeople, it was inscribed on bronze and publicly displayed in the forum. The *tessera* probably pre-dates the construction of the forum, and so was moved to the *tabularium* from its original location as the more appropriate place to keep it.

Other inscriptions were displayed in the forum, but cannot be given a precise location. A statue of silver was dedicated to the Genius Municipii by Quintia Flaccina (*CILA* 2.1056), and it is possible that the entrance to the forum was also marked by a statue dedicated in honour of Quintia Flaccina to Ceres (*CILA* 2.1055). A pair of plaques recording the original donation of the forum have also been found in the area of the forum (*CILA* 2.1076–7).[32] In these, L. Valerius Firmus listed the component parts of his act of benefaction: the temple, the forum, the porticoes, an exedra and the *tabularium*. It has been suggested that the forum was the original location for a series of three dedications to successive Flavian emperors, although as they are eighteenth century finds, we cannot be certain (*CILA* 2.1064–6).[33] This collection of inscriptions from the forum of Munigua demonstrates the deliberate use of place. Set within niches along the porticoes, statues of members of the leading families atop dedicatory inscriptions added to the decoration of the forum, but also acquired additional authority through their context. The focus on the forum as the preferred locale for epigraphic display runs counter to the architectural layout of the town. The sanctuary at the top of the hill was the visual focus, with processional routes leading to it, and its preferential decoration with coloured marbles. In contrast, only two inscriptions have been recovered from this area (*CILA* 2.1057, 1060). Similarly, there are relatively few funerary inscriptions from the town, despite the monumental necropolis surrounding it.[34] This is presumably because few of the townspeople actually lived within the town itself, and so most would have been commemorated in the countryside. It presents an interesting contrast to the impression gained from the various corpora of inscriptions, which are generally dominated by epitaphs: in this case, they formed a small part of the encounters with written text on the urban stage.

The inscriptions from the Forum demonstrate how powerful individuals and leading families could use the political heart of the town to legitimate their social position. One of the leading families was the Quintii, judging from the inscriptions they set up. Statues were dedicated to the father and son, Rufinus and Rufus, in the west portico: the statue to Rufus by the *municipes* of the town, and that to Rufinus by Rufus. Each inscription records that the recipient held the post of *duovir* on two occasions, gives the full title of the town and states that the statues were approved by decree of the *ordo decurionum*. Marcus Quintius Rufus, the son, also dedicated a statue to Hercules Augustus in the main temple complex (*CILA* 2.1060), and a second statue to Hercules Augustus with an identical text in the area of modern Algerciras on the Straits of Gibraltar.[35] These two inscriptions have identical texts, in spite of being set up in different places, demonstrating the extent to which such inscriptions conformed to an expected style. That Marcus is also the only inhabitant of Munigua to be known of from outside the town reinforces this impression of the standing of the family. Quintia Flaccina was probably related, and she held the title of *flaminica* of the provincial imperial cult. She set up the silver statue to the Genius Municipii in the forum, possibly a second with an identical text in an unknown location, and after her death, a statue was dedicated to Ceres in her honour and placed outside the entrance to the forum (*CILA* 2.1056, 1059 and 1055 respectively).

Although we do not see other families represented as prominently, there are instances of other magistrates being honoured within the forum. L. Valerius Firmus, whose benefaction paid for the construction of the forum was, like the Quintii, also elected *duovir* twice. Slightly different is the case of Severinus, who dedicated the statue to Bonus Eventus. He was a *libertus*, and dedicated the statue to celebrate the honour of being made *sevir*, and in this case, we can see how a social outsider would use this public platform to announce his growing importance.[36] Like the Quintii, he acknowledged that he was granted permission to set up the statue within the boundary of the forum by decree of the *ordo*. The inscriptions form part of the definition, creation and maintenance of power relations within the community. Political and social authority was derived through a number of related institutions, and the relationships between them are expressed in the single texts. We see the social and political power of specific individuals and their families: these inscriptions record the fact that they were considered worthy of honours, but also the donations to the community which justified these honours. In addition, we see the articulation of their relationship with their peers (or rivals) in the *ordo*: these honours were approved and allowed by the *ordo*, and the explicit mention of this permission within the text demonstrates its importance in the whole process. It is not only that these individuals held political authority, but that they needed the consent of others to display this authority. In the process of these individuals being honoured, we also see the process of naming and defining the other elements of the political community, such as the *municipes* and the urban community.

Other inscriptions show how the forum was used as an arena for the maintenance of relationships with those outside of the town. Such inscriptions slotted the town into the wider relationships of patronage and obligation which connected the local with the global within the imperial system. Dedications were made to Vespasian and Titus during Titus' reign; later, after his death, Titus' dedication had the title DIVUS added to his name, and the group was completed with a dedication to Domitian. All three were probably bases for statues, and formed a group of imperial sculpture, of the kind most frequently found in fora. They were all dedicated by men from the prominent families of Munigua: L. Aelius Fronto, and two members of the Licinii family. The *hospitium* agreement, also a bronze plaque, recorded a formal agreement between the senate and people of Munigua and Sex. Curvius Silvinus, an imperial quaestor and part of a senatorial family from Narbonensis (*CILA* 2.1053).[37] This was a formal relationship, connecting the town of Munigua into the wider network of political influence and obligation which stretched throughout the provinces of the empire, linking them ultimately with Rome.[38] The expected longevity of the relationship is emphasized in the wording, which stipulated that the agreement was to continue into the time of their sons and descendants. Both the imperial dedications and the *tessera* cemented these relationships between the town and these more powerful individuals, but they also served as a reminder that Munigua was no longer an independent community, but instead acted on a wider stage. For the local people, the town was the interface between them and the Empire.

Singilia Barba

Many of the characteristics seen at Munigua also occur in the town of Singilia Barba. Like Munigua, it developed from a pre-Roman settlement, and was given municipal status in the Flavian period. The site of the town has been known since the sixteenth century, and the forum was partially excavated by the University of Malaga between 1985 and 1992.³⁹ The rather incomplete plan consists of a paved square with a series of staircases leading to associated buildings. The excavations also produced 23 inscriptions from the forum: four in their original position, three built into later walls, and 16 without precise location.

Of the four inscriptions whose original location can be reconstructed, we can again see an attention to the placement, as all four flanked staircases. Two bases for bronze statues were dedicated to members of the Hirii family, probably father and son (*CIL* 2.5.786, 799). At around the same time or shortly afterwards, an inscription was set up to one side of the neighbouring staircase to the *duovir* Marcus Valerius Proculinus (*CIL* 2.5.789). The text states that Proculinus, who was given his choice of where to be honoured, specifically chose this area, and used the key nodal point of the staircase to increase its prominence. Public thanks were then offered to him in the forum, providing a glimpse of the activities through which the space was given its political meaning. A third staircase on the south side of the forum was also flanked by a dedication, in this case a post-mortem dedication to Marcus Cornelius Saturninus from his parents (*CIL* 2.5.797). All four bases were over 1.5 metres high, and assuming the statues they bore were life-size, each would have been over 3 metres high. They would have dominated the open space of the forum, enhancing it, but in turn, being enhanced by its social and political importance.

These inscriptions constitute only a portion of those which originally decorated this area. There was a series of three imperial dedications, to third and fourth century emperors in the name of the *Res Publica Barbensium* (*CIL* 2.5.777–9). Others include a marble plaque recording an act of benefaction (*CIL* 2.5.794), another honorific statue (*CIL* 2.5.801), a series of bronze letters possibly from more than one inscription (*CIL* 2.5.817), and more fragments of inscriptions on stone too fragmentary to reconstruct. The careful positioning of the inscriptions represents a desire for self-representation within the most prestigious area of the town. This was a cumulative process, as over time specific individuals or families added new monuments. However, the later incorporation of two second century inscriptions into fourth century walls suggests that they did not maintain their significance through to the end of the life of the town, and eventually came to be seen as no more than building stone (*CIL* 2.5.785, 824).

The inscriptions from the forum again demonstrate how the political institutions of the Roman town became the way through which this community framed their understanding of themselves and the relationships between them. The most articulate is the statue to Marcus Valerius Proculinus (*CIL* 2.5.789) commemorating his year as *duovir*, his acts of munificence to the community, and his capable administration of the town (*ob rem publicam bene atministratam* sic). Various constituent groups within the community are named within the text: the citizens and *incolae* of the town paid for the statue through public subscription, and the *ordo* passed a decree allowing it. Furthermore, his magisterial title has been reconstructed as as *duovir municipium municipii liberi Singiliensis*, again mentioning the name of the town, but also the townspeople. This rather wordy way of describing the town not only recalls similar phrasing in inscriptions from Munigua, but also the phrasing in the *lex Irnitana*. It articulates the idea that this was now an urban community, and that the local inhabitants were defined as *municipes*, and moreover, *municipes* of a specific town, a core element of the Roman ideology of urbanism.[40]

The inscription also records the public ceremonies surrounding its dedication: on the day Proculinus left office, public thanks were given in the forum, and sacrifices were carried out. It lists a series of acts of benefaction from him to the citizen body as a whole, and to various sections within it. During his year in office, he donated public games, and the same number of days of private games. It is not stated how many this was, but the *lex Coloniae Genetivae* required that the *duovir* provide four days of public games spending no less than 2,000 sesterces of his own money and the same from public money, therefore it is possible that Proculinus provided four days of public games as required, and an additional four days of private games.[41] He also provided free visits to the baths and oil for the whole *populus* and the *incolae*, and free entry to the baths and the gymnasium for men and women. The inscription compresses these multiple acts which constituted this ongoing relationship into a single text, to be recalled in the future through a single act of reading.

Although other inscriptions lack the wealth of details of the Proculinus dedication, we can see the same ideologies repeated within them. Both statues of the Hirii were honorific dedications (*CIL* 2.5.786, 799), and similarities in the wording, stone, lettering and style of decoration suggest that they were set up at the same time, at the end of the first century or beginning of the second century. Although we cannot be certain, the Hirii were probably father and son. The son was a *duovir*, but the father does not seem to have held any form of political office. Both statues were set up by the citizens and the *incolae* of the *Municipium Liberi Singiliensis* from money raised by public subscription (*ex aere conlato*), pointing to the active role of the wider community. Other inscriptions record further acts of benefaction, such as Lucius Clodius Montanus paying for the repaving of the floor of the basilica with marble, and for banquets in celebration of this. Two further fragments could also be honorific dedications, with acts of benefaction in recompense, including the payment for circus games (*CIL* 2.5.801, 816). Finally, a plaque recorded the dedication of a statue to Venus in celebration of receiving citizenship, either Roman citizenship, or citizenship of the town (*CIL* 2.5.774).

One noticeable feature within the texts of the inscriptions from the forum, repeated among those without context, is the emphasis on the act of naming the urban institutions of the town. It points to an internalization of the legal language of charters by the townspeople. They are categorized as the *muncipes* of the *municipium*, as we saw in the Proculinus inscriptions, and this is also seen in a second inscription where a priesthood is described as the *pontifex perpetuus municipum municipii liberi Singiliensis* (*CIL* 2.5.785). While the inscriptions create the united citizen body, they also serve to differentiate the various sub-groups within it. Some inscriptions differentiate between the *municipes* and the *incolae*, while in contrast, presenting them as acting in accord. Thus, for example both dedications to the Hirii are dedicated by the *cives et incolae municipii Liberi Sinigiliensis*, both separating them, but at the same time uniting them as part of the town. This emphasis on the naming of the various sections of the community may relate to the possible dual community hinted at in a dedicatory inscription (*CIL* 2.5.792).[42] The text refers to two different *ordines*: the *ordo Singiliensis* and the *ordo Singiliens(is) vetus*, and the decision taken by both to grant citizenship of the town to a *sevir Augustalis* from Cordoba. This is the only explicit reference to the two *ordines*, although the *ordo Singiliensis vetus* is hinted at in a further inscription (*CIL* 2.5.794). It is unclear how these twin communities originated, but the inscription provided one means of publicly declaring unity within the community overall. At the same time as the individual elements are named, it is made clear that they act in concert, be it the different *ordines*, or the *cives et incolae*. Whether this harmony existed in reality is an unanswerable question, but the inscriptions were part of the maintenance of the ideology that it should.

Writing Roman urban ideology

These three towns from Roman Baetica all demonstrate how the forum played a role in the creation and maintenance of an urban ideology. For the townspeople, their knowledge of how their world should be organized was reinforced through their experience of the forum and their reception of the messages it communicated through the inscriptions on display. Part of this was the significance of the space itself: the importance of the forum in the identity of the urban community, and political activities in maintaining the coherence of the community. A number of inscriptions refer to acts of benefaction in terms of paying for the construction of parts of the forum, or for the statues and other paraphernalia which adorned them. The wording of these accords with a value system where the public spaces of a town were important and part of the self-pride of the entire community. The materiality of the inscriptions was deliberately used to enhance the forum in preference to other spaces within the town, adding to its prestige, but in turn taking added authority from their position. However, we can take this further. As Zanker has argued: '[the townscape] not only shapes the inhabitants, but is shaped by them, for the buildings and spaces, having been constructed to embody certain messages and values, continue to communicate these same messages to succeeding generations'.[43] This is not only true for the buildings, but also for the inscriptions which adorned them. We tend to concentrate on the immediate message of these inscriptions, but they also embodied deeper values, and the ongoing act of reading the text and acknowledging these values formed one of the repeated acts which maintained the ideology of urbanism.

The smooth working of Roman urbanism was based around ideas of political activity, with political participation forming part of the self-definition of the overall community, but also of the various unequal political roles within that. Inscriptions formed part of the way in which that communal identity was created and maintained through their role in naming, for example, through the use of the phrase *municipes municipii Flavii Muniguensium* at Munigua. This picks up the language of the legal charters, suggesting the internalization of the new legally-constituted definition of the pre-existing community. At the same time, these inscriptions created the various elements within the community. This appears in its most extreme form at Singilia Barba, where one inscription distinguishes between *universus populus in municipio habitans et incolae* (*CIL* 2.5.789). A further example of this is the inscriptions which record the acts of the *ordo decurionum*: the frequent reminder that activities were carried out by the decree of the decurions was not only a statement of their authority, but helped to create it. In this way, inscriptions were embedded in the power relations within the community. This was particularly true for the individual members of the elite families who served as magistrates. The inscriptions which recorded their actions in the community not only demonstrated their authority, but legitimated it through the new political structure of urban magistracies and benefaction.

In such ways, the political inscriptions not only acted as a memorialization of certain acts, they also communicated the underlying ideology. They demonstrated that the town was well-ordered, a harmonious community, held together by communal political activity, and that this was the correct way to be. However, it also raises the question of whether there are elements which are distinctive to Baetica. The duplication of inscriptions at Munigua and Singilia Barba is notable, whether sets of identical inscriptions or paired inscriptions to father and son. In both cases, the inscribing habit seems to be dominated by a number of families, and at Munigua, the duovirate seems to have frequently been held by the same person on more than one occasion. We are used to thinking of honorific dedications being the product of a competitive magisterial system. However, in these more insignificant urban centres, are we in fact seeing restricted competition? Perhaps in these cases, the more important message was the adoption of new forms of socio-political organization through the legal framework of the urban ideology. This interpretation could be supported by the way in which some of the inscriptions echo the legal phrasing of the municipal charter, suggesting the internalization of this particular Roman interpretation of urbanism. It is impossible to say how far this was unique to Baetica. Ultimately, more comparative work between regions is needed to first trace the extent of variability in the use and language of political dedications, and then to interpret its significance in terms of urban ideologies.[44]

The act of inscribing is too complex a phenomenon to reduce to a single explanation, and others have proposed explanations which complement those outlined here.[45] The decision to set up an inscription was the product of the desire to communicate a complicated series of messages, both explicit and implicit, and each inscription can be understood as articulating these to varying degrees according to the wishes of the patron and the requirements of the specific circumstance. Nevertheless, underpinning these political inscriptions is an acceptance of a particular Roman ideology of urbanism, and it is through this ideology that we can understand the significance of the written city.

Notes

1　Bowman and Woolf, 1994, pp. 1–16, in particular, pp. 1–2.
2　MacMullen, 1982, pp. 233–46. Also, Barrett, 1993; Meyer, 1990; Woolf, 1996.
3　Papers in Cooley, 2000a.
4　For example, Garnsey and Saller, 1987, p. 26.
5　Revell, 2009.

6   Rykwert, 1988; Zanker, 2000, pp. 25–41; Richardson, 1995; Roda, 1995.
7   The most complete collection of urban charters is Crawford, 1988. See also González and Crawford 1986; González, 2008, pp. 11–165. Revell, 2009, pp. 49–54 argues that the Spanish charters reflect a specific ideology of urbanism.
8   Miller and Tilley, 1984; Shanks and Tilley, 1982, pp. 129–54.
9   Harris, 1989; see also Lomas et al., 2007.
10 See Corbier this volume.
11 There is a substantial literature on the form and the significance of the forum; see for example Laurence et al., 2011.
12 González and Crawford, 1986.
13 Revell, 2007.
14 Stewart, 2003.
15 González and Crawford, 1986, Chapter 51.
16 The most recent corpus of inscriptions from Baelo Claudia is Bonneville et al., 1988. For the history and archaeology of the town, Sillières, 1995.
17 González and Crawford, 1986.
18 González and Crawford, 1986, Chapter 95.
19 Crawford, 1996.
20 Williamson, 1987, pp. 160–83. This is refuted by Crawford in Crawford, 1988.
21 González and Crawford, 1986, p. 147.
22 Garriguet, 2004; Ney and Paillet, 2006.
23 Loza Azegua, 2010.
24 Sillières, 1995.
25 Dunbabin, 1990.
26 Gager, 1992.
27 Beard 1991.
28 The up-dated corpus of inscriptions from Munigua is published in González Fernández, 1996. See also Collantes de Terán and Fernández-Chicarro, 1972–4.
29 Schattner, 2003.
30 Hauschild, 1969–70; Hauschild, 1991.
31 Millar, 1977, pp. 441–2.
32 Schattner, 2003, p. 61.
33 Garriguet, 2004. Schattner, 2003, p. 213, n. 12 alternatively argues that they were from the two storeyed portico opposite the forum.
34 Schattner, 2003, pp. 210–4.
35 Stylow and Gimeno Pascual, 2002, pp. 335–6.
36 This contrasts with towns in Italy, see Mouritsen, 2005.
37 Alföldy, 1969.
38 Nichols, 2001, pp. 99–108.
39 The inscriptions from the excavations are reproduced in *CIL* 2.5; their positions are taken from p. 212. See also Serrano Ramos et al., 1991–2; Serrano Ramos and Rodríguez Oliva, 1988. The only excavations of the forum are described in Serrano Ramos, 1988. For the history and finds from the town, Atencia Páez, 1988.
40 Discussed more fully in Revell, 2009.
41 Crawford, 1988; Chapter 92 refers to the provision of games.
42 Ordóñes Agulla, 1987–8.
43 Zanker, 1998, p. 3.
44 See Blagg, 1990 for an example of this.
45 For example, Mackie, 1990, pp. 171–89.

15

Afterword

Peter Keegan

Admiror paries te non cecidisse ruinis qui tot scriptorum taedia sustineas

CIL IV.1904, 1906, 2461, 2487 = *CLE* 937

I am amazed, O wall, that you have not fallen in ruins, you who bear the weight of so many boring inscriptions.

Space – the final frontier?

We are told that we live in an age of information, bombarded with an extraordinary array of data. Though more often than not what we see or hear is extremely ordinary in nature and significance, we are nevertheless never far removed from the transmitters of much of this discourse: the internet, 24-hour television and mobile phones. Each day we find ourselves churning through email, Twitter, social networking sites and text messages, and our quotidian journeys often entail encounters with digital news feed scrolling live across department-store screens and advertising displays on the sides and rear of public transport, roadside hoardings, and throughout commuter precincts. The written spaces of the city in the twenty-first century are ubiquitous and pervasive.

What is striking is that those who lived, worked, and moved through the urban and peri-urban landscapes of the western Mediterranean under Roman rule (200 BC–AD 400) negotiated spatial environments replete with a proliferation of verbal and non-verbal messages – marked in a range of forms within the architectural fabric of cities and towns, displayed across a spectrum of civic, domestic, and occupational contexts, and produced for a variety of purposes and a broad cross-section of society. As the graffito in the epigraph of this chapter reflects, the sheer density of written space and the diversity of locations, functions, and producers/consumers of meaning permeating the architectural contexts of town and city in the Latin West speak to a spatially dynamic cultural practice – an epigraphic phenomenon that instantiates and encapsulates on a plethora of durable surfaces the ideas, customs, and social behaviour of women and men disparate in geographical terms but constituted collectively under a structurally common politico-military system of laws and principles. Distilled to its essential ingredients, this collocation of official and non-official texts and images

– within, on and across the purpose-built environments of the Latin-speaking world – interpenetrates and characterizes the settings for a gamut of human activities: the lives, livelihoods, learning and leavetakings of persons from every stratum of Roman society. As a consequence, thinking about written space in the western Mediterranean from the defeat of Hannibal to the Visigoth invasion of Italy requires us to consider not only how space changes perception but also how perception changes space.

Space > perception

As we move through cities in our daily lives, we are constantly transforming the spaces around us. The form and essence of urban space directly affects people's behaviour, describing in their perception what is possible or impossible, allowed or prohibited, suggested or advised against. We are now able to fill and stratify space/time with digital information layers, completely wrapping cities in a membrane of information and of opportunities for interaction and communication. As noted above, mobile devices, smartphones, wearables, digital tags, near field communication devices, location-based services and mixed/augmented reality have gone much further in this direction, turning the world into an essentially read/write, ubiquitous publishing surface. The usage of mobile devices and technologies alters the understanding of place. In this process, the definition of urban landscape powerfully shifts from a definition which is purely administrative to one that is multiplied according to all individuals which experience that location; as a lossless sum of their perceptions; as a stratification of interpretations and activities which forms our cognition of space and time.

During the course of this volume the contributors have investigated perspectives of the ancient city which see urban spaces in precisely this way: progressively filling with multiple layers of inscribed information. No matter how big (the monumental epigraphy of the forum and its associated civic infrastructure) or small (graffiti clusters on *palaestra* columns, *libelli* on commemorative sculpture), studying the discursive interdependencies of written space has demonstrated the possibilities available for modern eyes to reconceptualize how those who worked in and passed through these spaces perceived the nature of their particular urban environment and how the discourse which surrounded them shaped their perceptions – of themselves, their place in the world, their city, and their society. Indeed, studying the uses of space in ancient urban contexts demonstrates how possible it was for persons and groups living at the time to create multiple layers of narrative which traversed the city, and allows us to read them in different ways. The different strategies and methodologies deployed by each contributor have enabled us to highlight how cities in the Latin West expressed points of view on ideas and issues affecting every stratum in Roman society. From the lowliest slave to the emperor himself, written space in post-classical urban contexts encapsulated opportunities to inscribe one's identity (e.g., age, benefaction, culture, death, the economy, education, gender, occupation, politics, power, property, religion, status, and time).

Identity, of course, is a term which is very popular and which is commonly used in a number of disciplines concerned with the study of human behaviour, conduct and societal structures in general. Importantly for our purposes, Lynch defines identity as 'the extent to which a person can recognize or recall a place as being distinct from other places'.[1] Like individuals, cities should have character and distinctiveness; like individuals, these qualities comprise numerous characteristics, or identifiable elements that mark 'a sense of place'.[2] City spaces created through intentional design and incidental accretion reflect an array of determining and guiding parameters with respect to urban identity.[3] We can use the term 'collective built identity' to encompass the facets of identity which are represented through the built environment in an urban context.[4]

Hannah's survey of official and non-official *fasti*, for example, demonstrates precisely this point. The spaces within which religious and civic calendars were marked – predominantly public contexts (the meeting places of priestly colleges, associations and rural settlements; walls of buildings on the grounds of elite residences) – and the manner in which these chronological lists were recorded – inscribed on durable surfaces or painted as wall-decoration (*Fasti Antiates Maiores, Fasti Praenestini, Fasti porticus*); compiled as condensed, often abbreviated synthetic or exegetical items with/without pertinent symbols or illustrations of singular and/or seasonal activities – reflect spatio-temporal collocations – diachronic/cyclical (*Fasti Anni, Fasti Consulares*) and synchronic/episodic (*Fasti Triumphales*) – that underpin socio-political trends in late republican and imperial Rome, especially abbreviated demarcation of days (F, C, N, NP) on which political and legal business and the registration of magisterial actions integral to the maintenance of civic order and stability (consular elections, censorial lustrations, military victories) may take place.

These uses of the urban fabric in order to categorize, catalogue and characterize time exemplify how space shapes perception; in this instance, perception of socio-economic and political identity during the epistemic shift from Caesarian *res publica* to Augustan *imperium*. Simply put, architectural form can govern conceptual function: for example the semi-circular hemicycle on which was inscribed the *Fasti Praenestini*, governing line-of-sight and perspectival focus, set up in the civic centre, encouraging visual and conceptual associations with proximal civic architecture. Similarly, inclusion of nundinal letters (A–H) in *fasti* displayed in public contexts – whether these were civic spaces (marketplaces, civic buildings, temple precincts) or spaces in shared workplace, leisure, or domestic spaces (fulleries, exercise areas, shops, peristyle courtyards in private homes) – associate quotidian socio-economic cycles of production and exchange with a spectrum of spatial settings. The insertion of monumental epigraphy that charted the passage of time on a daily, seasonal, and annual basis into the fabric of regional and imperial urban spaces – whether erected on a scale suited to a particular local context (the sundial on a column with inscribed plaque in the precinct of the Temple of Apollo at Pompeii) or in a far more concept-rich metropolitan context (the obelisk with inscribed base comprising the Augustan *horologium* in the Campus Martius at Rome) – denotes such contexts as visual and spatial locations for storing and processing information keyed to complex elements of economic and state organization (Hannah).

We can locate a corollary to this reconfiguration of social identity in contexts denoting calendrical space by reference to Trifilò's examination of the *platea*. The broad descriptive term *platea* – comprising architectural and topographical elements (the broad monumental street, the open public space) – provides an entry-point into those nodes of written space described as '*lieux de la convergence*'.[5] As we have seen, the popularity of the term as a designation of building activity relates to the period from the death of Hadrian to the fifth century AD, increasing from the first to the second century and decreasing gradually thereafter. The efflorescence of inscriptions using the term can therefore be associated with towns under expansion or change rather than new foundations. Significantly, the monumental dedications bearing the term *platea* are united in their display of acts of *dignitas* and euergetism that consolidate social hierarchy *and* embellish the urban fabric. Not only would the use of the term appear to be part of a ranked calibration of street-types but also of a collective strategy in the determination of *loci celeberrimi*, what Trifilò refers to as 'the re-birth of the central place' (p. 178).

Reading written space in Pompeii draws out a correlation between the form and function of monumental epigraphy and graffiti as products *and* producers of meaning. Comparing commemorative statues on inscribed bases in dominant public spaces, in the chapters by Sears on the *fora* of North African cities or that by Cooley on baths in Roman Italy, and informal representations of gladiators and gladiatorial combat marked at Pompeii on the façades of buildings and the interior spaces of houses (palaestra of Large Theatre, Large Palaestra, 'House of the Gladiators') suggests that graffiti should be interpreted in precisely the same way as official epigraphy: namely, in relation to the architectural spaces in which they are situated. This is evident with respect to the graffiti located in the 'House of the Gladiators' (V.5.3) – a context configured very differently from the spatial arrangement of domestic spaces; one which conforms, therefore, with public spaces used by various groups, and, in particular, compares far more favourably with peristyle courtyards and *atria* in homes and columnated palestral spaces near large gathering areas (the Large Theatre, the Amphitheatre) than strictly delimited contexts like residential quarters for specific groups or *ludi* for training gladiators. Again, the physical context – denoted by the circulation of different categories of person through permeable social spaces framed by columns – reflects the use of graffiti, like certain types of formal epigraphy, as marking to be written and/or to be read.

Perception > space

Defining the city in the Latin West as a historical entity should be comparatively easy, given the Roman empire shared similar administrative, cultural and topographical developments. *Fora* appeared in all conquered cities as well as baths, temples and triumphal arches. As we have seen, however, textual and pictorial markings on durable surfaces – pervasive and highly visible, displayed in relation to the repertoire of buildings, architectural features, and sculpture (constituting the aggregated articulation of Roman culture and ideology), within and across contexts in the urban fabric of the western Mediterranean – act to express and shape (potentially and in reality) perceptions of the city and of individual and group identity during this period. The transformative principle underlying written space, its form and function as a conduit for changing perceptions, requires us to incorporate epigraphic culture as a constitutive element in the design and development of the classical city under Roman rule.

Importantly for any refinement of definitions of the Roman city, what the contributions in this volume reveal is that, like our gradual reconceptualization of Romanization[6] as a negotiated, diachronic process (of acculturation and integration) rather than a prescribed, synchronic episode (of conquest and cultural adoption), the principle of transformation inherent in written space should be understood as belonging to a spectrum of exchange. In other words, the features which embody the urban fabric of the Latin West should not be seen solely in terms of a single, linear imperative on perceptions of identity (person *and* place). Instead, written space is both part of the forces and means of socio-cultural production *and* a material product of the range of socio-cultural formations, shaped by elements of the prevailing economic, political and ideological systems, by their combinations and the social practices deriving from them.[7] It is on the ways in which perception changes space that this section will now focus attention.

Hemelrijk demonstrates how the activities underwriting female participation in the phenomenon of monumental epigraphy reflect the extent to which social perceptions shaped the spatial markers of urbanization and Romanization in the civic fabric of Roman Italy and the Latin West. Prestigious inscriptions on public buildings financed by women and on public statuary set up for them (e.g. Mineia, Paestum; Salvia Postuma, Pola; Cornelia Valentina Tuccia, Thamugadi) or by them (for deities and relatives) may be associated with the spread of Roman citizenship and the introduction of Roman civil law, permitting Roman citizen-women from prominent indigenous families to own and control property in their own right. Using wealth for the benefit of their cities allowed some of these women to enter the written spaces of urban centres. Setting up honorific statues and inscriptions for and by women in urban centres performed a triptych of functions: public recognition; perpetual remembrance; and exemplarity. The display of women's names (and/or images) in the written spaces of Roman Italy and the Mediterranean regions of the Latin West ensured that female euergetism was recognized, that their own and their families' prestige would be inscribed in the collective memory of their local community, and that other women would 'read' a model for embedding social aspiration in the durable, visible surfaces of the urban fabric. Changing perceptions of the legal capacity of Roman women *sui iuris* as property owners under the empire, in concert with the spread of Roman citizenship and law (under mandate or as a function of municipal charters), drove the participation and display of women in the written spaces of coastal Mediterranean Roman cities.

The change in socio-political dynamics, its reflection in the gendering of civic benefaction and commemoration and its impact on the production of written space find further expression in the funerary landscape of peri-urban Rome (Keegan). Studies of tombstone inscriptions have focused on methods of assigning names in Roman society, the age at marriage and death of demographic populations across the Roman Empire, relations of kinship, marriage, amity and dependence among elite and subaltern families and communities, and the performance of acts in accordance with traditional forms of belief and custom. Keegan asks what conclusions can be drawn from the corpus of private Latin funerary inscriptions from the city of Rome and its environs about the identity, social condition and cultural activity of men and women participating in the process of epigraphic commemoration and dedication. Exploring certain conceptual and experiential aspects of the commemorative process – the abilities of Roman men and women of different ages, ethnic origins, social affiliations, and belief systems to understand the visual and textual complexities of epigraphic representation; and the cultural contexts within and through which men and women interacted with the material and linguistic traces of epigraphic discourse – demonstrates that women participated as significantly as men in the process in a variety of ways and contexts usually regarded as prominently or exclusively male, opening up the possibility that in certain circumstances they left behind the trace or residue of a uniquely female perspective on their world.

Esmonde Cleary's study of inscriptions in public contexts across Roman Aquitania confirms how funerary epigraphy inscribed socio-cultural perceptions into extra-mural space. Occupying the peri-urban fringes, the epigraphic landscape of the dead in provincial Aquitania displayed the written record of collective ancestral identity. Significantly, the series of altars from Lectoure (*ILS Lactorates* 3–6, 8–12, 15, 18–24) – commemorating the performance of the *taurobolium* to the Magna Mater – raises interesting questions about gendered written space. Set up in the later second and earlier third centuries, these altars adduce the ways in which a succession of women used devotion to and performance of a particular cult as a means of self-expression (individual and group) and as a means to present themselves in the public sphere and sometimes to associate themselves with male members of the elite such as magistrates. Displayed in markings of self-representation, age, gender, and status patterns, family and kinship structures, and legal declarations of occupation and property, inscriptions which characterize the epigraphic profile of urban and peri-urban spaces – whether on tombstones, altars, buildings or statues; whether in provincial Aquitania, Roman Italy, or the imperial city of Rome itself – incorporate perceptions of identity into the monumental fabric of the classical city, in the process reformulating the nature, density and categories of written space in the Latin West.

Writing messages and drawing images which do not conform to the repertoire of official inscriptions – namely, marking durable surfaces with graffiti, circulating or posting *libelli*, affixing to architectural features non-official placards – is a cultural practice that constitutes space in a variety of interrelated ways: transitory and conditional in terms of location; spontaneous or premeditated depending on circumstance and opportunity; responsive to existing patterns of movement and thought or engendering new directions and perspectives. If we understand the production and consumption of meaning in the Latin West as part of an epigraphic culture comprising specific contexts, materiality and techniques of marking and display, then the non-official texts of such an oral-literate society comprise an integral counterbalance to the highly visible monumental epigraphy surviving either *in situ* or repurposed as reusable building material. Both categories of inscription occupy and reshape the fabric of written space, whether in terms of education (Garraffoni-Laurence), economic organization (Hannah), political polemic (Hillard), ideological contestation (Newsome), or social categories of person (Baldwin-Moulden-Laurence).

What this means is that how we approach unpacking and understanding the mechanisms for transmission of knowledge and meaning in the cities of the Latin West requires modification. Acknowledging the existence of multiple configurations of written space across historical time predicates a reconceptualization of epigraphy in Roman antiquity as more than a static category of artefact: that is, as text-based, and therefore susceptible to purely philological analysis and interpretation. First and foremost, evidence reflecting the density of official *and* non-official inscriptions situated in public contexts in Italian and provincial cities across the western Mediterranean reflects a *preference* for displaying texts marked on durable surfaces or affixed to architectural features in monumental and frequented urban spaces. Repopulating the inscribed spaces of the urban fabric with texts marked rather than incised – namely, painted, or written in chalk, charcoal, or ink on media other than stone or metal (wood, papyrus), and displayed or distributed publicly – amplifies the nature, density, and avenues of meaning production and consumption in the written spaces of the Roman West. Second, negotiating the conceptual limits of this epigraphic habit requires as a matter of logic the inclusion of a spatial coordinate (where) in addition to the traditional defining features: chronology (when); inscribing population (who); content (what); and rationale (why). As a diagnostic tool, topographical context underwrites the use and efficacy of both categories of inscription.

A question which a few contributors (Corbier, Esmonde Cleary, Revell) identify as integral to our understanding of written space in the Latin West is this: were words inscribed, painted, affixed or otherwise displayed under civic sanction (i.e., official documents), texts written on durable surfaces in public contexts (monuments, statues), always meant to be read, and by whom? As Revell notes, the complexity of the location of some inscriptions on architectural spaces calls into question if a visitor was even expected to read them. As we have seen, written space in civic contexts is populated by texts incised on stone, metal, and wood; and it is a space within which texts are displayed in order that they were read (funerary commemorations, elite benefactions, monumental dedications) or seen (imperial or provincial edicts, legal formulations, or city foundations). According to this view, the function of epigraphic display was determined by textual content and spatial context. In certain contexts – for example, temples – civic and state expressions of power and meaning did not require understanding of the text but rather display of the marked surface in and of itself. As Esmonde Cleary observes (p. 225), 'it was writing as a nexus of symbolic expression that mattered, not necessarily the exact content.'

New approaches to the study of graffiti offer intriguing correlations with this feature of monumental epigraphy: namely, that graffiti should not be viewed solely as verbal or non-verbal markings to be 'read' – i.e., registered, decoded, and interpreted – but as evidence for the act of meaning production. In the same way that certain formal inscriptions may have been displayed in public contexts to be seen but not read, instantiating by virtue of location (monumental pediments, temple walls) and intent (keyed to the content of the inscribed text) a speech-act to be remembered, so certain informal markings perform the same function. Reading written space in Pompeii, as Garraffoni and Laurence do, reveals the Large Palaestra as a context dedicated explicitly to child education (*CIL* 4.8518–8814; cf. the famous punishment fresco in the Praedia of Julia Felix) – i.e. instruction in and practice of letter-forms (alphabets). Interestingly, while there are few alphabets marked on public buildings (the Building of Eumachia, the Macellum, the corridor leading to the Large Theatre, the Temple of Fortuna Augusta), the streets (Via dell'Abbondanza), side-streets off principal through-routes (Porta Marina) or pedestrian termina in/outside city gates (Vicolo del Labirinto, Vicolo del Modesto) demark a spatial context replete with alphabetic graffiti, a fact confirmed in literary references to contexts associated with teachers and pupils.[8] In sum, 'the learning of letters produced its own pattern that cannot be mapped onto other patterns of graffiti' (Garraffoni-Laurence, p. 129).

Conclusion

The global process of urbanization that we are experiencing in the early twenty-first century and the process of Romanizing urbanism in the Latin West are similarly characterized by the formation of a new spatial architecture, made up of global or Mediterranean-wide networks connecting major metropolitan regions and their areas of influence. Since modern urban studies[9] tell us that the networking form of territorial arrangements extends to the intra-metropolitan structure, our understanding of post-classical urbanism in Italy and the western provinces under Roman rule should start with the study of these networking dynamics in both the territories that are included in the networks (the *provincia* and *civitates* of the Latin West) and in the localities excluded from the dominant logic of Roman spatial integration (the rural settlements and inhabited productive districts of the Roman Mediterranean).

As part of this broader exploration of urban diversity in antiquity, we have seen how written space serves as an analytical tool to address the ways in which verbal and non-verbal discourse inhabits and shapes urban space. It is clear that the forum is the preferred location for certain types of inscription (honorific dedications, records of benefaction, legal texts). Locations within the forum privileging visual standpoint and connectivity and designated by use include: (1) the formal entrance to the forum; (2) the porticoes, especially niches for display of statues and inscribed bases, as well as portico pediments, columns and free-standing statuary for inscribing dedicatory and commemorative texts and affixing official notices (imperial *libelli*, *edicta*, urban charters, provincial *leges*, *senatus consulta*, lists of jurors, *alba* of *ordines*), symbols of *hospitium* (*tesserae hospitales*), votive declarations (*plantae pedum* inscriptions) and execrations (*defixiones*); (3) structures integral to the civic function of the forum, for example the basilica, the *macellum*, the *tabularium*; and (4) purpose-built architectural forms, for example the altar, *exedra*, fountain, pediment, and staircase.

However, written space is by no means limited to the marketplace. As we have seen throughout this volume, the contexts which feature textual, numerical, and/or pictorial markings – the extra-mural funerary precincts; the multi-functional sites of exercise, hygiene, learning, and socio-economic discourse; the building façades of heavily trafficked thoroughfares – are many, varied, and susceptible to the display of official *and* non-official epigraphic discourse. To appreciate the form and function of this densely inscribed network of sites (sanctioned and/or preferred; conditional and/ or transitory) requires appreciation of the sensory and cognitive connections that are part and parcel of oral-literate societies in the Latin West. First and foremost, the displayed message (or series of messages, inscribed across time and space) must be visible, relying on factors such as size of lettering/marking, contrast of text/image with surface, line-of-sight modality with respect to purposive or incidental eye-contact, and so on. Contemporaneously, visual recognition is essential (at a semantic or symbolic level) but cognitive understanding may vary (from the recognition of intent to complex processing of information). By the same token, the communication may be directed to a broad or specific audience – categorized in relation, but not limited to any combination or permutation of socio-cultural factors (age, education, ethnicity, gender, status, and the like) – and dependent on meaning – namely, content and purpose. Naturally enough, all facets comprising the marked nature and apprehension of urban and peri-urban space depend very much on the mode of reception (premeditated or incidental; stationary or mobile).

The Roman city in the Latin West should be viewed as a site and subject of contention and debate, connected – ideologically and in terms of the production of spatial meaning – with the concept of social organization: e.g., organized religious worship, codified law, and formalized family relationships; *ordines, cives, incolae*. The public display of text intersects with and underpins the maintenance of the ideal of the Roman city, informing the various groups that comprise the social fabric of the city of the conditions which satisfy the Roman ideology of urbanism. However, in the same way that David Newsome asks if space can be dynamic, so the context within which written space exists may be understood in relation either to the direction in which meaning is produced (as a medium by which community perceptions change) or by which the inscribed urban fabric is reconstituted (as a referent for transforming action and thought).

Notes

1 Lynch, 1984, p. 131.
2 C. W. Thompson, 2002, p. 60.
3 Lynch, 1960, p. 8.
4 Raja, 2003, p. 91.
5 Gros, 2005, pp. 191–214.
6 The bibliography on the process of Romanization is vast. For a useful overview of the changing concepts of Roman identity and social change subsumed under the heading of Romanization, see Hingley, 2005, pp. 14–48. On the importance of archaeology to historical redefinitions of Romanization, see Torelli, 1995.
7 Castells, 1977, p. 126.
8 Streets: Mart. *Ep.* 9.68, Dio. Chrys. 20.9; side-streets/gates: Hor. *Ep.* 1.20.18, Quint. 1.4.27.
9 E.g. Neal, 2012; Albeverio et al., 2008.

Bibliography

Clauss-Slaby Epigraphik-Datenbank: http://www.manfredclauss.de/gb/index.html (last accessed 8 January 2013)
Culture et Idéologie dans la Genèse de l'État moderne. Actes de la Table Ronde de Rome (15–17 Octobre 1984). Rome: CÉFR 82.
L'Urbs: Espace Urbain et Histoire (Ier siècle av. J.-C.– IIIe siècle ap. J.-C.): Actes du Colloque International Organisé par le Centre National de la Recherche Scientifique et l'École Française de Rome (Rome, 8–12 Mai 1985). Rome: CÉFR 98.

Adamo Muscettola, S. (2000), 'The sculptural evidence', in P. Miniero, *The Sacellum of the Augustales at Miseno,* trans. C. Fordham. Napoli: Electa Napoli, pp. 29–45.
Adams, J. N. (1982), *The Latin Sexual Vocabulary.* Baltimore: The Johns Hopkins University Press.
—(2003), *Bilingualism and the Latin Language.* Cambridge: Cambridge University Press.
—(2007), *The Regional Diversification of Latin 200 BC–AD 600.* Cambridge: Cambridge University Press.
Alarcão, J. and Étienne, R. (1979), *Fouilles de Conimbriga, VII: Trouvailles Diverses. Conclusions Générales.* Paris: De Boccard.
Albeverio, S., Denise, A., Giordano, P. and Vancheri, A. (eds) (2008), *The Dynamics of Complex Urban Systems – An Interdisciplinary Approach.* Heidelberg; New York: Physica-Verlag.
Alföldy, G. (1969), *Fasti Hispaniensis. Senatorishe Reichsbeamte und Offiziere in den spanischen Provinzen des Römischen Reiches von Augustus bis Diokletian.* Wiesbaden: F. Verlag.
—(1979), 'Bildprogramme in den römischen Städten des Conventus Tarraconensis. Das Zeugnis der Statuenpostamente', in *Homenaje a Garcia Bellido IV. Revista de la Universidad Complutense de Madrid,* pp. 177–275.
—(1984), *Römische Statuen in Venetia et Histria. Epigraphische Quellen.* Heidelberg: Carl Winter (Abhandlungen der Heidelberger Akademie der Wissenschaften, Philosophisch-historische Klasse, 3).
Allais, Y. (1938), *Djemila.* Paris: Les Belles Lettres.
—(1971), 'Le quartier occidental de Djemila (Cuicul)', *AntAfr.* 5, 95–120.
Allison, P. M. (1992), 'The distribution of Pompeian house contents and its significance'. PhD thesis, Sydney.
—(1997), 'Artefact distribution and spatial function in Pompeian houses', in B. Rawson and P. Weaver (eds), pp. 321–54.
—(2004), *Pompeian Households. An Analysis of the Material Culture.* Los Angeles: The Cotsen Institute of Archaeology, University of California.
Anderson, J. C. (1984), *The Historical Topography of the Imperial Fora.* Brussels: Collection Latomus 182.
Arnaud, P. (1992), 'À propos d'un prétendu itinéraire de Caracalla dans l'*Itinéraire d'Antonin*: les sources tardives de l'itinéraire de Rome à Hiérasycaminos', *BSAF,* 374–82.

Atencia Páez, R. (1988), *La ciudad romana de Singilia Barba (Antequera–Málaga)*. Malaga: Servicio de Publicaciones, Diputación Provincial de Málaga.

Aupert, P. (1991), 'Les thermes comme lieux de culte', in *Les thermes romains*. Rome: CÉFR 142, 185–92.

Baird, J. A. and Taylor, C. (eds) (2011), *Ancient Graffiti in Context*. London: Routledge.

Balland, A. (1984), 'La "casa Romuli" au Palatin et au Capitole', *Revue des Études Latines*, 62, 57–80.

Ballu, A. (1897), *Les Ruines de Timgad : Antique Thamugadi*. Paris: Ernest Leroux.

—(1903), *Les Ruines de Timgad Antique Thamugadi : Nouvelles Découvertes*. Paris: Ernest Leroux.

—(1911), *Les Ruines de Timgad Antique Thamugadi; Sept Années de Découvertes (1903–1910)*. Paris: Neurdein Frères.

—(1921), 'Ruines de Djemila (antique Cuicul)', *Revue Africaine*, 62, 201–74.

Baratte, F. (1983), 'Les portraits impériaux de Markouna et la sculpture officielle dans l'Afrique romaine', *MEFRA*, 95, (2), 785–815.

Barbet, A. and Miniero, P. (eds) (1999), *La Villa San Marco a Stabia*. Naples: Centre Jean Bérard.

Bargagli, B. and Grosso, C. (1997), *I Fasti Ostiensis, Documento della Storia di Ostia*. Ostia: Soprintendenza Archaeologica di Ostia.

Barrett, J. C. (1993), 'Chronologies of remembrance: the interpretation of some Roman inscriptions', *World Archaeology*, 25, (2), 236–47.

Basso, K. H. (1974), 'The ethnography of writing', in R. Bauman and J. Sherzer (eds) *Explorations in the Ethnography of Speaking*. Cambridge: Cambridge University Press, pp. 425–32.

Bauman, R. A. (1974), *Impietas in Principem: A Study of Treason against the Roman Emperor with Special Reference to the First Century AD*. Munich: Beck.

Baxter, J. (2005), *The Archaeology of Childhood: Children, Gender and Material Culture*. California: Altamira Press.

Beard, M. (1991), 'Ancient literacy and the function of the written word in Roman religion', in M. Beard et al., pp. 35–58.

—(2003), 'Picturing the Roman triumph: putting the fasti capitolini in context', *Apollo*, July, 23–28.

—(2008), *Pompeii. The Life of a Roman Town*. London: Profile Books.

Beard, M., Bowman, A. K., Corbier, M., Cornell, T., Franklin, J. L., Hanson, A., Hopkins, K. and Horsfall, N. (1991), *Literacy in the Roman World*. Ann Arbor, MI: JRA Supplementary Series 3.

Beard, M., North, J. and Price, S. (1998), *Religions of Rome*. 2 vols. Cambridge: Cambridge University Press.

Becatti, G. (1961), *Scavi di Ostia IV. I Mosaici e i Pavimenti Marmorei*. Rome: Istituto Poligrafico e Zecca dello Stato/Libreria dello Stato.

—(1973–4), 'Opere d'arte greca nella Roma di Tiberio', *Archeologia Classica*, 25–6, 18–53.

Becker, W. A. (1873), *Gallus, or Roman Scenes of the Time of Augustus*. London: Longmans.

Belloni, G. G. (1974), 'Sigificati storico-politici delle figurazioni e delle scritte delle monete da Augusto a Traiano', *ANRW*, II.1, 997–1144.

—(1976), 'Monete romane e propaganda. Impostazione di una problematica complessa', *Contributi dell'Istituto di Storia Antica*, 4, 131–95.

Ben Abdallah, Z. (1992), 'Nouveaux aspects de la vie religieuse à Ammaedara, camp de la 3e Légion Auguste, puis colonie de Vespasien en Afrique romaine', in *CRAI*, 136, (1), 11–27.

Ben Abed-Ben Khader, A., Fixot, M., Bonifay, M. and Roucole, S. (2004), *Sidi Jdidi. La Basilique Sud*. Rome: CÉFR 339.

Bénabou, M. (1976), *La Résistance Africaine à la Romanisation*. Paris: F. Maspero.

Benefiel, R. (2010a), 'Dialogues of ancient graffiti in the House of Maius Castricius in Pompeii', *AJA*, 114, 59–101.

—(2010b), 'Rome in Pompeii: wall inscriptions and GIS', in F. Feraudi-Gruénais (ed.), *Latin on Stone. Epigraphic Research and Computing*, Lanham, MD: Rowman & Littlefield, pp. 45–75.

—(2011), 'Dialogues of graffiti in the House of the Four Styles at Pompeii (*Casa dei Quattro Stili* I.8.17,11)', in J. A. Baird and C. Taylor (eds), pp. 20–48.

Beness, J. L. and Hillard, T. (2012), 'Another voice against the "tyranny" of Scipio Aemilianus in 129 BC.?', *Historia*, 61, 9–12.

Bérard, F. (1991), 'Tacite et les inscriptions', *ANRW*, II.33.4, 3007–50.

Berry, J. (2007), *The Complete Pompeii*. London: Thames and Hudson.

Beschaouch, A., Hanoune, R. and Thébert, Y. (1977), *Les ruines de Bulla Regia*, Rome: CÉFR 28.

Bianchi Bandinelli, R., Vergara Caffarelli, E. and Caputo, G. (1964), *Leptis Magna*. Verona: Arnoldo Mondadori.

Birley, A. R. (1988), *The African Emperor: Septimius Severus*. London: Batsford.

Bispam, E. (2000), 'Introduction', in E. Bispham and C. Smith (eds), pp. 1–18.

—and Smith, C. (eds) (2000), *Religion in Archaic and Republican Rome and Italy: Evidence and Experience*. London: Routledge.

Blagg, T. F. C. (1990), 'Architectural munificence in Britain: the evidence of inscriptions', *Britannia*, 21, 13–31

Blanchard, A (ed.) (1989), *Les Débuts du Codex: Actes de la Journée d'Étude Organisée à Paris les 3 et 4 Juillet 1985*. Turnhout: Brepols.

Blennow, A. (2008), 'The graffiti in the cryptoporticus of the horti sallustiani in the area of the embassy of the United States of America in Rome', in O. Brandt (eds), *Unexpected Voices: The Graffiti in the Cryptoporticus of the Horti Sallustiani and Papers from a Conference on Graffiti at the Swedish Institute in Rome, 7 March 2003*. Stockholm: Svenska Institutet i Rom, pp. 55–85.

Bloch, H. (1953), 'The name of the baths near the forum of Ostia', in G. E. Mylonas and D. Raymond (eds), *Studies Presented to D.M. Robinson* II, St Louis, MO: Washington University, pp. 412–18

Blonce, C. (2008), 'Le rôle des administrations municpales dans l'érection des arcs monumentaux en Afrique (de la Tingitane à la Tripolitaine) du 1er au siècle ap. J.-C', in C. Berrendonner, M. Cébeillac-Gervasoni and L. Lamoine (eds), *Le Quotidien Municipal dans l'Occident Romain*. Clermont-Ferrand: Presses Universitaires Blaise-Pascal, pp. 595–623

Blume, F., Lachmann, K. and Rudorff, A. (eds) (1848–52; repr. 1962), *Die Schriften der römischen Feldmesser*, 2 vols. Berlin: G. Reimer.

Bodei Giglione, G. (1973), *Lavori Pubblici e Occupazione nell'Antichità Classica*. Bologna: Pàtron.

Bodel, J. (ed.) (2001), *Epigraphic Evidence. Ancient History From Inscriptions*. London and New York: Routledge.

—(forthcoming), 'Roman tomb gardens', in W. Jashemski (ed.), *Gardens of the Roman Empire*. Cambridge: Cambridge University Press.

Boeswillwald, E., Cagnat, R. and Ballu, A. (1892–1904), *Timgad: Une cité africaine sous l'Empire Romain*. Paris: Ernest Leroux.

Bonnefond-Coudry, M. (1989) *Le Sénat de la République Romaine de la Guerre d'Hannibal à Auguste*. Rome: BEFAR 273, pp. 108–12.

Bonner, S. F. (1972), 'The street teacher: an educational scene in Horace', *AJPh*. 93, (4), 509–28.

Bonneville, J-N., Dardaine, S. and le Roux, P. (1988), *Belo V. L'Épigraphie. Les Inscriptions Romaines de Baelo Claudia*. Madrid: Casa de Velázquez.

Bost, J. P. and Fabre, G. (2001), *Inscriptions Latines d'Aquitaine (I.L.A.) Pétrucores*. Bordeaux: Ausonius.

Bouet, A. (2011), *Barzan III, Un Secteur d'Habitat dans le Quartier du Sanctuaire du Moulin du Fâ à Barzan (Charente-Maritime)'* Éditions de la Fédération Aquitania 27, Bordeaux: Ausonius.

Bouma, J. (1993), *Marcus Iunius Nipsus-Fluminis Varatio, Limitis Repositio. Introduction, Text, Translation and Commentary*. Frankfurt: Broschiert.

Bourdieu, P. (1977), *Outline of a Theory of Practice*. Cambridge: Cambridge University Press.

Bowman, A. K. and Thomas, J. D. (1983), *Vindolanda: The Latin Writing-Tablets*. Britannia Monograph Series 4. London: Society for the Promotion of Roman Studies.

—(1994), *The Vindolanda Writing-Tablets (Tabulae Vindolandenses II)*. London: British Museum Press.

—(2003), *The Vindolanda Writing-Tablets (Tabulae Vindolandenses III)*. London: British Museum Press.

Bowman, A. K. and Woolf, G. (1994), 'Literacy and power in the ancient world', in A. Bowman and G. Woolf (eds), *Literacy and Power in the Ancient World*. Cambridge: Cambridge University Press, pp. 1–16.

Bremen, H. C. van (1996), *The Limits of Participation. Women and Civic Life in the Greek East in the Hellenistic and Roman Periods*. Amsterdam: Gieben.

Briand-Ponsart, C. (2008), 'Pratiques et institutions municpales à Cuicul (Djemila), cité de Numidie', in C. Berrendonner, M. Cébeillac-Gervasoni and L. Lamoine (eds), *Le Quotidien Municipal dans l'Occident Romain*, Clermont-Ferrand: Presses Universitaires Blaise-Pascal, pp. 103–19.

Brilliant, R. (1967), *The Arch of Septimius Severus in the Roman Forum*. Rome: Memoirs of the American Academy in Rome, 11.

Brind'Amour, P. (1983), *Le Calendrier Romain: Recherches Chronologiques*. Ottawa: Éditions de l'Université d'Ottawa.

Broise, H. and Thébert, Y. (1993), *Recherches Archéologiques Franco-Tunisiennes à Bulla Regia. II. Les Architectures, 1. Les Thermes Memmiens, Étude Architectuale et Historie Urbaine*. Rome: CÉFR 28/II.1.

Brunt, P. A. (1980), 'Free labour and public works at Rome', *JRS*, 70, 81–100.

Buchner, E. (1982), *Die Sonnenuhr des Augustus*. Mainz: Von Zabern.

—(1993–4), 'Neues zur Sonnenuhr des Augustus', *Nürnberger Blätter zur Archäologie*, 10, 77–84.

Buck, C. H. (1940), 'A chronology of the plays of Plautus', PhD thesis, Johns Hopkins University, Baltimore.

Burford, A. (1971), 'The purpose of inscribed building accounts', in *Acta of the Fifth International Congress of Greek and Latin Epigraphy (Cambridge, 1967)*. Oxford: Blackwell, pp. 71–6.

Callu, J.-P. (1980), '"Pensa" et "follis" sur une inscription d'Afrique', *AntAfr*. 15, 273–83.

Campbell, B. (2000), *The Writings of the Roman Land Surveyors*. London: Society for the Promotion of Roman Studies

Carandini, A. (1985), 'Orti e frutteti', in *Misurare la Terra: Centurazione e Coloni nel Mondo Romano. Citta, Agricoltura, Commercio: Materiali da Roma e dal Suburbio*. Modena: Panini, 66–74.

Cardona, G. R. (1977), 'Sull' "etnografia della scrittura"', *Scrittua e civilità*, 1, 211–8.

—(1981), *Antropologia della Scrittura*. Turin: Loescher Editore.

—(1982), 'Culture dell'oralità e culture della scrittura', in *Letteratura italiana*, 1.2. Turin: Einaudi, pp. 25–101.

Carettoni, G., Colini, A. M., Cozz, L. and Gatti, G. (1960), *La Pianta Marmorea di Roma Antica: Formae Urbis Romae*, 2 vols. Rome: Ripartizione del Comune di Roma.

Carradice, I. (1982), 'Coins, monuments and literature: some smportant sestertii of Domitian', in T. Hackens and R. Weiller (eds), *Actes du 9ème Congrès International de Numismatique, Berne 1979, I. Numismatique Antique*. Louvain-la-Neuve: Association internationale des numismates professionnels, pp. 371–83.

Carroll, M. (2004), *Earthly Paradises. Ancient Gardens in History and Archaeology*. Los Angeles: Getty Publications.

—(2006), *Spirits of the Dead. Roman Funerary Commemoration in Western Europe*. Oxford: Oxford University Press.

Cartigny, C. (1984), *Le Carré Magique: Testament de Saint Paul*. Paris: Diffusion Picard.

Casson, L. (1974), *Travel in the Ancient World*. London: Allen and Unwin.

Castagnoli, F. (1957), *Foro Romano*. Milan: Domus.

—(1964), 'Note sulla topografia del Palatino e del Foro romano', *Archeologia Classica*, 16, 188–95.

Castells, M. (1972), *The Urban Question: A Marxist Approach*. Cambridge, MA: MIT Press.

Castrén, P. (1972), 'I Graffiti del vano XVI', *Atti della Pontificia Accademia Romana di Archeologia, Ser. III. Memorie*, 11, (1), 67–87.

—(2000), '*Vici* and *insulae*: The homes and addresses of the Romans', *Arctos* 34, 7–22.

Castrén, P. and Lilius, H. (1970), *Graffiti del Palatino: II. Domus Tiberiana*. Acta. Instituti Romani Finlandiae, 4, Helsinki: Tilgman.

Cavallo, G. (1978), 'Dal segno incompiuto al segno negato. Linee per una ricera su alfabetismo, produzione e circlazione di cultura scritta nella storia della società italiana', in *Alfabetismo e cultura Scritta nella Storia della Società Italiana, Atti del Seminario Tenutosi a Perugia il 29–30 Marzo 1977*. Perugia: Quaderni Storici, 38, pp. 466–87.

—(1989), 'Testo, libro, lettura', in G. Cavallo, P. Fedeli, A. Giardina (eds) *Lo Spazio Letterario di Roma Antica, vol. II. La Circolazione del Testo*. Rome: Salerno Editrice, pp. 307–41.

Cèbe, J.-P. (1966), *La Caricature et la Parodie dans le Monde Romain Antique des Arigines à Juvénal*. Paris: De Boccard.

Cencetti, G. (1953), 'Tabularium principis', in *Studi in Hnore di Cesare Manaresi*. Milan: Giuffrè, pp. 131–66.

Champlin, E. (1991), *Final Judgments. Duty and Emotion in Roman Wills 200 BC–AD 250*. Berkeley; LA and Oxford: University of California Press.

Chaniotis, A. (2011), 'Graffiti in Aphrodisias: images-texts-contexts', in J. A. Baird and C. Taylor (eds), pp. 191–208.

Chartier, R. (ed.) (1985), *Pratiques de la Lecture*. Marseille: Rivages.

Chastagnol, A. (1960), *La Préfecture Urbaine à Rome sous le Bas-Empire*. Paris: Publications de la Faculté des Lettres d'Alger, 34.

—(1978), *L'Album Municipal de Timgad*. Bonn: Rudolf Habelt Verlag GMBH.

Cherry, D. (1995), 'Re-figuring the Roman epigraphic habit', *Ancient History Bulletin*, 9, 143–56

Chevallier, R. (1972), *Épigraphie et Littérature à Rome*. Faenza: Fratelli Lega (Epigrafia e antichità 3).

—(1976), *Roman Roads*. Paris: Picard.

—(1997), *Les Voies Romaines*. Paris: Picard.

Chiavia, C. (2002), *Programmata. Manifesti Elettorali nella Colonia Romana di Pompei*. Turin: S. Zamorani.

Cicerchia, P. and Marinucci, A. (1992), *Scavi di Ostia XI. Le Terme del Foro o di Gavio Massimo*. Rome: Istituto Poligrafico e Zecca dello Stato/Libreria dello Stato.

Cima, M., and La Rocca, E. (eds) (1998), *Horti Romani. Atti del Convigno Latronazionale Roma 4–6 Maggio 1995*. Rome: 'L'Erma' di Bretschneider = Bullettino della Commissione Archeologico Communale di Roma.

Clanchy, M. T. (1979), *From Memory to Written Record: England 1066–1307*. London: Edward Arnold.

Claridge, A. (2010), *Rome: An Oxford Archaeological Guide*. Oxford: Oxford University Press.

—Herklotz, I. and Wright D. (2012), *The Paper Museum of Cassiano dal Pozzo. Series A. Part VI. Classical Manuscript Illustrations*. London: Royal Collection Enterprises and Harvey Miller.

Clark, A. J. (2007), *Divine Qualities: Cult and Community in Republican Rome*. Oxford: Oxford University Press.

Clarke, D. J. (1978), *Analytical Archaeology* (2nd edn revised by B. Chapman). New York: Columbia University Press.

Clarke, J. R. (1991), *The Houses of Roman Italy 100 B.C.–A.D. 250. Ritual, Space and Decoration*. Berkeley: University of California Press.

—(2003), *Art in the Lives of Ordinary Romans: Visual Representation and Non-Elite Viewers in Italy, 100 BC–AD 315*. Berkeley: University of California Press.

Coarelli, F. (1978) 'La statue de Cornélie, mère des Gracques, et la crise politique à Rome au temps de Saturninus', in *Le Dernier Siècle de la République Romaine et l'Époque Augustéenne. Journées d'Étude Strasbourg, 15–16 Février 1978*. Strasbourg: AECR, 13–28 (= 1996. *Revixit Ars*. Rome: Quasar, 280–99).

—(1981a), *Roma*. Rome-Bari: Guide Archeologiche Laterza.

—(1981b), *L'Area Sacra di Largo Argentina. Topografia e Storia*. Rome: Poliglotta Vaticana.

—(1983), *Il Foro Romano, I: Periodo Arcaico*. Rome: Quasar.

—(1985), *Il Foro Romano. II: Periodo Repubblicano e Augusteo*. Rome: Quasar.

—(1987), 'La situazione edilizia di Roma sotto Severo Alessandro', in *L'Urbs*, pp. 429–56.

—(2005), *Roma*. Rome-Bari: Guide Archeologiche Laterza.

—(2007), *Rome and Environs: an Archaeological Guide*. Berkeley: University of California Press.

Collantes de Terán, F. and Fernández-Chicarro, C. (1972–4), 'Epigrafía de Munigua (Mulva, Sevilla). *Archivo Español de Arqueología*, 45, (7), 337–410.

Condron, F. (1998), 'Ritual, space and politics: reflections in the archaeological record of social developments in Lepcis Magna, Tripolitania', *TRAC 97. Proceedings of the Seventh Annual Theoretical Roman Archaeological Conference*. Oxford: Oxbow Books, pp. 42–52.

Constans, L. (1916), *Gigthis, Étude d'Histoire et d'Archéologie sur un Emporium de la Petite Syrte*. Paris: Imprimerie Nationale.

Cooley, A. E. (ed.) (2000a), *The Epigraphic Landscape of Roman Italy*. London: BICS Supplement 73.

—(2000b), *The Afterlife of Inscriptions. Reusing, Rediscovering, Reinventing and Revitalizing Ancient Inscriptions*. London: BICS Supplement 75.

—(ed.) (2002a), *Becoming Roman, Writing Latin? Literacy and Epigraphy in the Roman West*. Portsmouth, RI: JRA Supplementary Series 48.

—(2002b), 'Introduction', in A. E. Cooley (ed.), pp. 9–13.

—(2007), 'Septimius Severus: the Augustan emperor', in S. Swain, S. Harrison, and J. Elsner (eds) *Severan Culture*. Cambridge: Cambridge University Press, pp. 290–326.

Cooley, A. E. (in press) 'Coming to terms with dynastic power, 30 BC–AD 69', in A. E. Cooley (ed.) *A Companion to Roman Italy*. Oxford: Wiley-Blackwell.

—and Cooley, M. G. L. (2004), *Pompeii: A Sourcebook*. Abingdon: Routledge.

Corbeill, A. (2002), 'Ciceronian invective', in J. M. May (ed.) *Brill's Companion to Cicero. Oratory and Rhetoric*. Leiden: Brill, pp. 197–218.

Corbier, M. (1984a), 'L'aerarium militare sur le Capitole', *Cahiers du Groupe Recherches sur l'Armée Romaine et les Provinces*, 3, 147–62.

—(1984b), 'De Volsinii à Sestinum : cura aquae et évergétisme municpal de l'eau en Italie', *Revue des Études Latines*, 62, 236–74.

—(1987a), 'L'écriture dans l'espace public romain', in *L'Urbs*, pp. 27–60.

—(1987b), 'Trésors et greniers dans la Rome impériale (Ier–IIIe siècles)', in E. Lévy (ed.) *Le système palatial en Orient, en Grèce et à Rome, Actes du Colloque de Strasbourg 19-22 Juin 1985*. Strasbourg: CRPOGA 9.

—(1997), 'Pallas et la statue de César. Affichage et espace public à Rome', *Revue Numismatique*, 152, 11–40.

—(2006), *Donner à Voir, Donner à Lire: Mémoire et Communication dans la Rome Ancienne*. Paris: CNRS Éditions.

—(2008), 'Texte et image: du Musée capitolin au British Museum. Tradition et interprétation', *Ktèma*, 33, 433–46.

—(2011), 'Présentation. L'écrit dans l'espace domestique', in M. Corbier and J.-P. Guilhembet (eds), *L'Écriture dans la maison Romaine*. Paris: De Boccard, pp. 7–46.

Corbier, P. (2009), 'Timgad son développement urbain, ses notables', in A. Groslambert (ed.), *Urbanisme et Urbanisation en Numidie Militaire: Actes du Colloque Organisé les 7 et 8 Mars 2008 par l'Université Lyon 3*. Paris: De Boccard, pp. 181–98.

Coriat, J.-P. (1997), *Le Prince Législateur. La Technique Législative des Sévères et les Méthodes de Création du Droit Impérial à la Fin du Principal*. Rome: BEFAR 294.

Cornell, T. and Matthews, J. (1982, repr. 1991), *Atlas of the Roman World*. Amsterdam: Time-Life Books.

Crawford, M. H. (1973), 'Paestum and Rome. The form and function of a subsidiary coinage', in *La Monetazione di Bronzo di Poseidonia-Paestum*. Rome: Istituto Italiano di Numismatica, pp. 47–109.

—(1983), 'Roman imperial coin types and the formation of public opinion', in C. N. L. Brooke, B. H. I. H. Stewart, J. G. Pollard and T. R. Volk (eds), *Studies in Numismatic Method*. Cambridge: Cambridge University Press, pp. 47–67.

—(ed.) (1996), *Roman Statutes*. London: BICS Supplement 64.

—(ed.) (2011), *Imagines Italicae: A Corpus of Italic Inscriptions*. London: BICS Supplement 110.

Cribiore, R. (2001), *Gymnastics of the Mind: Greek Education in Hellenistic and Roman Egypt*. Princeton: Princeton University Press.

Criniti, N. (1970), *L'epigrafe di Asculum di Gn. Pompeo Strabone*. Milan: Vita e Penisero.

Cumont, F. (1922), *After Life in Roman Paganism*. New Haven: Yale University Press.

Curti, E. (2000), 'From Concordia to the Quirinal: notes on religion and politics in mid-Republican/Hellenistic Rome', in E. Bispham and C. Smith (eds), pp. 77–91.

D'Ambra, E. (2002), 'Acquiring an ancestor: the importance of funerary statuary among the non-elite orders of Rome', in J. M. Hojte (ed.), *Images of Ancestors*. Aarhus: Aarhus University Press (*ASMA* 5), pp. 223–46.

Damianaki, C., Procaccioli, P. and Romano, A. (eds) (2006), *Ex Marmore: Pasquini, Pasquinisti, Pasquinate nell'Europa Moderna*. Rome: Vecchiarelli Editore.

D'Arms, J. H. (1970), *Romans on the Bay of Naples: a Social and Cultural Study of the Villas and Their Owners from 150 BC to AD 400*. Cambridge, MA: Harvard University Press.

Davies, P. J. E. (2000), *Death and the Emperor. Roman Imperial Funerary Monuments from Augustus to Marcus Aurelius*. Cambridge: Cambridge University Press.

De Certeau, M. (1984), *The Practice of Everyday Life*, trans. Steven Rendall. Berkeley: University of California Press.

Degrassi, A. (ed.) (1947), *Inscriptiones Italiae, XIII. 1*. Rome: La Libreria dello Stato.

—(1954), *Fasti Capitolini*. Turin: G. B. Paravia.

—(1957), *Inscriptiones Latinae Liberae Rei Publicae*. Firenze: La Nuova Italia.

—(1963), *Inscriptiones Italiae, XIII. 2*. Rome: Istituto Poligrafico dello Stato.

—(1965), *Inscriptiones Latinae Liberae Rei Publicae: Imagines*. Berlin: De Gruyter.

Della Corte, M. (1933), 'Le iscrizioni graffite della Basilica degli Argentari sul foro di Giulio Cesare', *Bullettino della Commissione Archeologica Comunale di Roma*, 61, 111–30.

—(1939), 'Le iscrizioni della "Grande Palestra" ad occidente dell'Anfiteatro', *Notizie degli Scavi*, 64, 239–327.

—(1947), 'Il campus di Pompei', *RAL*, 1947, 555–68.

—(1959a), 'La scuola di Epicuro in alcune pitture Pompeiane', *Studi Romani* 7, 129–44.

—(1959b), 'Scuole e maestri in Pompei antica', *Studi Romani* 7, 621–34.

Delumeau, J. (1957), *Vie Économique et Sociale de Rome dans la Seconde moitié du XVIe Siècle*, I. Paris: BEFAR 184.

Deneauve, J. (1990), 'Le centre monumental de Carthage', in C. Lepelley (ed.) *Carthage et son Territoire dans l'Antiquité. Histoire et Archéologie de l'Afrique du Nord. IVe Colloque*. Paris: CTHS, pp. 143–55.

De Ruyt, C. (1983), *Macellum: marché alimentaire des Romains*. Louvain-la-Neuve : Institut Supérieur d'Archéologie et d'Histoire de L'Art.

Detienne, M. (1964), *Les Maîtres de Vérité dans la Grèce Archaïque*. Paris: Le Livre de Poche (New edition 1994).

—(1988), 'L'écriture et ses nouveaux objets intellectuels en Grèce', in M. Detienne (ed.), *Les Savoirs de Lécriture en Grèce Ancienne*. Lille: Cahiers de Philologie 14.

De Vos, A. and De Vos. M. (1982), *Pompei, Ercolano, Stabia*. Roma: G. Laterza.

Dickmann, J. A. (2011), 'Space and social relations in the Roman west', in B. Rawson (eds), *A Companion to Families in the Greek and Roman Worlds*. Oxford: Wiley-Blackwell, pp. 53–73.

Di Vita, A. (1995), 'Leptis Magna. La ville des Sévères', *Karthago*, 23, 71–7.

Doisy, H. (1953), 'Inscriptions latines de Timgad', *MÉFRA*, 65, 99–137.

Doxa, M. (2001), 'Morphologies of co-presence and interaction in interior public space in places of performance: the Royal Festival Hall and the Royal National Theatre, London', in *Proceedings of the 3rd International Symposium on Space Syntax*, pp. 16.1–16.15.

Dubrocard, M. (1976), *Juvénal, Satires. Index Verborum. Relevés statistiques*. Hildesheim: Georg Olms Verlag.

Dunbabin, K. M. D. (1989), '*Baiarum grata voluptas*: pleasures and dangers of the baths', *PBSR*, 57, 6–46.

—(1990), '*Ipsae deae vestigia* … footprints divine and human on Graeco-Roman monuments', *JRA*, 3, 85–109.

Duncan-Jones, R. P. (1990), *Structure and Scale in the Roman Economy*. Cambridge: Cambridge University Press.

—(2004), 'Economic change and the transition to late antiquity', S. Swain, and M. Edwards (eds), *Approaching Late Antiquity. The Transformation from Early to Late Empire*. Oxford: Oxford University Press, pp. 20–52.

Durliat, J. (1981), *Les Dédicaces d'Ouvrages de Défense dans l'Afrique Byzantine*, Publications de l'École française de Rome, 49. Rome: L'École française de Rome.

Durry, M. (1938), *Les Cohortes Prétoriennes*. Paris: De Boccard.

Dušanić, S. (1984), 'Loci constitutionum fixarum', *Epigraphica*, 46, 91–115.

Eck, W. (1984), 'Senatorial self-representation. Developments in the Augustan period', in F. Millar and E. Segal (eds), *Caesar Augustus: Seven Aspects*, Oxford: Clarendon Press, pp. 129–67. (= —(1996), *Tra Epigrafia Prosopografia e Archeologia. Scritti Scelti, Rielaborati ed Aggiornati*. Rome: Vetera 10, pp. 271–98.

—(1992), 'Ehrungen für Personen hohen soziopolitischen Ranges im öffentlichen und privaten Bereich', in H.-J. Schalles, H. von Hesberg, and P. Zanker (eds), *Die römische Stadt im 2. Jahrhundert n. Chr. Der Funktionswandel des öffentlichen Raumes. Kolloquium in Xanten vom 2. bis 4. Mai 1990*. Cologne: Rheinland Verlag, pp. 359–76.

—(1997), 'Der Euergetismus im Funktionszusammenhang der Kaiserzeitlichen Städte', in M. Christol and O. Masson (eds), *Actes du Xe Congrès International d'Épigraphie Grecque et Latine. Nîmes, 4–9 Octobre 1992*. Paris: Sorbonne, pp. 305–31.

—(2005), 'Der Senator und die Öffentlichkeit – oder: Wie beeindruckt man das Publikum?', in W. Eck and M. Heil (eds), *Senatores Populi Romani: Realität und Mediale Präsentation einer Führrungsschicht*. Habes. Heidelberger Althistoriche Beiträge und Epigraphische Studien 40. Stuttgart: Franz Steiner,

—(2010), 'Propaganda, staged applause, or local politics? Public monuments from Augustus to Septimius Severus', in Ewald and Noreña, pp. 89–110.

—(forthcoming 2013), 'Frauen als Teil der kaiserzeitlichen Gesellschaft: Ihr Reflex in Inschriften Roms und der italischen Städte', in E. Hemelrijk and G. Woolf (eds), *Gender and the Roman City. Women and Civic Life in Italy and the Western Provinces*. Mnemosyne Supplements, History and Archaeology of Classical Antiquity. Leiden; Boston: Brill.

Eco, U. (2000), *Kant and the Platypus. Essays on Language and Cognition*, trans. A. McEwen. London: Vintage.

Edensor, T. (2010), 'Introduction: thinking about rhythm and space', in T. Edensor (ed.), *Geographies of Rhythm: Nature, Place, Mobilities and Bodies*. Farnham: Ashgate, pp. 1–18.

Eisenstein, E. L. (1979), *The Printing Press as an Agent of Change. Communications and Cultural Transformations in Early Modern Europe*. Cambridge: Cambridge University Press.

Ellis, S. (1997), 'Late-antique dining: architecture, furnishings and behaviour', in R. Laurence and A. Wallace-Hadrill (eds), pp. 41–53.

Esmonde Cleary, S. (2008), *Rome in the Pyrenees: Lugdunum and the Convenae from the First Century B.C. to the Seventh Century A.D.* London: Routledge.

Étienne, R. (1976), *Fouilles de Conimbriga, II*. Paris: De Boccard.

Euzennat, M. and Hallier, G. (1986), 'Les forums de Tingitane', *AntAfr.*, 22, 73–103.

Evans, J. D. (1990), 'Statues of the kings and Brutus on the Capitoline', *ORom*, 18, (5), 99–105.

Ewald B. C. and Noreña, C. F. (2010), *The Emperor and Rome: Space, Representation, and Ritual*. Yale Classical Studies 35. Cambridge: Cambridge University Press.

Fabre, G. (1981), *Libertus. Recherches sur les Rapports Patron-affranchi à la Fin de la République Romaine*. Rome: CÉFR, 50.

Fabre, G. and Sillières, P. (2000), *Inscriptions Latines d'Aquitaine (I.L.A.) Lectoure.* Bordeaux: Ausonius.

Fagan, G. G. (1999a), *Bathing in Public in the Roman World.* Ann Arbor: The University of Michigan Press.

—(1999b), 'Interpreting the evidence: did slaves bathe at the baths?', in J. DeLaine and D. E. Johnston (eds) *Roman Baths and Bathing,* Portsmouth, RI: JRA Supplementary Series 37, (1), pp. 25–34.

Farrar, L. (2000), *Roman Gardens.* Stroud: Sutton Publishing.

Fear, A. T. (1996), *Rome and Baetica. Urbanization in Southern Spain c. 50 BC–AD 150.* Oxford: Clarendon Press.

Fears, J. R. (1981), 'The cult of virtues', *ANRW,* II.17.2, pp. 828–946.

Feeney, D. (2007), *Caesar's Calendar: Ancient Time and the Beginnings of History.* Berkeley: University of California Press.

Fejfer, J. (2008), *Roman Portraits in Context. Image and Context.* Berlin; New York: De Gruyter.

Feitosa, L. M. G. C. (2005), *Amor e Sexualidade: O Masculino e O Feminino em Grafites de Pompéia.* São Paulo: Annablume–FAPESP.

Feitosa, L. M. G. C. and Garraffoni, R. S. (2010), 'Dignitas and infamia: rethinking marginalized masculinities in early Principate'. *Studia Historica Historia Antigua,* 28, 57–73.

Feldherr, A. (1998), *Spectacle and Society in Livy's History.* Berkeley; LA and London: University of California Press.

Fentress, E. (1984), 'Frontier culture and politics at Timgad', *BCTH,* n.s., 17B, 399–407.

Février, P.-A. (1961), 'Le sarcophage à inscription X lege filiciter (Narbonne, Aude)', *Annales du Midi,* 73, 53, 11–7.

—(1964), 'Notes sur le développement urbain en Afrique du Nord, les exemples compares de Djemila et de Sétif', *Cahiers Archéologiques,* 14, 1–47.

—(1968), *Djemila.* Alger: Ministère de l'Information et de la Culture.

Fitchtenau, H. (1946), *Mensch und Schrift im Mittelalter.* Vienna: Universum.

Floriani Squarciapino, M. (1987), 'Nuovi mosaici ostiensi', *RPAA,* 58, 87–114.

Flower, H. I. (1995), '*Fabulae Praetextae* in context: when were plays on contemporary subjects performed in Republican Rome?' *CQ,* 45, 170–90.

—(2010), *Roman Republics.* Princeton; Oxford: Princeton University Press.

Fol, W. (1877), 'Color', in C. Daremberg and E. Saglio (eds) *Dictionnaire des Antiquités,* I, 2. Paris: Hachette, pp. 1325–31.

Forbis, E.P. (1990), 'Women's public image in Italian honorary inscriptions', *AJPh.,* 111, (4), 493–512.

Foster, S. (1989), 'Analysis of spatial patterns in buildings (access analysis) as an insight into social structure: examples from the Scottish Atlantic Iron Age'. *Antiquity,* 63, (238), 40–50.

Franklin, J. L. (1980), *Pompeii: the Electoral Programmata. Campaigns and Politics, A.D. 71–79.* Rome: American Academy in Rome.

—(1991), 'Literacy and the parietal inscriptions of Pompeii', in M. Beard et al., pp. 77–98.

French, D. (1981–88), *Roman Roads and Milestones of Asia Minor.* 2 vols. BAR IntSer. 392. Oxford: Archaeopress.

Funari, P. P. A. (1986), 'Cultura(s) dominante(s) e cultura(s) subalterna(s) em Pompéia: da vertical da cidade ao horizonte do possível'. *Revista Brasileira de História,* series 7, 13, 33–48.

—(1989), *A Vida Popular na Antiguidade Clássica.* São Paulo: Contexto.

—(1993), 'Graphic caricature and the ethos of ordinary people at Pompeii'. *Journal of European Archaeology*, 1, (2), 133–50.

Furet, F. and Ozouf, J. (1977), *Lire et Écrire. L'Alphabétisation des Français de Calvin à Jules Ferry, I.* Paris: Les Éditions de Minuit.

Gagé, J. (1977), *Res gestae divi Augusti*, third edn. Paris: Belles Lettres.

Gager, J. G. (1992), *Curse Tablets and Binding Spells from the Ancient World*. Oxford: Oxford University Press.

García, P. A. (2008), 'Propaganda imperial de la dinastía Severa en el Norte de África', *L'Africa Romana*, 17, 327–35.

Gardner, J. F. (1990), *Women in Roman Law and Society*, 3rd edn. London: Routledge.

—(1993), *Being a Roman citizen*. London: Routledge.

—(1995), 'Gender-role assumptions in Roman law', *EMC/CV*, 39 (n.s., 14), 377–400.

—(1997), 'Legal stumbling-blocks for lower-class families in Rome', in B. Rawson and P. Weaver (eds), pp. 35–53.

—(2001), 'Making citizens: the operation of the *Lex Irnitana*', in L. de Blois (ed.), *Administration, Prosopography and Appointment Policies in the Roman Empire*. Amsterdam: Gieben, pp. 215–29.

Gargola, D. J. (2008), 'The Gracchan reform and Appian's representation of an agrarian crisis', in L. de Ligt and S. J. Northwood (eds), *People, Land, and Politics. Demographic Developments and the Transformation of Roman Italy, 300 BC–AD 14*. Leiden; Boston: Brill, pp. 487–518.

Garnsey, P. and Saller, R. (1987), *The Roman Empire: Economy, Society and Culture*. London: Duckworth.

Garraffoni, R. S. (2008), 'Gladiators' daily lives and epigraphy: a social archaeological approach to the Roman munera during the early Principate'. Nikephoros: Zeitschrift für Sport und Kultur im Altertum, 21, 223–41.

Garraffoni, R. S. and Funari, P. P. A. (2009), 'Reading Pompeii's walls: a social archaeological approach to gladiatorial grafitti', in T. Wilmott (ed.), *Roman Amphitheatres and Spectacula: a 21st Century Perspective*, BAR IntSer. 1946. Oxford: Archaeopress, pp. 185–93.

Garriguet, J. A. (2004), 'Grupos estatuarios imperiales de la Bética: la evidencia escultórica y epigráfica', in T. N. Basarrate and L. J. Gonçalves (eds), *Actas de la IV Reunión sobre Escultura Romana en Hispania*. Madrid: Ministerio de Cultura, pp. 67–101.

Gascou, J. (1984), *Suétone Historien*. Paris: BEFAR, 225.

Gatti, G. (1891), 'Frammenti epigrafici di editti prefettizi del secolo IV', *Bullettino della Commissione Archeologica Comunale di Roma*, 19, 342–9.

George, M. (1997a), 'Repopulating the Roman house', in B. Rawson and P. Weaver (eds), pp. 299–319.

—(1997b), 'Servus and domus: the slave in the Roman house', in R. Laurence and A. Wallace-Hadrill (eds), pp. 15–24.

—(2007), 'The lives of slaves', in J. J. Dobbins and P. W. Foss (eds), *The World of Pompeii*. London: Routledge, pp. 538–49.

Gesemann, B. (1998), 'Kultmetamorphosen. Drei ungewöhnliche Monumente des Compitalkults', *Saalburg Jahrbuch*, 49, 95–8.

Giacchero, M. (1974), *Edictum Diocletiani et Collegarum de Pretiis rerum Venalium in Integrum Fere Restitutum e Latinis Graecisque Fragmentis. I. Edictum*. Genoa: Pubbl. dell'Ist. di Storia Ant. dell'Univ. di Genova.

Gibbs, S. L. (1976), *Greek and Roman Sundials*. New Haven: Yale University Press.

Gigante, M. (1979), *Civiltà delle Forme Letterarie nell'Antica Pompei*. Naples: Bibliopolis.

Giordano, C. and Casale, A. (1991), 'Iscrizioni pompeiane inedited scoperte tra gli anni 1954-1978,. *Atti della Accademia Pontaniana*, 39, 273-378.

Goldbeck, F. (2010), *Salutationes: Die Morgenbegrüßungen in Rom in der Republik und der frühen Kaiserzeit*. Berlin: Akademie Verlag GmbH.

Golden, M. (2011), 'Other people's children', in B. Rawson (eds), *A Companion to Families in the Greek and Roman Worlds*, Oxford: Wiley-Blackwel, pp. 262-76.

González, J. (2008), *Epigrafía Juridica de la Bética*. Roma: 'L'Erma' di Bretschneider.

González, J. and Crawford, M. (1986), 'The Lex Irnitana: a new copy of the Flavian municipal law', *JRS*, 76, 147-243.

González Fernández, J. (1996), *Corpus de Inscripciones Latinas de Andalucía. Volumen II. Sevilla. Tomo IV*. Seville: Consejería de Cultura, Junta de Andalucía, pp. 51-94.

Goody, J. (1968), *Literacy in Traditional Societies*. Cambridge: Cambridge University Press.

—(1977), *The Domestication of the Savage Mind*. Cambridge: Cambridge University Press. (= La raison graphique. *La Domestication de la Pensée Sauvage*. Paris 1979).

—(1986), *The Logic of Writing and the Organization of Society*. Cambridge: Cambridge University Press.

—(1987), *The Interface between the Written and the Oral*. Cambridge: Cambridge University Press.

Gordon, A. E. (1958-1965), *Album of Dated Latin Inscriptions*, 7 vols. Berkeley, LA: University of California Press.

—(1983), *Illustrated Introduction to Latin Epigraphy*. Berkeley, LA; London: University of California Press.

Gordon, R., Beard, M., Reynolds, J. and Roueché, C. (1993), 'Roman inscriptions 1986-1990', *JRS*, 83, 131-58.

Grahame, M. (1997), 'Public and private in the Roman house: investigating the social order of the Casa del Fauno', in R. Laurence and A. Wallace-Hadrill (eds), pp. 137-65.

—(2000), *Reading Space: Social Interaction and Identity in the Houses of Roman Pompeii*, BAR Int.Ser. 886. Oxford: Archaeopress.

Green, P. (2005), *The Poems of Catullus: A Bilingual Edition*. Berkeley, LA and London: University of California Press.

Gregori, G. L. and Mattei, M. (ed.) (1999), *Supplementa Italica-Imagines: Supplementi Fotografici ai Volumi Italiani del CIL. Roma (CIL, VI)* 1. Musei Capitolini. Rome: Quasar.

Gros, P. (1976), *Aurea Templa. Recherches sur l'Architecture Religieuse de Rome à l'Époque d'Auguste*. Rome: BEFAR, 231.

—(1985), *Byrsa III Rapport sur les Campagnes de Fouilles de 1977 à 1980: La Basilique Orientale et ses Abords*. Rome: CÉFR, 41.

—(1986), 'Une hypothèse sur les plateae Antoninianae du Palatin', *MÉFRA*, 98, (1), 255-63.

—(1995), 'Le culte impérial dans la basilique judicaire du forum de Carthage', *Karthago*, 22, 45-56.

—(1996), *L'Architecture Romaine, 1*. Paris : Les Manuels d'Art et d'Archeologie Antiques.

—(2005), 'Le rôle du people de Rome dans la definition, l'organisation et le déplacement des lieux de la convergence sous l'empire', in G. Urso (ed.), *Popolo e Potere nel Mondo ntico*. Pisa: ETS, pp. 191-214.

Gsell, S. and Joly, C. A. (1914) *Khamissa, Mdaourouch, Announa*. Algiers; Paris: Adolphe Jourdan; Fontemoing.

Guarducci, M. (1962) 'Il tempio della De Concordia in un bassorilievo dei Musei Vaticani', *Rendiconti della Pontificia Accademia Romana di Archeologia*, 34, 93-110.

—(1978), 'Dal giorno letterale alla critografia mistica', *ANRW*, II.16.2, pp. 1736-73.

Guittard, C. (1983), 'La topographie du temple de Saturne d'après la notice varronienne du *De lingua latina* (V, 42)', in R. Chevallier (ed.), *Présence de l'Architecture et de l'Urbanisme Romains. Hommage à Paul Dufournet*. Tours: Caesarodunum, 18 bis.

Habinek, T. (2005), *The World of Roman Song from Ritualized Speech to Social Order*. Baltimore; London: Johns Hopkins University Press.

—(2009), 'Situating literacy at Rome', in W. A. Johnson and H. N. Parker (eds), *Ancient Literacies. The Culture of Reading in Greece and Rome*. Oxford: Oxford University Press, pp. 114-42.

Hannah, R. (2001), 'From orality to literacy? The case of the Parapegma', in J. Watson (ed.), *Speaking Volumes: Orality and Literacy in the Greek and Roman World*. Leiden: Brill, pp. 139-59.

—(2005), *Greek and Roman Calendars: Constructions of Time in the Classical World*. London: Duckworth.

—(2009), *Time in Antiquity*. London: Routledge.

—(2011), 'The horologium of Augustus as a sundial', *JRA*, 24, 41-9.

Harris, W. V. (1983), 'Literacy and epigraphy', *ZPE*, 52, 87-111.

—(1989), *Ancient Literacy*. Cambridge, MA: Harvard University Press.

Harrist, R. E. Jr. (2008), *The Landscape of Words: Stone Inscriptions from Early and Medieval China*. Seattle: University of Washington Press.

Harsh, P. W. (1937), 'Angiportum, platea, and vicus', *Classical Philology*, 32, (1), 44-58.

Harvey, B. K. (2004), *Roman Lives: Ancient Roman Life as Illustrated by Latin Inscriptions*. Newburyport: Focus Publishing/R. Pullins Co.

Harvey, D. L. (1989), *The Urban Experience*, Oxford: Blackwell.

Haselberger, L., Romano, D. G. and Dumser, E. A. (2002), *Mapping Augustan Rome*. Portsmouth, RI: JRA Supplementary Series 50.

Hauschild, T. (1969-70), 'Exploraciones en el area de la ciudad, al este del foro', *Noticiario Arquelógico Hispanico*, 13-4, 61-71.

—(1991), 'Munigua. Excavaciones en el muro de contencion del foro', *Annuario Arqueológico de Andalucía 1989, vol. II Actividades Systemáticas*, pp. 171-84.

Havelock, E. A. (1973), *Cultura Orale e Civiltà della Scrittura: da Omero a Platone*. Rome-Bari: Laterza.

—(1982), *The Literate Revolution in Greece and its Cultural Consequences*. Princeton: Princeton University Press.

Havelock, E. A. and Hershbell, J. P. (1978-81), *Communication Arts in the Roman World*. New York: Hastings House (= *Arte e communicazione nel mondo antico*. Bari 1981).

Haynes, D. E. L. and Hirst, P. E. D. (1939), *Porta Argentariorum*. London: Macmillan.

Hemelrijk, E. A. (1999), *Matrona Docta. Educated Women in the Roman Élite from Cornelia to Julia Domna*. London and New York: Routledge.

—(2004), 'City patronesses in the Roman Empire', *Historia*, 53, (2), 209-45.

—(2005), 'Octavian and the introduction of public statues for women in Rome', *Athenaeum*, 93, (1), 309-17.

—(2008), 'Patronesses and "mothers" of Roman *collegia*', *Classical Antiquity*, 27, (1), 115-62.

—(2010), 'Fictive kinship as a metaphor for women's civic roles', *Hermes*, 138, (4), 455-69.

—(2012), 'Public roles for women in the cities of the Latin West', in S. L. James, and S. Dillon (eds), *A Companion to Women in the Ancient World*. Oxford: Wiley-Blackwell, pp. 478-90.

—(2012) 'Fictive motherhood and female authority in Roman cities', *EuGeStA, Journal on Gender Studies in Antiquity*, 2, 201-20.

—(forthcoming 2013), 'Roman citizenship and the integration of women in the local towns of the Latin West', in S. Benoist, S. Demougin and G. de Kleijn (eds), *Integration at Rome and in the Roman World, Proceedings of the Tenth Workshop of the International Network Impact of Empire (Lille, June 23–25, 2011)*. Leiden, Boston: Brill (Impact of Empire vol. 11).

—(forthcoming), Hidden Lives – Public Personae. Women and Civic Life in Italy and the Latin West during the Roman Principate.

Hemelrijk, E. A. and Woolf, G. (eds) (forthcoming 2013), *Women and the Roman City in the Latin West*. Mnemosyne Supplements, History and Archaeology of Classical Antiquity. Leiden; Boston: Brill.

Hermansen, G. (1982), *Ostia: Aspects of Roman City Life*, Edmonton: University of Alberta Press.

Hernández, J. (2005), 'The Roman calendar as an expression of Augustan culture: an examination of the *Fasti Praenestini*', *Chrestomathy*, 4, 108–23.

Hesberg, H. von (1992), 'Bogenmonumente der frühen Kaiserzeit und des 2. Jahrhunderts n. Chr. Vom Ehrenbogen zum Festtor', in H.-J. Schalles, H. von Hesberg, and P. Zanker (eds), *Die römische Stadt im 2. Jahrhundert n. Chr. Der Funktionswandel des öffentlichen Raumes. Kolloquium in Xanten vom 2. bis 4. Mai 1990*. Cologne: Rheinland Verlag, pp. 277–99.

—(2005), 'Die Häuser der Senatoren in Rom: Gesellschaftliche und politische Funktion', in W. Eck and M. Heil (eds), *Senatores Populi Romani. Realität und mediale Präsentation einer Führrungsschicht*, Habes. Heidelberger Althistoriche Beiträge und Epigraphische Studien 40. Stuttgart: Franz Steiner, pp. 19–52.

Hesberg. H. Von and Zanker, P. (eds), (1987). *Römische Gräberstraßen. Selbstdarstellung – Status – Standard, Colloquium in Munich, 28–30 October 1985*. Munich: Verlag der Bayerische Akademie der Wissenschaften.

Heslin, P. (2007), 'Augustus, Domitian and the so-called Horologium Augusti', *JRS*, 97, 1–20.

Hillier, B. and Hanson, J. (1984), *The Social Logic of Space*. Cambridge: Cambridge University Press.

Hillier, B., Leaman A., Stansall P. and Bedford, M. (1976), 'Space syntax'. *Environment and Planning B: Planning and Design*, 3, 147–85.

Hinard, F. (1985), *Les Proscriptions de la Rome Républicaine*. Rome: CÉFR, 83.

Hingley, R. (2005), *Globalizing Roman Culture. Unity, Diversity, Empire*. London and New York: Routledge.

Hölkeskamp, K.-J. (2006), 'History and collective memory in the Middle Republic', in N. Rosenstein and R. Morstein-Marx (eds), *A Companion to The Roman Republic*. Oxford: Wiley-Blackwell, pp. 478–95.

Hope, V. M. (2000), 'Fighting for identity: the funerary commemoration of Italian gladiators', in A. Cooley (ed.), pp. 93–114.

—(2001), *Constructing Identity: The Roman Funerary Monuments of Aquileia, Mainz and Nimes*. Oxford: BAR IntSer. 960.

—(2007), *Death in Ancient Rome. A Sourcebook*. London and New York: Routledge.

Horsfall, N. (1996), *La Cultura della Plebs Romana*. Barcelona: PPU.

—(2003), *The Culture of the Roman Plebs*. London: Duckworth.

Huntley, K. V. (2011), 'Identifying children's graffiti in Roman Campania: a developmental psychological approach', in J. A. Baird and C. Taylor (eds), pp. 69–89.

Hurlet, F. (2000), 'Pouvoir des images, images du pouvoir impérial. La province d'Afrique aux deux premiers siècles de notre ère', *MEFRA*, 112, (1) : 297–364.

—(2001), 'L'image du pouvoir impérial et sa localisation dans la ville: la singularité de la province d'Afrique aux deux premiers siècles ap. J.-C.' in M. Molin (ed.), *Images et Représentations du Pouvoir et de l'Ordre Social dans l'Antiquité, Actes du Colloque d'Angers, 28–29/5/1999*. Paris: De Boccard, pp. 277–89.

Invernizzi, A. (1994), *Museo della Civiltà Romana: Vita e Costumi dei Romani Antichi. 16: Il Calendario.* Rome: Edizioni Quasar.

Jackson, R. (1988), *Doctors and Diseases in the Roman Empire.* London: British Museum Press.

Jacobelli, L. (1995), *Le Pitture Erotiche delle Terme Suburbane di Pompei.* Rome: Ministero per i Beni Culturali ed Ambientali/Soprintendenza Archeologica di Pompei: Monografie 10. Bretschneider.

Jal, P. (1963), *La Guerre Civile à Rome. Étude Littéraire et Morale.* Paris: Presses Universitaires de France.

—(1967), 'La publicatio bonorum dans la Rome de la fin de la République', *Bulletin de l'Association Guillaume Budé*, 26, 412–45.

Janvier, Y. (1969), *La Législation du Bas-Empire Romain sur les Édifices Publiques.* Aix-en-Provence: La Pensée Universitaire.

Jashemski, W. F. (1970–1), 'Tomb gardens at Pompeii', *The Classical Journal*, 66, (2), 97–115.

—(1979), *The Gardens of Pompeii, Herculaneum, and the Villas Destroyed by Vesuvius.* New York: Caratzas Brothers.

—(1993), *The Gardens of Pompeii Volume II: Appendices*, New York: Caratzas Brothers.

Jerphanion, G. de (1938), 'La voix des monuments', *Études d'Archéologie. Nouvelle Série*, Rome-Paris: Les Éditions d'Art et d'Histoire. pp. 38–94.

Johnson, A. C., Coleman-Norton, P. R. and Bourne, F. C. (eds) (1961), *Ancient Roman Statutes: A Translation with Introduction, Commentary, Glossary and Index.* Austin: University of Texas Press.

Johnson, W. A. and Parker, H. N. (eds) (2009), *Ancient Literacies. The Culture of Reading in Greece and Rome.* Oxford: Oxford University Press.

Jouffroy, H. (1986), *La Construction Publique en Italie et dans L'Afrique Romaine.* Strasbourg: AECR.

Jouhaud, C. (1985), *Mazarinades: La Fronde des Mots.* Paris: Aubier Montaigne.

Kaster, R. A. (ed., trans.) (2006), *Cicero: Speech on Behalf of Publius Sestius.* Oxford: Clarendon Press.

Keegan, P. (2011), 'Blogging Rome: graffiti as speech act and cultural discourse', in J. A. Baird and C. Taylor (eds), pp. 165–90.

Kerr, R. (2010), *Latino-Punic Epigraphy: A Descriptive Study of the Inscriptions.* Forschungen Zum Alten Testament: 2 Reihe; Tübingen: Mohr Siebeck Gmbh & Co.

Khanoussi, M. and Mastino, A. (2004), 'Il culto della Gens Septimia a Bulla Regia: Settimio Severo e Caracalla in tre basi inedite degli Agrii, dei Domitii e dei Lollii', in *Epigrafia di Confine, Confine dell'Wpigrafia: Atti del Colloquio AIEGL-Borghesi 2003, 10-12 Ottobre 2003, Bertinoro, Italia.* Faenza: Fratelli Lega Editori, pp. 371–414.

Kleiner, D. E. E. (1977), *Roman Group Portraiture. Funerary Reliefs of the Late Republic and Early Empire.* New York: Garland Publishing Inc.

Koloski Ostrow, A. (1990), *The Sarno Bath Complex.* Rome: Ministero per i Beni Culturali ed Ambientali/Soprintendenza Archeologica di Pompei: Monografie 4: Bretschneider.

Knox, B. M. W. (1968), 'Silent reading in antiquity', *GRBS*, 9, (4), 421–35.

Koortbojian, M. (1996), '*In commemorationem mortuorum*: text and image along the "streets of Rome"', in J. Elsner (ed.), *Art and Text in Roman Culture.* Cambridge: Cambridge University Press, pp. 210–33.

Kotula, T. (1985), 'Septime-Sévère, a-t-il, visité l'Afrique en tant qu'empereur?', *Eos*, 73, 151–65.

Kruschwitz, P. (2010), '*Romanes Eunt Domus!* Linguistic aspects of the sub-literary Latin in Pompeian wall inscriptions', in T. V. Evans and D. D. Obbink (eds), *The Language of Papyri*. Oxford: Oxford University Press, pp. 156–70.

Kuhoff, W. (1990), 'Il riflesso dell'autorappresentazione degli imperatori romani nelle province dell' Africa (I-III sec. d.C.)', *L'Africa Romana*, 7: 943–60.

Ladjimi Sebaï, L. (2005), La Colline de Byrsa à l'Époque Romaine: Étude Épigraphique en État de la Question, *Karthago*, 26.

Lahusen, G. (1983), *Untersuchungen zur Ehrenstatue in Rom. Literarische und epigraphische Zeugnisse*. Rome: 'L'Erma' di Bretschneider (Archaeologica, 35).

Lalou, É. (ed.) (1992), *Les Tablettes à Écrire. De l'Antiquité à l'Époque moderne. Actes du Colloque International du Centre National de la Recherche Scientifique, Paris, Institut de France, 10–11 Octobre 1990*. Turnhout: Brepols.

Lanciani, R. (1898), *Ancient Rome in the Light of Recent Discoveries*. Boston and New York: Houghton, Mifflin and Company.

—(1901), *New Tales of Old Rome*. London: Macmillan and Co.

Langeli, A. B. (1978), *Alfabetismo e Cultura Scritta nella Storia della Società Italiana, Atti del Seminario Tenutosi a Perugia il 29–30 Marzo 1977*. Perugia: Quaderni storici, 38.

Langner, M. (2001), *Antike Graffitizeichnungen – Motive, Gestaltung und Bedeutung*. Wiesbaden: Ludwig Reichert.

La Rocca, E. (1987), 'L'adesione senatoriale al "consensus": i modi della propaganda augustea e tiberiana nei monumenti "in circo Flaminio"', in *L'Urbs*, pp. 347–72.

La Rocca, E. and de Vos, A. (1994), *Pompei*. Milan: A. Mondadori.

Lassère, J.-M. (2005), *Manuel d'Épigraphie Romaine, 2. vols*. Paris: Editions A. & J. Picard.

Lassus, J. (1981), *La Forteresse Byzantine de Thamugadi: Fouilles á Timgad 1938–1956 1*. Paris: CNRS.

Lattimore, R. (1942), *Themes in Greek and Latin Epitaphs*. Urbana: University of Illinois Press.

Laurence, R. (1994a), *Roman Pompeii: Space and Society*. London; New York: Routledge.

—(1994b), 'Rumour and communication in Roman politics', *G&R*, 41, 62–74.

—(1997), 'Space and text', in R. Laurence and A. Wallace-Hadrill (eds), pp. 7–15.

—(2007a), *Roman Pompeii: Space and Society*, second edn. Abingdon: Routledge.

—(2007b), 'Gender, age and identity: the female life course at Pompeii', in M. Harlow and R. Laurence (eds), *Age and Ageing in the Roman Empire*. Portsmouth, RI: JRA Supplementary Series 65, pp. 95–110.

—(2008), 'City traffic and the archaeology of Roman streets', in D. Mertens (ed.) *Stadtverkehr in der antiken Welt. Internationales Kolloquium zur 175-Jahrfeier des Deutschen Archäologischen Insituts Rom (Palilia 13)*, Rome: Reichert Verlag, pp. 87–106

—(2011), 'From movement to mobility: future directions', in R. Laurence and D. J. Newsome (eds), pp. 386–401.

Laurence, R., Esmonde Cleary, S. and Sears, G. (2011), *The City in the Roman West c. 250 BC-c. AD 250*. Cambridge: Cambridge University Press.

Laurence, R. and Newsome, D. J. (eds) (2011), *Rome, Ostia, Pompeii: Movement and Space*. Oxford: Oxford University Press.

Laurence, R. and Trifilò, F. (2013), 'The global and the local in the Roman Empire: connectivity and mobility?' in M. Pitts and M. J. Versulys (eds), *Globalisation and the Roman World. Perspectives and Opportunities*. Cambridge: Cambridge University Press.

Laurence, R. and Wallace-Hadrill, A. (eds), (1997), *Domestic Space In The Roman World: Pompeii And Beyond*. Portsmouth, RI: JRA Supplementary Series 22.

Lazzarini, M. L. (1983), 'Iscrizione greca nelle "Terme del foro" di Ostia', *RAL*, 8, 38, 301–10.

—(1996), 'L'incremento del patrimonio epigrafico greco ostiense dopo *Roman Ostia*', in A. Gallina Zevi and A. Claridge (eds), *'Roman Ostia' Revisited*. London: British School at Rome/Soprintendenza Archeologica di Ostia, pp. 243–7.

Leach, E. (1978), 'Does space syntax really "constitute the social"?', in D. Green, C. Haselgrove and M. Spriggs (eds), *Social Organisation and Settlement: Contributions from Anthropology, Archaeology, and Geography*, BAR IntSer. 47. Oxford: Archaeopress, pp. 385–401.

Lefebvre, H. (1991), *The Production of Space*. Oxford: Blackwell.

—(1996), *Writings on Cities*, (trans. and ed.) E. Kofman and E. Lebas. Oxford: Blackwell.

Lefebvre, H. and Regulier-Lefebvre, C. (2004), *Rhythmanalysis: Space, Time and Everyday Life.*, trans. Stuart Elden. New York: Continuum.

Lefebvre, S. (2006), 'Le forum de Cuicul: un example de la gestion de l'espace public à travers l'étude des inscriptions martelées', *L'Africa Romana*, 16, (4), 2125–40.

Le Gall, J. (1979), 'Les habitants de Rome et la fiscalité', in *Points de vue sur la fiscalité antique*. Paris: Université de Paris I, pp. 113–26.

Leglay, M. (1966), *Saturne Africain: Monuments II*. Paris: CNRS.

—(1968), 'Le temple sévérien de l'Aqua Septimiana Felix (Timgad)', *BCTH*, n.s., 3, 262.

—(1978), 'Salus imperatoris Felicitas imperii', *BCTH*, n.s., 14, 241.

Leglay, M. and Tourrenc, S. (1985), 'Nouvelles inscriptions de Timgad sur des légats de la troisième Légion Auguste', *AntAfr*, 21, 103–36.

Lehoux, D. R. (2007), *Astronomy, Weather, and Calendars in the Ancient World: Parapegmata and Related Texts in Classical and Near-Eastern Societies*. Cambridge: Cambridge University Press.

—(forthcoming), 'Image, text, and pattern: reconstructing parapegmata', in A. Jones (ed.), *Reconstructing Ancient Texts*. Toronto: University of Toronto Press, https://qshare. queensu.ca/Users01/lehoux/www/Reconstructing%20Parapegmata.pdf (last accessed 8 January 2013).

Lendon, J. E. (1997), *Empire of Honour: The Art of Government in the Roman World*. Oxford: Clarendon Press.

Lenzi, P. (1998), '*Sita in loco qui vocatur calcaria*: attività di spoliazione e forni da calce a Ostia', *Archeologia medievale*, 25, 247–63.

Lepelley, C. (1981), 'La carrière municipale dans l'Afrique romaine sous l'Empire tardif', *Ktèma*, 6, 333–47.

—(2011), 'De la réaction païenne à la sécularisation: le témoignage d'inscriptions municipales romano-africaines tardives', in P. Brown and R. Lizzi Testa (eds), *Pagans and Christians in the Roman Empire: The Breaking of a Dialogue (IVth–VIth century AD). Proceedings of the International Conference at the Monastery of Bose (October 2008)*. Zurich, Munster: LIT, pp. 273–98.

Leschi, L. (1947), 'Découvertes récentes a Timgad: Aqua Septimiana Felix', *CRAI*, 87–99.

—(1957), *Études d'épigraphie, d'archéologie et d'histoire africaines*. Paris: AMG.

Letzner, W. (2005), *Das Römische Pula. Bilder einer Stadt in Istrien*. Mainz: Von Zabern.

Levi, M. (1967), *Itineraria Picta. Contributo allo Studio della Tabula Peutingeriana*. Rome: 'L'Erma' di Bretschneider.

Levick, B. (1972), 'Tiberius' retirement to Rhodes in 6 BC', *Latomus*, 13, 779–813.

—(1978), 'Concordia at Rome', in R. A. G. Carson and C. M. Kraay (eds), *Scripta Nummaria Romana: Essays Presented to Humphrey Sutherland*. London: Spink, pp. 217–33.

Lèzine, A. (1968), *Carthage, Utique. Études d'Architecture et d'Urbanisme*. Paris: CNRS Éditions.

Lintott, A. (1968), *Violence in Republican Rome*. Oxford: Clarendon Press.

—(1993), *Imperium Romanum. Politics and Administration*. London and New York: Routledge.

Littlewood, R. J. (2006), *Commentary on Ovid's Fasti Book 6*. Oxford: Oxford University Press.

Lomas, K., Whitehouse, R. D. and Wilkins, J. B. (2007), *Literacy and the State in the Ancient Mediterranean*. London: Accordia Research Institute.

Lott, J. B. (2004), *The Neighborhoods of Augustan Rome*. Cambridge: Cambridge University Press.

Loza Azuaga, L. M. (2010), 'Nuevas esculturas femeninas icónicas de la ciudad romana de Baelo Claudia (Bolonia, Tarifa, Cádiz)', in J. M. Abascal and R. Cebrián (eds), *Escultura Romana en Hispania VI*. Murcia: Tabularium, pp. 119–35.

Lusnia, S. S. (2004), 'Urban planning and sculptural display in Severan Rome: reconstructing the Septizodium and its role in dynastic politics', *AJA*, 108, 518–23.

Lynch, K. (1960), *The Image of the City*. Cambridge, MA: MIT Press.

—(1984), *Good City Form*. Cambridge, MA: MIT Press.

Macdonald, M. C. A. (2010), 'Ancient Arabia and the written word', in M. C. A. Macdonald (ed.), *The Development of Arabic as a Written Language, Supplement to the Proceedings of the Seminar for Arabian Studies*, 40, pp. 5–28.

MacDonald, W. L. (1986), *The Architecture of the Roman Empire. Volume II: An Urban Appraisal*. New Haven: Yale University Press.

MacDougall, E. B. (ed.) (1987), *Ancient Roman Villa Gardens*. Washington, DC: Dumbarton Oaks.

Mackie, N. (1990), 'Urban munificence and the growth of urban consciousness in Roman Spain', in T. F. C. Blagg and M. Millett (eds), *The Early Roman Empire in the West*. Oxford: Oxbow, pp. 179–91.

MacMullen, R. (1982), 'The epigraphic habit in the Roman Empire', *AJPh*, 103, (3), 233–46.

—(1984), 'The legion as a society', *Historia*, 33, 440–56.—(1986), 'Personal power in the Roman Empire', *AJPh*, 107, (4), 512–24.

Macqueron, J. (1982), *Contractus Scripturae. Contrats et Quittances dans la Pratique Romaine*. Camerino-Nice: Université de Nice.

Magdelain, A. (1978), *La Loi à Rome: Histoire d'un Concept*. Paris: Belles Lettres.

Magi, F. (1972), *Il Calendario Dipinto sotto S. Maria Maggiore*. Vatican City: Tipografia Poliglotta Vaticana.

Malissard, A. (1983), 'Incendium et ruinae. À propos des villes et des monuments dans les Histoires et les Annales de Tacite', in R. Chevallier (ed.) *Présence de l'Architecture et de l'Urbanisme Romains. Hommage à Paul Dufournet*. Tours: Caesarodunum, 18 bis, pp. 45–55.

Mallon, J. (1982–6), *De l'Écriture. Recueil d'Études Publiées de 1937 à 1981*, new edition 1986. Paris: CNRS.

Manderscheid, H. (1981), *Die Skulpturenausstattung der kaiserzeitlichen Thermenanlagen*. Berlin: Gebr. Mann Verlag.

Marichal, R. (1973), 'La scrittura', in *Storia d'Italia*, V.2. Turin: Einaudi, pp. 1265–317.

Marrou, H.-I. (1932), 'La vie intellectuelle au Forum de Trajan et au Forum d'Auguste', *Mélanges d'Archéologie et d'Histoire*, 49, 93–110.

Martin, D. B. (1996), 'The construction of the ancient family: methodological considerations', *JRS*, 86, 40–60.

Marx, F. (1915), *A. Cornelii Celsi quae supersunt. Corpus Medicorum Latinorum 1.* Leipzig: Teubner.

Mastino, A. (1999), 'I Severi nel Nord Africa', in *11. Congresso Internazionale di Epigrafia Greca e Latina: Atti, 18–24 Settembre 1997, Roma, Italia.* Rome: Quasar, pp. 359–417.

Mastino, A. and Teatini, A. (2001), 'Ancora sul discusso "trionfo" di Costantino dopo la battaglia del Ponte Milvio: nota a proposito di CIL, VIII, 9356 = 20941 (Caesarea)', in G. Angeli Bertinelli and A. Donati (eds) *Varia Epigraphica: Atti del Colloquio Internazionale di Epigrafia, 8–10 Giugno 2000, Bertinoro, Italia.* Faenza: Fratelli Lega Editori, pp. 274–327 (Epigrafia e antichità, 17).

Mattingly, D. J. (2011), *Imperialism, Power, and Identity. Experiencing the Roman Empire.* Princeton and Oxford: Princeton University Press.

Mau, A. (1893), 'Scavi di Pompei 1891–92 (Insula V.2)', *MDAI(R)* 8, pp. 3–61.

Maurice, J. (1908–12), *Numismatique constantinienne.* Paris: Ernest Leroux.

Maurin, L. (1994), *Inscriptions Latines d'Aquitaine (I.L.A.) Santones.* Bordeaux: Centre Pierre Paris.

Maurin, L. and Navarro Caballero, M. (2010), *Inscriptions Latines d'Aquitaine (I.L.A.) Bordeaux.* Bordeaux: Ausonius.

Mayer, E. (2010), 'Propaganda, staged applause, or local politics? Public monuments from Augustus to Septimius Severus', in Ewald and Noreña, pp. 111–34.

Meadows, A. and Williams, J. (2001), 'Moneta and the monuments: coinage and politics in Republican Rome', *JRS*, 91, 27–49.

Mecacci, L. (1984), *Identikit del cervello.* Rome; Bari: Laterza.

Meiggs, R. (1973), *Roman Ostia*, 2nd edn. Oxford: Clarendon Press.

Meneghini, R. and Santangeli Valenzani, R. (2007), *I Fori Imperiali: Gli scavi del Comune di Roma (1991–2007).* Rome: Viviani Editore.

Meyer, E. A. (1990), 'Explaining the epigraphic habit in the Roman empire: the evidence of the epitaphs', *JRS*, 80, 74–96.

Michels, A. K. (1967), *The Calendar of the Roman Republic.* Princeton: Princeton University Press.

Miles, G. B. (1995), *Livy: Reconstructing Early Rome.* Ithaca, NY and London: Cornell University Press. Miller, D. and Tilley, C. (1984), 'Ideology, power and prehistory: an introduction', in D. Miller and C. Tilley (eds), *Ideology, Power and Prehistory.* Cambridge: Cambridge University Press.

Millar, F. (1977), *The Emperor in the Roman World.* London: Duckworth.

Miller, K. (1916), *Itineraria Romana.* Stuttgart: Strecker und Schröder (new edition 1964, Rome).

Milnor, K. (2009), 'Literary literacy in Roman Pompeii: the case of Virgil's *Aeneid*', in W. Johnson and H. Parker (eds), *Ancient Literacies: The Culture of Reading in Greece and Rome.* Oxford: Oxford University Press, pp. 288–319.

Miniero, P. (ed.) (2000), *The Archaeological Museum of the Phlegrean Fields in the Castle of Baia. The Sacellum of the Augustales at Miseno.* Naples: Soprintendenza Archaeologica di Napoli e Caserta, Electa Napoli.

Mitchell, S. (1999), 'The administration of Roman Asia from 133 BC to AD 250' in W. Eck (ed.), *Lokale Autonomie und romische Ordnungsmacht in der kaiserzeilichen Provinzen vom 1. bis 3. Jahrhundert.* Munich: R. Oldenbourg Verlag, pp. 17–46.

Mitchell, S. and Waelkens, M. (1998), *Pisidian Antioch. The Site and its Monuments.* London: Duckworth.

Mocsy, A. (1970), *Gesellschaft und Romanisation in der romischen Provinz Moesia Superior*. Amsterdam: Hakkert.

Morris, I. (1998), 'Remaining invisible: the archaeology of the excluded in Classical Athens', in S. R. Joshel and S. Murnaghan (eds), *Women and Slaves in Graeco-Roman Culture: Different Equations*. London: Routledge, pp. 199–226.

Morstein-Marx, R. (2004), *Mass Oratory and Political Power in the Late Roman Republic*. Cambridge: Cambridge University Press.

—(2012), 'Political graffiti in the late Roman Republic: hidden transcripts and common knowledge', in C. Kuhn (ed.), *Politische Kommunikation und öffentliche Meinung in der antiken Welt*. Heidelberg: Franz Steiner Verlag, pp. 191–218.

Mouritsen, H. (2001), *Plebs and Politics in the Late Roman Republic*. Cambridge: Cambridge University Press.

—(2005), 'Freedmen and decurions: epitaphs and social history in Imperial Italy'. *JRS*, 95, 38–63

—(2011), 'The families of Roman slaves and freedmen', in B. Rawson (eds) *A Companion to Families in the Greek and Roman Worlds*. Oxford: Wiley-Blackwell, pp. 129–45.

—(forthcoming), 'The inscriptions of the Insula of the Menander', in H. Mouritsen, (ed.), *The Insula of the Menander at Pompeii, Volume 5*. Oxford: Clarendon Press.

Mrozek, S. (1973), 'A propos de la répartition chronologique des inscriptions latines dans le Haut Empire', *Epigraphica*, 35, pp. 113–18.

—(1988), *Die epigraphisch belegten sozialen Randgruppen in den Städten Italiens (Prinzipatszeit)*. Graz: Leykam.

Murer, C. E. (2013), *Ehrenstatuen für prominente Bürgerinnen. Aufstellungsorte und Funktionswandel statuarischer Ehrungen in kaiserzeitlichen Stadträumen Italiens und Nordafrikas*, Amsterdam Doc. Diss.

Myers, R. and Ormsby, R. J. (trans.) (1972), *Catullus: The Complete Poems for Modern Readers*. London: Allen & Unwin.

Naddari, S. A. (2008), 'Cérès et céréaliculture à travers le secteur méridional du Haut Tell tunisien', *L'Africa Romana*, 17, 935–50.

Nappo, S. C. (1989), 'Fregio dipinto dal "praedium" di Giulia Felice con rappresentazione del foro di Pompei'. *Rivista di Studi Pompeiani*, 3, 79–96.

Navarro Caballero, M. (2001), 'Les femmes de l'élite Hispano-Romaine, entre la famille et la vie publique', in M. Navarro Caballero and S. Demougin (eds), *Élites Hispaniques*. Paris: de Boccard, pp. 191–201.

—(2004), 'L'élite, les femmes et l'argent dans les provinces hispaniques', in L. De Ligt, E. A. Hemelrijk and H. S. Singor (eds) (2004), *Roman Rule and Civic Life: Local and Regional Perspectives (Proceedings of the Fourth Workshop of the International Network Impact of Empire, Leiden, June 25–28, 2003)*. Amsterdam: Gieben, pp. 389–400.

Neal, Z. P. (2012), *The Connected City. How Networks are Shaping the Modern Metropolis*. London and New York: Routledge.

Nevett, L. (2011), 'Family and household, ancient history and archaeology: a case study from Roman Egypt', in B. Rawson (ed.), *A Companion to Families in the Greek and Roman Worlds*. Oxford: Wiley-Blackwell, pp. 15–32.

Newby, Z. (2002), 'Greek athletics as Roman spectacle: the mosaics from Ostia and Rome', *PBSR*, 70, 177–203.

Newby, Z. and Leader-Newby, R. (eds) (2007), *Art and Inscriptions in the Ancient World*. Cambridge: Cambridge University Press.

Newsome, D. J. (2008), 'Traffic and congestion in Rome's Empire', *JRA*, 21, 442–6.

—(2009), 'Traffic, space and legal change around the Casa del Marinaio at Pompeii (vii 15.1–2)'. *BABesch*, 84, 121–42.

—(2010), 'The forum and the city: rethinking centrality in Rome and Pompeii Nylan, M. (2012), Unpublished PhD thesis, University of Birmingham.

—(2011a), 'Introduction: making movement meaningful', in R. Laurence and D. J. Newsome (eds), pp. 1–54.

—(2011b), 'Movement and fora in Rome (the late Republic to the first century CE)', in R. Laurence and D. J. Newsome (eds), pp. 290–311.

Ney, C. and Paillet, J.-L. (2006), 'La basilique de Baelo-Claudia: étude architecturale', in *Actas I Journadas Internationales de Baelo Claudia: Balance y Perspectiva (1966–2004)*. Seville: Consejería de Cultura, Junta de Andalucía, pp. 93–136.

Nicolet, C. (1976), *Le Métier de Citoyen dans la Rome Républicaine*. Paris: Gallimard.

—(1985), 'Centralisation d'État et problème des archives dans le monde gréco-romain', in *Culture et Idéologie dans la Genèse de l'État Moderne*, pp. 9–24.

—(1994), 'Avant-propos', in S. Demougin (ed.), *La Mémoire Perdue: À la Recherche des Archives Oubliées, Publiques et Privées, de la Rome Antique*. Paris: de Boccard (Publications de la Sorbonne Série Histoire Ancienne et Médiévale; 30).

—(1998), 'Introduction', in *La Mémoire Perdue: Recherches sur l'Administration Romaine*. Rome: CÉFR 243, pp. 201–4.

Nicols, J. (1987), 'Indigenous culture and the process of Romanisation in Iberian Galicia', *AJPh*. 108, pp. 129–51.

—(1989), '*Patrona civitatis*. Gender and civic patronage', in C. Deroux (ed.), *Studies in Latin Literature and Roman History V*. Brussels: Collection Latomus 206, pp. 117–42.

—(2001), '*Hospitium* and political friendship in the late Republic', in M. Peachin (ed.), *Aspects of Friendship in the Graeco-Roman World*. Portsmouth, RI: JRA Supplementary Series 43, pp. 99–108.

Nielsen, I. (1993a and b) *Thermae et Balnea. The Architecture and Cultural History of Roman Public Baths I. Text; II. Catalogue and Plates*, second edn. Aarhus: Aarhus University Press.

Nijf, O. M. van (2011), 'Public space and the political culture of Roman Termessos', in O. M. van Nijf and R. Alston (eds), *Political Culture in the Greek City after the Classical Age*. Leuven; Paris; Walpole, MA: Peeters, pp. 215–42.

Nylan, M. 2012. 'The Power of Networks during China's Classical Era (323 BCE–316 CE): Regulations, metaphors, rituals, and deities', in S. E. Alcock, J. Bodel, and R. J. A. Talbert (eds) *Highways, Byways, and Road Systems in the Pre-modern World*. Cambridge: Cambridge University Press: pp. 33–65.

Oliver, J. H. (1989), *Greek Constitutions of Early Roman Emperors from Inscriptions and Papyri*. Philadelphia: Memoirs of the American Philosophical Society, 178.

Ordóñes Agulla, S. (1987–8), 'Cuestiones en torno a Singilia Barba', *Habis*, 18–19, 319–44.

Ossi, A. J. and Harrington, J. M. (2011), 'Pisidian Antioch: the urban infrastructure and its development', in E. K. Gazda, and D. Y. Ng (eds), *Building a New Rome. The Imperial Colony of Pisidian Antioch (25 BC–AD 700)*. Ann Arbor, MI: Kelsey Museum Publication 5, pp. 11–32.

O'Sullivan, T. M. (2011), *Walking in Roman Culture*. Cambridge: Cambridge University Press.

Palet, J. M. and Orengo, H. A. (2011), 'The Roman centuriated landscape: conception, genesis, and development as inferred from the ager tarraconensis case', *AJA*, 115, 383–402.

Panciera, S. (1998), 'Claudio costruttore de sua pecunia! A proposito di una nuova iscrizione templare romana', Y. Burnand, Y. Le Bohec and J.-P. Martin (eds), *Claude de Lyon, Empereur Romain. Actes du Colloque Paris-Nancy-Lyon, Novembre 1992*. Paris: Presses de l'Université de Paris-Sorbonne.

Pavis d'Esurac, H. (1976), *La Préfecture de l'Annone Service Administratif Impérial d'Auguste à Constantin*. Rome: BEFAR, 225.

—(1985), 'Pline le Jeune et l'affranchi Pallas (Ep. 7.29; 8.6)', l'ideologia dell'arricchimento e l'ideologia dell'ascesa sociale a Roma e nel mondo romano: atti del XIV Colloquio GIREA, Lecce 19–24 settembre 1983, *Index*, 13, 313–25.

Pavolini, C. (2006), *Ostia*, second edn. Rome/Bari: Guide archeologiche Laterza.

Pelling, C. (2002), *Plutarch and History*. Swansea: The Classical Press of Wales and Duckworth.

Penn, A. and Turner, A. (2002), 'Space syntax based agent simulation', in *Proceedings of the First International Conference on Pedestrian and Evacuation Dynamics*, pp. 99–114.

Pensabene, P. (1992), 'Il tempio della Gens Septimia a Cuicul (Gemila)', *L'Africa Romana*, 9, 771–802.

Pesando, F. and Guidobaldi, M. P. (2006), *Pompei, Oplontis, Ercolano, Stabiae*. Rome/Bari: Guide archeologiche Laterza.

Petrucci, A. (1980), 'La scrittura fra ideologia e rappresentazione', in *Storia dell'Arte italiana, III.2.1. Scrittura; Miniatura; Disegno*. Turin, pp. 3–123.

—(1984), 'Lire au Moyen Âge', *MEFR, Moyen Âge–Temps Modernes*, 96, (2), 603–16.

Petrucci, A. (1985), '*Potere, spazi urbani, scritture esposte : proposte ed esami*', in *Culture et Idéologie dans la Genèse de l'État Moderne*. pp. 85–97.

—(1986–93), *Jeux de Lettres. Formes et Usages de l'Inscription en Italie, 11e–20e Siècles*. Paris: Éditions de l'École des Hautes Études en Sciences Sociales (= La Scrittura. Ideologia e Rappresentazione, Turin 1986).

Pfanner, M. (1983), *Der Titusbogen*. Mainz: Von Zabern.

Picard, G. C. (1957), 'Civitas Mactariana', *Karthago*, 8.

Piganiol, A. (1962), *Les Documents Cadastraux de la Colonie Romaine d'Orange*. Gallia Supplement 16. Paris: CNRS Éditions.

Pighi, G. B. (1965), *De Ludis Saecularibus Populi Romani Quiritium*. Amsterdam: P. Schippers.

Platner, S. B. and Ashby, T. (1929), *A Topographical Dictionary of Ancient Rome*. Oxford and London: Oxford University Press.

Pobjoy, M. (2000), 'Building inscriptions in republican Italy: euergetism, responsibility, and civic virtue', in A. E. Cooley (ed.) (2000a), pp. 77–92.

Posner, E. (1972), *Archives in the Ancient World*. Cambridge, MA: Harvard University Press.

Potter, T. W. (1995), *Towns in Late Antiquity: Iol Caesarea*. Sheffield: Ian Sanders Memorial Committee.

Purcell. N. (1987), 'Tomb and suburb', in H, von Hesberg ad P. Zanker (eds), *Römische Gräberstraßen. Selbstdarstellung – Status – Standard, Colloquium in Munich, 28–30 October 1985*. Munich: Verlag der Bayerische Akademie der Wissenschaften, pp. 25–41.

—(1995), 'The Roman *villa* and the landscape of production', in T. J. Cornell and K. Lomas (eds), *Urban Society in Roman Italy*. London: University College London Press, pp. 151–79

Raja, R. (2003), 'Urban development and built identities. The case of Aphrodisias in Caria in the late Republican period', *Digressus*, 1, 86–98.

Raper, R. A. (1977), 'The analysis of the urban structure of Pompeii: a sociological examination of land use (semi-micro)', in D. L. Clarke (ed.), *Spatial Archaeology*, New York: Academic Press, pp. 189–221.

Rawson, B. (1997), '"The family" in the Ancient Mediterranean: past, present, future', *ZPE*, 117, 294–6.

—(2003), *Children and Childhood in Roman Italy*. Oxford: Oxford University Press.

Rawson, B. and Weaver, P. (eds), (1997), *The Roman Family in Italy. Status, Sentiment, Space*. Canberra: Humanities Research Centre; Oxford: Clarendon Press.

Ray, N. (forthcoming), 'Investigating Pompeian urban open space: the grand palaestra and its Environs', in B. Croxford and J. Lucas (eds), *Experiencing Place and Space in the Roman World*. Oxford: Oxbow.

Rebuffat, R. (1987), 'Le poème de Q. Avidius Quintianus à la déesse Salus', *Karthago*, 21, 93–105.

Rehak, P. (2006), (ed. J. G. Younger) *Imperium and Cosmos: Augustus and the Northern Campus Martius*. Madison: University of Wisconsin Press.

Rémy, B. (1995), *Inscriptions Latines d'Aquitaine (I.L.A.) Vellaves*. Bordeaux: Centre Pierre Paris.

—(1996), *Inscriptions Latines d'Aquitaine (I.L.A.) Arvernes*. Bordeaux: Institut de Recherche sur l'Antiquité et le Moyen âge.

Revell, L. (2007), 'Architecture, power and politics: the forum-basilica in Roman Britain', in J. Sofaer (ed.), *Projecting Identities*. Oxford: Wiley-Blackwell.

—(2009), *Roman Imperialism and Local Identities*. Cambridge: Cambridge University Press.

Reynolds, A. (1985), 'Cardinal Oliviero Carafa and the early cinquecento tradition of the feast of Pasquino'. *Roma Humanistica: Journal of Neo-Latin Studies*, 34A, 178–209.

Reynolds, J. (1976), Review of F. Magi, *Il Calendario Dipinto sotto S. Maria Maggiore*, *JRS*, 66, 247–8.

Rich, J. W. (trans.) (1990), *Cassius Dio. The Augustan Settlement (Roman History 53–55.9)*. Eastbourne: Aris & Phillips.

—(2008), 'Lex licinia, lex sempronia: B. G. Niebuhr and the limitation of landholding in the Roman Republic', in L. de Ligt and S. J. Northwood (eds), *People, Land, and Politics: Demographic Developments and the Transformation of Roman Italy, 300 BC–AD 14*. Leiden; Boston: Brill, pp. 519–72.

Richardson, J. S. (1995), 'Neque elegantem, ut arbitrator, neques urbanum: reflections on Iberian urbanism', in B. Cunliffe and S. Keay (eds), *Social Complexity and the Development of Towns in Iberia: From the Copper Age to the Second Century AD*. Proceedings of the British Academy 86. Oxford: Oxford University Press, pp. 339–54.

Richardson, L. Jr. (1992), *A New Topographical Dictionary of Ancient Rome*. Baltimore; London: Johns Hopkins University Press.

Roberts, C. H. and Skeat, T. C. (1983), *The Birth of the Codex*. Oxford: Oxford University Press.

Roche, D. (1985), 'Les pratiques de l'écrit dans les villes françaises du XVIIIe siècle', in R. Chartier (ed.), *Pratiques de la Lecture*. Marseille: Rivages.

Roda, S. (1995), 'Forum et basilica: gli spazi della vita collettiva e l'identità citttadina', in. M. M. Roberti (ed.), *Forum et Basilica in Aquileia e nella Cisalpina Romana*. Udine: Arti Grafiche Friulane, pp. 15–46.

Roddaz, J.-M. (1984), *Marcus Agrippa*. Rome: BEFAR, 253.

Rodríguez-Almeida. E. (1981), *Forma Urbis Marmorea. Aggiornamento Generale 1980*. Rome: Quasar.

Roller, M. (2010), 'Demolished houses, monumentality and memory in Roman culture', *ClAnt*, 29, 117–80.

Romanelli, P. (1959), *Storia delle Province romane dell'Africa*. Rome: 'L'Erma' di Bretschneider.

—(1970), *Topografia e Archeologia dell'Africa Romana*. Turin: Società Editrice Internazionale.

Rotondi, G. (1912, repr. 1966), *Leges Publicae Populi Romani*. Hildesheim: G. Olms.

Rüdiger, U. (1973), 'Die Anaglypha Hadriani', *Antike Plastik*, 12, 161–73.

Rüpke, J. (1995a), 'Fasti: Quellen oder Produkte römischer Geschichtsschreibung?' *Klio*, 77, 184–202.

—(1995b), *Kalender und Öffentlichkeit: Die Geschichte der Repräsentation und religiösen Qualifikation von Zeit in Rom*. Berlin and New York: De Gruyter.

—(2006), 'Ennius's *Fasti* in Fulvius's temple: Greek rationality and Roman tradition', *Arethusa*, 39, 489–512.

—(2007), *Religion of the Romans*, (trans. and ed.) R. Gordon. Cambridge: Polity Press.

—(2011), *The Roman Calendar from Numa to Constantine: Time, History, and the Fasti*, trans. David M. B. Richardson). Oxford: Wiley-Blackwell.

Rykwert, J. (1988), *The Idea of a Town: The Anthropology of Urban Form in Rome, Italy and the Ancient World*. Cambridge, MA: MIT Press.

Sabbatini Tumolesi, P. (1980), *Gladiatorum Paria. Annunci di Spettacoli Gladiatorii a Pompei*. Rome: Edizini Storia e Letteratura (*Tituli*, 1).

Sablayrolles, R. (1996), *Libertinus Miles. Les Cohortes de Vigiles*. Rome: CÉFR, 224.

—(2006), 'La vie urbaine en vase clos: l'encadrement des lieux de la vie collective dans *Lugdunum* des Convènes (IIe siècle avant notre ère – IVe siècle de notre ère), *Caesarodunum*, XL, 83–116.

Sablayrolles, R., Beyrie, A. (2006), *Carte Archéologique de la Gaule: 31/2 Le Comminges (Haute Garonne)*. Paris: Maison des Sciences de l'Homme.

Salama, P. (1951), 'Les bornes milliaires de Djemila-Cuicul et leur intérêt pour l'histoire de la ville', *Revue Africaine*, 95, 213–72.

—(1951-2), 'Bornes milliaires inédites de Timgad et de sa région', *BCTH*, 226–72.

—(2004), 'Anomalies et aberrations recontrées sur des inscriptions milliaires de la voie Romaine Ammaedara-Capsa-Tacapes', *ZPE*, 149, 245–55

—(2010), 'Les voies antiques', in J. Desanges, N. Duval, C. Lepelley and S. Saint-Amans (eds) *Carte des Routes et des Cités de l'est de l'Africa à la Fin de l'Antiquité*. Turnhout: Brepols Publishers, pp. 36–47.

Saliou, C. (2008), 'La rue dans le droit Romain classique', in P. Ballet, N. Dieudonne-Glad and C. Saliou (eds), *La Rue dans l'Antiquité. Définition, Aménagement, Devenir*. Rennes: Presses Universitaires de Rennes.

Saller, R. P. and Shaw, B. (1984), 'Tombstones and Roman family relations in the Principate: civilians, soldiers and slaves', *JRS*, 74, 124–56.

Salzman, M. R. (1990), *On Roman Time: the Codex-Calendar of 354 and the Rhythms of Urban Life in Late Antiquity*. Berkeley: University of California Press.

Sampson, G. (1985), *Writing Systems*. London: Hutchinson.

Sanders, G. (1984), 'Texte et monument: l'arbitrage du musée épigraphique', in A. Donati (ed.) *Il Museo Epigrafico. Colloquio AIEGL-Borghesi 83 (Castrocaro Terme-Ferrara, 30 Settembre-2 Ottobre 1983)*. Faenza: Epigrafia e Antichità, 7, pp. 85–118.

—(1991), *Lapides Memores. Païens et Chrétiens Face à la Mort: Le Témoignage de l'épigraphie Funéraire Latine*. Faenza: Epigrafia e Antichità, 11.

Sanderson, B. and Keegan, P. (2011), 'Crowning Marsyas: the symbolism involved in the exile of Julia', *Studia Humaniora Tartuensia* 12.A.2: http://sht.ut.ee/index.php/sht/index (last accessed 8 January 2013).

San Juan, R.M. (2001), *Rome: A City Out of Print*. Minneapolis: University of Minnesota Press.

Santopuoli, N., Seccia, L. and Varone, A. (2007), 'Utilizzo di procedure informatiche come supporto per l'interpretazione di graffiti pompeiani', in S. A. Curuni and N. Santopuoli (eds), *Pompei – Via Dell'Abbondanza: Ricerche, Restauri e Nuove Tecnologie*. Milan: Skira, pp. 175–7.

Sassy, G. (1953), 'Note sur une statue impériale de Thubursicum Numidarum (Khamissa)', *Libyca*, 1, 109–14.

Scarborough, J. (1969), *Roman Medicine*. London: Thames and Hudson.

Schalles, H.-J., Hesberg, H. von, and Zanker, P. (eds) (1992), *Die römische Stadt im 2. Jahrhundert n. Chr. Der Funktionswandel des öffentlichen Raumes. Kolloquium in Xanten vom 2. bis 4. Mai 1990*. Cologne: Rheinland Verlag.

Schattner, T. G. (2003), *Munigua: Cuarenta Años de Investigaciones*. Seville: Junta de Andalucía, Consejería de Cultura.

Scheid, J. (1998), *Recherches Archéologiques à la Magliana: Commentarii Fratrum Arvalium qui Supersunt: Les Copies Épigraphiques des Protocoles Annuels de la Confrérie Arvale: 21 av.–304 ap. J.-C.* Rome: Roma Antica 4.

Schnegg-Köhler, B. (2002), *Die augusteischen Säkularspiele*. Munich (= Archiv für Religionsgeschichte): Saur.

Schütz, M. (1990), 'Zur Sonnenuhr des Augustus auf dem Marsfeld', *Gymnasium*, 97, 432–57.

Schwind, F. von (1940), *Zur Frage der Publikation im römischen Recht*. Munich: C. H. Beck'sche Verlagsbuchhandlung.

Sears, G. (2011), *The Cities of Roman Africa*. Stroud: The History Press.

Seeck, O. (1919), *Regesten der Kaiser und Päpste für die Jahre 311 bis 476 n. Chr.* Stuttgart: J. B. Metzler.

Segal, A. (1997), *From Function to Monument. Urban Landscapes of Roman Palestine, Syria and Provincia Arabia*. Oxford: Oxbow Books.

Sehlmeyer, M. (1999), *Stadtrömische Ehrenstatuen der republikanischen Zeit*. Historia Einzelschrift 130. Stuttgart: Franz Steiner Verlag.

Serrano Ramos, E. (1988), 'Singilia Barba, una ciudad de la Baetica', in E. Ripoll Perelló (ed.), *Actas del Congreso Internacional 'El estrecho de Gibraltar' Ceuta, 1987. Tomo 1: Prehistoria e Historia de la Antigüedad*. Madrid: Universidad Nacional de Educación a Distancia, pp. 821–31.

Serrano Ramos, E., Atencia Páez, R. and Rodríguez Oliva, P. (1991–2), 'Novedades epigráficas de Singilia Barba', *Mainake*, 13–14, 171–203.

Serrano Ramos, E. and Rodríguez Oliva, P. (1988), 'Tres nuevas inscriptiones de Singilia Barba (El Castillón, Antequera, Málaga)', *Baetica*, 11, 237–56.

Shanks, M. and Tilley, C. (1982), 'Ideology, symbolic power and ritual communication: a reinterpretation of Neolithic mortuary practices', in I. Hodder (ed.), *Symbolic and Structural Archaeology*. Cambridge: Cambridge University Press, pp. 129–54.

Sillières, P. (1978), 'Nouvelles inscriptions de Singilia Barba (El Castillón, Antequera, Málaga)', *Mélanges de la Casa Velázquez*, 14, 465–76.

—(1995), *Baelo Claudia: Une cité Romaine de Bétique*. Madrid: Casa de Velázquez.

Smith, A. T. (2003), *The Political Landscape. Constellations of Authority in Early Complex Polities*. Berkeley: University of California Press.

Smith, R. R. R. (1998), 'Cultural choice and political identity in honorific portrait statues in the Greek East in the second century AD', *JRS*, 88, 56–93.

—(2007), 'Statue life in the Hadrianic Baths at Aphrodisias, A.D. 100–600: Local Context and Historical Meaning', in F. A. Bauer and C. Witschel (eds), *Statuen in der Spätantike*. Wiesbaden: Reichert, pp. 203–25.

Sogliano, A. (1899), 'Pompei – relazione degli scavi fatti durante il mese di settembre 1899', *Notizie degli Scavi* 7, 339–58.

Solin, H. (1970), *L'Interpretazione delle Iscrizioni Parietali: Note e Discussion*. Faenza: Fratelli Lega.

—(1973), 'Review of *CIL* IV Suppl 4', *Gnomon*, 45, 258–77.

Solin, H. and Itkonen-Kaila, M. (1966), *Graffiti del Palatino, I. Paedagogium*. Helsinki: Tilgmann.

Sonnenschein, E. A. (ed.) (1901), *Plautus, Rudens*. Oxford: Clarendon Press.

Spaeth, Jr. J. W. (1939), 'Martial and the pasquinade', *TAPhA*, 70, 242–55.

Sparrow, J. (1969), *Visible Words. A Study of Inscriptions in and as Books and Works of Art*. Cambridge: Cambridge University Press.

Spickermann, W. (1994) *'Mulieres ex Voto'. Untersuchungen zur Götterverehrung von Frauen im römischen Gallien, Germanien und Rätien (1.-3. Jahrhundert n. Chr.)*. Bochum: Universitätsverlag Brockmeyer.

Stein, A. (1931), *Römische Inschriften in der antiken Literatur*. Prague: Taussig & Taussig,

Stein-Hölkeskamp, E. and Hölkeskamp, K.-J. (eds), (2006), *Erinnerungsorte der Antike: Die römische Welt*. Munich: C. H. Beck, pp. 300–20.

Stewart, P. (2003), *Statues in Roman Society: Representation and Response*. Cambridge: Cambridge University Press.

—(2010), 'Geographies of provincialism in Roman sculpture', *RIHA Journal* 0005, http://www.riha-journal.org/articles/2010/stewart-geographies-of-provincialism.

Strocka, V. M. (1972), 'Beobachtungen an den Attikareliefs des severischen Quadrifons von Lepcis Magna', *AntAfr.*, 6, 147–72.

Stylow, A. U. and Gimeno Pascual, H. (2002), 'Epigraphica baetica', *Habis*, 33, 325–46.

Susini, G. (1966), *Il lapicida romano*. Bologna: L'Erma' di Bretschneider.

—(1973), *The Roman Stonecutter. An Introduction to Latin Epigraphy*. (Eng. trans. A. M. Dabrowski, E. Badian (ed.). Oxford: Blackwell.

—(1982), *Epigrafia Romana*. Rome: Jouvence.

—(1985), *Scrittura e Produzione culturale dal Sossier Romano di Sarsina*. Faenza: Lega.

—(1988), 'Compitare per via. Antropologia del lettore antico: meglio, del lettore romano', *Alma Mater Studiorum*, 1, (1), 105–24.

—(1989), 'Le scritture esposte', in G. Cavallo, P. Fedeli and A. Giardina (eds) *Lo Spazio Letterario di Roma Antica, II. La Circolazione del Testo*. Rome: Salerno Editrice, pp. 271–305.

Syme, R. (1988), 'Journeys of Hadrian', *ZPE*, 73, 159–70.

Tantillo, I. (2010), 'I costumi epigrafici. Scritture, monumenti, pratiche', in I. Tantillo and F. Bigi (eds) *Leptis Magna una Città e le Sue Iscrizioni in Epoca Tardoromana*. Cassino: Università degli Studi di Cassino, pp. 173–203.

Tanzer, H. H. (1939), *The Common People of Pompeii Study of the Graffiti*. Baltimore: Johns Hopkins Press.

Tardy, D. (2005), *Le décor architectonique de Vesunna (Périgueux antique), Aquitania* supplement 12. Bordeaux: Fédération Aquitania.

Thébert, Y. (2003), *Thermes Romains d'Afrique du Nord et leur Contexte Méditerranéen*. Rome: BEFAR, 315.

Thomas, E. (2007), *Monumentality and the Roman Empire: Architecture in the Antonine Age*. Oxford: Oxford University Press.

Thompson, C. W. (2002) 'Urban open space in the twenty-first century', *Landscape and Urban Planning* 60: 59–72.

Thompson, F. H. (2002), *The Archaeology of Greek and Roman Slavery*. London: Duckworth.

Thulin, C. (1913; repr. 1971), *Corpus Agrimensorum Romanorum* 1/1. Leipzig: Teubner.

Tonkiss, F. (2005), *Space, the City, and Social Theory: Social Relations and Urban Forms*. London: Polity Press.

Torelli, M. (1982), *Typology and Structure of Roman Historical Reliefs*. Ann Arbor: University of Michigan Press (second edn 1992).

—(1995), 'The creation of Roman Italy: the contribution of archaeology', in H. Fracchia and M. Gualtieri (eds), *Studies in the Romanization of Italy*. Edmonton: University of Alberta Press.

—(1996), 'Donne, *domi nobiles* ed evergeti a Paestum tra la fine della Repubblica e l'inizio dell'Impero', in M. Cébeillac-Gervasoni (ed.), *Les Élites Municipales de l'Italie Péninsulaire des Gracques à Néron*. Naples; Rome: École Française de Rome, pp. 153–78.

—(1998), 'Struttura e linguaggio del rilievo storico romano', in E. A. Arslan (ed.) *La 'Parola' delle Immagini e delle Forme di Scrittura. Modi e Techniche della Communicazione nel Mondo Antico*. Messina: Di.Sc.A.M., pp. 133–50.

Tourrenc, S. (1968), 'La dédicace du temple du Génie de la colonie à Timgad', *AntAfr.*, 2, 197–220.

Toynbee, J. M. C. (1971), *Death and Burial in the Roman World*. Baltimore: Johns Hopkins University Press.

Trappes-Lomax, J. (2007), *Catullus: A Textual Appraisal*. Swansea: The Classical Press of Wales.

Treggiari, S. (1991), *Roman Marriage. Iusti Coniuges from the Time of Cicero to the Time of Ulpian*. Oxford: Clarendon Press.

Trifilò, F. (2008), 'Power, architecture and community in the distribution of honorary statues in Roman public space', in C. Fenwick, M. Wiggins and D. Wythe (eds), *TRAC 2007: Proceedings of the Seventeenth Annual Theoretical Roman Archaeology Conference, London 2007*. Oxford: Oxbow, pp. 109–20.

—(forthcoming 2013), 'Traffic, congestion and the creation of public space in cities of the Roman Empire: the archaeology of the *platea*'.

Trimble, J. (2011), *Women and Visual Replication in Roman Imperial Art and Culture*. Cambridge: Cambridge University Press.

Turchetti, R. (1994), 'Ostia', in *Il Lazio di Thomas Ashby 1891–1930* I. Rome: Fratelli Palombi, pp. 85–122.

Turner, A. (2001), 'Depthmap: a program to perform visibility graph analysis', *Proceedings of the Third International Symposium on Space Syntax*, pp. 31.1–31.9.

—(2004), *Depthmap v4.09: A Researcher's Handbook (Revision 1)*. London: UCL Bartlett School of Graduate Studies, http://www.vr.ucl.ac.uk/depthmap/handbook.html

Turner, A., Doxa, M., O'Sullivan, D. and Penn, A. (2001), 'From isovists to visibility graphs: a methodology for the analysis of architectural space', *Environment and Planning B: Planning and Design*, 28, 103–21.

Urry, J. (2000), *Sociology Beyond Societies*. London: Routledge.

Valette-Cagnac, E. (1997), *La Lecture à Rome. Rites et Pratiques*. Paris: Belin.

Varone, A. (1999), 'I graffiti', in A. Barbet and P. Miniero (eds), *La Villa San Marco a Stabia*, Naples: Centre Bérard, pp. 345–85.

—(2002), *Erotica Pompeiana: Love Inscriptions on the Walls of Pompeii*. Rome: L'Erma di Bretschneider.

—(2008), 'Inseguendo un'utopia. l'apporto delle nuove technologie informatiche alla lettura "obiettiva" delle oscrizioni parietali', in O. Brandt (eds), *Unexpected Voices: The Graffiti in the Cryptoporticus of the Horti Sallustiani and Papers from a Conference on Graffiti at the Swedish Institute in Rome, 7 March 2003*. Stockholm: Svenska Institutet i Rom, pp. 125–37.

Vernant, J.-P. (1962), *Les Origines de la Pensée Grecque*. Paris: PUF.

Veyne, P. (1961), 'Le mausolée des légats à Carthage', *BSAF*, 34–6.

—(1968), 'Le carré Sator ou beaucoup de bruit pour rien', *Bulletin de l'Association Guillaume Budé*, 427–60.

—(1976), *Le Pain et le Cirque*. Paris: Le Seuil (new edition 1995) (= *Bread and Circuses: Historical Sociology and Political Pluralism*. London: Allen Lane 1990).

—(1983), 'Titulus praelatus: offrande, solennisation et publicité dans les ex-voto gréco-romains', *RA*, 281–300.

—(1983–91), 'Le folklore à Rome et les droits de la conscience publique sur la conduit individuelle', *Latomus* 42, 3–30 (= 'Les droits de la conscience publique sur la conduite individuelle : un constat ethnologique' in id. 1991. *La société romaine*. Paris).

—(1985), 'L'Empire romain', in P. Ariès and G. Duby (ed.) *Histoire de la Vie Privée, 1. De l'Empire Romain à l'An Mil*. Paris: Le Seuil.

—(1991), *La Société Romaine*. Paris: Le Seuil.

Vidman, F. (1957), *Fasti Ostiensis*. Prague: Academia (second edn 1982).

Virlouvet, C. (1987), 'La topographie des distributions frumentaires avant la création de la Porticus Minucia frumentaria', in *L'Urbs*, pp. 175–89.

—(1995), *Tessera Frumentaria. Les Procédures de Distribution du Blé Publique à Rome à la Fin de la République et au Début de l'Empire*. Rome: BEFAR 286.

Vivolo, F. P. (1993), *Pompei: I Graffiti Figurati*. Foggia: Bastogi.

Volterra, E. (1969), 'Senatus consulta', *Nuovissimo Digesto Italiano*, 16, 1055–8.

Wallace-Hadrill, A. (1987), 'Time for Augustus: Ovid, Augustus, and the *Fasti*', in M. Whitby, P. Hardie and M. Whitby (eds), *Homo Viator: Classical Essays for John Brimble*. Bristol: Bristol Classical Press, pp. 221–30.

—(1988), 'The social structure of the Roman house', *PBSR*, 56, 43–97.

—(1994), *Houses and Society in Pompeii and Herculaneum*. Princeton: Princeton University Press.

—(1997), 'Rethinking the Roman atrium house', in R. Laurence and A. Wallace-Hadrill (eds), pp. 219–40.

—(2003), 'The streets of Rome as a representation of imperial power', in L. De Blois, P. Erdkamp, O. Hekster, G. De Kleijn and S. Mols (eds), *The Representation and Perception of Imperial Power. Proceedings of the Third Workshop of the International Network Impact of Empire (Roman Empire, c. 200 B.C.–A.D. 476)*. Amsterdam: J. C. Gieben, pp. 189–208.

Ward-Perkins, J. B. and Kenrick, P. (ed.) (1993), *The Severan Buildings of Lepcis Magna: An Architectural Survey*. London: Society for Libyan Studies.

Warmington, E. H. (1953), *Remains of Old Latin*. Loeb Classical Library. Cambridge, MA: Harvard University Press.

Weaver, P. R. C. (1990), 'Where have all the Junian Latins gone? Nomenclature and status in the Roman Empire', *Chiron* 20, 275–305.

Webster, J. (2008), 'Less beloved. *Roman Archaeology, Slavery, and the Failure to Compare*', *Archaeological Dialogues*, 15, (2), 103–23.

Wegner, M. (1931), 'Die kunstgeschichtliche Stellung der Marcussäule', *Jahrbuch des deutschen archäologischen Instituts*, 46, 61–71.

Weiss, P. (2005), 'The cities and their money', in C. Howgego, V. Heuchert and A. Burnett (eds), *Coinage and Identity in the Roman Provinces*. Oxford: Oxford University Press, pp. 57–68.

Wesch-Klein, G. (1989), 'Rechtliche Aspekte privater Stiftungen während der römischen Kaiserzeit', *Historia*, 38, 177–97.

White, P. (2009), 'Bookshops in the literary culture of Rome', in W. A. Johnson and H. Parker (eds), *Ancient Literacies*. Oxford: Oxford University Press, pp. 268–87.

Wightman, E. M. (1985), *Gallica Belgica*. London: Batsford.

Williams, C. A. (2010), *Roman Homosexuality. Ideologies of Masculinity in Classical Antiquity (Ideologies of Desire)*, second edn. Oxford: Oxford University Press.

Williamson, C. (1987), 'Monuments of bronze: Roman legal documents on bronze tablets', *Classical Antiquity*, 6, (1), 160–83.

Williamson, C. (2005), *The Laws of the Roman People: Public Law in the Expansion and Decline of the Roman Republic*. Ann Arbor: University of Michigan Press.

Wilson, A. (2007), 'Urban development in the Severan Empire', in S. Swain, S., Harrison and J. Elsner (eds), *Severan Culture*. Cambridge: Cambridge University Press, pp. 290–326.

Wirszubski, C. (1968), *Libertas as a Political Idea at Rome during the Late Republic and Early Principate*. Cambridge: Cambridge University Press.

Wiseman, T. P. (ed.) (1985), *Roman Political Life 90 B.C.–A.D. 69*. Exeter: Exeter University Press.

—(1985), *Catullus and his World: A Reappraisal*. Cambridge: Cambridge University Press.

—(1986), 'Monuments and the Roman annalists', in I. S. Moxon, J. D. Smart and A. J. Woodman (eds), *Past Perspectives: Studies in Greek and Roman Historical Writing*. Cambridge: Cambridge University Press, pp. 87–101 (= 1994 *Historiography and Imagination. Eight Essays on Roman Culture*. Exeter: Exeter University Press, pp. 37–48).

—(1987), 'Conspicui Postes Tectaque Digna Deo. The public image of aristocratic houses in the late Republic and early Empire', in *L'Urbs*, pp. 395–413 (= 1994 *Historiography and Imagination. Eight Essays on Roman Culture*. Exeter: Exeter University Press, pp. 98–115).

—(1995), *Remus*. Cambridge: Cambridge University Press.

Witschel, C. (1995), 'Statuen auf römischen Platzanlagen unter besonderer Berücksichtigung von Timgad (Algerien)', in K. Stemmer (ed.), *Standorte. Kontext und Funktion antiker Skulptur*. Berlin: Ausstellungskatalog Abguss-Sammlung antiker Plastik, pp. 332–58.

—(forthcoming 2013) 'The public presence of women in the cities of North Africa. Two case studies: Thamugadi (Timgad) and Cuicul (Djemila)', in E. Hemelrijk and G. Woolf (eds), *Gender and the Roman City. Women and Civic Life in Italy and the Western Provinces*. Mnemosyne Supplements, History and Archaeology of Classical Antiquity. Leiden; Boston: Brill.

Wood, N. (1988), *Cicero's Social and Political Thought*. Berkeley, LA and Oxford: University of California Press.

Woodhull, M. L. (2004), 'Matronly patrons in the early Roman Empire. The case of Salvia Postuma', in F. McHardy and E. Marshall (eds), *Women's Influence on Classical Civilization*. London: Routledge, pp. 75–91.

Woolf, G. (1996), 'Monumental writing and the expansion of Roman society in the early empire', *JRS*, 86, 22–39.

—(1998), *Becoming Roman: The Origins of Provincial Civilization in Gaul*. Cambridge: Cambridge University Press.

—(2009), 'Literacy or literacies of Rome?' in W. A. Johnson and H. N. Parker (eds), *Ancient Literacies. The Culture of Reading in Greece and Rome*. Oxford: Oxford University Press, pp. 46–68.

Wuilleumier, P. (1963), *Inscriptions Latines des Trois Gaules*, XVIIe supplement à *Gallia*. Paris: CNRS.

Yakobson, A. (1999), *Elections and Electioneering in Rome: A Study in the Political System of the Late Republic*. Hist. Einzel. 128, Stuttgart, Franz Steiner, 1999.

Yates, F. A. (1975), *L'Art de la Mémoire*. Paris: Gallimard.

Yegül, F. (1992), *Baths and Bathing in Classical Antiquity*. Cambridge, MA and London: MIT Press.

—(1996), 'The thermo-mineral complex at Baiae and *De balneis puteolanis*', *Art Bulletin*, 78, 1, 137–61.

Youtie, H. C. (1973), *Scriptiunculae*. Amsterdam: Hakkert.

—(1975–81), 'Ὑπογραφεύς. The social impact of illiteracy in Graeco-Roman Egypt', *ZPE*, 17, 201–21 (= id. 1981, 179–221).

—(1981), *Scriptiunculae Posteriores*. Bonn: Rudolf Habelt Verlag GMBH.

Zadorojnyi, A. V. (2011), 'Transcripts of dissent? Political graffiti and elite ideology under the Principate', in J. A. Baird and C. Taylor (eds), pp. 110–33.

Zanker, P. (1970), 'Das Trajansforum in Rome', *Archäologischer Anzeiger*, 85, 499–544.

—(1988), *The Power of Images in the Age of Augustus*, trans. A. Shapiro. Ann Arbor: University of Michigan Press.

—(1998), *Pompeii: Public and Private Life*, trans. D. Lucas Schneider. Cambridge, MA: Harvard University Press.

—(2000), 'The city as symbol: Rome and the creation of an urban image', in E. Fentress (ed.), *Romanization and the City: Creation, Transformations and Failures*. Portsmouth, RI: JRA Supplementary Series 38, pp. 25–41.

Zadorojnyi, A.V. (2011), 'Transcripts of dissent? Political graffiti and elite ideology under the Principate', in J. A. Baird and C. Taylor (eds), pp. 110–33.

Zeller, J. (1906), 'Vicus, Platea, Platiodanni', *Archiv für lateinische Lexikographie und Grammatik*, 14, 301–16.

Zevi, F. (1971), 'Miscellanea ostiense', *RAL* ser.8, 26, 449–79.

Zimmer, G. (1989), *Locus datus decreto decurionum. Zur statuenafstellung zweier Forumsanlagen im römischen Afrika*. München: Bayerische Akademie der Wissenschaften.

—(1992), 'Statuenaufstellung auf Forumsanlagen des 2. Jahrhunderts n. Chr', in H.-J. Schalles, H. von Hesberg, and P. Zanker (eds), *Die römische Stadt im 2. Jahrhundert n. Chr. Der Funktionswandel des öffentlichen Raumes. Kolloquium in Xanten vom 2. bis 4. Mai 1990*. Cologne: Rheinland Verlag, pp. 301–13.

Index

Page references in bold denote a table, entries in italics denote a figure.